THE INHE

William Ayot

William Ayot first worked in London's gaming industry while developing as a playwright and poet. Following a personal crisis, he studied poetry, story and ritual under a remarkable series of teachers and shamans. By the mid nineties he was facilitating groups in rehab centres, and leading initiatory Rites of Passage for men. As a co-founding director of Olivier Mythodrama, he worked to bring narrative, imagination and poetry to organisations and business schools around the world. After reducing his business commitments, he set up *On the Border*, a groundbreaking poetry initiative in South East Wales. This led to the realisation of a long-held dream, the formation of NaCOT, the UK's first dedicated centre for spoken poetry, storytelling, and oratory. William also designs and leads rituals and works as a leadership coach. He lives with his wife, Juliet Grayson, in a restored Monmouthshire Gentry House near Chepstow.

also by William Ayot

Poetry

Small Things that Matter

Theatre

Bengal Lancer
Shakespeare's Ear

THE INHERITANCE

William Ayot

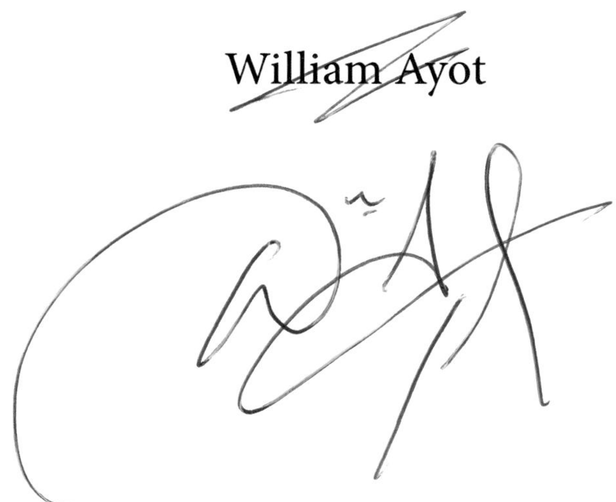

Sleeping Mountain Press

Second Edition 2014 Published by Sleeping Mountain Press
Previously published in the UK in 2011 by PS Avalon
Sleeping Mountain Press
Courtyard House,
Mathern
Chepstow
Monmouthshire
South Wales NP16 6HZ
www.williamayot.com

Design: Will Parfitt

Cover image – 'Quinces' – by Jenny Barron
Water colour – From the author's collection

Back cover photo: Castle Portraits

ISBN 978-0-9930306-1-1

CONTENTS

ACKNOWLEDGEMENTS

Some of these poems were first published
in the following publications:
Achilles Heel, Acumen, Candelabrum,
Poetry London Newsletter, Psychopoetica,
Spokes, Still, Weyfarers,
The Making of Them (Lone Arrow Press),
Writing for Self-Discovery (Element),
The Water-Cage (Sleeping Mountain)
and *Into the Further Reaches* (PS Avalon)

— To the Grandfathers —

THANKS

are due to the following artists, teachers,
practitioners and individuals who at various times
have given the author guidance, help or support:
Robert Bly, James Hillman, Martín Prechtel,
Lowijs Perquin, Malidoma Somé, Sobonfu Somé,
Shi Jing, Ron Pyatt, Richard Olivier, Steve Banks,
Mark Rylance, Geoff Mead, Jeremy King,
Paul Smith-Pickard, Robert Sherman,
Simon Powell, Myra Schneider, Paul Groves,
Jay Ramsey, John Hegley,
and Juliet Grayson Ayot.

I

BLOOD AND BONE

NEW YEAR'S EVE

Year's end, and the grief is with me,
unshed tears at the back of my throat
for those I failed, who didn't make it;
the ones who fell, who stumbled, reeling,
who would not, could not, make a change,
whose lives were lit by other stars
than those that shine so thinly now.

I will place a candle in my window —
not to guide them, still less to heal,
but to show them, wherever they are,
that I have kept faith, that I remember
their crooked smiles, their tipsy laughter,
heads thrown back in wild hilarity;
glasses raised, tall tales untold,
the dogs of disaster still on the leash;
dreams untarnished, dawns undimmed,
my foolish, frail, unforgettable dead.

HISTORY

I close my eyes, and imagine my parents
standing behind me, one at each shoulder;
behind them, and behind them, and behind them
two parents, travelling back in a vee through time.
Two, four, eight, sixteen, thirty-two, sixty-four —
in twenty generations I have a million ancestors.
I am the tip of an arrow. That's history.

I have a father in me, his frail heart breaking
on the battered anvil of his unlived life,
and a mother whose fear still trembles inside me,
reaching like a scold for the easy mask of anger.
They were good people. They made me who I am.
They left me ashamed of my body and my kind.

I have two grandfathers and two grandmothers,
on the one side dirt poor, on the other middle-class.
My grandfathers stare out of sepia photographs,
stiff in their uniforms like khaki butterflies,
chloroformed and pinned by the coming of war.
One granny died giving birth to my father,
the other endured, and drank herself to death.

I have war in me then, and the greed of Empire,
cruelties born of the ledger and the lash —
the boss's swagger, and the box-wallah's blag,
the foreman's snarl, and the slaver's dull-eyed stare.
I also have a pauper in me, driven from the fields,
grieving the memory of every pond and pasture.

There's a puritan in me who fought his brother,
and a Cavalier who wept as he buried his sons,
a whey-faced villager who pointed the finger,

tied his neighbour to a stake and watched her burn.
The neighbour's in me too, and she's not a witch;
and she did none harm, and she spoke none harm.

There's a monk, and a bishop, and a starveling curate,
and a hermit who went crazy alone in a cave;
each one giving their life to prayer and service,
each one stumbling on the unpaved road to God.
And there's a wet nurse too, and a silent midwife
who buried more children than she ever welcomed.

I've a troubadour inside me, and a crusader
prepared to do murders in the name of the Lord.
Their flags and their pennons flutter forlornly —
there's a bit of me that never got to Jerusalem.
Behind them there's a file of hard-faced warriors
and the sullen churls they ground into the mud.

There's a Celt, and a Pict, and a roaring berserker,
calling on the spirit of the Great White Bear;
and a völva in her trance, and a shaman drumming,
staving off the coming of hunger and pestilence.
These are my ancestors, my blood and my bone.
They make me who I am. I carry them with me.

ROMANTIC

Much thinner than he ought to be,
he begs no more than a smile or a blessing.

Head bent forward, shoulders hunched,
chapped hands deep in his empty pockets.

You could look into his flint-grey eyes
and see the stories of a thousand sons

brought to this city by hope or despair
at one last crop of thistles and stones.

You can hear him in the underpasses,
the delicate agonies of his dulcimer playing,

and all the while you can place him exactly
on the brow of a vast and motherly hill,

in silhouette against the skyline, a dreamer,
held down by nothing but the grasping clay.

THE INHERITANCE

This is the fear
my mother carried
like a cold, wet stone;
her rough hands cracked
with the handling of it,
her love worn thin
by its abrasions.

This is the fear
my father suppressed
like a squalling child;
his strong arms forcing
the pillow down on it,
tenderly, tenderly,
whispering a lullaby.

And this is the fear
I cannot own,
that I have wrapped
in the cloths of anger:
red for a warning
to keep me safe,
white for the grief
and the isolation.

This is the fear
of my generations,
handed down with
the bottle and the flask;
sharp as a cracked whip,
dull as a goad;
driving me, driving me
as they were driven.

FATHER AND DAUGHTER

(October, 1950)

A long black funeral car, nondescript as the age,
and you – austerity itself – in homburg and gloves
sitting with a tiny white coffin beside you,
stunned into silence by eight short days
of worry and gratitude, cruel choice and loss.

I'll take her myself, May. I can hear you say
though I was never there. *Better I do this alone.*

The scrunch of gravel, whispering conifers,
pity, and the doffing of hats and caps;
wreath-bearing visitors held by the sight of you
walking like a robot down the rows of graves,
holding out your offering, mechanised by death.

THE MADE BED

It would have been dark, or nearly dark,
and in the dark their loneliness would have been complete.
She would have waited beside him, listening to his breathing,
would have sensed his hand before it reached her,
might even have shrunk a little before it touched.
He would have whispered, like a beggar, abashed,
or the ghost of a child that has yet to let go. *Please.*
In the darkness she would have mouthed the word, *No*,
but as the hand took possession of her she would have sighed
and her body would have said, *Yes*, in spite of itself.
Neither of them would have been naked.
                                                            The nightdress
he bought her would have been hoisted over her breasts
and his pyjama buttons would have scraped her skin
as he pulled himself on top of her. They would have kissed
through habit, the beer on his breath meeting the port on hers,
and, as the mattress began to creak and protest,
she would have heard her mother's querulous voice,
clear and distinct above the comedy of his breathing.
Well, you've made your bed, so you'd better lie in it.
Abruptly, her body would have flared and kindled.
She would have turned to him, peered at him, held his face.
For a second they would have been lovers again.
His need and her pity would have melted away,
would have dissolved into feeling, into clouds and light.
There would have been birds and a single cry
                                            and then it would have been over.
Safe in the darkness she would have wept,
her lone grief bobbing on the swell of his snores,
while deep within her something would have quickened,
would have wriggled aggressively, demanded and joined;
then split, and split, and split again, both needed and unwanted.

A SUSSEX POEM

The years have all vanished like old Slindon Wood.
They lie shattered and broken, torn by the wind
While I, revisiting old familiar haunts,
Breathing rich downland air as I did of old,
Remember — Time makes tourists of us all.

Down off the hill with a church clock striking six,
A distant dog barking as if to test the stillness
And the scent of wood smoke, sweet apple and pear.
I was only passing through I know but in Sussex,
For a perfect moment, I belonged and was blessed.

Walking through woods in late October sunshine,
Beeches ablaze in restless glades of autumn gold,
Cherries already stripped of their dazzling brocade
And friends, kicking through the leaves, arm in arm,
Laughing — mocking the chill and the onset of the end.

Christmas Lunch and endless conversations
Spilling across the dunes and down to East Head.
Homeward like rooks across the pale December sky
To hot teas and presents and dogs by the fire.
Warmed through with love yet calling it company.

It's Christmas time once more. The years are long gone,
Gone with Belloc's plowman from Ha'nacker Hill.
Nothing is final. The windmill is turning again.
I am older, sadder. I can admit love now.
I knew it once in Sussex. They say I could return.

ANOTHER FUNERAL

Not the mourners with their drizzled faces,
nor the service with its dry embarrassments,
its gawky, shuffling infelicities,
nor yet the burial with its thud and wrench,
its dull flat, cauterising realisations —

but the involuntary halt by the cemetery gate,
the turn, the call, the sudden seeking
for the tiny grave hidden by the hedge,
a three-penny bit memorial, all but forgotten
yet found by that part in us that brings us home,
that listens to dreams and waits at thresholds,
reminding us of the might-have-beens,
the wraiths of our maybes, our lost potentials.

My sister the ghost-baby, unknown to me,
though she was a constant childhood presence,
a loss inexplicable, too huge for tears;
the hole in her heart a hole in our lives
that split us into assorted solitudes.

Now all our griefs come together in me:
renamed, acknowledged, mapped and followed:
each brook and stream, each tributary loss,
each laden, meandering river of bereavement.
We are heavy with the silt of our parents' tragedies,
un-grieved except in angers and busy-ness.
We are sluggish with them, ponderous, saturated.
My sister beckons me to weep down to the sea.

II

THE LAND OF GIANTS

WIRELESS

I am a radio station broadcasting to the world.
I am seven years old and I am sitting on a fence-post
overlooking the storm-field and the village beyond.

Being a radio station's more fun than being a train.
I was a train for ages: an express, then a sleeper,
then a goods, and then an angry little shunter.

Nobody speaks to trains because they're too busy.
But now I am a radio station, transmitting daily
to the far horizon — which is miles.

It's a varied programme including music, religion
and talks, and remembered bits of *Round the Horne*
that I take in on my crystal set before I fall asleep.

Every ten minutes I recite the news — What Miss Sims
said to my mum and how Dolly Feaver the postmistress
is still beating Pickles with a stick — which is cruel.

Sometimes I run out of news and then I sing things.
My song becomes a naming and my naming is a world:
Robin Hood and Little John and a pair of long trousers,

and Brock's Wood and the Hill and someone to talk to,
and the cedar and the elder and the elm and the oaks,
and the silver-backed mole and the pheasant and the lark,

and the weasel that steals the pheasant's eggs,
and the rooks and the rabbits, and nettles and docks
and the storm on the corn, and the clouds, and God....

COUNTING THE MARIGOLDS

The fist came out of nowhere.

He was nine years old and running up the garden path,
excited as only a boy can be
when he sees his father coming home.

Daddy, Daddy. I scored a goal!

It caught him right on the button.
Something split and he could taste the metal in his blood
before he hit the ground.

He was staring at a bed of marigolds,
concentrating, counting leaves and petals,
when his father picked him up and looked him in the eye.

I must have told you a dozen times, he slurred.
Never leave yourself open.

THE DELIVERY

The kilderkins lying in the cool of the cellar
manhandled, racked up, waiting to be drawn,
dumped off the dray on a rope pad, grabbed
and spun by expert hands. Billy Christmas
and his draymen calling out, *'ware below*,
and my father waiting as the barrels tumbled in,
upending them, grunting them into place,
smiling at the achievement, holding a mallet
ready to check the bung, to broach and tap.
Heavy tubs those barrels, eighteen gallons,
with every now and then a heavier thirty-six,
sitting there foaming through their wooden spiles,
the dank cellar cradling them, the delicious
cool of them, waiting on a hot September day.

And outside, Harry, cutting nettles in the orchard,
his one tooth beaming as he sharpened the scythe,
arcing it sharp with a sweep of the whetstone,
waving great circles with a practised air. Old Harry,
who'd always stop to make a boy an aeroplane,
with two bits of kindling, a nail and a story.
Harry, who could slice himself to the bone
and calmly wrap the gash in a paisley handkerchief.
Harry, who knew the time to the nearest half-pint,
and always arrived as my father was drawing
the first foaming glass of a new delivery.

The two of them, old friends, in the sunlit bar,
with the dust motes settling on the faded lino.
My father drawing off the old ale in the pipe,
Harry respectfully waiting for him to finish,
to pour and offer the first glass of the new.

Their ritual was for my father to draw the pint
but never to drink from it. He would hold it aloft
(beers were cloudier in those days), nod sagely
and declare it, *Clear as a bell*. Then he'd sniff
at it and hand it to Harry who would take it,
just as solemnly, sip it and proclaim it… *Passable*,
winking at me as I watched from the door.

I remember the day when Harry came in,
smelling of leather and nettles and grass.
A thin man, old, and wrinkled, and toothless,
full of tales, and the expectation of a pint.
My father nodded, pulled on the beer-engine,
a half-glass, then one he threw away.
Two strong pulls and he held up a pint of mild,
the rich nut-brown ale, glowing like a conker,
the thin foam spilling over his powerful hand.
That's perfect, he said as if to judge and jury.

Harry took the glass but then raised it in salute —
to me who was nine and going away to school.
Here's to you, old'n. Don't forget Old Harry.
Then he put the schooner to his lips and drank it
down in one.
He was dead when I came home,
had joined the ranks of those we never spoke about,
for speaking meant remembering and remembering
meant pain. But I held on to his scraps of kindling,
their tang of creosote, and the little nail of love.
and I remembered that morning in the sunlit bar
when old Harry toasted me like a Saxon eoldorman,
his Adam's apple bobbing as he drank my health.
The tilt of his head and the sadness in his eyes.
The passing on of something as old as the beer.

NINETY-SEVEN

He remembered the little black suitcase,
the journeying at peculiar times,
the panic in his mother's eyes,
but he couldn't remember understanding
or having it explained to him
why he was going to Ninety-Seven again
or why his father had become someone else.

He remembered feeling safe at Ninety-Seven,
climbing the stairs to a warm feather bed,
Cornish Wafers and scalded milk,
being tucked-in with a rubber hot-water bottle,
good-night kisses that didn't smell of beer;
but he was still too afraid to ask
how his father could become someone else.

He remembered whisperings at Ninety-Seven,
telephone talk about the coast being clear;
being scrubbed and made presentable,
getting in the back of a big black car.
He remembered the cold as he left Ninety-Seven,
frost on the car and the moonlit road.
He remembered thinking the moon might tell him
why his father had become someone else.

BACK TO THE NUMBERS

You go back to the numbers,
Apollonian numbers,
sky-dry and rarified,
as clean as abstract time.
Back to the numbers,
the mystery of numbers.
Numbers are worth the climb.

When his old Headmaster beat him
in the library at night
while the other boys were sleeping,
when the Hand of Authority slipped and strayed
from neck to back and down between his legs,
he counted things; anything,
volumes of Churchill, T.E. Lawrence
or sometimes the dozens of little punched holes
that covered Authority's polished brogues.

It was back to the numbers,
the safety in numbers,
sky-dry and rarified,
as rare as you can find.
Back to the numbers,
the sanctuary of numbers,
leaving all feeling behind.

LITTLE SOLDIERS

They used to come to her at night, the nine-year-olds,
long after lights out when everything was lonesome.

Maclean had been the first, and later young Bracey,
Bracey who was so much gentler than the others.

He'd knocked so quietly that she hadn't heard him
till his slippers had squeaked on the polished linoleum.

He'd been walking away when she called him back,
head down, hands in his dressing-gown pockets.

Maclean said you might have an aspirin, Matron.
And then through the fog of tiredness. *Can't sleep.*

She took him into her room and sat him on her bed
while the little pill fizzed in its tumbler of water

and then she sat beside him, waited as he drank,
waited till he sagged against her, like a tired pup.

He smelled the same as most young boarders, of piss
and polish and abandonment, yet he seemed different,

so she had cuddled him, like her own, until he sobbed,
and run a tender hand through his corn-coloured hair.

Then like her own, she had gently sent him back to bed
only this time the Head's wife had been lying in wait.

We think it only proper that we keep a certain distance.
And of course, at the end of term, they had to let her go.

Driving her to the station, the Head had been quite direct.
Fact of the matter is we're paid to turn out soldiers.

DEBTOR'S MOON

Two o'clock in the morning and the moon
is fingering the furniture like a bailiff.

The father, in flight from the shame
that nails him to the moment, is lying

unconscious, an outstretched hulk,
a pissed and dissipated Sistine Adam,

nicotine-gilded fingers pointing
towards his empty, brown-bottle god.

The boy has tried to drag him to bed.
He is twelve now. He has failed.

As he sits, benumbed, a foraging mouse
appears in the crook of his father's arm.

The boy calls out but nothing happens.
He is empty, dumb, becoming invisible.

The father mutters, shifts and snores.
The mouse takes fright and vanishes.

The boy stays, watching over his father,
and the moon slips through the trees.

EDDIES AND VORTICES

It had become a house of dull knives,
tattered cuffs and empty bottles.
There were no pictures on the walls
and music had long since fled.
The clock was a run-down contemptuous
Buddha, withdrawn into sullen silence.
In his room, my father was sleeping
it off while, in the kitchen, my mother
was putting the dishes away with just
enough righteous indignation to make
the dogs flinch at every resentful clatter.
The very air was thick with the ghosts
of arguments, unfinished and withheld,
spinning through the angry atmosphere,
creating eddies and vortices, feeding
the house's circular rage.
                                        Somewhere
a draught whistled in the woodwork,
howled and hooted, moaned and died,
as my father began to sing in his sleep.

NEVER

The night my father died
he hit me.
In an extremity of pain

or whisky-rage or both,
one arm dead already,
he lashed out with the other

to send me spinning
across the floor,
more shamed than truly hurt.

I took my tears and hid them,
nursed them
till I heard him on the stairs.

I'm sorry I hit you, he said
and I waited.
Let's make it up, old son.

Never — I spat out years
of resentment.
Never — and I turned away.

He left me then, and later
when I found him
the word was in the air.

Never — the dead forget
but a single word
can ride the living for life.

HIS SUIT

Can't remember much about the funeral
except that I wore my father's suit.
Not his Sunday best, there wasn't one,
but a blue serge striped affair that hung
at odd places on my adolescent body
whilst elsewhere it seemed unnaturally tight.
I'm not sure whose idea it was,
but I wore that suit like a shaman wears
an animal skin, the smell of his tobacco
lingering in the material, the memory
of his final, mad descent enveloping me
like a cloak of tribal secrets.
                                                            Back home,
amongst the bridge rolls and the whispers,
my severe Aunt Vera buttonholed me.
She must have spotted the suit because
she held me, gently fingering the lapels.
You're the head of the family now, she said,
and suddenly that old suit stank of beer.
I nodded back at her, just like my father,
smiling weakly as my shoulders sagged.

AROUND AND BELOW AND BEHIND

Across his shoulders anger
and down his knotted spine,
coiled and writhing, captive, bound;
the anger of a thousand yeses
in place of a solitary no.

Moulded round the anger,
corroded, cracked and dangerous,
the armour of his given-shame;
a second hand-me-down inheritance
from those who could not, would not love.

Far below the shame a grief,
unacknowledged, unexpressed;
the oily sea beneath a cliff;
quiescent now but never leaving,
eroding all with a lap and a kiss.

Behind all this a staring child,
alone, abandoned, terrified;
the quintessential orphan,
frozen by the fear of death
and life, and love, and all he knows.

THE BADGER

Today my hands
want to rip and slash,
my jaws to crush
and my teeth to rend.
I have no shred
of forgiveness in me,
no finer feeling,
no liberal felicities.
Today I am one with
the world's dark verities;
with beak and claw,
with talon and tooth.
Today I am hurting,
and I am dangerous.

PROCESSIONAL

I saw a man give way to grief
As the coffin entered in.
Being strangely moved, I stopped
And kindly said to him.

Did you know her long ago?
He, turning, shook his head.
He looked at me from far away,
Then quietly he said,

I grieve here in my father's place.
I openly weep in the crowd.
I shed the tears he could not shed
As death was not allowed.

You do not grieve. You do not weep.
You do not honour the shroud.
How can you ever learn to live
When death is not allowed?

I waited at the churchyard gate.
I thought that he might stay.
I hoped he'd teach me how to grieve
But he'd quietly slipped away.

THE WATER-CAGE

The grief came up unbidden, like water
slowly percolating through the strata
of the past. It found its level and stayed.

It stayed through the iron days of work
and exhaustion, through the brittle days
of disbelief and thoughtless solicitude.

It dripped through the hollow nights
spent clinging artfully to strangers
and leeched the hope out of crawling mornings.

In staying, it was joined by other griefs,
that through the years had washed together,
grief on grief, eroding chasms and ravines

until in time it was a stream of pain, a river
and at last a sea where I was held immobile,
drowning, in a cage that was a second skin.

The grief came up unbidden, like water
slowly percolating through the strata
of the past. It found its own level. It stayed.

A BREAK IN THE LINE

I tried to find him,
tried to put together all the pieces,
make some sense of who he was,
of who my father's father
might have been.

I never knew him,
never saw but one stiff picture of him
in a uniform behind my grandma,
caught between her softness
and his fear.

Twice I asked my uncle,
begged him for the story of his father,
hoping he would help me mend the line
that linked me to the fathers
of the past.

All he gave me was his silence
and the sense of something other, lying
like a wound between the generations,
something raw and tender
like a bruise.

Nothing but an emptiness,
a silence and the shame that set my father
like an animal against the world,
against the line, against himself,
against his son.

HE WRITES A LETTER TO HIS SON

My son, there are things you need to know,
things about your old man and your family
that have been lying in the darkness
unspoken, denied for over thirty years.

My father, your grandfather, wasn't a monster,
just lonely and driven by the ghosts of the past,
but when he was drunk he was another man
and that man could make a childhood a desert.
Sometimes he wanted to fight me, to wrestle.
Fingers locked, he'd force me to my knees,
to prove he was still my unbeatable father,
though the truth was his world was falling apart
and the only one he could beat was his boy.

The darkest times were the sunny afternoons
when he ordered me to strip while he stood there
screaming at me; flaying my fat, adolescent body,
skinning me alive with the rasp of his tongue.
And yes, of course, he had used me earlier,
had drifted from cuddles and little secrets
to the kind of things that make a mockery
of the link between a father and his son.
The maggot on the hook was that even though
he hurt me, he remained my only source
of love - or so it seemed to the wounded kid
who retreated into food and dreamy isolation.

I like to think that it wasn't my dad
who did these things — that it was the whisky,
the brandy, or some dark incubus — but on days
when I'm living without my skin, I remember
his eyes and my flesh begins to creep.

Then the numbness of the moment comes over me
and I know that it was him, my father,
who crossed the line from neediness to using,
and then blamed me for being abused.

I used to fantasise about telling you
the stories my father made up for me,
before the madness and the drink took hold;
and sometimes I dreamt of taking you to visit
the graves of the old folk I ran to in my loneliness.
I imagined telling you their stories,
and my pride as I introduced you to them,
knowing that their loves would not be forgotten.
At other times I knew that the wounds,
though largely healed, had cut too deep;
that I would never hold you in my arms,
nor show you off, nor promise you the world.

More commonly, I was somewhere in between;
travelling in hope of love and kindness
and a woman who could teach me how to trust.
Well, I faced my edge, and I found the woman
and she showed me how to grow my life.
Nowadays, when my father calls to me
from the depths of his particular hell,
I keep on walking, I hold on to my reality.
Which brings me back to this letter,
to you — the son I will never have.

SAVED

My father doesn't haunt me anymore.
The fear has burned off with the mourning
and the loathing has somehow dissipated.
I'm glad I managed to stop forgiving him.
The holy road of the righteous victim
had become a low, deceitful path.
The truth was, I needed to loathe him first,
to gorge myself on delicate hatreds,
eat till I was sated, bloated like a leech.
Only then could I fall away to forgiveness.

Now when I see him, it's sideways on:
a young man of thirty, before I was born,
matinée-idol looks and a crisp cotton shirt,
silk tie, homburg, maybe even spats.
More often than not he's vulnerable,
an orphan, fitfully whistling to the silence.
He's just seen a girl who is strangely familiar,
and he's watching her, hungering with his eyes.
Now he's a comet, falling towards her —
thinking she is beautiful, thinking he is saved.

CUT GRASS AND NICOTINE

I could tell you about the pity and the waste,
the way I watched him disintegrating,
slowly becoming the bloated wreck
that lay on the floor in a drunken puddle.
Or I could talk about the shame —
that's dangerous because I get stuck again
in the acid limbo that held me back then.
I could tell you about the shock of finding him,
snarling in death and grinning obscenely;
of magically thinking that I had murdered him,
killed my own father with my ill will;
of carrying his corpse for twenty years; falling
to my knees with the weight of his memory.
But it's harder, much harder, even now
to talk about the ache for the spaces where
the quiet atonements might have been made;
to say
          to say
                              to say that I still love him,
and that somewhere inside me there's a boy
who pines for the warm and comforting
odour of him, the starched-cotton crispness
softened with sweat and brilliantine,
the cut-grass freshness and the stale cigarettes;
to say after years of bile and bitterness
that sometimes I miss and yearn for my father.

OLD DOGS

Sunday was my father's birthday.
It came and went without my remembering
which is no bad thing considering the extremes
of love and hate that I have felt for him.
Had he lived he would have been a hundred,
a venerable old gentleman, frail and white.
Maybe he could have outlived his ruin,
have transcended the shambles that was his life.
Then again he might simply have wallowed,
waited like a baby in his puddle of Scotch,
hoping for a mother to come to his rescue,
or a wife, or a son, or the Seventh Cavalry.
My guess is that old dogs can't be bothered
and that old drunks rarely redeem themselves.
Still, it's good to think of him at his centenary,
ennobled by the journey, finally arrived,
clean and sober with his dignity recovered.
He may have been dead for half a lifetime
but the son he slumped against still has hope.

III

VOICES IN THE DARK

SURVIVORS

He found a veiled woman
who had seen too much
then tortured her further
by asking her — Why?

She looked at him sadly
through stricken eyes
that seemed to say — Have
you no pain of your own?

Roaring waters filled him.
She blessed his arid eyes.
Better sad than blind — but
better blind than screaming.

DANSE MACABRE

For P. T.

You see something behind their eyes,
a look that says I'd like to hurt you,
a message in the body as it reaches forward,
straining towards you like a dog on a leash;
mouth made cruel, muscles corded,
a flare of the nostrils, an involuntary snarl,
the malevolent flicker of a pink, wet tongue.

In an instant you are shutting down
as if nature itself were compressing you.
Your muscles go limp and volition fails.
The whole world seems to move in treacle.

On the outside no one notices a thing —
people who know you see nothing wrong —
while inside, past and present merge,
conjoining in a dance of ancient finality.
At this point a breath could make a signal
as broad as the gestures of a wild flamenco;
the slightest move confirms your submission
as clearly as if you had offered your neck.

So you freeze, like a fallow deer in the forest,
one hoof raised, in total attention, waiting
for the crash of the clumsy hunter, waiting
for the coming of the shadow of death.
And in your head an old tune circulates —
a nursery rhyme, or the ghost of a song.
The words are lost in a roaring silence
but the message is simple: endure, endure.

TAKE HER DOWN

Maria has been shamed so many times
she apologises with her every move.
Something in her cringes as she listens
to the jangled voices, the inner jury,
rigged always to find her wanting.
She lives in the tentative hope of love
and the luscious fear of what love might bring
but when she faces the bedroom mirror
she can see that love's an exclusive gift
exchanged by the beautiful, not the ugly;
not the fat, the stupid, the disgusting,
the obscene, the dull and the unlovable.

And now she's naked, in his room again,
in his terrible, smiling, sunlit room;
watching his shadow on the dove-grey carpet
as he moves towards her, snarling again.
His words, once tender, now spill like vitriol
over her breasts and her podgy white belly,
eating their way down to burn out her sex;
empty and wasted at thirteen years old...

You make me want to vomit. You're a whore.

She wraps herself in a grease-stained kimono,
sparing the mirror too long a sight of her,
and tiptoes down to the kitchen once more
where she soothes herself with midnight ice-cream,
licking her wounds on the back of a spoon.

CHIRON'S AUBADE

In the end nothing really heals.
The wound remains a hideous wound.
We may lay claim to powers,
knowledge, method and skill,
but all we have is a yen for wellbeing,
a modicum of hope and a desperate need
to make good, to fix, to rearrange the evidence.
What we do is pick at the scab,
peel it away for the sake of knowing,
worry and tug until tissue comes too,
opening the flesh to the old invasions.
Let us not pretend to healing —
better admit to our own desire
for meaning and control in an arbitrary world
that knows neither peace nor restitution.
They order things better in the forest —
revenge then learning, blood then understanding:
no chatter, no white coats, no pointless erudition,
just retribution and a cold dry wisdom
bleeding into the truth of the world.

FLASHBACK

It's like this. Something kicks it off –
a sharp word, a noise, the soughing of the wind,
an unexpected, complex animal smell –
a thing that is not exactly of the event
but close enough to make the leap,
to confound the present and loop back to the past,
to make of a breeze, or the lemon scent of polish,
a trigger that re-enacts the moment.
Not a drama, with its little lies and embellishments,
its opportunities for creating a bit of mileage,
but the real thing, complete and inescapable,
total immersion in the event itself;
exactly as it happened, in every fibre of your body:
the skin becoming clammy, the chill, the rigidity,
the shutting down of your stomach and liver,
the bile in your throat that is really adrenaline,
the bitter taste that comes with survival.
What you see without seeing, what you hear
without hearing, are the crystals
of memory dissolving in your blood.
Suddenly you are acting from another, older place,
living in two times simultaneously:
your mind alerted, with its calculating edge,
your subtle heart banished to unreachable safety;
the old reptile part of you hanging on,
ready to do anything to get back to the dark,
to peace, to the cool embrace of silence;
and if that means lashing out or hurting, if that
means wounding with tooth, or tongue, or blade,
so be it.

Afterwards the shame, the shaky hands, the staring,
the reinventions of history, the never-ever-agains.
I have hurt the people that I have loved most dearly,
and try as I may, the truth is, I could hurt them again.
My hope, as the spiral winds down to its centre,
is that they might come to look at me
without an edge of fear.

THE MEDICAL ROOM

On learning that D.H. his old teacher
had been tried and convicted

He remembered being marked out as a liar,
being made to stand on an Ercol chair
adrift on a sea of polished parquet
while the rest of the school ate prunes around him.

He remembered the letter which informed his parents
that he was no more than a rotten apple
in danger of contaminating the rest of the barrel —
no mean feat for an eleven-year-old.

And he certainly remembered the ritual after games,
the shivering queue of naked schoolboys
running the gauntlet of six hot showers,
each boy halted under the cold;
made to pirouette three times in front of him,
juddering and jumping, as he stood there,
naked too — *making sure no one caught a cold.*

But he couldn't remember a single teacher
Saying, *Something's wrong*, or stepping in to stop it,
though they must have noticed the breakdowns
and the truancy, the gradual diminishment,
the shrinking of the boys who waited after school,
shame-faced, silent, outside the Medical Room.

And that was the thing, the cruel thing,
the one dark thing he could never remember.

Not after years of counselling and therapy,
of 12-step meetings and self-help seminars,
circles and processes, group work and anger work,
of coming to terms with the rage and the childlessness;
learning that victims need not turn into perpetrators,
discovering that he wasn't rotten to the core,
discovering that sometimes the gift is to forget.

Even after finding and accepting love,
of allowing himself to be held by another;
even when he learned about the trial and conviction,
that some last part of him was finally safe;
even then, though he tried, he could never remember
what happened in the Medical Room.

IV

WALKING DOWN INTO THE WATER

MAN TO MAN

I shall spare you my pain
because I am English,
because I am understated,
because I am my father's son
and because the tipsy ghosts
of our forefathers
are floating in the air about us
like a regiment of butlers,
swaying slightly to and fro,
eyeing me suspiciously.

I can spare you my pain
because I am strong,
because I am practised,
because I'm a right-hard bastard
and because the dogs I've kicked
like the women I've fucked
know that I'm well-tasty,
that I like a drink on Fridays,
and if they want goodies
that's part of the deal.

I will spare you my pain
because I am numb,
because I am vulnerable,
because I'm up against the wall
and because the wall holds back
the boundless waters of my grief.
If it gave we'd all be swept away
but I daren't tell you that
because you're a man
and nobody trusts a man — ever.

GATHERING AT THE GATE

Deep suspicion darkly rounded
Bodies nursing fears well founded
Hungry ghosts by fathers hounded
To our meeting by the gate

Some in awe of rage unspoken
Most in boyhood nearly broken
All prepared to pay the token
Pay in passing through the gate

Work-bound men achievement driven
Long lost boys their shames unshriven
Men who ache to be forgiven
At our meeting by the gate

Without prompting without urging
Comes a story comes a purging
One by one their truths emerging
From the shadows by the gate

Somewhere in those shadows prowling
Near to pain and close to howling
Something stirring something growling
In the darkness by the gate

Maleness stronger for its weeping
Kept the man-child safely sleeping
There's a sense that we'll be keeping
To our meeting by the gate
In the shadows by the gate
In the darkness by the gate

COMFORT

For P. A.

A solid man, he's seen a thing or two,
enough to be assured of his place in the world.
The lines that are deepening into creases,
the greying stubble and the clear, kindly gaze,
speak of the journey from naivety to despair
and on to a hard-won, tempered acceptance.
Tonight though, his eyes are moist with memories
evoked by the awkward, tentative sound
of his friends in the kitchen singing hymns.
There are fragments, verses, starts and beginnings,
followed by the swoop of remembered choruses —
the rumbling summons of a half-forgotten past.

Gripped by more than musical nostalgia,
he's caught on the point of a genuine grief.
Images surface to discomfit and unsettle him,
the washed-out snaps of a sepia time.

As a lad I never thought Suffolk was flat.
The elms were like hills around the village,
and the towers of the churches split the sky:
Southwold, Blythburgh, Walberwick.
They were my Alps, my Himalayas....

A rousing chorus floats in from the kitchen,
carrying a remembrance of harvest homes.
There are tears now, welling and tumbling,
and the threat of a deep irrepressible sob.
He doesn't fight it, he lets it come
and with it the memory of consolations
that made rural poverty bearable:

the rooky fields, the stark November trees,
and the sonorous calling of the village bells:
Sundays and holidays, Christmas and Easter,
the careful monotony of the passing bell,
and once in a blue moon, now and again,
the rolling glory that was ringing the changes:
over the fields, through the wide Suffolk sky,
the comforting call of a long-forgotten god.

THE LADS IN THE PARK

Why do the young lads bellow in the park
and spoil the calm of a long summer's evening?

Perhaps they've forgotten something.
Perhaps they want salt but not vinegar.
Perhaps their little-boy voices just broke
and they think they need some man-practice.

Maybe they're in the movies.
Maybe they're on a mission.
Maybe there's suddenly a girl across the way
with a smile that only responds to bellowing.

Perhaps they're feeling isolated.
Perhaps they're feeling inadequate.
Perhaps they're feeling abandoned — though
the odds are they're not feeling anything at all.

Maybe if they didn't bellow they'd explode.
Maybe they're going to explode anyway.
Maybe the stillness scares them so much
they need the simple reassurance of an explosion.

Perhaps they're waiting to be told to shut up.
Perhaps they've been told to shut up already.
Perhaps they're sick of being called boys
long after their forefathers would have been men.

Then again they might just bellow 'cos they're lads,
'cos that's what lads have to do to get noticed,
and 'cos this sad and middle-aged world of ours
needs shaking, every generation, with a shout.

SMALL PARTING

Larry, the flatmate, left today.
We'd shared the place for a year or two;
argued over rent, laughed sometimes
and, on one occasion, grieved together
when his cat was killed by a careless driver.
Nothing remarkable about this small parting
except he couldn't bring himself to say goodbye
and I couldn't be fussed to cross the hall
as he slammed and banged and swore at boxes,
letting us know he was leaving in mid-dudgeon.
Odd how he needed to be angry to leave.
I used to quit jobs that way, one after the other,
using petty quarrels to break my attachments
like an eaglet, squabbling its way from the eyrie,
when all it has to do is fly.
Anyway, he left,
while I sat at the kitchen table and waited,
thinking to wave when he passed outside.
I heard him swearing his way along the hallway
and the crustle of his last black plastic bag.
There was a pause before the door shut, finally,
and he clumped his way past the kitchen window.
I raised my hand with a certain practiced irony
but he was deliberately looking away –
eyes down, jaw set, unable even to look at me.
Thus we parted, me feeling graceless, shabby
and cheap, and him with all his baggage.

DARSHAN

For 'Carlos' who didn't make it

A lattice of scar tissue covers his face,
and the eyes are hooded by swollen brows.
What you see is what you get: a wreck,
a boxer who's taken too many blows,
a man who's come in like a wandering pi-dog,
anxious yet hungry, desperate to settle.

Fuck it, I'm tired, fellas. I'm really tired.

He wants to do good, he says, to serve;
like the time in Calcutta when he was a kid.
He was just a junkie with nowhere to go
but the Sisters of Charity gave him a job
and a few rupees to keep him going.
All he had to do was bring in the dying.

I was using their money to buy my dope.

His head goes down and suddenly he's sobbing.
The story comes out in a series of grunts.
One time Mother Theresa was in the passageway.
He was pushed towards her by Sister Audrey.

Mother, this is Carl. He wants to see you.

Carlos froze as the tiny avatar cocked her head,
looked at him from beneath her blue-lined sari

He's fifty now and will never get sober,
but that was a moment that saw him through:
the blessing from the wrinkled little woman,
the eyes that saw, and loved, and forgave.

I'm a piece of shit – you know that, fellas –
but while she was looking at me, I was clean.

TEARS ON THE DRUM

For R.B.

We are standing together, my long-lost brother and I,
On the sloping deck of a holed and dying luxury liner.
We are sharing a fine cigar because we have no jokes.
He is talking about the grandfathers who went before.

Today I understand how these proud men,
Lonely and afraid, could rise up smiling
In far-off, strange, unhallowed places
With mud on their tongues and tears on the drum;

How they could gather, to pick sweet poppies,
The red, red poppies, and when they were gathered,
To walk together, into the morning,
The misty morning, and die together.

We need to weep awhile, my long-lost brother and I
But we both know the score — there's never the time.
So we wave once more at the distant boats. Then
We smile, hold hands, and walk down into the water.

MAKING FOR BENARES

We sat awhile and contemplated the departing river
And, as we flowed together in companionable silence,
We saw our fathers' giant lives becoming smaller,
No more than the wrack of their driftwood dreams.

It wasn't the abuse that broke us but the absence,
The ragged, gaping hole that's felt by bitter sons in exile.
We would have been warriors but there was no land.
We could have been lovers but we knew no love.

Instead, we burned like pyres in the angry copper light,
Our hearts too full to open to the whispers of the past.
Let us now consign our rusted armour to the river.
We tried. We failed. We learned to weep;
We deserve this tender peace.

SOMETHING WE DON'T TALK ABOUT

The beauty of men lies in the doing:
in a love that notices when things need fixing;
that mows the lawn, that feeds the dog,
that crosses vast oceans to bring home a nutmeg.

The beauty of men lies in the dancing:
in the wildness of youth, in the cackle of age,
in the furious stamp and the delicate gesture
that flies like a hawk from the wrist of a huntress.

The beauty of men lies in the silence:
the silence that speaks of the bloody fields;
of the distant wave, the encouraging smile,
and the song that was lost on the long road home.

MAMMA'S BOY

Wanting to say something to his mother;
wanting to say no, or, more exactly,
not now, not here, not in this room
with all these familiar people watching,

Wanting to say something to his mother
about love and control and the gift
of manhood – which isn't really hers to give
but his to claim, or steal, or simply demand
by holding up a firm, implacable hand.

Wanting all this but managing no more
than another rueful, apologetic smile;
the dip of the head and the yielding silence
which killers know as a rage deferred.

STANDING IS A GIFT

He comes at me because he must.
Sitting there, fat and in my fifties,
I am everything he loathes, and fears.
In his sight, I'm all the bosses,
teachers, badges, caps and uniforms,
all the bullies he's had to defer to.
I am the enemy. I am dad.

He snaps a sidelong scowl at me,
burning eyes under hooded lids,
but in that fire, if you cared to look,
you might catch the glint of something
slithering, ancient and implacable,
towards this thing he needs to kill.

It doesn't land straight, of course,
not in these sideways, sophisticated days;
it arrives as a sly yet casual aside;
a petty, sneering, yet practiced swipe
that shows a clear intellectual grasp
but has the slick of bile about it,
the sticky slick of a young man's hate.

I'm struck by a blast of desiccating heat
that emanates from the rage inside this boy
though what comes to mind is a desert street
where a tired sheriff is being stalked
by a kid who wants to shoot him in the back
because it's the Wild West and he knows
there's only one way to become a gunslinger.

So we sit there, sizing each other up
me with my worn and battered badge,
him with a look between murder and tears,
I want to say, *Does it have to be this way?*
but I know that it does – at least for him.

And that decides me. Standing is my gift.
I cross to the swing-doors of the saloon
which clatter as I step out into the sunshine.
I pause a moment to be sure of his footfall
then leave the sidewalk for the dusty street.

FAMOUS LAST WORDS

Someone once explained to me, patiently,
as if to an idiot, that Horatio Nelson
had never said *Kiss me Hardy*,
he merely said, *Kismet*, meaning fate,
meaning that's how the ship's biscuit crumbles.
But I've been spending time this summer
listening to men, and observing them;
watching how their worried shoulders speak,
their capable hands, their constant tension,
their silences, their yearning for affection.
I've been thinking of that tiny admiral's uniform,
the one with the Nile Star and the bullet hole,
and I have a sense of Nelson dying, shot
through the back in his moment of triumph;
Nelson, after years of hardtack and seasickness,
of discipline, and 'the exigencies of the service'.
Nelson, self-sacrificed piecemeal over the years,
dying on the altar of a nation's yearning.
And I have a sense of a great door opening
in a heart long starved of tenderness;
I see him looking at the faces in the Cockpit,
waiting for his friends and followers to join him,
and I see his eyes, through the telescope of pain,
holding on to Hardy as they waited for the ebb.
I see the feeling that a man can hold for another
when they've worked together for half a lifetime.
It was love that spoke – and not to history.
Of course he said it: *Kiss me, Hardy*

V

DWINDLING IN THE DUSK

A CERTAIN CLOSENESS

He picks up the phone and calls his mother.
It's been a while. They're not that close.

The tremble in her voice reminds him she's afraid.
A generation is dying around her, falling away
in ones and twos: today a friend, yesterday a brother-in-law,
tomorrow the woman across the way she always smiled at
but never got close to.

They talk around things – jobs and bosses, aches and pains –
but the silences speak of resentment and regret,
of the lost opportunities that made them who they are,
of passing trains that sped through the night.
How could they even begin to get close?

This grey-haired old darling, popular and well-beloved,
was once the terror of his childhood:
brittle, unpredictable, scared into lovelessness.
This was the mother of the shrivelled heart
who mocked him in public and shamed him in private,
the goddess who cursed him, who walked away.
And now she wants to get close.

On the telephone she says, *I love you* – words
he chased for thirty years; and when he visits, once a month,
she seems reluctant to let him go. Then, when he leaves
to catch his train, she follows him out into the night
whispering, *Love you*, to his retreating back.

So sometimes, when the day leaves him chopped inside,
he thinks of calling her and saying how he feels,
though that would risk a certain closeness.

Instead he sits by his window and thinks of her,
waiting in the stillness as the evening falls.
The two tied together, separated by continents,
scant miles apart, and dwindling in the dusk.

HER MANTRA

I'm so worried. I'm so worried. I'm so worried.
What's wrong, Mother?
I'm so worried. I'm so worried. I'm so worried.
What's the matter?
I'm so worried. I'm so worried. I'm so worried.
What is it?
I haven't got any clothes.

Alright, we'll find you some, says my wife.
Any excuse to get out of the nursing home.
Marks and Sparks suit you? John Lewis?
Come on then. Let's take you out for the day.

Her tiny frame beetling down racks of pastels,
grim mouth practising disappointment.
Right size, wrong colour. Right colour, wrong size.
And then the shock of something scarlet —
screaming, no-better-than-she-ought-to-be red.
A thick, heavy cardigan with military buttons.
A guilty little smile gives her pleasure away
as smell and touch now do their work
and her birdlike hand drifts over the material.
Soon there's a basket of silky white blouses,
slips and things she insists on calling 'smalls'.

At the checkout she beams like a visiting duchess,
tells an assistant that her hair looks pretty.
In the car she hums a long-forgotten tune.
Then, back in her room, she sinks onto the bed....

I'm so worried. I'm so worried. I'm so worried.
What is it now, Mother?
I'm so worried. I'm so worried. I'm so worried.
What's wrong?
I'm so worried. I'm so worried. I'm so worried.
But we got you clothes!
I've got nowhere to put them.

A LITTLE YES

My mother doesn't really know me.
A look comes over her, as she bolts her food
or gulps her scalding, nursing-home tea,
that says, who's this dodgy-looking man
with his stuck-up voice and work-shy hands?

I should be hurt by this, but I'm not.
Firstly, she never had much of a handle on me,
was always too self-absorbed to listen
to my desperate attempts to impress or inform.
And secondly, she's tiny now, diminished,
less than half the woman who used to scare me
by telling me she was going to kill herself,
or throw herself downstairs, or run away;
who at twelve I once found in the bathroom,
pissed and staring at a razorblade,
unable to live but unwilling to do the deed.

Before she was diagnosed, we'd got to the stage
where we practised the love
that we thought we should feel, but even then
she would occasionally whack me
with a royally casual, *What is it you do, dear?*

Today I am sitting with her, on her bed,
in the beige little room that is now her world.
She is quiet, and trembling, like a little girl,
a bundle of old shames, fears and loneliness.

I try to make conversation. It doesn't work.
We lapse into emptiness more than silence.
Do you want a cuddle? I say at last.
She nods a little, *Yes*, and sags against me.
There is nothing of her. She's almost gone.
I put my arm around her — still trying hard.

THE GRANDMOTHERS

The Grandmothers hover in the spaces
where long-dismantled walls once met;
in bricked-up casements and lost galleries;
resigned, abiding, waiting to be asked.

Beneath this old lintel, two sisters
lean against each other, gently
swaying backwards and forwards,
their feelings bleeding into the masonry.

That threshold over there still resonates
to childbed fears, to moans and cries.
A midwife leaves, a coffin arrives,
a family's sobs and sighs remain.

And when at last a building crumbles,
falling away like flesh from the bone,
these presences are left, imprinted,
hanging like cobwebs in the trembling air.

These are the places where, in our hurry,
We leave little pieces of our souls behind.
Some part of me then has departed already.
The Grandmothers welcome me, hovering, kind.

A VISIT

This evening, for a while,
as I sat in the gathering darkness, alone,
my mother, who died some years ago,
came to me – or rather surfaced within me –
so that my pursed lips became her pursed lips,
her fidgety hands my fidgety hands,
her wary eyes my wary eyes.
                                        We sat together
no more than a moment, my mother and I,
and then, in the flutter of an eyelid,
she gently moved on – though for that second,
while I sat in her tired, anxious skin,
I understood, and forgave, and was terrified.

VI

MEETING THE GODDESS

MY LITTLE MAN

What's all the shouting about?
asks one of two thin Islington women,
indicating the hall next door.

Some kind of uniformed organisation,
says the other, darkly,
squinting through the narrow glass.

Nazis…? No, Wolf Cubs, says the elder.
Little Nazis. Quite harmless actually.
Only six or seven years old.

All be over soon then, says the first.
They'll all be turning into eight-year-olds.
Ghastly! they say together.

Just then, as if to prove the point,
in a burst of boisterous caps and badges,
the pack comes tumbling through:

a dozen energised, excited boys,
each full of life and yelling his part in it,
till, just as quickly, they're off and away.

The women shudder involuntarily,
repelled, as if they've seen a crime.
They hold a battered, trampled silence.

I know a boy, says the elder at last.
You'd never catch him behaving like that.
But then he's from a very good family.

And as she speaks she conjures up
a pale and thoughtful eight-year-old,
standing alone at the foot of her bed.

She reaches out a hand and strokes him,
feeling his resistance fade.
Perfect, she whispers. *My little man.*

FROZEN RABBIT

Was it Sue? Forgive me, I've forgotten her name
though I've never forgotten the taste of her mouth
or the tantalising smell of her cheap perfume.
Yes, and the unbelievable fullness of her
when she gave me the keys to her young body.
Me, the fat and spotty fourteen-year-old
who could barely imagine what sex might be like.

The party, I remember, was decorous and tidy,
on a tidy estate in a tidy little town.
The music was the Beatles, and I was a rebel,
waiting for love and a whiff of Sgt Pepper.

Somehow we'd got into the dangerous dark
that beckoned around the side of the house. She let me
kiss her, kissed me back, till, like a record-player,
we went automatic and I became a Rolling Stone.
My hands, the same clumsy adolescent hands
that had failed the tests of button and bra-strap,
were suddenly as accomplished as a violinist,
as safe as Gordon Banks. I cupped her breasts,
like Bobby Moore holding two World Cups,
and for the first time I sensed a woman opening
to me — ardent, willing and unashamed.

I also remember that this was the moment
when the headlights caught us, pinning us to the wall,
and that my hands became fused to her breasts,
immovable, frozen, rigid with astonishment
as I recognised her father coming to take her
home.

ACROSS A CROWDED ROOM

Who's that? What an extraordinary face.
And look at those eyes, amazing eyes.
Kind of — familiar. She's looking over here.
You could get lost in those eyes.

I wonder if we've met before?
It's as if we know each other already.
Maybe we were lovers in another life,
long ago, like Antony and Cleopatra.

Yes, we're probably an ongoing item.
We came together: we were torn apart.
We loved, we lost, we betrayed each other,
compelled by an all-consuming passion.

And now we've spotted each other again.
Venus and Mars will collide right here.
There'll be sparks, desire, a couple of children,
separations and tearful reconciliations.

Finally one of us is going to call it a day.
They're going to croak and desert the other one.
I don't know why we bother, really.
Here she comes... *What are you looking at?*

NIGHT MUSIC

Tonight the stars are broken glass.
He has no one to touch but himself.

He could go back to the midnight shop,
cruise the high metallic racks,
buy himself a pliant lover,
take her home and slowly undress her,
page by glossy page

but the stars would still be broken glass.
There'd be no one to touch but himself.

Later, he might cross the river,
take his ever-growing compulsion
to meet the girls that businessmen meet
under the arches of excitement
where money and numbers no longer do it

but the stars would still be broken glass.
After the business he'd be alone.

He could call her, right now, call her
and say that he wanted to hold her,
meaning he wanted her to hold him
but they both know that he'd be lying.
They never held. He cut straight to sex.

Tonight the stars are broken glass.
He has no one to hold but himself.

BOWERBIRDS

Basically it's their youth he hates,
even more than their beauty;

the lustrous, not-quite-ripeness
of them, the endless possibilities.

Everyone's in love this evening,
and worse, they're only twenty-one.

Couples dotted along the river,
staking out their mating territories;

turning bench after public bench
into deeply private arbours

where, like bowerbirds,
they mime the wordless rituals

of gift and tentative gift; of blush
and glance and touch and kiss.

Alone now, he has come to loathe
their easy, unforced intimacies;

the gazing and the stroking,
and the play of lips on grateful skin.

Their hungry kisses make him shrink
as his skin crawls to the kiss of envy

and every elegant, youthful gesture
makes him older, sadder, emptier.

THE SAME OLD SONG

Fuck, fuck, fuck!
I've done it now.
Said far too much.
Said all the things
I promised
I'd never, ever say again.

Fuck! I can't believe it.
I've given it all away.
Muttered those little truths
That leave you
Feeling like offal
Slithering down a pipe.

Fuck! I've really blown it.
I've made declarations,
Unreasonable demands.
Oh fuck — I've even made a deal.
Thing is, I'm all confused:
Am I in love again,
Or is this just bronchitis?

IN FROM THE DARK

Barely house-broken, he comes to her
downcast but alert, offering her a stone,
a leaf, a feather that he hopes might show
the wonder that he feels and needs to share.
Every tiny gift, each incremental gesture,
brings the timber wolf closer to the fire.
Now trembling, now curious, now aching
for affection, he stalks the warmth and light.
Sidling in from the forest of experience,
mind alive to the first false move, tense
body listening for the dry snap of memory,
he circles slowly round the flames, shudders,
then lays his head upon her lap.
This is how
the wildness dies. This is how we come in.

A TRUCE TOO SOON

I have no answer to the anger of women,
the resentment I see in a small, balled fist,
in a wire-taut smile, in a trembling chin.

I have no response to the hatred I see
that defers and defers and defers to the male
yet revenges itself upon innocent boys.

I have no reply to the old, cold loathing
that slithers behind my lover's eyes,
keeping me watchful and wakeful beside her.

No, I've no answer to the anger of women,
no answer beyond a slow understanding,
a terror, and the age-old rage of men.

SPENT

A thick August night
with the slow air stunned
and the world come down
to a melting maze
of arms and legs
and heads on thighs;
to the rising and falling
of bellies and nipples,
and to one hand moving,
exhausted but demanding,
running beads of sweat
together as it slides,
beyond all relief,
from pleasure to pleasure,
to pleasure, to pleasure....

AS EASY AS FALLING

Love me she said, opening to him like a well
but
love me
became
save me
and
save me
became
use me
and
use me
became
hurt me,
like they
hurt me
before.
So
he did,
he
hurt her
and
it was
all
so easy,
as easy
as using,
as easy
as losing,
as easy
as
falling
down
a well-
used
well.

THE DECENT THING

It was her body, of course, her call, her choice.
What their awkwardness had made together
was a burden, an encumbrance to her. Palely
he had offered marriage, had felt the chains
of responsibility leap as the hull of his life
had careered down the slipway; gone before
even the band arrived.
I don't want it, she said
and he had winced... *You'd better get it fixed...*
So he had done the decent thing, had found
the money she despised, had borrowed
and worked the extra hours; then gone with her
to the seaside town where he had stood, alone
and ashamed, as the bright assistants had fussed
around her, and the busy consultant had done
the business, had made all safe, and clean,
and forgettable.
Outside, on the beach, as he waited in the rain,
he heard the words he would never speak,
would never throw at her, even in temper, even
on the day that she walked away. Some poor
idiot was shouting at the shingle, his flat
voice skimming over the rain-stunned water.
It was my kid too, you know. It was my kid too.

STAG

Oooh Lovely!

What is it about the very word 'marriage'
that has rational people squealing like pigs?
What part of this trite, commercial transaction
sets their eyes agleam, like a fire sale or a car crash?
Is it the prospect of another empty ceremony,
the dull flat drone of the inauthentic minister,
the meaningless farrago of thees and thous?
Or is it the parading of trophy and conquest,
the public triumph of ownership:
the suppression of the singular,
the death of the wild, the extinction
in another of their own surrendered flame?

Aaah Bless!

SALT WOMAN *

Salt Woman, hidden in a world of tears,
I heard you sobbing but I would not comfort you;
Hearing not a lover but the mother of sores,
Banished and shunned in a hundred tellings.

I had forgotten you. I had abandoned you
Yet still you came to me in birdsong and dreaming.
And I was afraid of you, afraid of your giving —
your wild embrace, impassioned as the wind.

Heart Woman, vanished to a lake of salt,
I heard you calling but I could not answer you.
And now that I see you, now that I can honour you,
Everything has savour, but you are gone.

* The Story of Salt Woman – from the Pueblo peoples of the South Western United States – speaks of a fabled woman made of salt who was shunned by the people until they belatedly realised that her crystal fingers could give their food savour – by which time she had vanished into the Great Salt Lake. Since then it has been the task of men to pan for salt in the distant lake – and to do so by panning backwards whilst weeping – a sacred atonement to the divine feminine.

A WORD

(For B & L on the occasion of their marriage)

It's sad to think we might have lost
Those rich and rumbling Jacobean cadences
Which stirred and comforted our ancestors
In times of woe and joy and need,
Those weighted, freighted, archaic words
That uplifted, admonished and held the soul.

Blessed art thou...
Let not your heart be troubled...
Faith, hope, charity, these three —
But the greatest of these is charity....

I've heard that the Inuit of Alaska
Have a hundred ways of describing snow,
That the Ifaluk on their atoll in the South Pacific
Have innumerable words for kinds of anger —
Lingeringer, nguch, tipmochmoch, song.
Once we had charity, now we just have love,
And love is an overburdened word.

Let us then wish our dear friends charity,
A broadening and a deepening, a growing care,
A kinder, wiser, more courageous caritas
That meets the world and all that it can do;
A love that can soothe an ailing toddler,
Yet still burn bright at the end of the day;
A love that travels, out there and back again,
A love that can wait, in patience, and awe;
A love that accepts, a love that allows,
A love that can trust when it doesn't understand;

A living companionship, a learnt compassion,
A quiet meeting of hands, and hearts, and minds.

So, let us now vouchsafe them both this quality,
Which *vaunteth not itself* and *is not puffed up*.
May they cleave together many years in charity.
May they come to know more than just plain love.

CONISTON WATER

Going down
for the first time,
all he could hear
was the water in his ears
and the squeal of a toddler
somewhere on the shore.
The second time,
he heard the rush
of a lifetime,
polishing the stones
of his inadequacies.
But the third time,
the last time,
he felt the sound
and it ripped at him,
tore him like a tooth.
What filled his ears
when he finally went
under was the rending
ripple of her laughter.

HE TAKES A LITTLE POP AT THE MOTHER-IN-LAW

Families again — hers this time, not his.
What you don't want, you get. What you need,
they can never give you.
                                        Her mother takes
a small, slightly nondescript molehill
and turns it into a veritable alp: a loose word
here, some family politics there, a couple
of assumptions and a downright lie.
Within hours the whole demented pack
of us are seething, twisted, ready to pop
while she, the architect of countless dramas,
sits feigning innocence and baffled incomprehension.
There's a certain kind of selfish old woman
who cannot relinquish the power of motherhood,
whose latter years are a rearguard action,
a resentful retreat in the face of youth.
Defeat follows defeat and slowly, inevitably,
the things that could have been gracefully surrendered
are snatched away by exasperated children.
There are victories, of course, nasty little routs,
triumphs to be carried to the grave and beyond.
Her daughter is left with the corrosive certainty
that she will always be less than mummy,
while her son, her darling, the apple of her eye,
stays emasculated, tied to the stake of her charm.
The loathing she felt for her children's father
drips like vitriol into their lives, drama by drama,
commotion by commotion, slowly weakening them,
making them smaller – stifling, silencing, murdering.

IT TURNS AND SOFTLY SPEAKS

Night after night the empty road,
the home-light diminishing then vanishing
as you travel out into the world again,
hungry for a love that you can never allow.

If only you could pause for a moment,
look down at your feet and not at the horizon,
you might spot the small grey pebble of love
lying discarded where you flung it as a child.

What was the hurt that made you a loner?
How did the wondrous gift become a wound?
You're alone. You're still giving
but you're giving from an exhausted place.
Listen to the call of love: admit, accept, receive.

VII

IN THE SECRETIVE NIGHT

CHASING THE FISHERMAN

Here it comes — another workshop poem,
quietly descriptive, and nicely judged;
a low-key, continent, and well-wrought lyric
imbued with an element of difficulty:
not quite obscure but acceptably mysterious;
furnished and burnished with liberal angst.

Oh bollocks! – I want to write a poem
filled with a rage of ancestral bones;
a poem of old chants, challenges and hakas,
a howl, a snarl, an indictment, a charm,
a mantra with anger flying like spittle,
a piece with a blood-price, with dirt on its hands;

that poem from Porlock, from Reading, from Chile,
that poem from Belsen, from over the wire;
a poem by Crow out of Anna Akhmatova,
a poem that gets me to the passionate dawn.

HAMLET IN HAIKU

Hamlet in haiku
A few syllabiloquies
And the kid snuffs it

THREE HAIKU

i

Pheasants on a branch
The last rooks trailing homeward
Rosehips in the mud

ii

Finches quarrelling
A painted hedgerow plundered
God, I hate haiku!

WE KNOW WHAT WE LIKE

We're going to see
that blockbuster movie:
the one based on
the smash hit musical,
which came from
the big television series,
inspired by the show,
whose book derived
from the documentary
about the film,
of the play, of the opera,
adapted from the novel
which came from
that brilliant radio play;
or was it the best-selling
audio book, adapted
from the biography
that won that award,
about the guy on television.
You know, whatshisname.
We love anything original.

PERFECT

Like this, like a revelation, here and now,
a moment that a lifetime's work has led to.
Here, in the kitchen, in the middle of the night
with Juliet asleep and the moonlit world made
transitory.
                    A stirring, an idea, a latent image,
something waiting to be fashioned, to be born.
But then, when it manifests, to simply let it go:
no making, no object; no lens to catch or capture it;
neither canvas, nor paper, nor limiting stone.
Just a moment of itself, like a sunset or a kiss:
like the time Mark Rylance stepped aside
to let Shakespeare himself appear before us;
or the night Nigel North with his delicate lute
became the very strength and comfort of Bach.
Yes, to surrender, to embrace the ephemeral,
to allow what is perfect to vanish away.
Maybe now, sitting here in the secretive night
with the old house settling, grumbling around me.
A man, alone, with the pieces of his life,
the immensity of death, and the sweetness
                                                                      of everything.

DEAD POET

It's good to be dead, to have the leisure
to talk to someone who might want to listen;
to be a poet at last, I mean a real poet, dead
as a doornail and so somehow more believable.
There's no denying it was tough for a while
wandering around with all those feelings in a culture
where feelings were increasingly unwelcome,
where ultimately they were seen as a kind of curse,
where even poets were afraid of words like soul
and pain and spirituality.
                                        So, it's good to be dead,
to have given up all claim to being Percy Perfect,
the man whose mind was a series of rooms
graciously opened to an appreciative public;
good to have given up the fruitless quest
for an approval that led right back to the cradle;
good to be shot of the body I was shackled to,
aching to be free, to be some body else.

Of course, being dead has its compensations;
lazing down the years on this yellowing page,
waiting for you to browse your way towards me,
to find me 'accidentally' when we both know
there's really no such thing as an accident.
I feel like the Raven, just three books along,
who waited for the Hero on the road to his doom.
From here you look shiny, young and invulnerable.
Bend closer. Listen. I have something to tell you.

PRAISE SONG TO THE EARTH

Azima wo he, azima wo...
Praise chant of the Dagara people
Burkina Faso

I praise the Earth, still young and rounded,
full and fecund, blowsy in her greening.

I praise the Earth, long-sorrowing mother,
withered, wounded to the point of death
by sons who take the spike to her passivity.

I praise the Earth, awesome and indifferent,
who neither turns nor lashes out but shrugs,
who cannot count, who kills without rancour.

I praise the Earth, her giving and taking,
her generational exchange of life for life,
new flesh for bone, of moistness for aridity.

I praise her but my culture has no words,
no richly polished words of deliciousness
to pour in her honour, to pour like a balm.

I praise the Earth but even here I'm stealing.
These words are my brother's — *Azima Wo.*

VIII

GETTING INTO GREY

A TRAVELLER'S TALE

Well, it finally happened:
I caught myself wearing sandals and socks.
Oh, they were special-import-mountaineering
lightweight-velcro-fastening numbers
but the fact is I was wearing them, voluntarily.
Sandals and socks, there's no excuse.
I'm a wally, a wuss, an ageing hippie.
My hair has opinions; it goes its own way.
I've started dressing like a jumble sale.
Worse, I listen to folk songs — and enjoy them.
It started as a week-end thing
— secretly doing what I used to sneer at —
but now it seems to have bled into my life,
crept up on me, like eating pasta and muesli.
Sometimes I can scarcely believe
that the man in the anorak is actually me,
walking deliberately up a hill
just so that he can walk down the other side;
and the man who stops to smell the hawthorn,
who smiles at strangers and says good morning,
the one who is sad when he hears a sad story,
who wants to go deeper, who doesn't know.
Then I remember another man,
impeccably turned out, booted and suited,
who wore his reserve like a full set of armour,
and I think of the day when, like Sir Parsifal,
he met a band of palmers on the wasted road.
Sir Knight, said the travellers, *what are you doing,*
wearing your armour on a holy day?
The knight errant stopped and looked at himself.
I'm a fool, he said, *I'm a fool*, and he wept.

AFTER THE BEEP

When friends are protected from friendship's call
And machines bar the way like a maid in the hall,
When a click has you gripping the hollow-voiced phone
And your sigh binds the silence that follows the tone,

When the dark in the day and the midsummer chill
Leaves the soul like a vacuum nothing can fill,
When a prayer gives way to an echoing shout
With the knowledge that God, like the others, is out

Then go to the mirror and stare at the face
And study each line and the pain and the grace,
Then know that the face and the eyes and the heart
Are all that you have. It's enough — make a start.

TO A TALENTED YOUNG FRIEND

For J. V.

Take a walk in the woods. Follow any path.
Slip your city shoes off and feel the mud
oozing between your shocked, wet toes.
Get messy, get lost, get rat-arsed if you need to,
but remember to allow the daemon beside you
to whisper his charm when you step out on the ledge.
Take care to squander your years effectively.
Enjoy the moment, the tingle and the rush;
and when the Grail Castle opens its secretive door
to offer you a kingdom for a question answered,
don't worry if you stumble, or get it wrong —
wrong is the right thing to be doing right now.
The Wasteland will come with its tears and cinders,
its shaming Damoselles, and confining armour.
For the moment feel the wind as it rakes your skin,
calls on you to make that first incredible leap.
Trust it. Lean on it. You're a young hawk. Fly.

TEARAWAY

Above the falls it looks so easy.
The trickle from your soggy field
is an invitation to the world,
while the brook that runs from this beginning
is clear curiosity, a promise of adventure.
It draws you like a tender leaf;
new-fallen, floating; already separate.

The growing pull brings on the shallows:
movement, noise and fast-cut images;
sudden tunnels of hurried green, made loud
by the gathering of talkative waters;
bends that open onto dazzling reaches
of rippling spill and wordless chatter.

Ahead of you, you wouldn't know it
from the passing banks and nodding reeds,
something awaits you, something unthinking,
slow and pike-like, of sinuous cruelty.
In the calm, your reflection smiles up at you.
You shatter it with a casual hand.
The water lifts you, carries you forward.

UP FROM HAIGHT ASHBURY

He finally gets to San Francisco

The raven sits on the arm of a lamppost,
his croak distinct in the piney air.
He's watching a hopelessness of dossers,
gathering, blinking, scratching their arses
as they climb out of their cardboard barrio
just by the entrance to Golden Gate Park.

The raven sharpens his beak on the metalwork,
tapping out a warning from the Other World.
You'd expect the dossers here to be old hippies —
washed-out tattoos and toothless chucklings,
but they are all young — American innocents,
blown in from Idaho and the lonely Dakotas.

I'm in mid-swerve, and turning to leave
in my just-been-clocked-by-a-crack-dealer way,
when I realise that this is what I was here for,
a glimpse of my yearned-for-yet-unlived youth.
The crack dealer smiles, and promptly forgets me.
The raven follows me all the way home.

MORNINGS

I love these mornings, these do-nothing mornings:
the old house, still, accepting, idling;
jackdaws squabbling around the chimney tops
while a robin rehearses on the quince;
the slow light, warming the tired stone,
and the nearby bleat of March-born lambs.

Windy mornings too — their shallow bluster,
their wheedling question, and complaint:
the casements rattling, the fluttering glass,
the whole house protesting, talking to itself:
resentful draughts, shrill and needy,
the angry slam of a put-upon door.

And those other mornings, like a shapeless prayer,
mumbled, incoherent, yet of infinite solace:
the settling-in of a day-long drizzle,
the amplified drip of air-become-water —
stasis, surrender, saturation —
gathered and gentled by the constant rain.

MEMENTO

On my wall I have a stone, a remnant
which I liberated from a public park,
from a midden littered with empty cans,
discarded bottles and foul-smelling rubbish.
It's the shoulder of a broken gravestone,
a smashed-off wedge from a limestone truckle.
It boasts a single, barely recognisable face
of careful lettering that says no more than

IN MEM...
and
FRANCES...
WHO DEPAR...
and then
... YEARS...

I know little about it, except that the park
was once the graveyard of a debtor's prison,
home to the frivolous and the impecunious.
I saved it one damp and wintry morning
after I'd seen it hurled by a wino who screamed
like Moses throwing down the Tablets,
red-faced, indignant, inspired in his rage.
I got it home and hosed it down, scraped it
then scrubbed it, then left it in a tub of bleach.
I wanted, or rather I needed, to make it clean.
Now it's a memorial to my own prodigal dead:
the bellicose lads and the sad inebriate women,
the blowsy wives and their bitter defeated men.
At times I can almost smell the tap-rooms,
with their fug of yeast and rough-cut tobacco.
I imagine the faces, determined and cheerful,
three-sheets-to-the-wind or melancholy-sour.

I see the bravery, the fear, the constant striving,
the recurring failure and the turning-away.

On my wall, a fragment of broken headstone
to remind me of people who are all but forgotten.
Sometimes I can sit and ponder it, fondly;
at other times, I still need to scrub it clean.

BAD DAY

I'm watching bluebells nodding in the orchard
when I think of my father for the first time in years.
A breeze of grief stirs the damson blossom
then dances away among the trees.

If there's a measure for us, it's our parents,
and in those terms I haven't done too badly:
real love, a home, some genuine friendships —
but I would have liked a body of work, something
for the memory to run its fingers over,
something to leave with a chance of lasting.

I can't count the projects I've left unfinished,
dumped because of a negative word
that carried the edge of my parents' contempt.

What I wanted, what I lacked, was a sense of blessing.
What I got was the acid burning of their scorn.
And now I'm angry. It's the same old pattern:
first grief, then shame, then ruinous anger.

The buzzards have left their nest down the lane.
They circle over the house, rising on a thermal.

I'm looking at sixty, and still having bad days.
Sometimes you just want to fly away.

THREE RAGAS

(i)

Morning

The music comes to me,
drifting over the lake,
as a breeze strokes the face
of the smoky waters.

I am eating the air of India
but I am a coach-party wallah
and very young. My English shoes
have barely stirred the dust.

The music speaks of Siva
the Destroyer and his Sakti
though I am blind to him
dancing in his circle of fire.

As for Kali, the Smiling One
with her terrible necklace,
I have no patience to sit
with her and count the skulls.

The ache in my body says,
Stay. Sit and listen,
but my head says. *Look!*
Over there, an elephant!

I'm off down the road again.
The music fades behind me.
My shoes keep their polish
in spite of the dust.

THREE RAGAS

(ii)

Afternoon

The Delhi kites are circling
and a fever is upon me
as my rickshaw threads
its way against the flow.

On a time-out from business
thirty years later
I'm staring at some pi-dogs
as they squabble for scraps.

One noses something
that catches my eye – a man
laid out upon the ground
in a strange and listless pose.

He's lying in a clearing
left by the multitude
that eddies around him
on its way to the Mosque.

This man is no drunkard.
This man is no junkie.
This man is dying,
alone, on the pavement.

I look back, a sick, fat man
on a rickshaw. Our dull eyes
meet for a moment,
then he covers his face.

THREE RAGAS

(iii)

Evening

In the City of Ghats
overlooking Mother Ganga
Siva is dancing
as the pyres crackle and spit.

I am lying on a day bed
humouring a doctor
as a lizard smiles above me:
Kali waiting for lunch.

The doctor is a kindly soul
but he doesn't know
what's wrong. I am weak.
He is sweet. I am afraid.

Below on a mud bank
a herdsman beats a buffalo.
The whack of his lathi
offends the sandalwood air.

Outside in the alleyway
someone is chanting.
I'm held by it, ambushed,
taken by surprise.

My journeyed heart begins
to open. I am by a lake,
enchanted by an older music,
dusty – ready to hear.

FOUND WANTING

Late afternoon in early April,
a wisp of cloud in a clear blue sky.
The scent of balsam is sweetening the air
while the greens of young larch, willow, and hazel
combine to form the first rush of spring.
I'm watching the buzzards cruising their territories,
cadging an updraft to the lip of the cwm,
where they hover to note the scavenging options:
a wounded roebuck, a stillborn lamb, a rabbit
too far from the safety of the warren.
They circle languidly back to the edge again,
lazing on a thermal, waiting for a death.

Watching them, I think of my cousin Anne.
A natural connection, she just soars into my mind,
and hangs there the way the dead sometimes do.
I felt ashamed when she died, having failed to find her
when she lay dying, and I was in the area.
We write, we call – make the minimum effort –
but the news of a death still leaves us judged.
Prepare to feel guilty, she said to me once
when we were anticipating the deaths of our mothers.

I wish she had come here, had stayed in this house.
I wanted her to see me settled at last, to be witness
to my landing, my joy and good fortune.
But it wasn't to happen, we didn't reconnect,
so a part of me will stay the callow nonentity
she would have considered me right up to the end.

It's going to be a beautiful evening.
Things are gathering for the little revelation
that often occurs here, around this time. The alders still
and begin to darken as the shadows of the hanger
pour like honey and the larches point towards the indigo.
Everything waits for the evening star.

OTHERWISE

It could have been otherwise. The world
might have been baked a different shape.
We could have been sovereigns, or simple
saints, lovers of earth or seaborne wanderers.
But no, we are ourselves and torn between
the need for love and what we call our duty.
Life can be cruel, has never been otherwise,
so we have learned some iron truths:
that hardships lead to a hardness in the heart
and that work often serves in place of love.
But on a rolling blue afternoon in April
we can sit and watch the world unwinding,
remembering the light as well as the darkness,
and see ourselves for what we really are:
plain people, good, for all we feel otherwise,
gifted with a talent for thought and kindness.
That's when we gently reopen to the world,
to the drifting blossom and the scent of lilac.
It's another spring. The world has survived.
Life has a beauty and — admit it — so do we.

AN AFTERWORD:

THE INHERITANCE AND THE UNDERWORLD

These poems were not originally written with a collection in mind. Over a period of nearly twenty years they have spoken to live audiences: affirming, comforting and occasionally enlightening people about their own struggles and obsessions. They were written to be spoken, often with specific groups and gatherings in mind. As such they were put to work – in the room – and so served their purpose.

They have rarely been published, either because of sheer laziness on my part or because they don't fit into the current mold of what poetry ought to be. Though I would have liked it to be otherwise, they have been variously dismissed as "straightforward", "uncomplicated" or downright "simple". From a high literary point of view then, they may not be great literature, but from the point of view of an audience member who distrusts poetry – who may have felt belittled or shunned by it in its modern dress – they are clear, direct, and accessible. Together, they chart a journey from a largely unconscious and wounded victimhood to a hard-won, if still partial, self-awareness and acceptance. They change over the years in quality, density and focus, reflecting developments in character and style. It's uneven and occasionally rough stuff but it's honest, and of its moment, and as such I decided to hang it together as a sequence or collection, rather than jettison parts of it as a form of juvenilia or 'therapeutic poetry' (such a contemptuous phrase).

In fact, the underworld journey this collection points to did involve numerous therapies, both psychotherapeutic and physical. There were also innumerable workshops and seminars, men's groups and gatherings, initiatory rituals, retreats and shamanic explorations. The poems reflect this eclectic mix of influences in their assorted styles and responses. Over time, some did get published in magazines while others lay in drawers until they were dusted off and brought out for the readings and events, which evolved out of my work.

I have acknowledged individual publishers and thanked my teachers and guides elsewhere, but I would also like to acknowledge the men and women who shared this journey and allowed me to join them in their own particular versions of the underworld. Though many of them remain un-named, and occasionally anonymous, that doesn't mean they have been overlooked or forgotten. We all have an inheritance and many of us struggle to speak our truth. Some never get to say a word, still less receive a hearing. This book charts one journey from silence to self-expression – sometimes just speaking is a victory.

William Ayot
Mathern
2011

INDEX OF FIRST LINES

Lightning Source UK Ltd.
Milton Keynes UK
UKOW04f1301220615

253925UK00002B/35/P

The Hidden Motor

The Psychology of Cycling

Martijn Veltkamp

An imprint of Bennion Kearny

Published by Dark River, an imprint of Bennion Kearny Ltd

Original Title: De verborgen motor
This edition published by agreement with Uitgeverij Prometheus

ISBN: 978-1-911121-11-4

Published by Dark River, an imprint of Bennion Kearny Limited
6 Woodside
Churnet View Road
Oakamoor
ST10 3AE

About the Author

Martijn Veltkamp is a psychologist based in The Netherlands. He obtained his PhD from the University of Utrecht in 2009, and specializes in motivation and behaviour. He is a passionate cyclist, writer, and follower of cycling.

For more information, please visit www.martijnveltkamp.nl

Twitter: @MartVelt

Acknowledgements

I would like to thank a number of people who were of great help during the process of writing this book. First the (former) pro riders and experts for sharing their experiences with me, namely Greg van Avermaet, Gert Jakobs, Harm Kuipers, Henk Lubberding, Steven Rooks and Tom Veelers. Matthijs Nikolai Bal, Olivia Butterman, Thomas van Rompay, Gert Veltkamp and Johan Fjodor Verwoerd provided valuable suggestions and constructive comments on early versions of several chapters in the book, for which I would like to thank them a lot. I am very grateful to Michiel Rouwenhorst and Egbert Veltkamp for critically reading the entire first draft of the manuscript, and Marieke van Oostrom, Mariska Kortie and Inez Veneberg at Prometheus for their endless detailed comments and suggestions while editing the manuscript; it really translated to a much better end result! A great thank you to Niels Stegeman for the good and swift translation of 'de Verborgen motor' into 'The Hidden Motor', and James Lumsden-Cook at Bennion-Kearny for the many suggestions to optimize the English text. Finally, and last but not least I like to thank Laura, for the many discussions on the content as a fellow psychologist, but also for providing me with the opportunity to spend so much time on this book, time that for sure could have been spent elsewhere.

Table of Contents

Prologue

There was a time when almost everyone was just dying to take apart Fabian "Spartacus" Cancellara's bicycle.

A conspiracy theory, in 2010, claimed that the vigorous Swiss had won both the Tour of Flanders and Paris-Roubaix with the help of a motor hidden somewhere in his bicycle, and not on his own merit. Even now, the internet still abounds with clips showing Cancellara speeding away from Tom Boonen on the Kapelmuur in the final lap. Large, red arrows pointing towards the Swiss' handlebars, combined with frames so enlarged they become vague, near Impressionist smears, suggest that Spartacus used so-called 'mechanical doping' or, in other words, activated his mysterious motor.[1] The question, therefore, is – would we uncover the Swiss' big secret were we to cut up his bicycle?

When a racing cyclist performs so splendidly that he outraces his competitors with apparent ease, as Cancellara did in 2010, is it any wonder that both friend and foe want to figure out the secret to a rider's success? And, aside from speculation about hidden motors, what about more likely suppositions regarding illicit substances? Especially when we take into account the abundance of doping scandals in the 1990s. Whatever the case, when a supreme performance is delivered, to many people, mysterious forces appear to be at work.

*

Mysterious Forces at Work in Sport was a book that was published way back in 1941. Its author, sports journalist Joris van den Bergh, described how people in many different branches of sport are capable of extraordinary achievements based on their mental strength. There is a reason why people such as Gert-Jan Theunisse – mountain jersey and Alpe d'Huez stage winner in the Tour de France back in the 1980s – commented that, as far as he was concerned, the mind is the key to success. Or, as he put it: "Climbing is, above all, mental labour. Whatever the head is grinding away at, when you're in the mountains, it affects the body nearly 100%."[2]

As we shall see in this book, what Theunisse says about climbing applies equally to all other race elements and terrains. The mind is the invisible, mysterious power they were already writing about in 1941, but it is also the power that, with all the doping scandals nowadays, seems to be in danger of being forgotten.

When viewed in this light, Fabian Cancellara is indeed racing with a hidden motor. A very strong and silent one: his mind. A few years after the rumours about a hidden motor in his bicycle, he won the Hell of the North for the third time in his career. Unlike previous victories, the champion that year was decided at the finish line itself, in a duel with the Flem Sep Vanmarcke.

Cancellara's preparation for the race was far from ideal, falling twice in the week before Paris-Roubaix. In the race itself, no one wanted to take the lead in Cancellara's group. He was the absolute and only favourite, and his competitors felt that if they raced him to the finish, they'd lose well before the end.

The race turned out to be an incredibly tough event, with Cancellara cycling from a practically hopeless position to the lead position, finally defeating Vanmarcke in the final dash. Once across the finish line, he dropped from his bicycle in total exhaustion. He lay stretched on the grassy centre of the historic cycling track of Roubaix, and needed to be supported by two aides as he made his way to the stage, completely spent.

He produced only barely coherent words in the interview following the ceremony. He explained, in English far worse than people were used to, that finishing solo was always good, but that today he had to fight the entire way – all the way to the end. But it was a fight he fought nonetheless: "My head and my legs simply wanted to take me this far."

This statement is a testament to pure willpower. When your body is aching and every fibre cries out that it's time to stop and you can't go on, willpower stubbornly gets you across the finish line, to victory.

There are times when a sportsman can go beyond the limitations of his body. The French cyclist Joël Pelier, for example, was so driven to finish well on the 17th stage of the 1986 Tour de France, that immediately upon arriving on the Col de Granon, he had to be put on a ventilator and ended up in a 7-hour coma.[3] That is the powerful, hidden strength of the mind.

Prologue

Ever since the publication of *Mysterious Forces* in 1941, there have been many changes in the world of sport, and cycling, but also in psychology. The past decades have seen many studies that better explain why sportsmen and women behave the way they do. With cycling, a number of profound questions have been asked. Why is cycling alone – as per a time trial – so much harder than in a group? Why does one bad day in a grand Tour mean nothing but bad luck for one team, while another team with double the effort and enthusiasm succeeds in every escape? Why can a cyclist who just became a father suddenly perform so much better than before? Why does a lead group with five riders work so much better together than a group of 15? These are all questions that can be explained by looking at the sport through the lens of psychology.

The purpose of this book is to provide insights into the mental aspects of cycling and sport by examining examples from big cycling races and psychological studies that explain the course of these races. We'll find out how Bradley Wiggins developed a sudden fear of descents in the 2013 Giro d'Italia, and what he could have learned from Gianni Bugno in this regard. We'll see why Filippo Pozzato lost the 2009 Paris-Roubaix, and why Fausto Coppi made incredible getaways that no one else dared.

This book is an overview of the most *important* mental aspects of sports cycling. These are aspects people will find easy to recognise watching a race on television, and which cyclists will also feel themselves… when they're trying to motivate themselves, and when preparing for or participating in races.

To set us off on our journey, the first chapter will discuss cycling as both a team sport and a solo venture. Let's get started!

1

Time Trials: How Strong is the Lonely Cyclist?

Despite cycling being a team sport at heart, to many outsiders it seems more like a solo sport. After all, there are a handful of favourites (nearly always mavericks) and races are won by individual riders not complete teams.

However, as followers of cycling know all too well, a rider cannot compete successfully without being part of a team, and within any team – riders have individual roles to play. They contribute in their own way to the group's strategy to help ensure that *one* rider in the team ultimately triumphs.

Time trials form a special discipline in cycling. While cycling in and of itself is a real team sport, it is here that a rider must suddenly bike alone, followed only by a car with a team manager. Time trials are viewed by riders themselves as the most difficult discipline because the rider has only himself to rely on. So, why is cycling alone so much harder than in a group?

To find the answer to that question we have to go back to 1898. At the time, professional sports cycling was still relatively new, as was behavioural psychology. This period, at the close of the 19th century, saw the birth of one cycling race after another, such as the first edition of Paris-Roubaix which was inaugurated in 1896. In 1898, this race was won in an impressive manner by the Frenchman Maurice Garin, who won by more than 20 minutes over the second place finisher. Garin, known as the 'little chimney sweeper' (he was only 1.63 metres tall and was indeed a professional chimney sweeper), is mostly known nowadays for winning the first Tour de France in 1903.

1898 was also the year when American researcher Norman Triplett performed a ground-breaking study that marked the rise of two psychological movements: social psychology and sports psychology.[1] Triplett was an ardent cycling enthusiast (he followed American races with great interest); his study was therefore about cycling.

Triplett noticed that, depending on the type of race, the average speed proved very changeable. This was only partially a surprise, as in those days (in America) it was very much in vogue to ride behind a motorised pacesetter. Indeed, some events saw cyclists ride behind them for the entire race! Nowadays, this discipline (known as a *derny race*, thanks to the anorexic motors made by the French manufacturer Derny) has almost completely disappeared from the racing schedule. As anyone who has ever ridden behind a motor car or other cyclist will know, it's easy to gain higher speeds in a slipstream compared to battling the wind head on. It follows that a cyclist will ride more slowly in an individual time trial, when not behind a motor vehicle.

But there's another factor aside from the effects of slipstream and wind. Triplett requested the results of all American cycling races from 1897 and calculated the average speed of each race. Based on more than 2,000 pieces of data, he reached the following average speeds for each type of race:

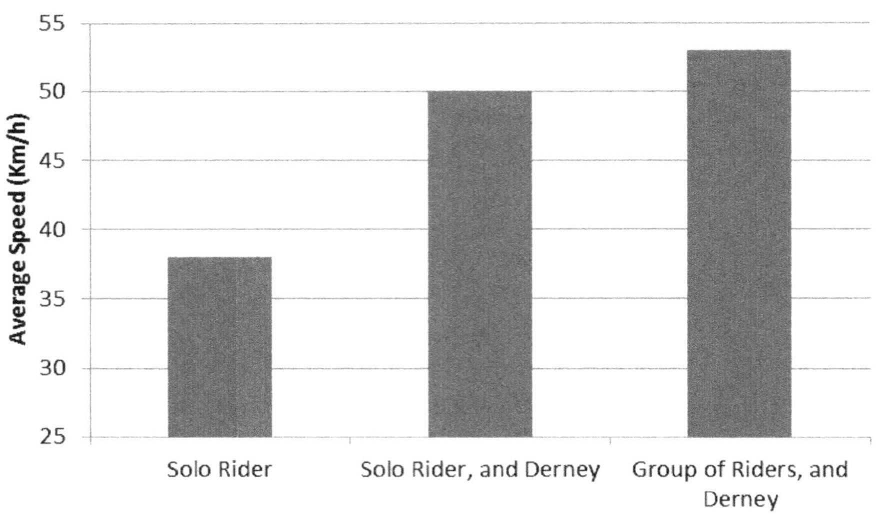

As expected, the riders in individual time trials were significantly slower than those in individual derny races. What was interesting, however, were the higher race speeds attained when riding in groups with a derny. The objective circumstances were almost the same for both individual derny and group races with riders experiencing the same effects with regards to wind and slipstream.

Certain factors may explain these differences. Individual but not group races have a flying start, and group but not individual races benefit from a slipstream advantage. In derny races, this advantage remains for group riders where in the final laps the derny motor leaves the track. But Triplett took such differences into account. Apparently, there was another factor causing cyclists riding in groups to go faster.

The difference in speeds intrigued Triplett. He suspected it had nothing to do with factors like physical conditions, equipment or race circumstances. Rather, or so he reasoned, it was the presence of other riders which made those groups perform better.

To confirm his suspicions, Triplett did the same research in a different setting, where factors such as equipment, wind and weather were not relevant.[1] He invited children to visit his laboratory at the University of Indiana, and fashioned a simple game using fishing rod reels. By attaching a red flag to the fishing line and running the line out along a 4-metre long ‘race track’, the children could wind the reel and make the flag go from A (the ‘start’) to B (the ‘finish’). During the experiment, the children were asked to race the flag to the finish line a number of times, as fast as they could. Half the children did this game alone (thus simulating the individual time trial); the other half did the game in a group – all starting on their own race track together. And as with the results of the 1897 cycling season, the children playing in a group finished faster than those children playing alone.

In short, when a rider races as part of a group it releases, as Triplett put it, “hidden powers that a rider normally does not possess.” Psychology calls the effect Triplett demonstrated ‘social facilitation’. You could therefore say that while time trials are not, by definition, a more difficult discipline, cycling as part of a group is easier.

The phenomenon that cyclists have things a bit easier when in a group is robust, and still has an enormous influence on sports cycling more than 100 years after Triplett’s research. The same phenomenon applies to training, too: training in a small group is easier than training solo. There are several explanations as to why riders in a group have it just a little bit easier mentally.

First of all, the competitive element is more present. While a rider in a time trial is battling for victory, he never sees his competitors, and can therefore never be motivated by their speed or tired gazes to push his boundaries that little bit more. Furthermore, a rider in a group can rely on his teammates for mental support at times when he's completely done in. And finally, a rider in a time trial, not being distracted by other cyclists, necessarily reflects much more on his own thoughts and worries. This doesn't have to present a problem as long as he feels he's riding a good time trial, but should things not be going well, doubts soon settle in and concentration goes out the window.

All these mental factors, combined, can cause a rider to lose minutes over large distances in a time trial – even when a rider is physically and conditionally as strong as anyone else. The best time trial champions of the current generation all confirm this. Take the German Tony Martin, multiple time trial world champion, who has the rather tasteless nickname *der Panzerwagen* (the armoured car). He summarises the reason for his dominance in time trials since 2011: "To me, riding time trials is all about the mind. You need goals to drive you. I need that pressure at the starting line to really want to win. That will is what drives me. It's the only way I know how." [2]

Another example is Swiss cyclist Fabian Cancellara: Olympic time trial champion in 2008, and no less than a four-time world champion. Year after year would see "Spartacus" don the rainbow jersey. His supremacy suddenly came to an end after 2010, and yet, Cancellara didn't seem to be weaker than his closest rival Tony Martin. In fact, the Swiss' performances outside time trials, like in the Flemish spring classics, were better than ever before. The charismatic rider admitted that his early career had been dominated by an iron will to win time trials, and this will had weakened over time. Other than the classics, he was simply less able to focus on this discipline and viewed it more as, to quote the man himself, "business as usual."[3] At the end of his career however, at the 2016 Olympics, the Swiss focused on the time trial. It was to be his final quest for gold before retirement and his physical capabilities as a time triallist turned out not to have diminished as he easily beat the competition and rode to glory on the roads around Rio de Janeiro.

The best example of the advantage gained by riding with others is when a rider is overtaken during a time trial. Usually, this means the rider has already lost around two minutes to the person overtaking him. Suppose time trials came down to pure physical stamina and strength. If so, it would be the easiest thing in the world to predict the outcome. The rider who has just gained two minutes, overtakes the person in front of him and (continuing to progress) immediately leaves him eating dust. However, this almost never happens. Most of the time, the rider being overtaken seems to suddenly get back his fighting spirit. He will remain close to the person who overtook him for many kilometres. This has nothing to do with slipstream effects. The international cycling federation UCI has a rule in place that riders in time trials cannot ride too closely behind one another for too long a time, to prevent them benefitting from slipstreams. No, the effect we see time and time again is social facilitation in the flesh: the other's presence is all it takes. The rider has something to aim for once more. After all, he is directly and visibly competing with someone else and this is sufficient to release those hidden powers.

The explanations summed up so far as to why someone in a group can ride faster than someone alone, are mostly aimed at the conscious thoughts a rider has: thoughts which can distract him from the race; doubts that can catch him by surprise; a lack of faith in his own abilities; the desire to defeat the rider cycling ahead of them (thus lifting performance). However, the phenomenon demonstrated by Triplett so long ago has another cause.

In the late 1960s, psychologist Robert Zajonc wanted to show that people performed better in groups due to reasons other than conscious thoughts. So, in 1969, he decided to research this by way of a test involving cockroaches.[4]

Zajonc got hold of a number of cockroaches. He placed half of them in a tube by themselves such that they had to move towards a light at the other end of the tube in order to find food. The remaining cockroaches had to traverse the same tube in the same way, but had to do so with other cockroaches. As it turned out, just as with humans, the cockroaches were faster when in a group. Cockroaches, however, have no conscious thinking capability and therefore cannot ruminate about their performance or that of their competitors. Zajonc concluded that the presence of others makes you perform better at a very basic level.

Zajonc posited that a person's performance improved as a result of bodily tension evoked by the presence of others. Both people and cockroaches experience this tension, and lead to one's body going on autopilot. The energy in your body focuses much more on those tasks you do well – cycling for a cyclist, for example – and less on other tasks. Indeed, research shows that the presence of others has a positive influence on simple tasks (such as cycling), but that more difficult tasks (such as solving a riddle) are negatively influenced by the presence of others.

This switch to autopilot makes it a lot easier, mentally, for a cyclist to ride in a peloton. For pro-cyclists, cycling is so ingrained in their behavioural repertoire that bodily tension often means that a rider will focus more easily on cycling itself. Consequently, since conscious focus and thoughts are centred on performance, a rider has less room in his mind to worry about things and – perhaps more importantly – he pays less attention to his body. Any indications of tiredness setting into the legs or pangs of pain elsewhere in the body become muffled background noise.

This phenomenon can be compared to the experience of pain almost everyone has experienced at one time or another. The days when you feel under the weather: a headache, sore throat, painful muscles. In short, the flu. And, because you agreed, ages ago, to go to that birthday party – you go. Once you're there, you feel much better. You're having a good time and your throat suddenly hurts much less. The headache is seemingly gone. It's only once the party's over and you're home that all those ailments come hurtling back. The point is, those complaints were never gone; through the distraction and the presence of other people you were just less aware of your body and therefore in less pain.

The same applies to a rider in the peloton as opposed to the solo rider. A rider will feel the burning in his legs much sooner in a time trial than when riding in a peloton. Specialist Tony Martin summarises the secret of riding a time trial as follows: "You have to have a strong mind, and you need to love pain."[2] A side note here is that the German's remark is not entirely psychologically accurate: it's likely time trial cyclists don't like pain so much, but they feel less pain by focusing more on the race and less on themselves.[5]

Similar observations arose in a conversation I had with Henk Lubberding, former Dutch professional road racer. Lubberding spoke from a great deal of experience when it came to the difference between an individual time trial and a solo run from the peloton. His professional career started in 1978 and continued all the way to 1992.

Over those years, Lubberding rode in the team of Peter Post, who was the reigning king of the peloton at the time. Lubberding rode good time trials especially in the first years of his career with, for example, a win during the prologue of the always brutal Tour de Romandie (1979). He regularly won races mostly by sprinting away from the lead group in the final part of the race and reaching the finishing line solo. It wasn't the little races he won, either. He was two-time Dutch champion, won Gent-Wevelgem, and was the victor on four stages of the Tour de France. And yet Lubberding, who was often the centre of attention with his long hair, was known as the lackey of Jan Raas and Gerrie Knetemann. In short, he rode more for others than himself.

Later in his career, his time trial results worsened. Lubberding attributes this decline in performance to his mind. "Time trials are trials you have to do alone, constantly battling the pain and your own limits. A rider who knows he's got a chance for a good result can last longer. He can focus fully on the moment. A time trial is no place for thinking. You have to have a lot of faith in your own abilities. As soon as you start thinking on the days ahead (with stage races), or if you continually wonder why you're cycling full speed ahead, you've already lost. As soon as you start thinking, the ability to deal with the pain is gone."

Apparently, somewhere along the line in his time trials, there was a shift. "I was very focused in the early years. Later on, there were time trials where I had to save my energy. The day after one of those stages, I had to give my all again for Jan Raas, you know. I just lost focus over time. I started thinking more. There was a moment I thought: 'what will I get out of it, I'll end up coming in fourth or fifth anyway'. You can kiss a good result goodbye right there."

When it comes to the difference between riding a time trial solo or racing in front of a peloton solo, Lubberding confirms what the psychological study showed us: it's easier to surge ahead by yourself during a regular stage. "A solo run is really something else. You are able to leave *other people* behind you, so your confidence is up. You already know: I can make that finish line. Nobody was able to challenge your breakaway. Everyone is exhausted. Whenever I escaped from a lead group, when I was able to ditch the others, I knew I could finish it. A time trial simply doesn't give you these references. You're on your own, and you need to figure out what to do."

It is probably clear by now that most cyclists prefer the protected surroundings of a peloton over a solo time trial. But that's not the end of the story – it's not just fellow cyclists who have a positive effect on the rider, the spectators do as well. While the public's influence may not be as great as those of fellow cyclists, the research definitively shows that a person performs better when there's a crowd of onlookers.[6] Naturally, this does not only apply to sports cycling, but to most other sports as well.

It's a positive for riders that cycling races are so well-attended in countries such as the Netherlands and Belgium. A race like the Tour of Flanders is not only very popular amongst cyclists for its long history, but also for the special atmosphere surrounding it: the incredible feeling of cycling past an overwhelmingly enthusiastic crowd of supporters. Compare this scenario to that of an average stage of the Vuelta a España. The race-course is all but deserted there.

One exception to usually desolate Vuelta stages was the prologue of the 2009 event on the TT Circuit in Assen. The winner, prologue specialist Fabian Cancellara, called that day's race a battle of the heavyweights due to the setting and the sheer number of spectators. He also said the enormous number of people was an extra motivation to bike a good race.[7] The transit to the abandoned roads of Spain a few days later was a stark difference.

To summarise, cycling alone can be quite a challenge, and riding alone is likely to be slower when compared to riding in a group. Or will it? In the next chapter we dig deeper…

2

Lead Groups: Speedsters versus Slowpokes

Cycling in a group is easier than cycling alone and, on average, a group will bike faster than soloists. But *if* cyclists bike so much faster in a peloton, why do they often bike so slowly? And if a peloton is so fast, why do big races have so-called 'slow stages'? And if we examine lead groups that manage to escape the clutches of the peloton, there are countless examples of frontrunners who do not work well together and who bike slower than they could. Why?

Lead groups are an interesting phenomenon. A lead group usually has somewhere between two and seven riders. Larger groups (e.g. say 15) don't take the lead for very long as they are often swallowed back up by the peloton fairly quickly, or they disintegrate into smaller groups, one of which then usually takes the lead. Examples of a large lead group successfully staying ahead are rare, to say the least.

But when they do, the consequences are quite often immense. Take the 13th stage of the 2006 Tour de France, when a large lead group – including Óscar Pereiro Sio – managed to break away from the peloton. At the finishing line, the group turned out to have a lead of over 30 minutes. Pereiro Sio, who started the day with an arrears of 25 minutes, really had no chance of gaining a good spot in the classification at the time but obtained the yellow jersey this way – and kept it all the way to Paris. This shows that, even though it only happens rarely, *if* a large lead group manages to come to an accord, it immediately makes the riders in that group hunker down and perform better than they normally would.

The fact that there are examples of large groups biking faster than solo bikers does not mean that the opposite (soloists cycling faster than groups) is not possible. Indeed, whilst Norman Triplett observed that bikers perform better in a group than alone – in 1913, Frenchman Maximilien Ringelmann described the exact opposite.[1]

Chapter 2

Ringelmann was an agricultural engineer. His work consisted of researching possible improvements to labour processes in the countryside. He was no psychologist, and therefore did not concern himself with questions of a psychological nature, and yet he has become famous as one of the pioneers of psychological research.

In 1913, Ringelmann published the results of research that he had performed back in 1883. As farming included the frequent movement of heavy equipment – carts, ploughs, and the like – Ringelmann wanted to know with what number of people this could be done most effectively. To test this, he got test subjects to engage in a tug-of-war and measured the amount of strength they exerted. The tug-of-war had to be done in different arrangements: alone, with someone else, with three people, etc. The graph below shows how much strength participants exerted in each situation, taken on average over several test runs.

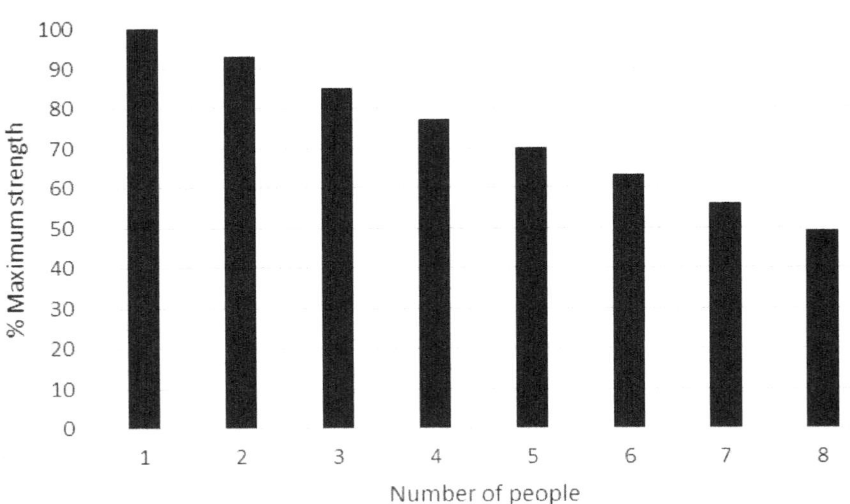

Ringelmann's results contradicted Triplett's findings. Ringelmann observed that the bigger the group, the worse the individual performances became. Indeed, later research, done across different test environments, demonstrates that the ideal group size is between four and eight people.[2] It's no coincidence that most lead groups in cycling that escape the peloton consist of somewhere between three and eight riders. When the numbers get below three, one is not able to get the full benefits of cycling in groups, and as we will see later on in this chapter large group sizes are also not favourable.

With Triplett's and Ringelmann's studies in mind, you could say that cyclists, when biking in a group, sometimes go faster and sometimes slower. Of course, this information doesn't really help us. What would be useful to determine is *when* a group of riders are likely to perform better or worse!

The first studies into this were done by the previously mentioned Robert Zajonc.[3] He showed that the presence of others is beneficial when doing simple tasks, but their presence is a hindrance when performing more complex tasks.

This explains why a cyclist, who is encouraged by supporters along the route, starts to perform better; while a rock climber facing an extremely technical challenge will not. Still, this does not really help us understand why one lead group cooperates better than another. After all, each cyclist has the same task to perform. Of course, this task can weigh more heavily on one body than another, and one cyclist can handle it better than his teammate. But it's all the same to the mind: it doesn't make the cycling itself easier or more difficult.

In 1987, almost a century after Ringelmann's and Triplett's studies, the American academic Arthur Harkins published research in which he tried to combine all of the previous studies into group performance into one model.[4] What his model showed was that the performances of a group depend on whether the people in those groups feel their contribution is (or can be) *evaluated*. In other words: does a rider feel that his contribution to the lead group is noticed by others?

The Tour de France sometimes shows statistics when a lead group makes a breakaway. The viewer can see exactly which cyclist has ridden point the most and which one the least. Riders don't need such statistics. When you're part of a lead group, you don't need stats to tell you which riders are giving their all and which aren't. To a certain degree this is true.

Based on Harkins' research, cyclists will perform better when they think their performance can be evaluated by others. But when they think nobody's noticing how well they're riding point, cyclists are tempted to rely on the performance of others, and a lead group's performance as a whole declines. It's in big groups that cyclists feel their contribution is not noticed, as the sheer number of riders makes it near impossible for an individual cyclist to ascertain whether or not everyone in the group is pulling their weight. This leads us back to the Ringelmann effect that started the chapter: the bigger the group, the less noticeable the contribution of each individual rider, and the less they will actually contribute. After all, they need to conserve their strength for the finale.

There's a reason why there's much more talking between cyclists in big lead groups as opposed to smaller ones. Such big groups often have a number of riders permanently stuck at the rear, and thus you get riders who don't act like they're in a lead group at all. Explanations for this behaviour are often given in a tactical light ('My manager won't let me race, as my team captain still needs to make his move'). And yet, there are times when you see these cyclists confer for a while and then contribute.

Indeed, it would seem that speaking to cyclists who are barely pulling their weight is a psychologically effective tool. A rider who's part of a noticeable breakaway, and thinks nobody will notice when he skips a few turns, will quickly come around when addressed on the matter by his fellow cyclists! This feeling – that there's a chance of being evaluated – makes all the difference between a group that works together well or not at all. Addressing cyclists who don't pull their weight can be quite effective in forcing a simpering breakaway into becoming an efficient getaway.

Incidentally, there is a second much simpler reason why big lead groups see a lot of discussion: a larger group is difficult to coordinate and cooperation is harder to achieve. A single look of understanding may suffice in a smaller group, but this won't work in a big group. Such a group requires dialogue to try and get the members' different interests to align – of which there are more than one in a smaller group.

The discovery that a rider in a group bikes faster than when he's alone (large groups excepted) does not mean that small groups of cyclists *always* manage to set a higher pace than a solo rider. Performance depends on the quantity of shared motivation that the riders comprising the group develop.[5]

A lead group that is *motivated* to stay ahead, will be able to hunker down and give it their all, while a less motivated group may not. At first glance, examining the effects of motivation may seem curious. You would expect the lead group that comes out ahead in a cycling race such as the Tour or the Giro, or in an exhilarating one-day race such as Liège-Bastogne-Liège, to always have highly motivated riders.

However, this is not the whole truth. The group's motivation depends on the chances their escape will succeed. In the first week of a big race, when the roads are often flat and the sprinters ambitious, there are hardly any escapes which last all the way to the finishing line. Later on, when there are hilly stages interspersed between the mountain stages and the sprinters are all spent, or even disillusioned, the chances of success are much higher. Everyone knows this. In short, escapees will be less motivated to give it their all on day 2 than on day 12, as they will have less faith in a good end result when the race is only just underway. The consequence is that a lead group bikes relatively faster and cooperates better on day 12 compared to day 2.

Naturally – thankfully – there are personal differences. There will always be riders who hold the perpetual belief in a good outcome, who always seem to give it their all. These are the solo riders, the champions of the long run; the riders who, even when the chances of succeeding are so very slim, still make that escape and give a racing stage its flair. They give no thought to the 'sucker' effect (to use a not so very subtle term).

This sucker effect is yet another factor contributing to the fact that groups (both lead groups and complete pelotons) often ride slower than they're capable of. Nobody wants to be that clod occupying first position for most of the stage, only to be ditched in the final round. And no one wants to be in the team that struggles to stay ahead of the peloton before seeing their first rider cross the finish line 30th. To prevent such scenes, a lot of riders and teams will strenuously avoid doing more work than someone else. As cycling lingo will have it, they prefer to 'first finish what is on someone else's plate'.

Chapter 2

Thankfully, there are exceptions: riders who are always ready to work and not sit around calculating whether or not they may be doing too much of it. These are the men of long-lasting escapes and no-holds-barred attacks, men like Jens Voigt, Juan-Antonio Flecha, Adam Hansen or 90's star Jacky Durand.

Jacky Durand was a professional cyclist between 1990 and 2004. He was known for being a part of long-lasting escapes (which he rarely won). Durand was always motivated to bike whether there was a high chance of success or not. He couldn't care less. "I'd rather finish last and completely exhausted, having attacked on the road 100 times, than finish 25th without having tried a thing." In the end, those long-lasting escapes became so notorious that the French cycling magazine *Vélo* published a 'Jackymètre', keeping track of how many kilometres Jacky had spent riding in front of the peloton each month.[6]

Durand didn't have a lot of success with his insatiable lust for attacking, but he was part of that special breed of riders that cycling absolutely cannot do without. It's their motivation and insusceptibility to the sucker effect that gets a lead group going; they also enhance the chances of such a group cooperating well (social facilitation) and staying ahead against the odds. And while Durand may not have enjoyed a lot of success, he still won three stages of the Tour de France. An even more vivid example is his performance during the Tour of Flanders in 1992…

With 217 of the 260 kilometres to go, Durand and the German Thomas Wegmüller took off from the peloton in a completely hopeless escape. Everyone involved is typically happy with an escape like that: the sponsors (because a breakaway at the least gives them airtime) and the peloton with the favourites (including, in this case, Museeuw, Ballerini and Fondriest) as they can safely let the twosome gain some distance, and then overtake them about 20 kilometres before the finishing line.

But not in 1992.

The favourites kept their pace slow for a long time, and kept looking after each other; they let Durand and Wegmüller stay ahead by themselves. With 12 kilometres to go Durand, in his Castorama jersey, defied all expectations. Sticking to his principles of attack, he left his companion behind on the Bosberg. It was the day the sucker won the Tour of Flanders. Solo!

The previous chapter explained that the simple presence of others can make a cyclist perform better. Whether those 'others' are cyclists or spectators is pretty much irrelevant. And yet, conflicting research from the 80's shows that the presence of an audience could actually make athletes perform *worse*.[7]

So, what can cause the performance of a cyclist to plummet when cheered on by a crowd? The answer to this question has really already been answered. Whether a lead group bikes better or worse depends, as the research initially showed, on the degree of difficulty with which people perceive the task. If the task is easy, performance levels go up. If the task is difficult, performance levels go down.

The study that demonstrated how performance can be affected by the presence of an audience saw its subjects play pool. A number of the pool players were very experienced, while others less so. What was interesting was that the experienced players did better when there were spectators, whilst the crowd got on the nerves of the less experienced players. As a result, they played worse.

When we look at cycling races with this information, it would seem the older, more experienced cyclists are more likely to profit from a jubilant crowd than the freshmen. Riders who have just transferred to the professional peloton are inexperienced and they still need to discover their place in the pecking order. Their insecurity can result in reduced performances when everyone in the crowd (and the camera) is looking at them.

Indeed, recent studies have shown that the *insecurity* of inexperienced athletes – and not so much inexperience in and of itself – is a major cause for reduced performance in groups, or when there are a great many spectators.[8] Apparently, with cycling, the important thing is not so much the difficulty of the task (this is the same for both inexperienced and experienced cyclists) – the crucial aspect is the degree to which a cyclist *feels he is a good cyclist*. When confidence is high, a cyclist will profit from having spectators around but not when confidence is low.

Chapter 2

There are experienced cyclists who'd rather go without the adoration (or the opposite!) of spectators and confident youngsters who get a boost from riding alongside the cameras and getting the crowd's attention. However, generally speaking, experienced (and therefore more often older) cyclists have more self-confidence than less experienced cyclists. As such, experienced athletes will be more positively influenced by the presence of spectators than the other way around. Looking at it that way, it may be a stroke of luck that experienced athletes are the ones who draw the biggest crowds.

Up unto this moment a group of riders consisted mainly of a bunch of individual cyclists temporarily brought together. Sometimes however, a group of riders is much more than that… they are a real team. In the next chapter, we will therefore dive a little deeper into this special form of cycling in groups.

3

Team Spirit: A Team is More than its Members

In 2004, a relatively new team came into the world of professional cycling and started making headlines almost immediately. A team that would, in just a few years, make its way to the top of the pile and head the UCI Team Ranking from 2005 to 2008. Ivan Basso and Carlos Sastre were the team's stars, and the 2004 season would also see the team introduce a new Luxembourgian rider: Andy Schleck. The slender boy was rumoured to be even better than his talented brother Frank, who debuted two years earlier.

The Dane Bjarne Riis – who won the Tour de France himself in 1996 – was the captain of all these established and up-and-coming names. He was seen as a master tactician by the peloton, the key to the team's success. And, indeed, Riis turned out to be the brains behind *Team CSC*. He was the inventor of what, in 2004, was a revolutionary philosophy about the functioning of a cycling team.[1]

Riis' philosophy caught on with other teams. It was a way of thinking and working that didn't just bring success after success, but which also enriched the minds of riders themselves. As Sastre explained, "I never would have thought I'd find a team that would make me grow as a human being the way this team has." Or as Bobby Julich added, "This is the first time in my career I'm learning something that I can use after I stop cycling."[1]

At the heart of this new philosophy was something not all that shocking or even innovative: teambuilding. Trusting each other completely, being ready, and wanting to commit absolutely everything you have for a teammate. This is what Riis' vision boiled down to.

In a way, this philosophy is as ancient as the sport itself. A winner who has crossed the finish line and gets accosted by a journalist for a first response, invariably thanks his amazing teammates, who took themselves out of contention for him. This seems to happen irrespective of the team the cyclist is from, and regardless of the year victory is attained.

It was not so much the concept of teambuilding that was innovative. Rather, it was Riis' execution that made all the difference. Up until then, a close-knit team was a kind of by-product of mutual training and racing. CSC turned that radically around: teambuilding *became a goal in and of itself*. Obviously, camaraderie and fellowship amongst cyclists is important to each professional cycling team, but the methods used by CSC to generate a positive atmosphere went far beyond what other teams were doing.

Team Sky, starting in 2010, did something similar. All professional cycling teams were serious about training schedules and techniques for their cyclists, but the British team took it to another level by following a rigorous scientific approach.

But back to CSC, for now.

CSC was probably the first cycling team to regularly organise training camps where there were no race bikes and no strength training facilities in sight. Indeed, in early 2004, Ivan Basso found himself in a veritable no man's land, somewhere on a cliff overlooking the sea. His teammates were there as well. Riis asked the Italian if he'd be so kind as to throw himself off the cliff.[1] Basso's first response was that he couldn't swim. "And that's exactly why I asked you," was Riis' reply.

This turned out to be an exercise that would serve Basso when racing. An exercise designed to help him overcome his fears. He needed to learn to trust in his fellow teammates lending him a hand; they would be the ones who would jump after the North-Italian rider and get him safely back onto dry land.

At CSC, the goal was to create a team where the riders completely trusted one another and where everyone was committed to giving 100% for their teammates. Other teams may only have had an 80% success rate, by comparison. During his time as team captain, Riis had analysed sports cycling from a distance and concluded that this – *total commitment* – was the key to success.

The world of sports cycling was, at first, reluctant to embrace Riis' new methodology. However, the success of the CSC approach soon started to sway others and turn them into believers.

Psychologically, the added value of active teambuilding is not really all that surprising. An old and well-known school of German psychology, gestalt psychology, had – as its core principle – the idea that the sum is greater than its parts.[2] Nowadays, that movement is mostly known for its insights into visual perception: that what people see is more than the meaning of each individual piece of visual information. We have a tendency to automatically look further than those separate pieces, to combine them into something meaningful (added value).

The idea of the gestalt movement went further, however, and can equally be applied to groups of people – in this case, cyclists. A team is more than the nine individual riders a team manager can select before the race. Incidentally, we've seen this before: the social facilitation effect and its core principle that a rider in a group (in other words, a part of the whole) is capable of more than a solo cyclist.

But being part of a team has added advantages.[3] Practically speaking, a lead cyclist could never win a single lap or even a single stage without teammates backing him up. Riders who fall back to the support cars each day to fetch water for their captain are the ones who close the gaps to other lead riders; they keep the wind away. That takes willing sacrifice.

A good team atmosphere, furthermore, leads to a clear division of roles where everyone knows what to do and when to do it. And when it comes down to it – like when a rival makes his attack – there are no doubts as to whom has to give chase first. That way, the team avoids a late response and a bird that's flown the nest.

Communication is also stronger between riders from a close-knit team. It keeps everyone better informed during a race, but it also has its advantages when outside competition: you learn from each other through talking. When there's a good atmosphere in the team, young cyclists will feel more comfortable and want to learn more from the experienced old-timers.

Finally, but certainly no less important, is the trust and emotional support teammates can provide for one another. Races such as the Tour of Flanders and the Tour de France have become so important that previously unseen levels of stress for riders are commonplace. It's at times like these that cyclists need to depend on each other, to feel supported. Indeed, research has shown that people in a close-knit group can handle stressful situations better through both mutual trust and communication (where people actually discuss their concerns!). Both factors are more extensive and common in close-knit teams.

All these positive effects, put together, provide cyclists with the feeling that it's very special to be a part of a close-knit coherent team. It makes them feel like they are part of something unique. A certain kind of chemistry is created that empowers teammates to do anything for each other.[5] It's therefore not really all that strange that many teams actively started working on teambuilding in the wake of CSC's success.

Riis' team didn't head the classifications for too long though. At the end of the CSC era – around 2008 – the façade started showing cracks. The stable, safe environment the team once offered its riders vanished due to ever-changing (sub)sponsors and team captains. That close-knit team feeling also turned out to have a dark side to it after a string of doping confessions: those teammates who would do anything for each other also protected those that doped.

More recently, we don't have to look far to find the most professional and progressive team with regards to creating a close-knit group of riders: Team Giant-Alpecin, riding under a German license and situated in the east of the Netherlands. Since 2012, the team's motto has been 1T4I, where the T stands for Team Spirit (and the 4Is stand for Inspiration, Improvement, Innovation, Integrity).

Since 2008, sprinter and sprint lead-out Tom Veelers has been cycling for Team Giant–Alpecin (formerly known as Skil-Shimano, amongst others). He has been very aware of how management has worked on creating team spirit. Intense activities strongly resonate within the team, says Veelers, "We are a very close team, and have been from the start. In 2008 we were 16 guys. And I'm even counting the support staff in that figure. That small group quickly became very close-knit. Now, we've got a crew of 100: the riders themselves, including a women's team and youth training, medical assistants, mechanics – you name it.

We've put a lot of effort into keeping the atmosphere within the team the same, despite the size we're at now. And the team's mood is still generally good. That's why, whenever we select new cyclists, we take a close look at the type of person they are. What makes this guy tick? Is he a fit for the team? If not, he won't make the cut, no matter what his achievements."

Putting the team's interests before personal interest is not something just any team can achieve. It takes time and energy, both from the team and individual cyclists, so says Veelers. "The first six months I rode for Skil really took some getting used to. In the Rabo training team [Veelers rode for them until 2008], I was much more used to riding for myself. You absolutely need some time to make that switch, to start thinking and riding for the team. Our recruitment process reflects that. The new guys really need to get used to the focus on team spirit during training camps, and they need to put in effort to learn to act according to the same philosophy. It helps that you spend time with each other socially, away from the races and the sport. You get to know each other in a different way. It pays off in the end."

Most professional and even amateur teams spend time working on team atmosphere. The question is what does a team like Giant-Alpecin do so *differently* that leads to increased success? Veelers can only draw a comparison with the Rabo training team from his early years. According to him, while you were part of the Rabo team, everyone still wanted to show off their individual skills. "We all wanted to be the best, to get into the picture and get a professional contract." On the one hand it was advantageous for him, because it stimulated him to go that extra mile. But on the flip side the team's performance suffered. Also, Veelers indicates that a lot of teams work with premiums. The whole team gets a bonus when a rider from the team wins, but the winning rider gets an extra fee *above that*. That way, you promote individualism and make the athletes in the team less prepared to cooperate.

"Look, as a pro, you get about 10 years of professional cycling, and you've got to earn your living that way. If you get into a position during a race where you have the opportunity to put your own chances and interests ahead of others, you are more inclined to do so. It literally pays off. We don't have a reward system like that at Giant. There is 100% trust that teammates are biking for the designated team captain. The old Rabobank team is now going through a similar turnaround.

You know they have to work towards creating a team spirit. And that takes time, because they're coming from such a different place."

I asked Veelers what 'gains' a good team atmosphere can bring to races. "You notice it throughout the entire race course. You know your teammates are with you when you're biking – literally and figuratively. We bike physically close to one another, so that when, for example, Marcel [Kittel] ends up in a wrong sweep, there are plenty of riders close by to react immediately. But in a figurative sense too, because you can rely completely on your teammates."

A close unit is also very important for a team such as Giant, as they are fully committed to doing mass sprints. The number of successful solo sprinters is small. Sprinting is typically dependent on the so-called 'train' – a number of teammates who incrementally increase the pace during the last few kilometres of the race. The sprinter himself will only need to step up during the final 200 metres. Tom Veelers, often the last man in the train, finds being a close-knit team essential to a good train. "We're very well-attuned to each other: everyone knows exactly what to do. If you need to fix something, like a sprinter needing to be tempered back into place during a full-on final, everyone knows which two guys need to sacrifice themselves. Good team coordination is also really important during the sprint train. We all know exactly what each of our places and tasks are in the train. As soon as new riders join the team, you can immediately tell they still need to get used to that."

And yet Veelers says he finds the learning curve for new and young cyclists in a team with a good, close-knit atmosphere to be shorter than with other teams. "Because you're thinking from the team's point of view, you become driven to share experiences. I notice that I like sharing my knowledge with new, talented guys in our team, like Sinkeldam or Mezgec. By sharing knowledge and experience, the team as a whole becomes better. If you're not thinking primarily about the team's interests, you don't expend much energy on it."

The strength of Team Giant-Alpecin's approach was nicely demonstrated during the 2012 Tour de France. The Dutch team – then named Giant-Shimano – travelled to Liege with big expectation; that year's race would start with enormous public interest. The team had spent years developing the perfect sprint train, with the talented Marcel

Kittel at the end. Those many years of focused investment now needed to pay off with a stage win for the German. But fate would intervene. Kittel started feeling ill and had to back out fairly quickly. Decapitated like that, many teams would have been unable to perform at all, and might have simply tried to gain some television time by sending their riders along in hopeless escapes. But not this team. They immediately flipped a switch and started riding for Veelers. And not without reward: alongside the best sprinters in the world, the substitute ended up in fourth place on the 2nd stage and took third place on the 4th stage.

How did Tom experience the enormous pressure on him and on his team? “It was a big disappointment that Marcel took ill. But pretty soon the team was saying: ‘Tom is now the last man on the sprint train. He is the fastest after Marcel and has the most sprinting experience.’ Everyone believed that. And we knew that if luck came our way, we had a shot at winning. That mind-set was our key to victory. I knew everyone was biking full steam ahead for me those days – just like I had planned on biking my all for, let’s say, my teammate Koen de Kort if that had been the plan. That’s the way it works.”

What the cyclist is describing here is one of the most powerful features of a close-knit team. It is the emergence of full mutual trust based on the fact that the efforts a rider needs to make for his teammates will be delivered equally unto him when the roles become reversed. A consequence is the willingness for sacrifice. Veelers beautifully summarised the result of the active focus on team spirit within the group. “Because we were a real team, even if the individual cyclists weren’t the best in the world, we were able to achieve real success.” It’s a cycling spin of the earlier-mentioned gestalt slogan that the ‘sum is more than its parts’.

A close-knit team spirit is apparently essential for team performance. The question that remains, therefore, is *how to stimulate that feeling.* The methods that aid in the creation of a tight team do not deviate a great deal from the earlier-mentioned practical examples.[3] When searching for new cyclists, it’s a good idea to look at their personalities and ambitions and determine whether or not these fit within the team. It’s also good to encourage interactions outside races and training. This allows riders to get to know one another in different settings, and thus create an open atmosphere sooner.

Chapter 3

The best practical example of creating tight-knit groups comes from the military. In the army, it is vital that soldiers do anything for one another, and that everyone knows what each person's role is and when they need to perform that role. To effectively teambuild within CSC training camps, Bjarne Riis contacted the military. And so it happened that Bjarne Christiansen, a former commander in the Danish military, found himself present and correct. He was the one who organised the practical teambuilding activities. He would drop the cyclists off somewhere in the wilderness with a small supply of food, and tell them to 'figure it out' from there together.

What the two Bjarnes had thought up boils down to this: drop a group of riders far from society, give them extreme assignments to prove themselves to the team (think of Basso having to jump off a cliff) and let them face all manner of deprivation together. These elements – isolating the team, giving them extreme assignments and facing crises together – are a ubiquitous part of groups where strong team cohesion is valued.[3] Not just in the army, but also during student initiations, or the ceremonies of sectarian groups.

As far back as 1957, pre-eminent psychologist Elliot Aronson was researching team cohesion, together with a colleague from the US Army.[6] His work clearly showed a number of things. People place more value on something for which they have had to make a lot of sacrifice. If a group is placed in isolation, it makes the members more attuned to an 'us versus them' attitude. Hardships and extreme assignments add the value – the feeling that team members are part of a beautiful whole.

Aronson makes the comparison with watching a film in the theatre[6]: when you've just paid money to see a film, one you may have spent weeks anticipating, you are more inclined to consider it to be better than when watched on television for free. Seen in that light, the appreciation for the team you've invested in is no different to the appreciation you feel for the newest Johnny Depp movie or the latest iPhone.

Finally, it would be remiss to automatically assume a close-knit team is superior to less solid groups, by definition. This is not always the case. In the end, a team's success is mostly determined by its ambition and its goals. [3] A team's culture, including its values, is of the utmost importance. A close-knit team that is motivated and ambitious will indeed perform better than a fragmented team without any cohesion, such as the small Spanish and Italian teams where everyone seems to bike for themselves.

And yet, a team that doesn't focus on the right races or which bungles training schedules – no matter how harmonious and consistent – will probably perform worse than a less bonded team. The point is you need a good team atmosphere on the one hand, but also fleshed out team goals and the knowledge of how team members view these goals on the other. That's what the whole group needs to focus on.

You can see this nicely in the two teams that we've discussed previously, CSC and Giant-Alpecin. Both teams are clearly aware of the fact that you not only need a tight group of riders, but you also need to indicate what's expected of these riders. Both teams set down core values that the riders know by heart. The content of these values differs quite a lot between the teams, as do the consequences.

On one side we have Team CSC, which stands for: respect (respect others for their efforts), communication, dedication and loyalty (be loyal to your team and your colleagues). Team Giant-Shimano, on the other, bikes under its 1T4I-rules. As a reminder, T stands for Team Spirit, whilst the I's provide the direction: Inspiration, Improvement, Innovation and (moral) Integrity.

The most striking difference between the two teams is the last core value – loyalty (CSC) versus integrity (Giant). There exists quite a substantial difference; especially in the light of cycling's difficult relationship with performance-enhancing drugs. Here we have witnessed the German-Dutch team, with in its focus on integrity, taking a moral stand condemning the use of doping. The Danish formation, however, places loyalty above everything else; a loyalty to the team and your teammates. This loyalty can present a danger when it comes to doping. A cycling team quickly creates an atmosphere in which cyclists would never disavow their teammates, or the team as a whole, even when they are aware they're venturing down an unacceptable path.

Despite it being very difficult to substantiate – the glory days of Riis' formation coincided with the latter days of a culture that seemed to view doping as normal – while the cyclists in the German-Dutch team vehemently disapproved of doping in interviews, the riders in Riis' team kept falling into one doping scandal after the next (Ivan Basso, Frank Schleck, Bobby Julich). Tyler Hamilton, who biked for this team for two years, even wrote a book about the alleged drugs culture within the team.[7] Probably, he wouldn't have written the book if he'd still been employed by the team; after all, he too remained loyal to his team and fellow teammates.

In the next chapter we will shift to a rather different psychological topic. Up until this point, we have covered subjects that are quite typical for team sports, such as the effects of group size and the importance of a good team spirit for performance. Instead, we shall look at the individual cyclist and how her or his expectations affect performance…

4

Great Expectations: Coppi's and Giant-Alpecin's Trust

In the previous chapter, we saw that cyclists in a lead group are more inclined to work together when they're confident that the end result will be good. This confidence is mostly to do with expectation: the expectation athletes have that they're 'in it to win it'.

Such expectations are an essential part of cycling.

This chapter will therefore dive into the role these expectations play in the emergence of talent and achieving success. We'll see that these expectations not only influence individual riders, but complete cycling teams as well. Firstly, we'll examine how even the expectations of an athlete's support staff can influence race performance.

In the 1960's[1], psychologist Robert Rosenthal and his colleagues conducted research to test the idea that a student's performance partially depended on the expectations of their teachers.

At the start of the first semester, pupils from a school in Boston participated in a number of intelligence tests. Subsequently, researchers interviewed the school's teachers and flagged up that particular pupils from the class had scored so well on the tests that they were likely to get very good grades that school year. At least, that was what the researchers told the teachers. In reality, the pupils in question had not performed any better than the others; they were randomly-selected average pupils.

Rosenthal's research sought to address what was going to happen to the 'chosen' pupils. Would they perform better or worse than others? Would the teachers' (inaccurate) thoughts about their abilities lead to differences in actual performance?

Chapter 4

At the end of the school year, the pupils retook the intelligence tests from earlier in the year. The IQs of the pupils whom the teachers *thought* would be excellent pupils rose by 10 points compared to the control group (for whom no predictions of success were made) even though – at the beginning of the year – they scored the same. The pupils, whom the teachers expected to be smarter, actually became smarter!

Rosenthal offered an explanation. The teachers – subconsciously or not – treated the pupils whom they thought would perform better differently. The so-called 'talented' pupils were treated much more benevolently by their teachers and, at the same time, these pupils were given higher demands: they received more challenging and more difficult assignments than the others, and were therefore given more opportunity to learn.

They were also allowed more speaking time in class and allowed to demonstrate their knowledge more often. In short, the chosen pupils were given more chances to develop their talent – even if that talent did not differ from other pupils.

Rosenthal's findings became known as the Pygmalion effect and later studies have shown that this effect works both ways.[2] If you, as a teacher, coach, parent or other type of tutor, expect someone to perform badly, that person will end up doing exactly that.[3] Again, the expectations determine how the tutor interacts with a pupil. Negative expectations essentially mean that the pupil is considered unable to improve much due to limited personal qualities. A lost cause. Thus, from the tutor's perspective, less effort will be put into trying to improve someone he or she thinks cannot be improved to begin with. Additionally, these expectations will be verbally and nonverbally communicated to the pupil, which in turn can negatively affect self-confidence and eventually performance. Thus, a person's expectation of someone is a major influence on the outcome.

A young cyclist is like a school pupil in Rosenthal's study, an unpolished rock that may reveal a rough diamond – after some grinding and polishing by support staff. When a trainer has high expectations of him, the rider will perform increasingly better. Of course, there is always the risk that a young unpolished cyclist, even with intense grinding and polishing efforts, will be exactly what he appeared to be:

nothing more than a rock. That rock will appear to glitter after a lot of guidance, no doubt, but it will never be a diamond. And conversely, a rider that's a diamond in the rough will never be able to shine without a guiding team who sees and nurtures his talent.

Training talent is a delicate yet crucial part of sports cycling. The history of sport is riddled with examples of mediocre cyclists who were – to no avail – trained as future Tour winners. History is also filled with a plethora of forgotten cyclists with a great deal of potential who remained undiscovered and who subsequently gave up their cycling careers for less illustrious occupations. The same patterns can be seen in other sports, like soccer, skating, swimming and hockey. If finding and training talent is such a complicated matter, the question is – how can cycling teams handle it?

The Giant-Alpecin team is, once again, an interesting case study when it comes to the development of talent. To obtain their victories this team (in a way) made itself dependent on the success of their talent development program, ever since they started back in 2008. For example, the team never acquired established riders which, for most professional teams, is *the* standard strategy for quick success. From the beginning, Giant placed their focus on drawing in fresh talent and then, through intensive training, guided them to their peak performance. Indeed, team manager Iwan Spekenbrink, when asked as to his strategy for climbers and one-day specialists in his team, said the following: "We really want *major* talents. [Established] classification riders you can find, but […] should we invest in a rider who can place tenth or twelfth in a major tour? If you look at *our* team now [2013], we've recruited *talent* to win multi-stage races: Daan Olivier, Warren Barguil, Tom Dumoulin, Tobias Ludvigsson and Lawson Craddock. We want to ensure our boys are developed into true classification riders."[4] In 2014, this focus on young talent was further underlined with the arrival of an official youth development team.

That this (perhaps) daring strategy has paid off for the team hardly needs explaining. The technical staff have moulded a boatload of pretty promises into a wonderful team, and developed one big favourite: Marcel Kittel. The German sprinter, under the care of Giant until 2016, has already ridden many victories, including stage wins in the Vuelta a España and the Tour de France. The story of this German rider's rise speaks volumes as to the effectiveness of the team's training.

Chapter 4

Kittel was already getting good results at an early age. He was undoubtedly talented but if we look at the young Thuringian's list of accomplishments his path seemed clear: a candidate pegged to succeed his fellow countryman Tony Martin as the king of time trials.

At 17 and 18, he won the junior road time trial world championship; at age 20, he repeated this achievement in the Under-23 category. And yet, the team saw something else in him: "When he transitioned from the promising riders to the professionals, we soon figured out that sprinting is his real specialty. So that's what you work on with him," said Spekenbrink.[4] Thus everything was aimed at developing Kittel into what his trainers, with their excellent vision, saw him to be: the biggest German sprint gun since Erik Zabel. Without this foresight and guidance, and without the support of his team, Kittel would never have become the champion that waited inside him.

Giant-Alpecin's strength is perhaps even better demonstrated by the fact that Kittel isn't the only favourite the team has produced; they have developed other riders including John Degenkolb, and Tom Veelers whom we heard of in the previous chapter. The team itself is so well thought-out and so balanced, that it automatically increases the chances for each individual. For example, the team has carefully selected its riders to operate well in a train, and prepares each rider for his *specific* part in that train.[4] The principle that the sum is more than its parts once again applies.

Team Giant-Alpecin has an arsenal of talents in its ranks, each of whom is trained for a specific function in the team. The question is how they look for, and entice, new and promising talent. Iwan Spekenbrink has the following to say: "By scouting for talented young guys that surface from time to time [a rider] will stand out at first because he produces good results. The next step is to penetrate to his core. What kind of guy is he? Where is he from? How long has he been cycling? Does he show the potential for growth? All those kinds of things."[4]

Looking at its results, Team Giant-Alpecin must have developed a good gut feeling for scouting, but Spekenbrink says that success is not always up to them. "True talent is scarce. Achievements are, in the end, made by the rider. Not the team, not the trainers – the deciding factor is the athlete. And that's where we try to add as much guidance as we can. The same applies to obtaining talent. You need a stroke of luck."[4]

Just like Boston schools where teachers, through intense mentoring, improved the scholastic performance of average students whom they thought were talented, team managers will sometimes put a great deal of energy into enhancing the qualities of a cyclist whom they just *believe* is talented. The cyclist will undoubtedly perform better, but he'll never attain the level of a champion. Giant is well aware of this risk. Spekenbrink tells of two Chinese riders (Ji Cheng and Yan Dong Xing) in the team in whom they had invested a lot of time, as both had the ability to become potential good fits. "Cheng truly has the talent to become a valuable pawn for a team, much more so than Dong, I must say. In Dong's case, this turned out to be less true."[4] Dong no longer rides for the team.

It's not just a herculean job to fish for the stars of tomorrow from the enormous pond of young cyclists – the subsequent step is no less easy. A promising rider whom you've just acquired for the team must then be developed in a certain direction, and this chosen direction is not always that obvious. Marcel Kittel, our example above, was a seemingly incredible time trial cyclist, but was eventually steered onto the path of the mass sprint by management.

Although not so much for Giant-Alpecin, most teams consider the wish to be the father to the thought. Take France as an example. The country has spent years waiting for the next Bernard Hinault, who won the Tour five times. Each young cyclist who does a half decent job cycling uphill or against the clock becomes *the* new French hope for that kind of work and is then trained in that field. Take Sandy Casar, David Moncoutié, Jonathan Hivert, Cristophe Rinero, Eric Boyer, Charly Mottet, Blel Kadri, Jérôme Coppel, Luc Leblanc, Christophe Moreau, François Simon, Laurent Jalabert, Brice Feillu, Cristophe Riblon or Rémi di Grégorio. So far, no good. It might just be that if French talent had been trained less for all-round work and more based on their individual talents – as seems more frequent at the start of the 21st century – they *would* have made French hopes come true.

Giant-Alpecin therefore shines a light on using the intrinsic qualities of each cyclist optimally. The goal, at first, is to discover talents before exploring them further. Indeed, the team guards itself from thinking the other way around. Take, for example, the promising Dutch cyclist Daan Olivier. Spekenbrink says of him: "He's just someone whom we have to put through the system, to develop him as best we can. He's a good climber, but too young to focus solely on climbing. The boy needs to broaden his development first. He may need that later on in his career. It's a way of figuring out where special attention is needed in his case."[4]

When we look at the training of talented cyclists, for example at Giant, we can conclude that the team manager may appear to be similar to the teacher and his class, but contrary to the teachers in the Rosenthal study, the manager is well-informed. He doesn't just rely on the results of a talented rider – 'this cyclist does good time trials, so we'll turn him into an excellent time trial cyclist' – but collects as much information as he possibly can about the person and starts him off on general training. This way, the cyclist himself takes centre stage and his true skills are allowed to surface.

As we pointed out at the start of the chapter, a manager's great expectations for any team member are certainly not unique. No less important are the expectations the athlete has *for himself*, whether as a professional sportsman or enthusiastic amateur. *Does he believe he has what it takes*?

At first glance it may seem obvious to assume that talented riders and established names are not beset with doubt. They win and are often physically stronger than their colleagues – so there's little room left for misgivings. One would assume that doubt mostly arises when you step down the ladder, away from the elite, into the lower pool of professionals and leisure cyclists. And yet, established cyclists can be perennial doubters while a less-talented rider can be completely convinced of his own abilities. The controversial Italian cyclist Riccardo Ricco, for example, never doubted himself – after all, nobody could come close to his divine prowess, could they? And on the other side of the aisle we have someone like Andy Schleck, the hit-and-miss Luxembourgian, who is said to be a doubter.[5]

Years of psychological study shows that people's belief in their own abilities does not directly link to what they should – objectively – be capable of. It depends more on what people *attribute* their good or bad achievements to: is it their own strength or the weaknesses (or invincibility) of others?

Consciously or subconsciously, people spend a large portion of their day dealing with questions like these. The Viennese professor Fritz Heider wrote back in the early 1940s that, generally speaking, people are like amateur psychologists.[6] All day we strive to give meaning to our own behaviour and the behaviour of others. If someone at work argues with a colleague, we'll wonder why he snapped. Was he in a bad mood, was there trouble at home? Or was the colleague being unreasonable, and he was justified to lash out? These are the questions we ask ourselves – and we should for they help us to make sense of the world and help us adjust our own behaviour. If a co-worker blames himself for an argument with his colleague, they'll likely apologise. If it was the colleague's fault, however, he'll think twice before apologising.

Athletes do the exact same thing. They're constantly evaluating their performance. They try to understand to what degree their achievements can be attributed to factors they themselves control (to what degree *they* are responsible for victories and defeats) or whether outcomes are the consequence of luck or the aptitude of their colleagues.[7]

Psychological studies show that three questions are important when evaluating performance.[8]

1. Do others behave the same way (consensus)?
2. Is the situation unique (distinctiveness)?
3. Do you always act like this (consistency)?

To illustrate these questions, I'll use the example of a cyclist participating in the Tour of Lombardy…

As happens so often on this tour, it's been raining the whole day. Our rider is part of a long-lasting and ongoing escape, climbing up the legendary hill of Madonna del Ghisallo. As the climb progresses, more and more of his strength is sapped from him and, eventually, he has no choice but to forfeit. He drops back and eventually crosses the rain-soaked finish line far behind the winner. How will our cyclist evaluate his own performance at the end of the race?

He'll have to ask himself the previously noted three questions.[7,8] The first is whether or not his performance was the only one of its kind, or whether others had the exact same thing happen to them. If he was the only one to forego victory this way, chances are that he had a lot of influence on the result. If other cyclists had a similar experience, the performance will have been largely influenced by the circumstances. The latter is not unrealistic in our example scenario. After all, it's well known that bad weather makes a lot of cyclists perform poorly and puts them on a downward performance slide.

The second question concerns factors that differentiate this race (or parts of it) from other races. Did this edition of Lombardy have any unique circumstances (e.g., storm, exceptionally strong line-up); something that deviated from normal race conditions? The bad weather again provides one simple answer. However, an effective evaluation of one's performance demands further digging, where one looks at other distinguishing characteristics during all phases of the race. Were there, despite the bad end result, phases during the race that the cyclist *is* happy about? The rider was part of a long-lasting escape, after all, and that's no small feat. The fact that he was able to join this escape is an achievement in and of itself.

Finally, we have the consistency question. Does the cyclist perform consistently badly; does he *always* fall back at the end of a race? Most professionals can (reassuringly) answer this question in the negative. Again, it's useful to examine things a bit further, to spot patterns in the achievements gained. Does a bad performance *always* happen during long-lasting escapes? Does under-performance come about in autumn classics, such as the Tour of Lombardy? By finding the answers to all these questions a cyclist can analyse his performance and expose his strengths and his weaknesses. And a cyclist who knows where his strengths lie, and what he is less good at, can bike efficiently. He will become a cyclist who, *when* he attacks, immediately becomes a danger. Attacking, after all, is only done when the rider is certain he has a chance.

Heider was right when he argued that all people are amateur psychologists who continually question their own (and others') behaviour. However, he also revealed a relative weakness at the same time: *an amateur is not a professional psychologist*. In real life, it is rare that the analysis described above is carried out systematically and to its fullest extent. It often gets stuck in summary judgements which – depending on someone's personality – vary from baseless feelings of superiority to unjustified insecurities.

A wonderful example in the 'superiority' category is Chris Horner. In 2013, he won the Vuelta a España and in doing so set a record of being the oldest Grand Tour winner ever. He analysed his victory as a 41-year-old in the following, rather me-me-me manner in the cycling magazine *ProCycling:* "What I have demonstrated in the Vuelta has never been done before. I couldn't care less who won which races this year; my victory is the greatest achievement professional cycling has seen for a long, long time. I have achieved something which no one has been able to do in the past hundred years. And possibly no one will in the coming hundred years, unless, of course, I'm part of it. My advanced sporting age makes it epic. My achievement is legendary."[9] To be sure, Horner won two stages and the GC which is an enormous achievement, but at the same time previous Vuelta winners did that as well so it's not *that* unique. In addition, the gap to the runner-up, Vincenzo Nibali, was merely 37 seconds after three weeks of riding.

It's the second category of cyclists, those with a predominantly fatalistic mind-set, which garners the attention of psychologists though. These thoughts, with which individuals undermine themselves, are especially dangerous as they eventually – when they keep returning – can lead to so-called 'learned helplessness' which we'll talk about more extensively in the following chapter. There is a reason why sports psychologists are good at helping athletes analyse their performances effectively. They do so by asking the right questions and, more so, by continuing to ask the right questions when many people stop.

The main reason why sport psychologists or trainers and coaches spend a great deal of time unpicking a cyclist's achievements is simple: these achievements help determine the *future* success of an athlete. In the end, it doesn't matter whether a rider wins or loses a lot, it matters how he attributes his achievements, and this comes down to only four real possibilities:

1. *The rider performs well and attributes this to himself.* He will be happy, gain self-confidence, and see himself as a capable cyclist.
2. *The rider performs well and attributes this to circumstances or to others*. He will be very grateful and feel lucky, but will not gain any self-confidence.

3. *The rider performs badly and attributes this to himself.* He will start feeling guilty, possibly become ashamed, and consider himself incompetent.
4. *The rider performs badly and attributes this to circumstances or to others.* In this case he will mostly be angry with everything but himself.

Research has shown us that self-confidence is incredibly important to performing well.[10] Americans succinctly talk about a 'can-do' mentality – *yes, you can* – and this roughly equates to an athlete choosing to attribute successes to himself, and failures to circumstances.

Attributing successes to oneself increases self-confidence, attributing bad performances to oneself decreases this confidence. Athletes who have learned to attribute previous successes to their own strengths are often *so* confident they appear ready to tackle anything. You can find countless wonderful examples of this including Fausto Coppi, the rider who (together with the Belgian Eddy Merckx) is often seen as the greatest sports cyclist of all time.

Coppi was loved and notorious for his absurd enterprises; unbelievable escapes which only he could do. Most famous is Coppi's stubborn venture in the Giro d'Italia on the 10th of June 1949, during the 17th stage. It was the Queen stage: a staggering 254 kilometres. The course included five exhausting climbs, over roads that were barely passable due to bad weather and a lack of asphalt.[11] The start in Cuneo saw Coppi's main rival, Gino Bartali, wearing the pink jersey. Despite Bartali being close to retirement age for a sports cyclist, and Coppi having time on his side, Bartali was probably not very worried. The mountains were the 'demesne' of Bartali. Coppi, on the other hand, was the king of time trials.

But something improbable happened early on in the race. The roadside supporters could hardly believe their eyes as on the Colle della Maddalena, the first climb, with 192 kilometres left to go, Coppi accelerated. Sports journalist and author Dino Buzzati, who was covering the tour of Italy that year and was able to watch Coppi's escape live, wrote that evening, "We realised that this episode would be talked about interminably for years to come, even though it didn't seem that special: just a man on a bicycle, leaving a group of fellow cyclists behind."[12]

Nowadays, such a long-lasting escape is doomed to fail; perhaps viewed as an act of despair. It wasn't much different back then… as was demonstrated by the reaction of Coppi's rivals. Buzzatti wrote, "And Bartali? Did the champion not move at all? He did, [he chased him]. But it was strange, his heart didn't seem to be in it, like he didn't believe in it, as if he considered it all a harmless feint."[12] Cycling 192 kilometres alone, through bad weather, over bad roads, climbing steeply, with a peloton breathing down your neck – it seemed a pointless exercise from the get-go.

Yet Coppi persevered. The bad weather may even have worked to his advantage. Instead of a large peloton chasing him, the race quickly evolved into a battle of two: Coppi versus Bartali. The result was astounding. In Pinerolo, Coppi sent his Bianchi across the finish line in first place, after nine hours of biking. Bartali placed second, but was a staggering 12 minutes behind. That pink jersey was for Coppi.

Why did Coppi decide to attack so early on this legendary stage, whilst others would probably not have countenanced the thought? On the one hand, Coppi was only second placed in the general classification but this is not a good enough explanation on its own. Most cyclists who choose to attack and take risks in order to go from second place to the top of the GC always take into consideration that risks present dangers; instead of gaining one place, one might lose multiple places far more easily. A big escape that hasn't a snowball's chance in hell of succeeding is therefore too risky. The chance of someone overtaking them is enormous, and a cyclist can lose his place on the podium through such careless actions.

Coppi didn't care much for the podium, as many of the greats do. Only first place mattered. That mind-set makes it easier to take risks: if you think second place is just as bad a result as 100th place then you can focus totally on just one thing – the number one position – rather than strategically trying to ensure a top-10 position, as many cyclists do.

A much more important reason for Fausto Coppi's early flight was the result of his earlier performances, and his analysis. He had built up confidence. Indeed, long-lasting escapes are a frequent presence in

Coppi's cycling career and became something of a trademark. He knew from experience that extremely long-lasting solos could lead to victory, but more importantly, he knew that those solos could lead to victory *because this was his strength, because he possessed this strength.* And what he didn't do was attribute his solo escape victories to fate, or to weak or inattentive rivals. If Coppi had, he most likely would never have attempted his long flight in the Giro.

Fausto Coppi's heroic escape illustrates the idea that behaviour in a race and a cyclist's strength aren't so much driven by previous successes or failures as by a rider's interpretation of those outcomes (e.g. attributing successes to personal strengths and failures to circumstance). Many athletes do not do this. In fact, some are inclined to do the exact opposite: when they win they are so thunderstruck as to not realise what just happened… they were just lucky. But if something goes wrong, they see it as confirmation of how little they are worth.

Exactly because these thoughts have so much influence on an athlete's performance, is it important they are addressed, and it is often helpful if someone has another person around to ask the right questions: do you always perform the same in this situation? Do others do the same or are you unique? This is something an athlete can train for, too. Just as a cyclist's training is meant to strengthen the body, a training of the mind can strengthen the brain.

This way, an athlete learns to ask the right questions and attribute his performance to circumstances he *controls.*[10] Further analysis of underperformance, say during bad weather, may show that the cyclist eats less regularly in such weather conditions, or drinks less. Or perhaps he is more sensitive to cold and the team's regular rain outfit is not optimal for him. Food, drink, and clothing are matters a cyclist can influence and can work on, as opposed to the weather.

The effect of this mind training on sports performance was studied a few years ago by a number of French psychologists.[13] The researchers divided reasonably experienced golfers into three groups [A, B, C]. One of the groups [A] had to putt over four sessions, were given no motivational feedback, and were allowed to practice in-between sessions. The two other groups were the ones that mattered. After a session of putting, one of the other groups [B] was told their performance depended greatly on their concentration, efforts and strategy. Meanwhile, the final group [C] was told they really had very little influence on their performance. The result would predominantly depend on the difficulty of the task itself. In other words, one group [B] was trained to attribute their sports performance to things they themselves influenced and which they could work on. The other group [C] was told the opposite; they were given a demotivating message.

After these instructions, both groups were told to do the same thing as the first group: putt three more sessions, and practice as much in-between as they wanted.

The research showed that the feedback had the intended effect; the golfers attributed their performance to their own skills or (bad) luck respectively. The most important result of the study was that thought training turned out to have a *direct influence* on physical training – the practice in-between. The group that did not receive instructions [A] kept practicing for equal amounts of time. The group that was taught that their behaviour would barely affect their performance [C] spent less and less time practicing. The golfers who believed they had lots of influence on their performance [B] *increased* their practice time. In short, what the study suggests is that a cyclist's expectations of himself not only affect his behaviour *during* a race, but also his training rhythm and motivation. And that makes that influence possibly greater than we had, at first, envisaged.

A lion that sees a mouse when looking in the mirror will not race well: he's afraid to rely on his own strength. A mouse whose coach sees him as a lion, will exceed his own limitations. That is the power of expectation, the power of belief. These expectations don't apply to just individual athletes or their support staff; it even applies to whole teams.

In the 1990s, the Rabobank cycling team, for example, often started out very well during the first few days of a big race, and then managed to keep that energy going right up to the finish line. They seemed to have a good team atmosphere. They believed in winning the stage, they believed in a positive end result. The team joined in with the right escapes – if it wasn't Boogerd, it was Denis Menchov or Erik Dekker. Everyone was able to give that little bit of extra effort. However, if they experienced setbacks in the first week – a fall, or a flat tire for the team captain at an inopportune moment – their thoughts quickly segued into 'this is not our race'. The riders appeared to bike around unmotivated, only out 'on duty', and with no zest for attack.

Eventually, one thing applies to all teams. When the team is confident that the cyclists are capable of racing well, then all riders in that team will profit. Tom Veelers, who is the last man in the sprint train for Team Giant-Alpecin in many races, acknowledges this. "When you're with Marcel [Kittel] at the starting line, you just have a very good chance of winning. When we bike for Mezgec, who's very talented, we get extra satisfaction when he wins. But other guys, like Marcel, allow you to go that extra mile, because you know it's there and the chances of winning are very good. It's the same for John [Degenkolb] when arriving at slightly uphill stages, because that's his speciality. But when you get to a flat stretch of a stage, everything has to be perfect for him, it's the only way he can win. That puts a lot more pressure on the team."

There are also races where a team truly has very little chance of racing well. The Tour of the Basque Country with its mountainous terrain was one of those races for Veelers' team that specialized on flat sprint stages. He succinctly summarises many of his team mates' thoughts during the Vuelta al Pais Vasco: "What am I doing here?!" The expectations within the team for that tour were usually quite low. Such an attitude might be viewed as realistic (rather than pessimistic) and yet, as Veelers indicates, it doesn't mean the motivation to bike such a tour is non-existent. The Tour of the Basque Country is a very good preparation race for races later in the season, explains the Giant cyclist, "to grow some uphill backbone."

It's really only for the three major races (the Giro, Tour and Vuelta) that all participating teams have prepared optimally. The first stage of these races has all teams biking with full confidence in their own abilities. Each team thinks they have a runner in their midst. Even teams that have a runner at the starting line whom the crowd doesn't know about will bike that first stage as if they have Cavendish or Kittel in their side. Each team naturally wants to be at the head, resulting in two hundred cyclists continually trying to bike at the front of the peloton. That's a reason why Veelers says: "The tension and stress in that first stage is incomparable." This is why most of the major collisions happen in these first stages of cycling races.

Gradually, during the first week, most teams notice that their primary rider can't meet expectations. They lose faith, attribute bad performances to themselves and think other teams are simply too strong – just like an individual rider would. The power balance becomes clearer and clearer. Halfway through the race there's only about three teams on point. The rest of the teams let them do the hard work and no longer interfere. One advantage of this resignation is that nerves in the peloton become less frayed.

The risk for teams that achieve little during the first few days of a race is that they'll have very few expectations left for the rest of the race. Asking the right questions whilst evaluating those days is therefore crucial in order to flexibly adjust plans and keep the fighting spirit for the remainder of the race. A team that hits the mark right away experiences the opposite. In 2013, for example, Giant-Shimano rode an unlikely successful Tour de France. Marcel Kittel won the mass sprint on day 1 and repeated the feat another three times in the following weeks. Tom Veelers reminisces: "It was amazing, us winning the first stage. Now, we could take it easier after stage 1, and bike with less stress. I was cycling with more confidence, and of course Marcel had more confidence as well." These words beautifully encapsulate this chapter: a first victory creates positive expectations for the team and all individuals in that team, and these expectations subsequently form the basis of further success. Without that first victory, the other three might never have happened, in the absence of positive or even the presence of negative expectations.

In the next chapter, we will focus a bit more on those negative expectations, since there is a specific case where such expectations can really block performance to the extreme.

5

Mental Breaking Points: How to Lose the Tour de France

In the previous chapter, we saw how the expectations of a sportsman or team are like a counter-weight that can both improve and degrade performances.

On the positive side, an athlete can achieve better results than he would normally do when he expects to perform well, whilst an athlete with negative expectations often performs worse than his physical capabilities.

Occasionally, however, something unexpected happens where an athlete does not just underperform – but drops completely off the bottom of the scale. It's as if all hope is lost. When this is the case, a cyclist can lose the Tour de France within a single day, even on a potentially 'uneventful' flat stage. Such results cannot be solely explained on the basis of expectations. Rather, they are related to a fundamental human need that is linked to such expectations… something that can make people break mentally.

In this chapter, we will look at what it means to break mentally both in the short and the long term, and see how not only individual athletes but entire teams can break as well.

One particular race is, by the nature of its route and roads, exceptionally rich with illustrations of cyclists breaking mentally: the 'Hell of the North' or Paris-Roubaix. It is a one-day race of over 250 kilometres with more than fifty of them on poorly accessible cobble stones. The race takes place in a French mining area, and the riders often look like mineworkers by the end of the race with faces caked with dust and mud thanks to the condition of the roads. Indeed, many cyclists are barely recognizable when they cross the line. It's an environment where Belgian cyclists feel at home. From 1896 to 2016 Belgian racers have taken 55 victories in the race. One of them was even given the nickname ‘Monsieur Paris-Roubaix’: Roger de Vlaeminck. Four times he won the Hell, and just as many times he came second.

Not surprisingly, given Belgium’s history with this race, in 2009 helicopter images showed the pavements along the 260 kilometre long route dressed in yellow and black Flemish flags. Most of the main contenders departing that day were from the Flemish part of Belgium. Stijn Devolder, Tom Boonen, Leif Hoste – they were all hoping for victory as they mingled on the start line that morning, under a grey but dry sky.

Paris-Roubaix is one of the few – maybe the only – races that is already exceptionally exciting to watch 100 kilometres before the finish line. The riders have already been on their bikes for 160 kilometres, and the first physical effects – like muscle and joint aches resulting from bouncing over the cobbles – are taking their toll. And then suddenly the tempo goes up even further. The peloton passes a final village, some desolate meadows, and then all of a sudden they enter a narrow trap: the forest of Wallers, or La Trouée d’Arenberg. A 2,700 metre long five-star cobblestone section. Completely covered in a thin green layer of moss it is there, in the middle of a forest with masses of supporters on both sides of the road, that a cyclist finds he has nowhere to go. He just has to enter the trap and hope that he will be able to exit it unscathed and preferably well-placed.

Back in 2009, a large peloton entered the forest, but only a small group came out. A massive crash left many behind – some permanently, others at a big distance. Another incident took place shortly afterwards, at the Mons-en-Pévèle. Six men remained. Pozzato, Flecha, Hushovd and – how could it be any different – three Flemish riders: Boonen, Hoste and Vansummeren. Soon, Vansummeren had dropped off the pace.

The Italian rider Filippo ‘Pippo’ Pozzato was not very popular in Belgium. Often he followed the main contenders in races where he was also strong, without ever attacking himself. The lead favourite in this type of race was usually Belgium’s hero Tom Boonen. Pozzato was therefore considered Boonen’s shadow, a chicken-hearted athlete to some, a master tactician by others.

Eventually, the race wound up to its grand finale in Roubaix with both Pozzato and Boonen in contention. At the Carrefour de l'Arbre, another hellish cobblestone section, one after another of the leading contenders literally dropped out. First the Rabobank rider Juan-Antonio Flecha slipped away in a corner, taking Leif Hoste with him. In the next corner, in the same kilometre, it was Norwegian Thor Hushovd's turn. He fell, at the precise moment that Boonen attacked.

Boonen immediately had a gap on Pozzato, although he didn't really get away. At the end of the bouncy road of Arbre, with 16 kilometres still to go, the difference was exactly 11 seconds. Boonen had manufactured this gap within a kilometre. He was not able, however, to continue the trend and the Italian kept pushing with the difference staying ever-constant. Boonen was not making a single metre anymore. Indeed, six kilometres later, the difference was constant at 13 seconds.

Still, although Boonen was not gaining a single metre, Pozzato was not making any time back either. He lagged behind, and was not getting any closer as the finish line drew near. Ultimately Pozzato broke. With six kilometres to go, the time difference was almost identical to that when Boonen took off but the Italian's faith had gone and his head started to hang down. He was mentally shot to pieces and in the last five kilometres the Italian lost over half a minute. Ultimately, 47 seconds after Tornado Tom crossed the finish line, Pozzato followed.

Anyone who finds themselves on a racing bike, and who has encountered a situation like that of Pozzato, will be able to imagine the frustration Pozzato must have felt: racing with all you've got, and yet it not making the slightest difference. Trying as hard as you can and not even closing an inch on the cyclist in front of you. On the contrary, inch by inch your rival is gaining territory. Commonly, such situations end up with the chaser breaking, like with Pozzato. Physically one is often quite able to maintain the gap to the cyclist in front, to control the damage. So it is not so much the body but the mind that breaks.

From a psychological point of view this is not that surprising. In a situation where a rider tries everything to get back to the front of the race without any result, a certain psychological need is not fulfilled, namely that of control. Just as humans have physiological needs – like those for food, water and oxygen – they also have psychological needs. And just as not meeting physiological needs makes people ill, the same eventually goes for psychological needs.[1] These needs therefore have an enormous impact on human behaviour.

The need to have meaningful relationships with other people and to be socially accepted, for example, is one of man's most essential psychological needs.[2] Research shows that people who are socially excluded experience pain. The same brain areas involved in processing physical pain (such as when you bump your knee) are also active when people are rejected.[3] And when this need for meaningful relationships is not met over a prolonged period of time, people have a higher chance of getting depressed or becoming physically ill.[2]

Another important psychological need is that of control. This does not refer to objective control, like controlling whether a door is properly closed. Nor is it about controlling a race, like the cat-and-mouse game that the peloton and a small breakaway group so often play in stages that are destined to result in a bunch sprint. It is about a more subjective form of control, namely about the *feeling* that you have control over a situation through your behaviours and actions.[4] A feeling that what you do (e.g. cycling with everything you've got) is of influence to what you want to achieve (e.g. closing a gap). If you feel that your behaviour has no effect, then the important need for subjective control is no longer met. Being deprived of the feeling of control has a big impact on performance. Without it, motivation will crumble.

One of the most important psychological theories – attribution theory – states that human behaviour is predicted by three main factors.[5] Applied to cycling these are:

1. How badly do you want it? This is related to the motivation to win.
2. Is it appropriate? The appropriateness of behaviour is dependent on norms and values. For example, there is an unwritten rule in cycling that it is inappropriate to attack at a moment when your competitor crashes or punctures; this is considered unfair play.
3. Do you feel you have control over the situation through your behaviour? If a cyclist thinks that what he does will be pointless, he will not start any initiative at all.

If we apply this to Pozzato breaking in the final phase of Paris-Roubaix, then it is clear that this was not the result of a lack of motivation to win. If he had won the classic Paris-Roubaix then – in a single day – his entire year would have been a huge success. So, the will to win was not a problem. Pozzato was also *allowed* to win, it was appropriate. In 2009 Pozzato was riding in the Katusha team, while Boonen was wearing a Quickstep jersey. They were direct competitors without any special circumstances; just one rider against another. The essential element is therefore the third factor. Pozzato broke because he felt that his efforts did not influence the situation: he gave it all he had but got nothing back in return. This feeling caused the breakpoint, the juncture where the status quo was shattered and the time difference suddenly increased rapidly. Indeed, more generally speaking, a breaking point in a race is almost without exception the consequence of feeling that one's efforts no longer impact the race outcome. The feeling that you do not possess the power to close a gap, the feeling that you are no longer able to keep a certain speed. The entire enterprise may seem meaningless in such cases: the goals seems unattainable, the motivation is gone. The body is hanging in, but the mind breaks.

It will come as no surprise that the experience of control is an important factor within sport psychology.[6] It should be noted that, in the end, we are talking about *perception* here. It is not about whether you are objectively able to achieve success – most riders are physically able to achieve success – but about your judgment of the situation. Some riders always keep fighting no matter how hopeless (objectively) the situation may seem. The German cyclist Jens Voigt was a typical example. Other cyclists, conversely, appear to abandon hope quite easily, even when the course of events is pretty much undecided.

Keeping faith in one's capabilities – namely, how your performance affects the progression of the race – can be difficult. Some athletes are by nature better able to do this than others, and will therefore be less likely to break mentally. Research, however, shows that there is a trick for minimizing damage in cases like Pozzato's, in cases where an athlete feels they have lost control over the situation: a kind of *resetting*.[4,6] Instead of giving up, it can prove very beneficial for an athlete to adjust targets. For example, rather than focusing solely on victory, one may set a spot on the podium as a new goal.

In the case of Pozzato, whose breakpoint in Paris-Roubaix was close to the finish with the chasers at a comfortable distance, it did not matter much how he dealt with his gap to Boonen. He would secure second place anyway. But there are plenty of examples where it *could* have affected the results. Let's examine an instance that illustrates the difference between a mental breakdown versus resetting targets, and which also shows how a loss of control applies not only to individual athletes like Pozzato, but at a group level as well. Consequently, it follows that a loss of control can hinder athletes who compete in individual sports, and also teams in prototypical team sports.

During the 13th stage of the *Centennaire,* the hundredth edition of the Tour de France, the peloton finally appeared to split in two. The days prior to this stage, which went through Brittany, had seen journalists and supporters vainly anticipating the sight of a peloton being torn to pieces by fierce gusts of the coastal wind (although, surprisingly, this only happened after the peloton left the coast behind).

Sprinter Mark Cavendish won that day and for a flat stage it therefore seemed business as usual. But this was not the story of the day. Although the little British rider won, he sprinted to victory from a group of just 14 cyclists – they were the only ones left from the bunch. The peloton was split into pieces thanks to the wind and so the riders passed the finish line in small groups, so-called echelons. As has happened so often in the Tour, crosswinds shook up the general classification. And, as has happened so many times before, the major victims were predominantly South-European riders.

With 84 kilometres to go overall, Spanish contender Alejandro Valverde got into problems. Just when team Omega-Pharma and Belkin hit the front and forced the peloton to split into small groups, the Spaniard punctured. His Movistar teammates waited and supported him and virtually the entire team chased hard to bring Valverde back into contention. Just like with Boonen and Pozzato, and despite their best efforts, the time difference remained constant with the peloton riding 30 seconds in front of them, and not an inch being gained. The entire team tried even harder, but to no avail. They worked together like a single human being and, more importantly, they *thought* like a single person. As they failed to make up the lost ground as a group, they lost the feeling that their pedal strokes influenced the situation; after all, they were not getting any closer. Without affecting the distance to the peloton themselves, they became dependent on others, on Belkin or Omega-Pharma, to slow the overall pace. But those teams were too strong and then – suddenly – the entire Movistar team broke. In a very short period, the gap quickly increased and spectators could see how the faces of the Movistar riders changed. Their heads hung down and it became noticeable that they were becoming more physically relaxed. The will had gone and their speed dropped. Valverde's hopes for a Tour victory were literally gone with the wind here, like so many Spaniards had done before him over stages characterized by strong winds. It would have saved the Movistar team minutes if they had readjusted their expectations and switched to damage control rather than stubbornly trying to get back to the *tête de la course*.

A cyclist is able to gain seconds thanks to superior bike and clothing materials over competitors, and further seconds with better nutrition. Indeed, one may win the Tour because of it. On the other hand, one mental breakdown is enough to lose minute upon minute. On that 13th Tour de France stage, in 2013, Valverde lost a stunning 9 minutes and 54 seconds. And with it, all chance of making the podium in Paris.

On the same 13th stage, in 2013, something very similar happened with 30 kilometres to go. Team Saxo-Tinkoff and Belkin accelerated, and it was race leader Chris Froome who ended up in the chasing group. The gap of 10 seconds remained constant, even though three teams were leading the chase: Sky, BMC and Katusha. Two of them broke, eventually, and the gap between them and the leaders rose to almost a minute. Team Sky, however, did not break and were able to control the damage.

In an interview later that day with Sky leader Froome, it became clear why his team was able to minimize any time loss. While the stage was unfolding, he had already realized that he would be losing the yellow jersey that day. But instantly he looked forward to subsequent stages and knew that if he did not lose too much time, he would find plenty of opportunities *later on* to regain the leader's jersey. Team Sky had thus done exactly what the research says is the best thing to do; as soon as you start to lose control, adjust your goals in such a way that you regain control. Team Sky had switched from defending the yellow jersey to the goal of limiting time losses, and it saved their day.

A single stage (or tour) where an athlete or team breaks, like the examples we have seen above, will not have much impact over the longer term as far as the need to 'feel in control' is concerned. Valverde lost a potential podium spot in the Tour de France but his career did not nose-dive following his disappointment. Things become different, however, when one gets disappointed time after time, when a rider gives it his all but does not see a clear connection between these efforts and race results.

The effects of a more persistent feeling of 'no control' over one's life or achievements have been extensively researched.

Back in 1967, American psychologist Martin Seligman was doing research in the footsteps of Burrhus Frederic Skinner (commonly known as B.F. Skinner). Many years earlier, Skinner had found that animals can be trained to perform specific behaviours by rewarding them. Known as operant conditioning, when a pigeon learns that he will receive food by pressing a lever in his cage, he will press the lever continuously. He will even continue this behaviour if the lever press is no longer followed by the reward of food.[7]

Seligman did comparable research with dogs.[8] He wanted to see if dogs who received electric shocks, and who could end the shocks by pressing a button, would quickly learn to push the button. He divided the dogs into two groups. A pair of dogs (one from each group) was placed at opposite ends of a cage with a barrier that ran down the middle fully separating them. In each cage the electric shocks would stop immediately as soon as a dog on the selected end pressed the button whilst, unbeknownst to the dog, this button press also stopped the shock delivered to the dog at the other end of the cage. When the dog at the other end pressed his own button – nothing happened. In doing this, Seligman conditioned one group of dogs to control when the shocks would end; whilst the other group learned that whatever they did would not influence their unfortunate situation (their shocks would end, but not by their own doing).

After this first test a second followed, and it was at this point that a crucial discovery was made. The experimental setup was slightly altered so that the two dogs were placed in a cage separated by a different barrier – a barrier that both dogs were able to jump over quite easily. The dogs were placed at each end of the cage where – on one side – they would receive electric shocks delivered to them via the floor. On the other side of the cage there was no electricity. The only thing the animals needed to do, to end the pain, was to jump over the barrier.

Based on earlier studies by Skinner with pigeons, one would predict that all the dogs would quickly learn to jump over the barrier and avoid electric shocks. But this did not happen. Only the dogs that learned they had control over ending the shocks quickly jumped to the other side. The dogs that had become used to passively enduring the pain did nothing. They did not try to jump across the barrier, but lay howling on the electric floor. They had learned that there was nothing they could do to stop the pain. Seligman called this the 'learned helplessness' effect.

Humans experience learned helplessness as well, and if it affects one's entire life then this feeling of helplessness can result in acute depression. It is no coincidence that Martin Seligman did plenty of research on depressive disorders! But learned helplessness can also manifest itself in a very specific domain, like cycling, or even cycling in a specific country. This occurs when a rider experiences for a prolonged period, race after race, that whatever he or she does, does not matter. And just like the dog study, the consequence is that even if that rider finds himself in a position to win, he will not have any faith in a good outcome and will harbour extremely negative expectations. Consequently this rider will not give it the full 100%.

As an example, it seems that many Italian grand tour contenders have developed a kind of learned helplessness towards racing in France. In the Tour de France, Italian riders are often only a shadow of what they can demonstrate in their own country. Take Michele Scarponi, an Italian with an impressive record in races that take place in his home country, as an example. Every time he started in the Tour he looked like a different man… an anonymous rider.

Of course, for Italian cyclists, races in their own country are so important that they specifically prepare for them; for an Italian rider the Giro d'Italia is at least equally important to the Tour de France. Sub-par performances are therefore at least partly due to the fact that Italians start the Tour with suboptimal preparation. That is, generally speaking, a cyclist who gives it his all in the Giro will start the Tour a month later already fairly exhausted. But even when an Italian like Michele Scarponi skips the Giro, it does not show in France. It's as if the helplessness kicks in once the Italy-France border is crossed. All seems lost before it actually starts.

Chapter 5

The feeling of not having control is, in short, unfavourable for two main reasons. In the short term, it can cause an athlete to break mentally with all the associated negative consequences for performance. Next to that, there is a risk of long term consequences where an athlete develops chronically negative expectations until a point is reached where one feels completely helpless. This experienced 'lack of control' is considered one of the biggest hurdles for optimal sports achievements for both individuals and teams.

With individual athletes, however, there is another psychological aspect that is just as disturbing… maybe even more so. In the next chapter, therefore, we will zoom in on the causes of *fear*, and examine what an athlete can do to deal with his or her fears.

6

Fear: The Fall of Wiggins

Nowadays, Pescara is mostly known as a beach resort, but it is also a monument to Italian sports cycling – with a long history in the Giro d'Italia. The city has seen stages of the Giro pass through it on 18 occasions, the first time in 1912. Legends such as Alfredo Binda (in 1927 and 1931) and Freddy Maertens (1977) won the stage here. Even when the town was mostly in ruins after bombing during the Second World War, the Giro stopped here in 1947 and 1948, when the stars were Fausto Coppi and Gino Bartali.

Pescara was the stage for a Giro arrival in 2013 as well, with Bradley Wiggins as the major contender. He had won the Tour de France the year before, making the Briton from the all-powerful Team Sky the big favourite at the start in Naples.

The stage to Pescara departs from San Salvo and runs through the hilly landscape of Abruzzo to the Adriatic coast. It's the 10th of May, and the peloton is getting ready for the 7th stage. A day earlier, Mark Cavendish had won the 6th stage fairly easily, and had dedicated his victory to Wouter Weylandt who had died in a crash on the 3rd stage of the 2011 Giro; the text 'WW108' was seen many times that day, on banners and chalked onto the road. The previous day – the 9th of May – was exactly two years after the talented Belgian cyclist fell to his death during a descent. On the podium, two years later, Cavendish didn't hold up a trophy, a bunch of flowers, or a bottle of champagne, but the shirt number 108 – the number WW died wearing. The whole day highlighted the dangers that cyclists confront in their profession and the particular risks that a descending rider must face.

Pescara had a gloomy appearance on the 10th of May 2013, on account of rain. The riders would have to pass through San Silvestro, six kilometres before the finish line, a little village separated from Pescara by a serpentine descent.

Two dim lights and the heavy rumble of engines announced the riders' arrival in San Silvestro. Adam Hansen, the sole remaining rider from the day's escape and the designated winner in Pescara, passed first, followed closely by the group of favourites, of course including Wiggins, but also Nibali, Gesink, Evans, Scarponi and 2012's winner, Hesjedal. All of them were soaked to the bone. There was a mere handful of hairpin bends, and just 149 metres of descent, separating the riders from the finish line in Pescara.

As per the other descents that day, Wiggins quickly fell back among the favourites riding point. Taking it slow, not taking any chances, not losing the Giro because of a fall; these are thoughts that must have crossed the mind of the pride of British cycling. And in the meantime, the crowd saw Wiggins fall back further and further… bit by bit. His posture drew the attention of many and the television screens showed a somewhat cramped upper body, with hands tight on the brakes. For someone who didn't want to take risks, he did not seem to be all that careful when making turns.

That's when it happened – exactly what Wiggins was afraid of – a fall on an extremely slippery hairpin bend. Luckily, without any damage to body or bicycle, he quickly mounted his bike again and chased the other favourites, who, with less than five kilometres to go, were now out of sight. It became something you could not really call a chase anymore: an amateur would bike a better descent. Wiggins was now fully cramped up and came to a near stop at every turn. Not one turn was done properly. In less than five kilometres, 'Wiggo' lost almost a minute-and-a-half on his competition.

The fear that Wiggins took with him on the road to Pescara was not something he could discard at the end of that day. A day later there was a time trial scheduled and, as the reigning Olympic time trial champion, Wiggins was by far the favourite. But yet again, those bends were taken with little confidence, and he made error after error. His qualities as a time trial rider still won him second place, though!

During the 9th stage, a further day later, the same thing happened. It was raining and Wiggins forfeited time on a descent en route to Florence. Due to his strong team, he managed to return to the group of favourites before the finish line, but the effort the riders needed to make were enormous – and unnecessary. Finally, disillusioned and above all ill, the Briton gave up during stage 13. Over the following years, Wiggins never returned to his old skill levels during the big races, although he still achieved major successes in the velodrome like an incredibly fast hour record in London in 2015, and Olympic gold in the team pursuit at Rio 2016.

Descending is a technique one rider manages better than another. For example, Colombian cyclists are notorious for being bad at descents. Wiggins turned out to be the same. Or, in his own words, after the 2013 Giro: "Let's be honest. I descended like a bit of a girl. Not to disrespect girls, I have one at home. But that's life and we have to push on." And yet, during previous years and when riding other courses, no one ever really noticed that Wiggins wasn't good at descents. How can a cyclist, apparently from one moment to the next, become less capable at descents?

There was much speculation during the Giro as to what had happened to Wiggins, from bad equipment to the wrong tyres. Something like that may happen to a cyclist once, but not for several stages in a row. The more probable explanation is that Wiggins got scared. Fear has a substantial impact on mental functioning, and a scared rider will make mistakes quicker. Fear really is a handicap for a cyclist, certainly during a descent. A rider without fear, on the other hand, will take calculated risks and appear to be flying.

Perhaps the best-known example of such a cyclist is Paolo Savoldelli, whose nickname '*Il Falco*' (the falcon) was earned for good reason. A combination of good technique and an almost complete lack of fear made him the best cyclist in the peloton when it came to descents. It's no exaggeration to say that his 2002 and 2005 victories in the Giro d'Italia were mostly due to his capacities as a descender.

Savoldelli was also present during the 2013 Giro, but as a spectator (he quit professional cycling in 2008). He too saw Wiggins labouring down the mountain but his analysis made no mention of equipment issues. "It seems that he got a scare because he fell at a point where they weren't even descending quickly," Savoldelli said. "Even on the straights you could see that he was going very slowly, he wasn't pedalling and you could see that he was really afraid. Simply by looking at him, you could tell that he was really afraid on those descents." The angelic-faced Italian added, "I'd never have thought that a Tour de France winner would have a weakness of that kind."[1]

Chapter 6

And yet, from a psychological point of view, it's no wonder a big cycling champion can develop a fear for descents in a relatively short time, seemingly out of nowhere.

There are only six emotions present in all people, from birth and in all cultures, and which get expressed in the same way:[2]

1. Fear
2. Anger
3. Disgust
4. Sadness
5. Surprise
6. Happiness

Fear is a natural response to circumstances where a person feels threatened. The moment you see danger, fear quickly sets in; the consequence of which is you go into survival mode. When someone is scared, there are three natural responses: fight, flight or freeze.[2] These responses have been developed through evolution and are also instinctively present in other animals. When an animal sees or smells danger, say because there's a predator nearby, many will run away as quickly as they can to physically escape the predator. Or they attack. And yet, there are also animals that will literally freeze to escape a predator's attention, sometimes even with a leg still in the air, unmoving.

A cyclist who's afraid, whether it's due to the chaos in a mass sprint or an unclear descent, will also respond by fighting, fleeing or freezing. This response, however, is driven by the nature of the cause. The fear of a mass sprint is something one can easily flee from (i.e. quit), simply by not joining it. Fleeing during a descent is often not an option, though, as it usually equates to forfeiting the race, by joining the stragglers. Seeing as how quitting is not in the average cyclist's dictionary – and certainly not for a cyclist with classification ambitions, such as Bradley Wiggins – two options remain. A cyclist who fights will overbalance his fears, and start taking irresponsible risks (risks a rider without fear would never take). But the fear response most glaring, in reality, is freezing. The body literally locks up.[3]

While turning the pedals is a cyclist's most basic action, a frightened cyclist can suddenly forget how to move his legs. His responsiveness becomes slower, it can seem that every move is an enormous effort. The mind locks, too: the cyclist can no longer focus and images of his fear becoming reality continually flash before his eyes. Even before he makes a turn, he sees himself lying on the asphalt. A collection of images and short films run through his mind, all with the same theme: the cyclist falling, sliding over the wet asphalt, colliding head-on with a sand-coloured rock and hurtling into the chasm. Every possible fall comes to the fore. With such pictures haunting his mind, not even the best rider can bike a good descent.

An explanation on the natural response to fear provides insight into why Wiggins made such a terrible descent, but not why Wiggins didn't seem to be scared at all, *until* the 2013 Giro. How can someone seemingly from one moment to the next become scared of something like biking a descent?

On one hand, it has to do with the fact that the fear of falling is never really gone; it lurks in the back of most people's minds. A fear of heights is one of the most common fears around, and the fear of descending a mountain is related. By riding down a mountain (often without incident) a cyclist learns that he doesn't need to be afraid of a descent. The rider sees no danger and thus experiences no fear.

Children, however, are often afraid of falling from height at a young age. Indeed, researchers back in the 1960s sought to address the question of whether fears are derived from nature or nurture. To differentiate between congenital and acquired fears, the study was conducted with very young children.

To test a fear of falling, researchers Eleanor Gibson and Richard Walk made a 'visual cliff' in their research laboratory.[4] In essence, this cliff was a table with a checkerboard table cloth, on top of which sat thick plexiglass. The plexiglass extended well beyond the edge of the table whilst – underneath it – the table cloth was laid out some four feet below. In this way, they created the appearance of visual depth (and a drop 'off the edge' of the table) even though there was no actual drop (the Plexiglass would sustain an individual's weight). It just looked like there was.

During the study, six-month-old babies, who were able to crawl, were placed on the table on the side where the checkerboard cloth was directly beneath the glass. Their mother would go to the other side of the table. The researchers then studied whether or not the babies would crawl to their mothers (they'd have to crawl over the visual cliff). Of the 36 children participating in the study, only three crawled to their mothers. Nearly all the babies stopped at the exact spot where the checkerboard cloth was four feet lower. These children were already afraid of falling even at that young age. Babies who are not yet able to crawl, and who therefore have no personal experience with the potential danger of falling, are not afraid though.[5] This shows on the one hand that fears are learned (instead of innate) and on the other that the fear of falling is one of the earliest learned fears and quite ingrained in human nature.

A cyclist's fear is not dissimilar to a baby's fear of falling, and both can be 'learned' and *overcome* by biking a lot of descents. But it can return relatively easily the moment you lose faith in your ability to make descents. Generally speaking, an 'old' fear is sooner to return than a completely new fear develops. The question that then remains is how a rider in a race 'learns' to be afraid of, for example, a descent; like Wiggins did.

To find the answer to this question, we must go back to a world-famous psychological study. It was conducted in 1920 by the influential American psychologist John B. Watson and his assistant Rosalie Reyner.[6] Watson wanted to research how fear arises. In order to do so, he carried out several tests on a nine-month old baby, a hospital inpatient, called Albert. Nowadays, the study is commonly known as the *Little Albert* experiment.

In the first part of the study, Watson wanted to know what Little Albert was afraid of. The baby was therefore placed in an examination room where Watson's assistant kept bringing in different animals and objects. A white rabbit, a monkey, a rat, a dog, a piece of wool, a newspaper, etc. The brave baby (or more likely innocent and unknowing baby) wasn't afraid of anything. He looked around with his eyes wide open, taking everything in his stride. Albert did show, however, that he was afraid of loud noises (as do nearly all young babies).

Next, Watson tested whether the child could acquire fear. The curious Albert was once more placed in the examination room on a big, soft mattress in the middle of the room. He was accompanied by a white rat used for laboratory tests. The little baby was not afraid; he even started playing with the white, soft animal. Every time the rat came close to the boy, Albert tried to pet the rodent. Over time he even started having fun doing it.

Only after Albert had become used to the presence of the white rat – and it became clear that he wasn't the least bit scared of the little creature – did the real test take place. Watson positioned himself out of the baby's eyesight, with a hammer and a steel pipe whilst Albert played with the rat. This time, however, Watson would strike the steel pipe with the hammer every time Albert touched the rat. This loud bang would have Albert crying immediately: he was scared to death of the noise. By doing this every time the baby touched the white rat, Albert unconsciously made a link: touching the rat = terrifying noise.

Now came the most important part of the study. Albert was once again placed in the examination room on the mattress. After he got used to the environment, the white rat was reintroduced. As soon as Albert saw the small rodent, he started crying fearfully and tried to flee from the animal. The loud noise was no longer necessary: the boy had learned that the rat itself was scary. The researchers were thus able to demonstrate how fear is acquired.

A little over two weeks after the original study, Albert was still in hospital and a second assessment was done. The researchers wanted to see if his fear was permanent or only short-lasting. This session saw the now nearly 10-month old baby placed back in the test room. The same animals and objects shown a fortnight before were shown to Albert again. The results were striking. The boy was not afraid of objects like a newspaper, or animals like a monkey, but he was still deadly scared of the white rat. And not just that: Albert seemed to react fearfully to anything white and fluffy. He was almost equally afraid of a white rabbit, but also by something like Santa Claus' white beard.

When Albert was over a year old, Watson wanted to do a new experiment, hoping to demonstrate that fears can be untaught as well. To do so, he wanted to perform a test comparable to the one he used to teach the fear. However, Albert turned out to have been discharged from hospital so this test never took place. Chances are that Albert's acquired fears plagued him for a long time!

Chapter 6

The experiment with the very young Albert may be sad, but it was nonetheless very important in better understanding how fears develop. A cyclist's fear of descending may occur in the exact same way. Bradley Wiggins' descent can be compared to Albert's white rat. Albert became afraid of the rat when touching it was accompanied by the ear-splitting noise he was terrified of. A cyclist can very quickly become afraid of a descent in the same way. The moment the descent is accompanied by something very negative, a fear of descending *will* develop. This negative 'something' which makes a cyclist fearful can be anything at all. In Wiggins' case, it could have been a previous fall in similarly bad weather conditions or all the attention given to Wouter Weylandt. After all, he died after a fall during a descending stage and the exact day before Wiggins became so afraid, there was an enormous amount of attention for WW108. The Italian rider Gianni Bugno, for example, was known to have become afraid of descents after his teammate Ravasio died in a fall.[7] Bugno overcame his fears, by the way, but more on that in a bit.

Now that we know how fear develops, it's time to look at how to get rid of it. What could Wiggins have done during the rainy mountain stages of the 2013 Giro to overcome his fear? There are at least three known methods that have been proven to help in reducing fear or even eliminating it. The best-known method, and therefore perhaps the most commonly used and important one, is almost too simple: just do it. *Face your fears*. Psychology refers to this form of fear treatment as exposure. The word itself really gives it away: you try to reduce your fear by exposing yourself to the very same thing scaring you. Are you afraid of descents, or specifically descents in the rain? Then practice a whole bunch of descents (in the rain). By doing and especially – as that's what it's about in the end – by noticing that it's going well, that your fears are not coming true, you'll see your fears lessen over time.

At the same time, this method is not as simple as it appears at face value. There's a reason why people with a specific fear are given professional guidance when starting exposure. There is a risk of wanting to do too much all at once, where you rush into the situation you're fearful of. This can be so provocative that your fear does not lessen at all. Exposure is therefore most often done by applying a step-by-step approach.

Arachnophobia, for example, is a common fear. People who are extremely scared of spiders can develop their fear to a level where they start avoiding spaces where a spider may be, even if they've never seen one there before. This could be an attic, but also a completely different country (e.g. you avoid going to Australia because of leaping Huntsman spiders). Imagine someone like that, for their first exposure, being let into a room with a very large spider (a method called *flooding*). Such a meeting would undoubtedly not go well. The fear could become so overwhelming that the person could have a panic attack, freeze completely, and even scramble to leave the room. Nothing would have been accomplished: that person would not have been able to experience the baselessness of their fear, but only that their fear is justified by way of their intense reaction to the spider.

Such cases usually start with imaginary exposure: a method in which you visualise seeing a spider, or watch a spider in a virtual environment. Only when someone manages to handle these forms of exposure well and realise their fear is not rational (and that their fears are not becoming reality) is the next step made. For example, the supervised viewing of a real spider. That way, one step at a time, the person is exposed more and more, until they can independently handle spiders.

To apply this to cycling, it means you can reduce or even eliminate your fear by gaining experience. The French superstar Thibaut Pinot, who, the same as Wiggins, had a fear of descents, did this very thing. This fear was *the* major obstacle for him becoming a true elite member of the peloton. In the autumn of 2013, the former French racing driver Max Mamers felt for Pinot and decided to offer him his services. The driver, who had driven the 24 Hours of Le Mans multiple times and who was therefore probably not that sensitive to fear, took the Française des Jeux cyclist to Nevers, to the Magny-Cours race track. Pinot made his first steps towards overcoming his fear on the legendary Formula 1 race track. Mamers, by then well into his seventies, had the clear-cut and simple plan of having the French youngster in the relatively safe environment of a car on the deserted race track, and then letting him race around at speeds of nearly 200 kilometres an hour. "At first, he will have an instructor with him," said Mamers, "and then he will drive alone. With the run-offs at the Magny-Cours, he's not risking anything."[8]

It's a classic example of exposure. Once the first step has been perfected, someone can take the next one. After Pinot left the race track in Nevers, he took that next step: ascending and descending on his bike. He had to get used to taking turns at high speeds again; firstly, at his own pace, no pressure, then at greater and greater speeds. And finally, when that hurdle had been taken as well, came the ultimate test: descending during a race. Pinot passed all tests with flying colours. The 2014 Tour de France even saw him make the podium. It's all the more admirable when you realise it was during the mountain descents that he was attacked by his rival and fellow countryman Romain Bardet. Most likely he considered his riding more a victory over himself than over Bardet.

When we look at Wiggins, exposure as a solution presents us with an immediate and apparent problem. His fear seems to have developed during the 2013 Giro, thanks to rapid descents during ghastly weather. Exposure to descents in Wiggins' case is impossible to avoid. However, rather than being able to apply exposure treatment, his case was a typical example of flooding: forced by race circumstances Wiggins has to make steep and rapid descents in the rain all the time and day after day. Gradually getting used to biking descents, slowly building up confidence in his own abilities, and realising his fears are unjustified, as Thibaut Pinot did, is not an option. The Brit's competitors see his weakness, the man who started out as the favourite. Like a predator, they attack him where he's weak, going just that little bit faster in the descents, forcing Wiggins to take extra risks. This pushes Wiggins to almost bike through his fear, but he just can't. Exposure such as this doesn't lessen fear; if anything, it increases it. If you want to use exposure to get rid of your fear, it needs to be done outside competition, without the accompanying pressure, just as Pinot did.

Aside from exposure, another method for overcoming fear is to focus on something else during moments of fear. This is really a distraction task, and distraction is known to weaken emotions, including fear.[9] The goal is to have less fear in one's mind by focusing on something else. By becoming less preoccupied with a fear, you notice that the situation is no longer that frightening.[10] For example, a cyclist can focus completely on the environment by looking at what he sees: the verdant trees near the bend, a traffic sign, a man with an extravagant moustache along the roadside. Or he can make himself aware of what he's hearing:

the sucking sound of a tire, the rumble of engines, the staccato pulse of helicopter blades. He can choose to be aware of the smells surrounding him or feel the wind on his face. They are all ways to lessen fear.

The final way to decrease fear is based on the method that John Watson wanted to do with Albert: *counter-conditioning*. The first example of this method being applied is actually indirectly linked to the Little Albert experiment. During his college seminars, Watson regularly referenced his findings with Albert and, one day, one of the people listening was Mary Cover Jones. She was so enthusiastic about this kind of research that she decided to pursue the same. In the early 20's, she met Peter,[11] a three-year-old boy who was afraid of rabbits. Watson had previously demonstrated with Albert that fear develops through an object or animal being coupled with something negative, such as a loud noise in Albert's case. When fear develops in this fashion, it can possibly be unlearned in a similar way, Jones reasoned. This hypothesis led to Peter's treatment.

Jones placed Peter in a study room. Every time a rabbit was brought into the same room, Peter was also served his favourite food. That way, a positive experience was coupled with seeing the rabbit each time. The boy soon became less fearful of the rabbit. Jones at first placed the rabbit a fair distance away from Peter, but was soon able to place the rabbit closer without him becoming scared. Eventually, he even wanted to pet and play with the rabbit even when he wasn't given his favourite food: Peter had overcome his fear.

The counter-conditioning method that Jones applied to the boy all those years ago is still in use today. It has been repeatedly shown to be successful with adults.[11] It is also an effective tool to lessen a fear of descents. A good story to illustrate is that of the cyclist who raced on Mozart: Gianni Bugno.

Gianni Bugno started his professional career in 1985, when he was 21-years-old. Despite immediate recognition as a promising cyclist, he only gained great successes from the 90's onwards. He became one of the peloton's leaders and topped the international cycling union UCI's world classification chart several times. He won the Giro d'Italia, was a two-time podium finalist of the Tour, won Milan-San Remo and the Tour of Flanders, and was a two-time world champion.

Chapter 6

I myself was but a young boy during Bugno's glory days, and he was one of my cycling heroes. An un-Italian Italian who, in his own country, never became as popular as his rival Claudio Chiappucci, despite his successes. Bugno was a modest, introverted, elegant cyclist – more a British gentleman than an Italian macho man. His posture on his bike was beautifully still; it was as if he considered cycling not just a sport, but an art form.

Bugno had a problem that severely impeded his progress during races.[7,12] This became glaringly obvious in 1988, for example, when he participated in Milano-Torino in October. During the final ascent, Bugno, perhaps the strongest man in the race, charged. The breakaway forged a rift and only one man, the German Rolf Gölz, could follow him all the way to the top. It seemed clear that these two riders would sprint for victory. But during the descent Bugno was overcome by fear. He was afraid to do anything, and lost whole minutes during the descent. Bugno referenced the catholic nature of Italians in his self-berating comment: "A priest in a soutane could have made it down faster."[13]

A fear of descents seemingly developed in Bugno due to two negative events. In 1986, two years before the Milano-Torino race in question, Bugno was still biking for his first professional team, Atala. During most races in that period, he shared a room with his team mate and friend, Emilio Ravasio. In 1986, they rode the Giro d'Italia together and on the 28th of May, during the 1st stage, Emilio – who wasn't wearing a helmet, as was common in those days – took a hard fall whilst making a turn. He died that same day. This tragic accident left a deep mark on Bugno. He lost his ability to take big risks, and descending became his Achilles heel. This was only made worse in the spring of 1988, when he had to leave the Giro after his own bad fall.

Bugno sought out therapy to deal with his fear (to hopefully get rid of it altogether). The treatment was a variation on the one used on three-year-old Peter, whose favourite food was coupled with his big fear. Bugno wasn't helped by food, but by classical music. In the middle of winter, far from any races, Bugno repeatedly listened to Mozart in a soothing context, a process which had a calming effect on him.

The moment the races started again, the Italian turned out to be quite the spectacle in the peloton. Even the *New York Times* wrote about him, and that was at a time when professional cycling was not a popular sport in America.[12] Bugno turned up at the starting line with earphones and a Walkman in his back pocket, descending the mountains whilst listening to Mozart's 'Jupiter Symphony'. And it worked: in 1990, his fear seemed to have been conquered. After a maddening dash down the Poggio, he won Milan-San Remo. Not much later, he would also take home a place in the final ranking of the Giro d'Italia, for the first time in his career. The teams he competed for changed, from Chateau d'Ax to Gatorade to Mapei, but his winning streak continued. The elegant Italian seemed to have overcome his fear for good. Although Bugno retired from professional cycling a long time ago, he's still present at the big races in a different capacity. The man with a fear of descents is nowadays permanently at high altitude on a professional basis: he is very likely the most famous helicopter pilot to document cycling races!

Despite fear potentially playing a large part in an athlete's success (or lack of it), it doesn't have to be the only one. An athlete can bend, but does not necessarily have to break.

Up to this point in the book we have looked at psychological factors that mostly operate at an individual level (such as fear in this chapter) alongside factors that also play a part at a group level (such as team atmosphere). That both individual and team factors are recurring features has to do with the quality of sports cycling which makes it so psychologically interesting: namely, that it is both a team sport (you ride as a team) and an individual sport (there is only one winner) at the same time. In the next chapter we will be looking at the intriguing tension that this dichotomy often creates within races.

7

Social Dilemmas: The Decision in the Amstel Gold Race

During a race, cyclists are constantly balancing between group interests (e.g., the team or an escape group they are part of) and individual interests (e.g., personal victory). This dichotomy can occasionally create a psychologically fascinating tension, as the group's interests and the cyclist's interest may be at odds. An example of such a dilemma could be found during the 2013 Amstel Gold Race.

The peloton participating in this edition of the Amstel Gold arrived in Southern Limburg in a quite surprised state. The sun was shining, the temperature was pleasant. Considering the exceptionally foul spring of 2013, that was really quite something. Milan-San Remo, normally a convivial spring race, was ridden in such terrible circumstances that an outsider like Tom-Jelte Slagter had to give up, frozen by the snows, "I was *so* cold during that blizzard. [...] I could hardly brake. [...] My first priority now is to recover and then get going again for the Tour of the Basque Country."[1]

The Tour of the Basque Country that Slagter was eyeing turned out to be one of the toughest editions in its history due to the combination of rain and cold. Races such as Kuurne-Brussels-Kuurne, Nokere Koerse, and the GP Lugano had to be cancelled completely due to the ferociously bad weather. A complete mountain stage in the Giro d'Italia had to be cancelled for the first time since 1989 because of the unprecedented amount of snow that had fallen; two other stages were shortened for the same reason. After all the abominable courses in Southern Europe, the peloton only found actual spring in the Netherlands.

The course of the Amstel Gold Race final was altered in 2013 for the first time in several years. Previously, the riders would enter the latter part of the race over the Eyserbosweg. Shortly after that, the Keutenberg would usually follow for the second time. After this terribly steep hill, the riders were normally sent down a relatively long and winding bit of road, where many escapees could be caught. And finally, on the Cauberg, the favourites would make the final sprint to victory.

In 2013, the organisers applied a trick they'd learned the previous autumn (when the world championship took place on the road to Valkenburg). Instead of placing the finishing line directly on the Cauberg, they added an extra lap of 20 kilometres. Those kilometres featured another three hills, namely the Geulhemmerberg, Bemelerberg and – why the hell not – the Cauberg once more. The finishing line was a kilometre beyond the top of the Cauberg. The goal, of course, was to stretch out the finale with the expectation that it would still begin on the Eyserbosweg but that it would give escapees just a little longer to try and stay ahead, and thus create more excitement for the spectators. In the end, the chances were still good – just as in previous years – that a renowned cyclist would take the victory. Men such as Gilbert, Rodriguez, Valverde, Sagan. After all, these are the names you want to add to your honours list as a race organiser.

As far as the above goes, the organisers got what they wanted – escapees were given more chances in the finale. But the predicted scenario that it would be won by one of the favourites did not come true. Indeed, the race organisers looked somewhat crestfallen when a dawdler from an escape group, the Czech Roman Kreuziger, who'd only escaped the peloton in the finale, won the race. At least, that's how the newspapers reported it.

It's actually quite strange that Kreuziger was not deemed a potential race winner by many cycling critics and enthusiasts. He had fallen from the pedestal of a 'good' cyclist some years earlier; most likely due to a meteoric start to his career which had subsequently tailed off.

Kreuziger had inherited his father's good genes. Roman senior was also a professional cyclist who, in the nineties, rode for the Italian Italbonificia-Navigare team. He wasn't an exceptional cyclist, but his record in the smaller tours was not without merit. For example, he won several stages and the final ranking of the 1991 Tour of Austria.

Roman junior followed in his father's footsteps. And how! He became the junior world champion in 2004, and was quick to join the professionals. He garnered good results in the big races, earning the white jersey and winning the 2009 Tour of Romandie. He also placed fifth in the 2010 Amstel Gold Race. It seemed a given that Kreuziger would be winning the Tour de France at some point down the line. However, the following years saw his development stagnate. Even though he was still biking good results, Roman never really won a big race. Which is why he was considered a write-off at the age of 26. A development from wonder boy to total loss.

That was until that sunny day in April, when Kreuziger took the lead together with four other escapees on the next-to-last climb up the Cauberg. And those others were not just anyone. Pieter Weening, who demonstrated his mettle in the Tour of the Basque Country not long before, was there. As were Nordhaug, Caruso and Grivko – all specialists in this discipline. Five racers from five different teams; competitors needing to work together temporarily to stay clear of the clutches of the peloton. At the time, his fellow escapees had no notion of the hidden stirrings within Kreuziger, "I said before the classics that I was on form. [...] When you ride a classic you have to bet all your money on one card. It is a do-or-die scenario. We only had an advantage of several seconds; I didn't want to play the waiting game."[2]

With only seven kilometres to go, Kreuziger made his escape. The actual stretch of road was inconsequential. Flat as a pancake. Not one spectator lining it. Exactly the part of the race track you're certain that nothing will happen. It's exactly there that Kreuziger took off, while the others on point had barely recovered from climbing the Bemelerberg. Behind Kreuziger followed Weening, who looked back first at Caruso and then at Nordhaug. The look on his face spoke volumes. Which one of you is going to close that gap? Weening slowed just a little, even going so far as to momentarily stop moving his legs, in order to put his arms in the air. "Come on, take over, I'm not doing this by myself," is what he wanted to make clear. But none of his fellow escapees wanted to do the dirty work. Finally, Nordhaug took over lackadaisically, while at the same time waiting to be relieved again, so that he could implement his plan to approach the leading man himself. In short, the coordination had all gone – just like Kreuziger had. He was nowhere to be seen. If *he* had any intention of putting his arms in the air, it would be to indicate victory.

Chapter 7

Psychologically speaking, a situation like the 2013 Amstel Gold Race is called a *social dilemma*, and it's not unique. In fact, nearly every race, stage or competition featuring an arrival uphill, ends with a finale in which the lead group determines the race in a comparable fashion. One racer attacks, the rest keep looking at each other, and in the meantime the bird has flown.

The social dilemma can best be explained by using a well-known example: the prisoner's dilemma.[3,4] This dilemma is about a situation where two people are suspected of a crime. Let's use John and Matthew as an example. They are suspected of breaking into a home together, and the police have enough evidence to prove they committed the crime. The only thing missing is the confession. The two men are therefore interrogated separately and are offered a plea bargain in return for a confession.

If John and Matthew both stay silent, no confession would mean a year in prison for both. If they both confess, that becomes a three-year prison sentence. It's therefore better for both of them if they remain silent. The problem is that John and Matthew are interrogated in separate rooms; they don't know whether the other will confess or stay quiet. It could well be that one of them confesses, while the other denies everything. The following table shows you the consequences:

		Matthew	
		Confesses	Denies
John	Confesses	Both serve 3 years	John is cleared, Matthew gets 5 years
	Denies	Matthew is cleared, John gets 5 years	Both serve 1 year

The dilemma becomes clear by looking at it from John's perspective. When he only considers his own situation, he'll confess to the crime, hoping that Matthew denies everything. He'll go free. The problem is that John doesn't know what Matthew will do; there's no way for him to steer Matthew in a certain direction. For example, if Matthew *also* confesses, John suddenly won't go free, but they'll both have to serve three years. And the chance that Matthew will confess is big; because just as a confession is John's ticket out, the same goes for Matthew. However, if John doesn't place his own self-interest – going free – first, but considers the shared interest he has with Matthew, he'll deny it all. Because if Matthew also denies the break-in, they won't get a three-year sentence, they'll each get one year.

The essence of this dilemma is therefore twofold. Namely, that you have to make a contrary choice, depending on the value you place on your own interest or the group interest, and where personal interest is more appealing but at the same time comes with greater risk. And this relates to the fundamental insecurity about what the others in the group will do.

The prisoner's dilemma has been extensively researched and has been very influential, as similar scenarios frequently occur in daily life, albeit with different consequences. Think, for example, about energy consumption. Everyone knows we have to try and consume less energy, as that helps save the environment. Turning the heating down a little, switching off appliances we're not using, etc. – these are simple ways of putting less strain on the environment. If everyone does it, it's going to have a beneficial effect on the environment. And yet, it's so nice to have a warm house; to let the computer run in the background so that you don't have to wait for it to boot up next time. It's so very tempting not to lower your own energy consumption, and just hope everyone else does. The problem, of course, is that when everyone thinks that way, nothing happens.

The prisoner's dilemma can also be seen in sports cycling. A situation where *one* rider from the lead group breaks away creates such a dilemma. In the 2013 Amstel Gold Race, Roman Kreuziger made his attack and four riders followed: Weening, Caruso, Nordhaug and Grivko. Who was going to close the gap?

The problem, however, is that closing a gap like that takes a great deal of energy, certainly in a race finale. The rider out front will be caught but the pursuit will have taken so much out of the cyclist who made the sacrifice that he'll be beaten by the other racers at the finish line. They will have profited from his hard work and saved their strength. It would be best if the pursuers worked together, and closed the gap one cyclist at a time… in this case, to Kreuziger. The leading cyclist is – in that way – brought back into the fold, and everyone will have spent an equal amount of energy.

Unfortunately, this is not how real life works. With the finishing line in sight, cyclists will think more and more about their personal interest. That interest informs the racer: let the others close the gap, save your strength for the sprint. Here, too, the following applies: if everyone thinks that way, no one will close the gap, immediately making the lead man the winner. The game of saving your strength as much as you can and letting the others do the dirty work will have gained you nothing more than a sprint for second place. And indeed, this is what happened in the 2013 Amstel Gold Race. Behind the escaping Kreuziger, Weening looked around and kept his legs still. Who's going for the chase? The others looked back without doing anything. No one wanted to do the dirty work – and no one did. Personal interest won, but made everyone a loser in the end.

In comparable race situations, there's almost always a rider who eventually gives chase, even though it might be far too late. It's never completely clear which rider from the lead group will try to close the gap. And yet, psychological studies have revealed a number of influential factors. Based on the riders who are a part of the chase group, and based on their personalities and interrelations, we can reasonably estimate who is most likely to do most of the chasing.

First of all, it's the composition of the chase group that is important.[5] During a race, it's known that if *one* pursuer has more to gain by closing the gap with the lead cyclist than the other pursuers, this cyclist will do more of the work. You can immediately see this when there's a sprinter in the lead group. He has everything to gain by approaching the finishing line together, and then winning during the final dash. And so, the sprinter will (have to) do most of the chasing.

On the flip side, it's mostly the team captains who are less inclined to give chase. Of course, this is more the case when the chase group consists of several cyclists from the same team. The captain is the scorpion: waiting and seemingly quiescent, he hovers at the back of the group and lets the others, especially his team mates, do the work. It's only just before the end that he shoots his way to the front, passes everyone and tries to sprint to victory.

When a leading cyclist in a race has joined the escape, the opposite is more likely to occur. He is oftentimes more inclined to do some legwork, for two reasons. Firstly, the leader has more of a staked interest – his lead jersey – in closing the gap to the riders in the lead, and so everyone expects him to do the work. And even if the lead group offers no threat to his position at the head of the ranking, he'll still do the lion's share of the work, because he's forced into that position by his direct competitors; they simply don't do anything. The second reason mostly applies at the end of multi-day cycling races. When the ranking leader has a somewhat comfortable lead, he will appropriate the hard work to show he has all his strength left, and that he's more energetic and powerful than everyone else.[5] Closing gaps in that situation have less to do with gaining on the cyclists ahead of him, and more to do with impressing the ones behind him.

One final race element that clearly influences the willingness of pursuers to work on gaining the lead is the arrears on the leader. If the gap is still small, and the pursuers think it will be easy to close it, the chances that proper cooperation will occur are slim – even though the benefits would be huge. Everyone's inclined to wait for the others to start racing. When the arrears are larger than the pursuers had foreseen, when the stage victory is in danger, the chances are much larger that cooperation will take place.

Of course, there is a chance that none of the lead group cyclists will respond to a rider's breakaway. Strategies will have been thought of in those cases as well. Research shows that one of these strategies is the best, and it's called 'tit-for-tat'.[6] It's really very simple. What a rider should do is firstly work with the riders nearby and then react to what they do (or don't do). The quick response after a breakaway leads the other riders to trust you, and entices them to do their share of the work as well.[7] After the initial work, the other riders should cooperate – tit-for-tat – so that the gap to the lead rider is closed cyclist-by-cyclist. If, after the initial work by the first cyclist, no one else takes over, he should not continue. By sticking to this strategy, a rider shows he is willing to cooperate, but at the same time that he's not going to be fooled with. Accordingly, a rider will never waste more energy than his competitors this way.

The best part of the tit-for-tat strategy is that it doesn't just increase the odds of gaining on a lead cyclist during the stage itself, but can also be useful to a cyclist during an entire race or even during an entire season. An active, cooperative attitude will earn a cyclist points. When a rider is generous in one race and does a lot of the legwork, he can expect to be rewarded in kind during another race. One logical consequence of this is that the history riders build up with one another influences their cooperation: it's a continual settling of outstanding bills. One racer helps the other because, a year ago, the tables were turned. One rider absolutely refuses to help another because he was not given any help himself during an earlier race.

This may appear strange to someone who doesn't know about the outstanding favours that riders have amongst each other. Take the 27th of May 2011, the 19th stage of the Giro d'Italia. The stage culminated (as do half of all Giro stages) up a mountain at Macugnana, some 1,360 metres above sea level, not far from the Swiss border. Seven kilometres before the top, Italian Paolo Tiralongo, who'd never won anything in his 12 year career, sped up. The favourites, including Alberto Contador in the pink leader's jersey, let him go. Tiralongo's decisive attack in this stage – meant to further the distance between him and his competitors – took place 1,500 metres before the finishing line but Contador caught up with Tiralongo easily, with a burst of speed that made the Italian look like an amateur.

And yet, it was the Italian who, 15 minutes later, was on the podium waving his flowers, emotional after his first career victory. The last four hundred metres saw Contador clearly not making an effort to bike away from Tiralongo. He was continually looking back, making himself the pacesetter for the old Italian, as if it was a derny race. From time to time, the man in the pink jersey had to keep his legs still, to let Tiralongo catch up again. The final dash was a farce… a gift.

A classification leader is known to hand out presents, but that a leader would make this much effort to let another win is extraordinary. Why this happened only becomes clear when we know the history between Contador and Tiralongo. In 2011, the riders were in different teams, but in 2010 they were on the same team. They both rode for the Kazakh team Astana. Contador won the Tour de France then, with some difficulty. It was the Tour that Lance Armstrong was biking anonymously for the first time after his hegemony of many years. After seven Tour victories – even though these were declared invalid afterwards – Armstrong, pretty much without fanfare, ended up in 23rd place in 2010, nearly 40 minutes behind the yellow jersey.

Contador was able to wear the yellow on the Champs-Élysées, but it was not an easy victory. On the contrary, his margin over the number two, Andy Schleck, hadn't been so tight in many years. The race outcome wasn't made so much by tactics or a difference in strength, but by a faltering chain. During the 15th stage, a route through the Pyrenees from Pamiers to Bagnères-de-Luchon, Andy Schleck's chain blocked (he was wearing the yellow jersey at that point), at the exact moment Contador sped up during the climb up the Port-de-Bales. Schleck ultimately lost 39 seconds, and the yellow jersey.

When two riders are so closely matched, as Andy Schleck and Alberto Contador were in 2010, the team becomes the deciding factor. Indeed, the domestiques (helpers) of both teams worked like mules. Whole days they rode point, closing all gaps. They did everything to allow the captain to stay in his team mates' cosy shelter. But one domestique is simply stronger than the other, can do more work, can keep at it longer. Paolo Tiralongo was that domestique to Contador: a super domestique, brutally slaving away.

Tit-for-tat. And so, a year later in 2011, Tiralongo got his reward, and won his first stage in his 12 year professional career. Tiralongo's good work was paid back by way of a stage win.

In 2013, Roman Kreuziger, in his blue-yellow Saxo Bank jersey, stood on the top level of the Amstel Gold Race podium. "I'm extremely happy," Kreuziger said of this victory, "it is my first victory at one of the classics and it makes me even happier that I pulled it off at the Amstel, a race I've always liked." Seven kilometres from the finishing line, the Czech took a gamble, took off – and won. Behind him, there were gambles as well, with some riders looking around for support before everyone else lost. Kreuziger's victory was due not only to his strength, but also to the failed strategy of the group chasing him.

Chapter 7

It's clear by now that the composition of the group chasing the strong Czech influenced their willingness to do the necessary work. We haven't even discussed the riders themselves and their personalities. Research has shown that there is one character trait that has a strong influence on what a rider will do when someone breaks away: their *social value orientation.*

Social value orientation means that people have stable preferences when it comes to achieving results for themselves when compared to others. This orientation can, for example, express itself in the degree that someone is inclined to help others, in relationships and during races. One of the biggest experts in this field of research is Dutch Professor Paul van Lange.

Van Lange and his colleagues differentiate between three types of value orientation.[8] Firstly, riders can be *prosocial* or *cooperative*. These types of riders are quickly inclined to work together. They want the best result for themselves and for their fellow escapees. When a rider breaks away from a lead group, they will be willing to take on part of the work sooner. After all, it's in their interest and in the interest of all the others that the escaping cyclist is caught up with. A typical example of such a rider was Juan-Antonio Flecha: a rider who biked with everything he had and was always willing to work with others.

Then there are *individualists*. These riders want the best result for themselves; they don't care what the others do. When a rider breaks away, as Kreuziger did in the Amstel, they'll be willing to do the work as it's in their own interest to catch up with the lead cyclist. Individualists, however, more than cooperative types, will try and save as much of their strength for the final sprint as they can, whilst cooperating during their relief on point. Chances are, however, that the fervour with which they give chase is somewhat lacking. An example of a more individualistic rider is Alberto Contador. Only placing first matters to him. The other places are all the same to him: whether he places second or twentieth in a race, he sees no difference.

And finally, we have *competitive* riders. This type of rider will want to perform the best they can compared to the others. On one hand, a competitive mindset in cycling might seem the best of the three to have. After all, cycling is, by its very definition, a competitive sport. Biking as fast as you can is not the point; the point is to be faster than the other cyclists and thus win races. Still, this reasoning is not entirely correct. A rider with a competitive value orientation, who's in the group behind the lead cyclist, won't be eager to do the work. He'd rather save his legs and wait for the others to do the dirty work – with the risk that the lead cyclist will never be caught. Even when that lead cyclist isn't caught, this type of rider will still be able to demonstrate to his fellow escapees that he's the fastest. The number of cyclists who fall into this category seems to be relatively high. Such riders in big races often compete for a place in the top ten; they'll still have performed relatively well then.

A spectator watching at home, or along the route, would have had a difficult time figuring out which value orientation Weening, Caruso, Nordhaug and Grivko held, riding behind Kreuziger the moment he made his escape. You can perhaps only deduce this information from previous races, and what these riders were inclined to do during an escape.

There are a few more factors which are now known to partially correlate with which orientation a person has.[8] Age, for example, is one of them: as people grow older, they become more cooperative. Or, in short, the older the rider, the greater the odds he is willing to ride point. It goes without saying that this cannot be heedlessly taken for granted, as is the case with all factors. Still, generally speaking, older cyclists are more obliging.

Furthermore, people who grow up in a more collectivist environment are generally more cooperative than people who come from an individualistic environment. This difference between environments is often associated with different countries. America is the poster boy for an individualistic society. You could deduce that American cyclists are generally not that inclined to cooperate with others… their personal interests come first. While this holds a kernel of truth, it is not the whole story. Generally speaking, you could also say that people from urban areas have a more individualistic mindset compared to those from rural areas.[9] Cyclists who grew up in the countryside are generally more inclined to work with others than cyclists who grew up in an urban space.

Finally, and this relates to the previous point, a correlation has been found between the size of the family a person grows up in and their value orientation.[8] People from families with many children often have a more cooperative mindset than people from families with few children. And this is even more the case when someone has a lot of sisters (instead of brothers). The reason for this is that people from a large family have to learn how to share and cooperate from birth. The effects of these seminal lessons reverberate across a lifetime, all the way into cycling races.

Note that, taken by themselves, there is a limited relationship between the aforementioned factors (like family size) and how a cyclist behaves in a cycling competition. Nonetheless, relationships have been found and, taken together (e.g., an older rider coming from a large family and living in the countryside) they help to increase our understanding of why a cyclist behaves the way he does.

We have seen in this chapter that one type of cyclist has a special role and how their presence makes all the difference: that of a team captain. Indeed, the presence of leaders in a group takes us beyond the psychology of social dilemmas. Power comes into play. In the next chapter, we will take a closer look at the function and role of power in cycling.

8

The Balance of Power: from Raleigh to Sky, from Badger to Spartacus

Nowadays, hardly anyone refers to his bicycle as a 'steel steed'. It's a synonym that should be restored to everyday parlance, though, especially in sports cycling. That's because the professional peloton, with its host of unwritten rules, clear-cut hierarchy, and continual power struggles, bears all the hallmarks of a small knightly order from the early Middle Ages![1] Riders are like modern knights, knights of the pedal. Just like those steel-armoured men on their horses did a thousand years ago, racers continually battle one another. The landlords of those days are today's lead cyclists. The patrons of the peloton are the kings of days past. They determine what happens, they bless any escape or hand out gifts by way of stage wins, as we saw Contador do in the previous chapter.

And just like in the Middle Ages, power lasts as long as physical strength. Some cyclists control everything, others follow. Those clear boundaries between leaders and followers in the world of cycling delineate everything, which is why it's good to pause and consider the use of that balance of power, to understand the mental advantages of being part of a powerful team.

The presence and impact of powerful leaders in the peloton is probably greater than you would expect, for their sphere of influence is not limited to what people can see on television. For example, in 2003, the young Bradley Wiggins participated in the Giro d'Italia. He had only turned professional shortly beforehand having focused mostly on track cycling where he was very successful. This was his first time participating in a big race. The peloton did not offer much attention to the newcomer; Pantani and Cipollini were the big favourites. All eyes were focused on them. And not just the eyes of fellow cyclists, but also those of the TV audience. Indeed, Wiggins stayed out of the camera's watchful eye, biking around anonymously at the back of the peloton. The future winner of the Tour de France would later give up, exhausted. Although, it was more like he was given up on. The 18th stage and the umpteenth mountain course were the limit for Wiggins. He did not complete the stage in the allotted time and was therefore no longer welcome for the following day's start.

The racer, then biking for Française des Jeux, told an interviewer later on that he had suffered much: "That Giro was the worst thing I've done in life!"[2] In passing, he also gave an example of how patrons can determine the course of a race, without television viewers being any the wiser. In this case it turned out that, for Bradley Wiggins, finishing or not finishing the 2003 Giro d'Italia depended on Mario Cipollini. Wiggins explained: "Marco Pantani was riding and Cipollini was in the rainbow jersey. When Cipo was still in the game, I was doing okay. Every time he thought they were biking too fast, especially uphill, he biked to the head of the peloton and made sure they slowed down. But then he left the race after he crashed, and all hell broke loose."[2] The mountain stages were suddenly lacking a leader who looked after the interests of the lesser climbing gods. Indirectly, the extravagant Italian dragged a lot of riders down with him in his fall.

At other times, the influence of patrons is clear to everyone. A leader, after all, cares little for the presence (or lack) of television cameras. Take the Tour de France on the 5th of July 2010, during the 2nd stage. When you looked at the race course from Brussels to Spa beforehand, you knew immediately that the Tour management had very carefully planned this route. Hills from the beautiful spring classic Liège–Bastogne–Liège were featured and a mass sprint could very well be in the works as well. Fireworks guaranteed! But the reality turned out to be quite different. No fireworks, no sprint, not one bit of action. *One* man was sufficient that day to cripple the entire peloton. A Swiss in a yellow jersey: Fabian 'Spartacus' Cancellara.

The reason why Spartacus directed the neutralised peloton to the finishing line that day was a series of falls in the last hour of the stage. That riders would crash was expected, mind you. The whole stage was as grey as the streets of Liège: the weather was right for accidents. And yet Cancellara decided to influence events after the descent down the Côte de Stockeu. During the descent down this notorious hill, riders fell in heaps on the shining, slippery pavement. It wasn't the little names that crashed. Allesandro Petacchi, Christian Vandevelde, and the Schleck brothers, podium candidates, as well. The younger brother,

Andy, even fell twice during the same descent. Because of this fall, the distance between the Schleck brothers and the peloton quickly extended to nearly four minutes.

Some riders smelt blood and wanted to keep up the pace. The Rabobank captains Menchov and Gesink watched on avidly: they were given the opportunity to take out two serious contenders for the classification on day three of a big race. And yet, they were told from up high that falling would no longer be decisive to that day's race. Cancellara decided that it would be irresponsible to have a peloton bike in such weather on serpentine and slippery roads. He biked to the head of the peloton, stretched out his colossal body, stopped his legs and spread out his arms: slow down. He made clear that the riders were going to wait and bike to the finish together. No sprint. And thus, the charismatic Swiss made a firm decision to which the whole peloton listened. Grudgingly and reluctantly it bent to the will of the man in the yellow jersey. Disappointed and frustrated, fellow riders watched the Schleck brothers return to the peloton. "Today fair play won," Andy Schleck concluded with relief once the stage was over.

After the rainy ride came the storm: the press was critical of Cancellara for stopping the race because of a few falls. Many team managers echoed these criticisms. "Crashes are part of the race and they should have kept on going," said Lotto manager Marc Sergeant. "I'd be interested in knowing if Cancellara would have made the same decision if the Schleck brothers hadn't fallen so far behind?"[3] Such remarks found eager fans among some of the other classification riders, who interpreted the event more as strategic team play than fair play. Finally, the sprinters spoke up, irritated as their chance for a stage win went up in smoke. After all, fair play had already won the day. "I feel like they have taken something away from us today," Thor Hushovd was heard exclaiming after reaching the finishing line.

This event during the most important cycling race in the world and in front of a global TV audience was a beautiful display of power. Team captains, classification riders and sprinters did not agree with the judgement of the yellow jersey bearer. And probably rightly so, because however much Spartacus made his move appear an act of solidarity – which it probably was, at least partially – it seemed more like a strategic decision to keep the Schleck brothers, his team mates, in the race. Despite all of this, despite the annoyed riders who wanted to continue racing, the Swiss still managed to influence the right people and, with a rock-solid conviction, cripple the entire peloton. Fabian Cancellara not only had power, he also possessed seemingly unheard-of leadership qualities. And that is another thing entirely, which we'll talk about later on.

The examples of Cipollini and Cancellara not only demonstrate that power in the peloton is most definitely present, but also that it, and the presence of leaders, can be useful. And it's really not that strange because – despite the balance of power being easier to recognise in sports cycling than in other sports – in the end there is no single sport and not even any group of people where power is distributed evenly. Indeed, research into the evolutionary origin and functions of power and leadership shows that there is no example in human history of a society without any form of rule. In fact, even groups that originally plan to function without a leader (e.g. group decision making) eventually see the rise of a leader-follower relationship.[4] It's only human that some lead where others follow.

The reason that a power balance is so ingrained in humans is exactly *because* it is useful and always has been. Whenever a group of people have to solve a problem together, it's important to avoid everyone randomly doing things their way; *one* person needs to take the initiative and then guide the others.[5] As primitive man, this leader-follower relationship was effective when finding water and food and chasing away predators or rival groups.[4] Nowadays, the factors that made leadership advantageous then are still present. Essentially, little has changed. The proven examples of leadership, some of which will be shown below, also play a part in sports cycling. And this is not only true of individual riders, but also of managers of cycling teams, even complete teams and their position as leaders of the peloton.

One of the most important and eye-catching advantages of a power hierarchy in sports cycling is, of course, that the captain saves his strength in order to be fresh when the finale of the race comes around. The power of the team as a whole is naturally also a deciding factor. Team Sky, *the* team since 2010, have utilised several captains and been able to play multiple cards during races due to the strength of the team as a whole. That's how Sky won the Tour de France both in 2012 and 2013, though with different – interchangeable, if you will – captains: Wiggins (2012) and Froome (2013).

This saving of strength works even better when the captain actually acts as a leader and coordinates the tasks of his team. Everyone then knows exactly what his job is: who has to give up his tire when the captain's goes flat, who carries the water, who joins in riding point early on in the stage, who does that later on, etc. That ability to coordinate is therefore in and of itself an important quality that benefits riders.[4] A good leader, alongside good training, allows an intrinsically slightly weaker team to compete properly against its stronger rivals.

Furthermore, the balance of power between captains and lieutenants, between patrons and the rest, creates structure and clarity. Each rider knows his place which promulgates order and quiet, sometimes even literally. For example, on Stage 15 of the 2012 Tour de France, after the first hour of the race was ridden at a terribly high pace with countless and pointless escapes, Edvald Boasson Hagen rode to the front with an angry and dominant look to indicate to everyone that enough was enough – in the name of yellow jersey bearer and Sky teammate Wiggins. "Let them go" or similar words were spoken to the fervent chasers of the umpteenth group of escapees. And thus it was done. The escapees made their escape and the peloton stayed where they were to the finale.

That a clear balance of power creates structure and order is something that can be seen in every multi-day race. Just watch: the chaos in the first few days of such races is enormous, but gradually diminishes. Why? Because all teams and their respective captains are full of hope on day one that they will be able to obtain the prized leader's jersey. There's still a struggle for power. After a few days, quiet descends as reality bites and a race order (based on results) develops. There's mostly two, or maybe three, captains who let their teams steer the peloton. The rest seem to follow them meekly around and let the powerhouses do their work. This strategy of letting the teams of the big favourites do all the work is in many cases everyday reality and may even seem logical but – according to a recent analysis[7] – is not the best way to promote success. Rather, a guerrilla strategy (frequent and unexpected attacks) would be a more suitable strategy to disrupt and defeat the more powerful competitor(s).[7]

Just as with previous topics in this book, the effect of power is not simply limited to individual athletes, but equally applies to whole teams. Other teams have their eyes on the leading team and let this group take the initiative. On one hand, this could be an advantage for the team in question as it allows them to mould the race to their liking. On the other hand, it does require a lot of energy to keep control of the race and ride at the head of the peloton all day. The question then is how cyclists from the most powerful teams of their time, such as Sky, US Postal, Banesto or Raleigh experience biking in such a powerful team for themselves. To answer this question I spoke with Henk Lubberding, a rider who was, for years, a part of perhaps the most illustrious team of all time: TI-Raleigh.

Raleigh was a professional Dutch team between 1974 and 1983, and is by far the best team the Netherlands has ever produced. The Raleigh team dominated the classics and was unbeatable in team time trials. Joop Zoetemelk, wearing the team's legendary red-and-yellow shirt, also won the 1980 Tour de France. Many riders who are now part of the Dutch hall of fame, such as Jan Raas, Hennie Kuiper, Johan van der Velde and Gerrie Knetemann, were all members of this incredibly strong team.

In a beautifully-illustrated book about this Dutch team, author Joop Holthausen described how Peter Post and his Raleigh team started a revolution in sports cycling.[7] The team had strong racers but this was not the reason they were able to become all-powerful; that was merely a basic condition. More importantly, the team brought in a working revolution at the time by, for example, having mechanics service the bikes of all riders every day during big races.

Truly crucial and revolutionary, however, were the team's tactics. While all teams in those years had been built up around one absolute captain, Post's team had several substitutes at their disposal. The advantage was that when the captain couldn't participate due to uncooperative legs or some mechanical failure, there was always another rider to take his place. Other teams facing this situation, by comparison, became headless, without options. Raleigh's level structure opened up many tactical avenues as each rider in the Raleigh team could play for the stage victory. Each attack featuring a rider from that feared Dutch team was a potential danger to their competitors. This was much less the case with other teams. For them, any escaping rider was not much more than a pawn to serve the captain in the finale. They would usually not even be allowed to try to win the race for themselves; they were really just there to support the captain strategically. Henk Lubberding was part of this Raleigh system for many years, and garnered two wins during the Dutch road cycling championships, amongst other things. Incidentally, his victories illustrate the effectiveness of the team's tactics yet again: he barely served as captain. He gained most of his victories while biking for Jan Raas or Gerrie Knetemann.

Lubberding joined the team in 1978, during its heyday, and recalled his time there with such vividness and detail that it seemed like yesterday. It's Lubberding's experience that racing for a powerful team (like Raleigh or a team like Sky since 2010) mostly comes with advantages. The disadvantages, such as having to be the man on point during a race are, more often than not, just part of the bargain. "Being a part of a team like that, that has so many victories, is just the most wonderful feeling. Just feeling part of it is good in and of itself, the 'I was there' feeling. There's this chemistry that forms that is an incredible motivator. It feels like you've already won, which as a team makes you constantly focused during a race. When one attack was parried, the next one from our team was already moving. The competition felt terribly demotivated."

"During Raleigh's glory days, we knew we would win when two of our guys were in the lead group. We were just better. Biking for a team like that gives you an enormous rush, and you'd see that even the least-abled rider in the team started to become a better cyclist. You can do so much more than you would normally when there's all that trust."

The enthusiastic former pro also explained how Raleigh's structure influenced performances. It mainly came down to this: as the whole team was performing so well, it became easier for the captain to also want to ride for someone else, like a lieutenant. Even then, the chances were still very good that someone from their own team would win. Furthermore, Raleigh, more so than other teams, had captains that were innately more disposed to working for someone else, men like Jan Raas and Gerrie Knetemann.

"I remember, as an example, an edition of Ghent-Wevelgem. There was a moment when a lead group formed that had seven[!] Raleigh men in it. And then Leo van Vliet surged ahead. They let him go, because everyone knew that he was the least-able rider in the Raleigh team at that time. They were all thinking: we'll get him later. They also gambled that Raas himself would want to win. But no. We didn't see Leo again that entire day." And that's how Leo van Vliet won this beautiful classic in 1983. At the same time, the example underlines once more how even the lowest-ranked rider can exceed his own abilities by biking for such an all-powerful team.

The willingness of men such as Raas and Knetemann to bike for others is so important, according to Lubberding, because it pleases everyone in the team. "We really got a rush from someone else in the team winning. But not everyone felt the same way. Those cyclists also needed to have their own benefits to being the team, and were thus given the opportunity every now and then to pursue their own chances. You could see Cavendish doing the same when he was biking for Sky, for example. He was competing in a world championship he had no business participating in. Just to help his English colleagues, who nearly all rode for Sky as well. Kilometre after kilometre, you saw Cav grinding away at the head of the peloton. That's the kind of thing that's very much appreciated by your team mates.'

What is most noticeable in Henk Lubberding's analysis, is that it's not so much that the captains profit from the powerful position of a team like Raleigh or Sky (we already know that), what's interesting and what Lubberding emphasises time and time again is that all the lieutenants also manage to profit. This is exactly what scientific research has shown: leadership is not just a positive thing for the captain himself, or the patrons of the peloton, but also for the followers.[8] This explains why the much delineated power structure in sports cycling has never changed over the years.

The balance of power in sport is not just advantageous to the leading athlete, but to everyone in a powerful team, and to a certain degree even to the ones drawing the short straw: the followers. Still, there is another function to this balance of power on a higher level. And that's something the entire professional peloton, perhaps even all of sports cycling, profits from: maintaining the unwritten rules of sports cycling.

Such unwritten rules naturally play a very important part in sports cycling,[9] as in other sports, associations or companies – even if not one cyclist has even been disqualified for breaking one of them. After all, these are rules that have not been written down or even maintained by the UCI cycling union. The unwritten laws of cycling are basically no different to the norms and values of our society as a whole. They dictate what is, and what is not, appropriate behaviour; how to deal with colleagues and competitors. They provide structure and create expectations. They form an essential part of identity, and therefore play an important role in professional cycling.

Take the rule of waiting when a direct competitor takes a fall. You can see an example of this in the 2001 Tour de France when, during the heat of the finale, Lance Armstrong decided to wait until his rival Jan Ullrich got back on his bike after a tumble. It turned out to be a favour not without some profit: in the 2003 Tour it was Armstrong himself lying on the ground with Ullrich waiting for him, allowing Armstrong to win the Tour once again.[10] Or take another rule (one that's quite controversial to outsiders, as it leads to discussions as to whether deals can be struck): I take the yellow jersey, you get some money or a stage win in exchange. Joop Zoetemelk confessed 25 years after the fact that exactly such a deal was crucial to him winning the 1980 Tour de France.

The thing was that on Stage 16, the day before a mountain stage that would take the riders over the almost mythical col du Galibier, Zoetemelk fell off his bike while wearing the yellow jersey. He started the next day, Stage 17, in pain and as a consequence lost touch with his major rivals on the first steep parts of the Galibier. The chances of taking the yellow jersey all the way to Paris were almost gone.

Luckily for Zoetemelk, there was still a fair amount of flat terrain where he could make up the time he'd lost on that massive climb in the Alps. However, Zoetemelk was completely isolated with no team-mates to be seen, only some French riders of various small French teams. So, he made a deal, and promised cash to various riders if they would help him to limit the gap to the front of the field. It worked and the Dutchman won the Tour that year![11]

Above, we examined how it is considered unacceptable to attack a rival when they crash and are on the ground. Despite cycling laws providing 'direction' in races, there are still people who violate them though. For example, Claudio Chiappucci and his whole team wasted no time in attacking when GC leader Greg LeMond had a flat on the 1990 Tour.[12] Just like official laws, some people consider them there to be broken...

Chapter 8

And this is where the most important function of power in sports cycling comes to the fore. As with the police and the judiciary upholding a country's penal code to prevent chaos from erupting, the *patrons* of the peloton are the leaders who have the strongest stake in upholding cycling morals. It is them who, in the end – or at least officially – are responsible for providing clarity and structure in the peloton, which gives the riders mental and sometimes literal peace.

You can find countless examples of this, with perhaps the most famous one being the altercation in 1985 between the by now forgotten Frenchman Joël Pellier and his famed countryman Bernard Hinault. It was the year Hinault – also known as The Badger – won his fifth and final Tour victory and when Miguel Indurain, the Spaniard who would follow in Hinault's footsteps as a five-time Tour winner, made his debut on the French Tour.

On the 10th of July 1985, the 12th stage of the Tour took place; it was a mountainous course no less than 270 kilometres long, from Morzine to Lans-en-Vercors. It had been a tough race thus far, and Bernard Hinault wanted the stage to be slow-paced. He did not take the young and overenthusiastic Joël Pellier (riding his first Tour) into consideration. The rider from the Skil-Sem team raced with all his might and made attack run after attack run. Right up until when Hinault had enough. The patron wanted the peloton to have an easy day, and you don't start racing like a maniac on a day like that. Pellier broke the rules.

When Pellier made another attack, Hinault jumped into action. With a determined face he biked away from the peloton in his yellow jersey. He careened with high speed towards his young compatriot. As soon as he had caught up with Pellier, Hinault gave him a very stern scolding in front of the camera: today we ride *en groupe*.[13] Fabio Parra would eventually win the stage, but the story that day was of the man in the yellow jersey showing his strength, and giving everyone a clear demonstration of cycling's morals. Just as Spartacus would do in 2010, one simple correction by The Badger was enough to literally and figuratively restore peace to the peloton.

Hinault indeed was a true leader, possessing power and knowing how to use it. Now we have looked at power, the next question is surely – what makes a good leader? Let's take a look.

9

Leadership: Oh Captain, My Captain

The previous chapter listed illustrious riders such as Mario Cipollini, Fabian Cancellara and Bernard Hinault – famous names to cycling enthusiasts. They are examples of cyclists with powerful positions in their teams, and the peloton, who seemingly created that position for themselves effortlessly. This type of person can be found in all sports: they seem natural-born leaders. True talents.

It cannot be said of Bernard Hinault that he became leader of the peloton against his will; that he gradually grew into this prominent position. Equally, the idea that it took him some time to get used to, is untrue. On the contrary, the Frenchman – who as the patron of patrons had a hugely powerful position – took on his role at a youthful age. In 1978, at 23 years-of-age, he participated in the Tour de France for the first time. In the same year, the peloton went on strike in Valence d'Agen, angry at the Tour's management for moving them around from stage to stage all the time. Heading this strike was a young rookie with a straight, confident gaze: Bernard Hinault.[1]

Despite Hinault being an exceptional champion and leader, it's fairly infrequent for the big leaders of the peloton to take on the role of captain – to make their mark – at such a young age. As well as Hinault, the same thing happened with Slovakian and multiple champion Peter Sagan. Even back in 2011, when he was only 20-years-old and in his second year of professional cycling, he took up the captaincy of the Liquigas team alongside renowned team mates including Ivan Basso and Vincenzo Nibali. In short, some riders seem born to take on the role of captain and leader.

Of course, it's not that simple for everyone. There are plenty of riders who struggle when taking charge, and who continue to struggle throughout their careers. So, how is it that one person leads with ease, and effortlessly takes on a position of power, whilst another does not?

Chapter 9

As it happens, more often than not, there is at least one clear-cut answer: those cyclists who obtain power and become captain, are simply very strong and talented cyclists. It seems obvious, does it not? Despite the unique manner in which Hinault led the peloton during the 1978 Tour (and thus being a surprise to many) the young Frenchman was already someone to take notice of. He'd previously won important races such as the Vuelta a España, Ghent-Wevelgem, Liège-Bastogne-Liège and the Dauphiné Liberé in 1977. The same goes for Sagan, who in 2010 seemed to effortlessly win a number of stages and points classifications in Paris-Nice and the Tour of California.

Winning stages and multi-day tours is, in and of itself, sufficient to gain influence over other racers. Psychological studies into power differentiate between several forms of power a person can have over others.[2] In sports cycling, three forms matter most (whilst the more types of power a rider has, the more influence he'll have over others).

The first form is a rider's power to educate others. This is something done mostly by the older riders in a team. They teach the younger riders the workings of the peloton; they teach them the skills of their trade.

The other two forms of power are directly linked to a rider's success: the power to reward, and the power one gets from others looking up to a cyclist due to race success. This third form sees an exceptionally well-performing rider routinely develop power. After all, when someone decisively and easily wins, it's only a matter of time before a large portion of the peloton develops respect for him.

The power to reward, on the contrary, is something a rider completely controls himself but which stems from good race performances. A rider who never wins himself, can hardly grant a stage win to others. Multiple champions can certainly gift stage wins, and thus put others in dependent positions. After all, they have to wait and see if one day they'll have to return the favour. Ranking leaders, for example, often grant the stage win to a fellow escapee. Teams also regularly see the captain forfeiting his stage win – as happened with the Raleigh team in the previous chapter. Raas and Knetemann were prepared to let their domestiques create their own chances and even support them in doing that. The system only works because captains win a lot themselves, and do not need to prove their positions as leaders for race after race.

Leaders in cycling are often awe-inspiring mountaineers, burly bears, or explosive greyhounds. They are typically not the riders who have to struggle, day after day and mountain after mountain, to avoid losing precious seconds and reach the finishing line after the time limit. Leaders are not the supposed sprinters who lose their position at the decisive moment race after race. They're not the riders who are taken off guard by an attack, or raise their hands in victory a hundred metres before the finishing line only to be passed by three others before crossing it. They're not riders who make a forceful display 60 kilometres from the finishing line, before arriving completely worn out. These riders will not quickly become leaders.

There are also plenty of strong riders who will never be captain, or at least not a proper one. Aside from physical strength, there are a large number of other factors that influence whether or not someone makes a good captain. And those factors, which in the end greatly determine the outcome, are mostly mental. Based on years of psychological studies it is now even possible to create a complete psychological profile of what makes someone a good captain.

Firstly, good captains (designated leading riders within a team), team managers (general leaders of teams), and *patrons* (unofficial leaders of the whole peloton) generally have high emotional intelligence. This means that they can empathise with others, that they *understand* others, and have good social skills. It also means they are not easily defeated and have a positive attitude.[3]

A large-scale study done in 1999 into the characteristics of good leaders fleshed out our understanding.[4] Conducted across 62 different cultures, it provided a list of characteristics that good captains or patrons possess. Good leaders are competent in what they do, although this is quite commonsensical. Furthermore, they are generally highly focused on performance and very self-confident. They are viewed as honest, have integrity, and can inspire those around them. They know how to motivate others and encourage them. Truly effective leaders are social and aim for cooperation. They know how to create a close-knit team, and keep that atmosphere going, even when their luck has turned.[4] A leader is also smart and can anticipate events. He's a visionary, and knows where the team must go. He is decisive, determined, and aware of what's going on. He's also a good negotiator.

He knows how to achieve the best result for all different parties, keeping everyone satisfied.[4]

This list of characteristics is quite long, perhaps too long. It's fair to ask whether someone who has all these qualities even exists. There is no definitive answer although it would be interesting if we could get the whole peloton to take a personality test! However, for the purposes of this story, that won't be necessary. We can conclude that when a rider has many of these characteristics, the more likely it is that he'll be a good captain. And as a good captain, the odds that he will eventually develop into a leader of the peloton grow.

To illustrate, I'll once more use the example from the previous chapter: Fabian Cancellara putting his foot down and neutralising the entire peloton during the rainy Ardennes stage of the 2010 Tour. The overlap between the psychological profile of a leader and this event is striking. The Swiss managed to curtail the peloton through the enormous self-confidence he demonstrated, combined with his determined hand gestures that brooked no dissent. And yet, that decisiveness alone was not enough. The action was a success because nearly the entire peloton saw Cancellara as a smart, honest and social man: he had garnered goodwill. Besides, the neutralisation of the stage was the result of negotiations taking place while biking the race between the Swiss and race management. All in all, it's hardly surprising that Cancellara has become a patron.

The previously described characterisation of a good captain started with a focus on physical strength, and ended in a long list of personal characteristics. What's striking is that all the characteristics on the list are positive ones; a good leader seems to have few negative qualities. The list also excels in its predictability. Were we to ask a random person to give a description of a good leader, the chances are that he or she would list the characteristics from the psychological profile. Or even more probably, the interviewee would summarise the entire list as 'charismatic' or someone with the 'x-factor'. Indeed, charisma sums up the profile quite well. The peloton's leaders have always been charismatic people, whether patrons such as the extravagant Mario Cipollini or the immovable Bernard Hinault, or someone like legendary team manager Cyrille Guimard (who triple Tour de France winner Greg LeMond even described the best coach in the world).

Generally speaking, people prefer being led by charismatic characters.[5] Imagine biking in a professional team and a young, talented team mate – not yet captain – matches your vision of what makes a good captain. Chances are you'll automatically be more influenced by him, valuing his ideas just a little more than those of other team mates. You unknowingly assign captaincy on him this way. The knife cuts both ways. The right combination of characteristics makes a rider a better leader, and at the same time makes his team mates *want* to be led by him.[5]

In practice, you can find plenty of examples where it's not entirely clear whether riders truly want their captain leading them and whether the captain has such positive characteristics – even if he is a clear and self-confident leader. Take Lance Armstrong. In hindsight, he was more a dictatorial captain than a compassionate one.

In the 2004 Tour, for example, the American was at the zenith of his power. He had won the Tour five times. He was the captain, the team manager, patron and friends with Hein Verbruggen (chair of the UCI back in the day) and thus king of cycling. On the 18th stage of that particular Tour, a small group of riders made an escape shortly after departure. The Italian Filippo Simeoni from the small Domina-Vacanze team, a complete non-danger in the rankings, was not part of it, but a bit later on he decided to sprint to the head of the race by himself. He didn't take Armstrong into consideration; furious, he raced to the Italian's position. Some words follow that we as the television audience did not quite catch, although we understood the general meaning.

Afterwards, Simeoni didn't want to disclose the exact choice of words the captain used, "It was too serious,"[6] but the upshot was that Simeoni dropped back to the peloton. At least part of Armstrong's actions towards Simeoni stemmed from a court case before the race during which he had testified against the famed Dr. Ferrari. Simeoni testified that Ferrari was involved in unsavoury practices, and that the doctor had shown him how to effectively use the doping drug EPO.

Despite Simeoni never once mentioning the name of Armstrong during the court case, reports afterwards suggested that the American felt he had been attacked and indirectly accused. That was the reason for the Texan's show of strength on the 18th stage; making a move in his personal feud with the Italian. After Simeoni let himself be led back to the peloton, as if he was a dog with Armstrong holding the leash, the American smugly looked around him. Smiling, he made a gesture across his lips of a zipper closing. To say the least, this behaviour is not very much in line with the profile of a leader we just presented!

When we look at psychological studies done in this area, the conclusion is remarkable. The positive qualities that define a good leader may allow a rider to quickly become one, but also, once he *is* a leader, allow for those same qualities to disappear over time as well.[7] To many people, the ancient cliché that 'power corrupts' is unfortunately very true. Research has shown that people become more dishonest, egotistical and impulsive once they have taken on a position of power. They do not consider other people as much. They do not empathise with others. And very importantly (in light of cycling's doping scandals) they consider themselves more justified in breaking rules, while at the same time wanting others to abide by those rules.[7] The true strength of a leader is therefore to continue embodying the qualities that brought him to power, even when power tantalises the individual with potential corruption and self-interest.

By now, we're able to understand the type of rider that makes a good leader. There's still a catch, though, for the problem is that cycling often operates according to the law of the jungle. The consequence of which is that riders who have everything it takes to make captain never make it that far; they don't win enough. On the flip side, there are plenty of riders who do not have the character needed to be captain, but who wind up in that position after a batch of good results.

One example in the latter category is Jevgeni Berzin, a Russian who, after several wins, was catapulted into the position of captain of the Gewiss-Ballan team at a young age. His response after his victory in the 1994 Giro d'Italia spoke volumes as to his qualities as a leader: "I would have won the Giro just as well without my team."[8]

The qualities that make a rider a good leader do not necessarily make him a bad one if he lacks them. Perhaps it's better to rephrase this… *they don't tell the whole story*. Becoming a captain brings pressure: the pressure to perform, to tell others what to do, to deal with ruthless critics, to bear responsibility. And it's that pressure that a lot of captains cannot handle.

Take Erik Breukink, one of the most successful Dutch grand Tour cyclists ever. In the late eighties, he was a two-time Giro podium finalist, and was also on the podium during the 1990 Tour de France. He was the kind of rider who performed better if he was able to bike in the shelter of the peloton but who could completely freeze the moment he was put forward as the captain on the starting line. To make the difference crystal clear, let's compare him to Peter Sagan: a rider who has no trouble whatsoever with the pressure of being a captain. He feels at home there and manages to maintain a certain playfulness, despite the pressure. It's not uncommon to see him working away with a smile on his face during important races like the Tour, entertaining the viewers and the spectators by doing uphill wheelies and other tricks.

Being a captain always comes with pressure, for both someone like Sagan and someone like Breukink. The difference has to do with the person and the way he handles it. One suffers – becoming paralysed by the pressure and the enormous stress – while the other seems to barely notice. The question then is *what* creates that difference.

How a rider manages the pressure of being a captain turns out to be largely related to a specific personality characteristic: anxiety.[9] People with high anxiety are more inclined to focus on negative emotions and insecurities by nature. When riders with this personality trait are put under pressure, their focus on the negative increases.[9] Instead of focusing on the race they quickly shift their focus to thoughts of insecurity, such as: "My legs are no good," or "I'm sure to disappoint my team mates." Riders with low anxiety suffer from this less; they can more easily focus on the race, even when the pressure ramps up.

Looking at research into performance pressure among athletes, two things happen to riders who cannot handle pressure well. First of all, they become more easily distracted; secondly, they become more self-aware. To achieve success, though, they need to completely focus on the race.

Captains with high anxiety are especially vulnerable to becoming distracted when pressured. Their thoughts will linger on the pressure and the responsibility of having to perform well: "As long as I don't lose any time" or "I *have* to show what I'm made of today." Distraction is a risk for all captains. The more important the race, the higher the pressure and the more the outside world demands a rider's attention.

Chapter 9

It's incredibly difficult to focus on the race when journalists ask you the same questions a hundred times a day. With the enormous media frenzy, the Tour de France is a hugely strenuous race psychologically.

And not to forget the other discomfort that the pressure to perform brings: focusing on yourself. At first glance, this may seem a positive thing. And yet, self-focus has two negative side effects for athletes. When you're more aware of yourself and your body, there is less mental capacity in your working memory left to focus simultaneously on what matters most: the race.[10] Self-focus becomes yet another form of distraction. And the more an athlete becomes distracted, the greater the odds that he'll choke under the pressure. A rider who's distracted by both media scrutiny and a focus on himself in the form of negative thoughts will almost certainly become paralysed by the pressure.

The other reason a greater inner focus negatively affects a rider under pressure is that he starts to focus more on how he bikes. Biking is an automatism, and many studies show that automated behaviour worsens when you become aware of doing it.[11] A pianist will make mistakes when he starts to actively look at what he's playing. The same thing happens to a cyclist: when he starts looking at his posture on the bicycle and how he makes turns, his posture will almost certainly worsen (he'll start moving around) and he will start making errors in steering. Other studies show us that people are sooner able to get into the flow of things, and thus bike better, under normal racing pressure, but that the flow evaporates when the pressure gets to be too much: it'll feel like you're pedalling in squares.[12] There's a reason why performing under pressure is sometimes referred to in psychology as paradoxical performance!

An example, par excellence, of how a rider can choke under such paradoxical performance is Michael Rasmussen, in particular his time trial during the 2005 Tour de France. Most people will remember the Dane for the interminable quarrel with Rabobank regarding his whereabouts which forced him to leave the 2007 Tour. But many cycling enthusiasts will also remember Rasmussen's 2005 Tour. Back then, Rasmussen was very much an unknown. He rode for the Rabobank team, captained by Michael Boogerd and Denis Menchov.

Rasmussen, who'd covertly joined the early escape on the 9th stage that was to last all the way to the finishing line, was suddenly high up in the rankings (second-place) with the polka dot jersey for best climber thrown in for good measure. And to everyone's surprise, he managed to hold on to his top three ranking and the polka dot jersey during the stages that followed. Rabobank had a climber on their hands! For the first time in the long history of the team, a Rabobank cyclist could end up on the podium in Paris. Rasmussen was immediately promoted to absolute captain and the pressure of an entire nation – or even two: the Netherlands and Denmark – came to rest on his shoulders.

With this pressure bearing down on him, Rasmussen started his next-to-final stage, a 55 kilometre time trial. The tension could be seen in his face quite clearly. He was completely withdrawn and focused on himself. His ride was paradoxical performance in action: so motivated to do everything perfectly, that his entire time trial ended up a complete failure. He continually changed his posture and his attempts to make perfect turns resulted in the very opposite. Three falls and four bike changes later, and all his chances for the Paris podium had disintegrated.

The pressure of being captain, and performance pressure in general, are big impediments to many riders getting good results. Luckily, there are three aids that have been demonstrated to help in coping with pressure.

First of all, when someone is distracted from the race by all manner of thoughts, it can help to simply vocalise them. When someone bottles everything up inside, those thoughts will influence performance. Riders should say them aloud, whether it's to a team mate, team manager, or the media, and those thoughts of insecurity and doubt will dissipate allowing focus to be regained.[13]

A second tool is regularity. A captain or star performer won't escape media attention and all its attendant worries. But it helps to spend one's remaining time as normally as possible. You like to read books? Just like multi-time Tour de France winner Laurent Fignon? Make sure you take time out of your evenings to read a bit.

One final aid, which links to the previous two, is relaxation. A good team atmosphere can help a lot in this regard, but it obviously depends on a rider's team. A rider can take control here and do things that actively relax him before an important race. It can be anything, as long as it is calming and relaxing. Listening to music, playing guitar, taking a stroll, etc. If this can be done *before* a race, it will help a rider to relax *during* the race and forget about the pressure. Because completely focusing on the race for three whole weeks is impossible, focusing one hundred per cent *during* a stage is already an achievement in and of itself. And even that is only possible when one regularly takes time to create moments when complete relaxation can be encouraged. The 1980 Tour de France winner Joop Zoetemelk summed it up best: the Tour is won in bed!

10
Motivation: Fondriest's Milan-San Remo

The themes discussed in this book, so far, offer insight into how an athlete's brain affects athletic performance and what psychological aspects are important when competing in a group. The themes have concerned the cyclist 'in action' but author Willem Frederik Hermans has posited a broader question: "Why would a cyclist bike across the length and breadth of France when the country has an extensive railway network?"[1]

The question of why someone bikes or takes part in sport at all is an interesting one. Generally speaking, the most important questions every athlete should ask themselves are: What drives you to do this sport? What's it all for? Why do you train every day, adjust your diet and daily schedule, and stop socialising? Why do you suffer? The answer to these questions is directly linked to an athlete's motivation, and therefore his performance.

To illustrate the power that motivation has over performance, we travel to a hotel just outside of Milan. It's the middle of the night when a young cyclist's dreams are interrupted by the telephone ringing. The phone call announces the birth of his daughter. The cyclist is ecstatic at the birth of his child – Maria Vittoria – so much so that he can't sleep (at all) for the rest of the night. Not the best of circumstances to start an important race one would think. And yet, later on, the Italian sports daily *Corriere dello Sport* summarised the 1993 *Primavera* race, also known as Milan-San Remo, with the headline '*La festa del papà*' (The feast of the father) for the 20th of March turned out to be a very good race for new father Maurizio Fondriest.[2] Enthused, determined and pumping with adrenaline, he had no doubt as to how he would perform in the race.

Chapter 10

Even before the start, when the Lampre team was going over its strategy, things were clear. The plan Fondriest shared was brief: "I'm going to win today. For Maria Vittoria."[2]

And so it came to pass.

The happy Italian was praised by the Italian crowd throughout the race following the media's reporting of his fatherhood. The many supporters formed a festive chain of sound along Fondriest's route, *"Sei forte, papà!"* they shouted at him: "You're strong, papa!" (a reference to the eponymous Italian hit from the seventies by Gianni Morandi).

On the legendary Poggio, once the radiant symbol of the lush Italian Riviera, now an ugly hill of dilapidated greenhouses, Fondriest made his escape. Driven and stronger than anyone else, he quickly found himself alone. He passed the top of Poggio solo, and all attempts to catch up with him floundered. Fondriest seemed to effortlessly celebrate his daughter's birth on the streets of San Remo.

Maurizio Fondriest was an exceptional cyclist, there can be no doubt about that. Mediocre cyclists do not become a two-time world champion. Yet his performance in the 1993 Milan-San Remo was exceptional even for him. He simply could not be beaten. His victory was due to unequalled motivation: an unbreakable will to get that one victory on that day. He knew exactly what he was biking for that day. To Fondriest, Milan-San Remo was no longer a race, but a pilgrimage.

Fondriest's Primavera shows how incredibly important motivation is to a rider. No matter what the strength of his legs, how well trained his body, or how strong his stamina, without motivation no rider will ever get good results. A high degree of motivation in athletes is therefore directly linked to better performance, greater determination, and more creativity. [3] And that applies to both races and training.

That motivation plays such a large role in the world of sports is not all that surprising when we take a look at what the term means exactly. Motivation can be defined as the catalyst that initiates a certain behaviour, that focuses it and determines its intensity and persistence.[2] When translated to cycling, this means that a motivated rider will want to train more often (initiation), for a clearer goal (focus), and that he will be able to bike at his limits for a longer period of time (intensity and persistence). Despite the phenomenon being a mental one, motivation directly affects the things a rider is physically capable of.

When a rider doesn't really know what he's biking for anymore, his motivation will quickly dissipate. It will then be nearly impossible to perform well. This is known to happen to cyclists who have decided to end their careers, but who still want to finish the season. Such a rider will be thinking about the period *after* his professional career and much less on the actual biking: his focus is gone. This was exactly what the Saxo-Tinkoff rider Karsten Kroon (according to himself) experienced at the end of his career.[4] The drive to bike disappears, and so does motivation.[5]

Many cycling enthusiasts and amateurs will recognise the effect that being motivated can have. It's much easier to train intensively when you know you are biking a *cyclosportive* like La Marmotte in two months. That tour becomes your motivation. On the other hand, if you have nothing planned, the temptation to sit at home becomes much greater than getting on your bicycle.

Professionally speaking, there are hardly any unmotivated riders. The demands on pro riders are high and each rider is expected to persevere and be willing to make sacrifices to such a degree that someone who is not highly motivated will never make it to the professional level. Still, there are clear differences to be observed amongst the professionals. Riders don't all have the same reasons for biking, and different incentives can generally be divided into two psychological categories: intrinsic and extrinsic; motivation from within and from outside.[3,6]

Intrinsic motivation means that a rider bikes mainly for the joy of biking itself. He enjoys getting on his bicycle in the morning, putting on the miles and racing. He could talk about biking all day and enjoys bettering himself, especially when he's biked his usual training lap faster than ever.[3] The best example of an intrinsically motivated rider is possibly Jens Voigt who, despite being well past the age of 40, was still riding in the peloton with fervour. Another example is the talented Belgian Greg van Avermaet, from the ranks of BMC. When asked about his biggest motivation to bike, his immediate answer was: "My biggest drive is to just have fun biking! Even on hectic days, like the Tour of Flanders, I just try to enjoy everything as best I can."

Chapter 10

An extrinsically motivated rider doesn't just bike for fun, but also for the rewards that come with it. This usually boils down to money, fame, attention, or beautiful women, although nobler things can also be involved. To such a rider, biking is only a means to an end – the true motivation lies outside biking. If that type of rider happened to be poor at cycling, but better at driving a car or singing, he'd be driving a car or singing. A well-known example in this category is the less-than-loved Riccardo Riccò, also known as 'Il Cobra'. A blonde-haired Italian who seized every opportunity to make headlines or get his face on television.

Another terrific example is the Italian Ivan Quaranta, whose wonderful nickname was '*Il Ghetopardo'* – 'the Leopard'. Quaranta was a very talented sprinter, the designated successor to superstar Mario Cipollini (nicknamed the Lion King). In 1999, both the old Lion Cipollini and the young Leopard Quaranta rode in the Giro d'Italia. Quaranta was unequalled in speed and almost immediately won two massed sprints; pretty boy Mario was biting dust. It seemed a new star had been born. But Il Ghetopardo wasn't looking at the future. He had defeated Cipollini twice; now the time had come to reap the reward, to brag about his status. The day after his second victory, the team managers of Mobilvetta told the world that their sprinter could not continue due to complaints of exhaustion. That exhaustion turned out to have little to do with biking: the young Ivan had spent the previous night in a disco until 4 a.m., drinking and dancing with women to celebrate his success.[7] It turned out he preferred that to biking around Italy for three weeks.

Lion King Cipollini is himself a good example of how a rider can have different motivations for biking. At first glance, the sprinter sometimes seemed to be biking for fame and glory: he was the stereotypical example of an Italian who cared for nothing but outward appearance. He would show up at every time trial wearing yet another loud tiger-striped jersey. Of course, the Italian enjoyed all that attention and yet, at the same time, he got enormous satisfaction from biking itself. This is most likely the reason he still frequently got on his race bike long after his professional career was over – and not just for fun.

As it turns out, whether a rider is intrinsically or extrinsically motivated is quite important. Time and time again, research has demonstrated that intrinsic motivation gets you farther and makes you more successful over the long run. [6] This may not come as much of surprise. Someone very passionate about biking can much more easily build his life around it. It's the very thing he wants! He'll start training and won't mind adjusting his diet. It's also easier to train throughout the winter, to really study up on training methods and bike materials. To an intrinsically motivated rider, biking is part of his life, his identity.

Someone biking for other reasons, such as money or (media) attention, will consider the above as sacrifices, something done away with as soon as it's possible. Also, with extrinsic motivation come risks: the moment you have a bad streak – the moment success is not immediately present – it becomes very difficult to keep going. You're not biking for fun, and you're not achieving the thing you are biking for. You try to give your all in a situation like that. It's extremely difficult for extrinsically motivated people under such circumstances and they give up sooner and accomplish less over the long run.[6]

The positive effect of an intrinsic motivation to bike was demonstrated quite nicely several years ago with '*der Jan*': Jan Ullrich. This rider was originally more extrinsically motivated. He was very good at biking and could make quite a bit of money doing it. To him, biking was not much more than making a living but he still managed to do well; he won the Tour in 1997 and was a frequent runner-up to Lance Armstrong after that. The battle with the American, however, was mostly on paper. Ullrich spent his winters living like a king and not biking much, and never really amounted to much of a threat to Armstrong in the subsequent Tours. His lack of success was due to his undisciplined winters, and combined with Armstrong's hegemony, made the German lose all faith. His old Telekom colleague Jacques Hanegraaf saw it happen: "I saw a cyclist in trouble, who didn't know what was going on."[8]

But, in 2003, this turned around completely and we saw the most exciting Tour de France in years. Even in the final weekend, after three weeks of racing, it was still unclear whether a determined American or a pulverised German would win the Tour. The difference in ranking was only a few seconds. Eventually, during a rainy time trial when he gave it his all, Ullrich once again – partially due to a fall – had to acknowledge Armstrong as his superior. And yet we still got to see a completely different Ullrich. For the first time, he had managed to truly make the American work for his victory. He had also been transformed from a rider who was very happy with second place into one who'd rather place one hundredth than second. Only gold was important to him. He seemed stronger than ever before in his magenta Bianchi tricot.

What had happened to Ullrich to explain this turnaround? It wasn't novel training methods or the like: the main difference was that Jan Ullrich was no longer biking for money. He had (re)discovered his love for the sport. During a presentation organised by the Tour management on the occasion of its hundredth anniversary in the winter of 2002, Ullrich suddenly came eye to eye with cycling legends including Eddy Merckx and Felice Gimondi. It struck him how special it was to have won the Tour, how amazing it was to be a professional racer. "Until that moment, I never understood the true value of my victory in 1997 from the perspective of cycling history," Ullrich explained.[8]

From that moment, his passion for cycling grew. He wanted to bike and made self-improvement his goal. He was a different person. Jacques Hanegraaf, who was hired around the same time to coach Ullrich, noticed it too. "The conviction is coming from inside now, that's what's different from before. He's no longer doing assignments because they're assignments. It's in his mind. He knows what's necessary. He *wants* to do it."[8] Ullrich's turnaround is a beautiful example of how an intrinsically motivated rider can go that extra mile when compared to a rider who is driven by outside motivation.

Despite 'a love of the sport' underpinning the better bikers, it's true, at the same time, that *every* successful cyclist earns well. The money, the fame and the media frenzy – it's all part of the game. The same holds for racers who are not in it for 'the fame', riders who mostly want to enjoy the races themselves. So, what is the effect of external rewards such as attention, power, and extravagant sponsor deals on such riders?

It seems obvious that a rider who bikes for the love of biking would care little for all the 'fuss' surrounding it. This may be the first response of intrinsically motivated riders but years of research in this area has shown that external rewards come with a somewhat ironic effect.[6] Because of extrinsic rewards, people can eventually lose their intrinsic drive. Someone who started cycling for the love of it and then becomes successful and thus rewarded will become less motivated to bike after the rewards dwindle – for example because the rider has been less successful over a period of time. In essence, there's no reward anymore and there's not much enjoyment to be found either.

A good illustration of the above comes from 1973 when the American psychologist Mark Lepper and colleagues undertook research at a primary school with children between the ages of three and five. It was at a time when primary schools increasingly utilised a method whereby children who acted in an exemplary manner were rewarded. Children would get stickers when they read from a book. If they did some maths without being asked to, they would get a cross on a stamp card; a full card could eventually be traded in for a physical reward such as an apple or something similar. The parallel with cycling is obvious: a child is rewarded for doing something he/she was probably already doing by their own volition.

Lepper and his colleagues were interested in the effect of this reward approach to children's behaviour.[9] During the first part of the study the children were free to draw on a large piece of white paper with marker pens during class. This way, the researchers could easily observe which children innately liked drawing (and were thus intrinsically motivated) and which children were less interested.

A few weeks after this session, Lepper and his associates returned to the school. This time, *some* of the children were given a metaphorical carrot: they were told they would get a diploma with a gold star if they drew a beautiful drawing. Just as several weeks beforehand, the children were allowed to draw, but this time for a reward. The remaining children were not told anything; they were allowed to draw whatever they wanted, when they wanted, and however much they wanted (exactly like before). A diploma was never mentioned.

Another two weeks passed before the three researchers visited for the last time, to conduct the portion of the study that they were truly interested in. The set-up was identical to the first session: all children were allowed to draw as long as they wanted. Rewards were not given. On this third day of testing, Mark Lepper wondered what would happen with the children who had fun drawing the first time and who were given a reward for their drawing the second time. Would they still be contentedly colouring away on the last day?

The answer was clear.[9] The children who'd never received a reward, were still motivated to draw; after all, they were having fun every time! But the children who got diplomas for their drawings on day two, had lost their appetite for it. Their intrinsic motivation had been broken. The children who were having fun drawing, without thought of a diploma, attributed their behaviour (drawing) to themselves: "I draw because I like doing it." The children who were offered the reward (the diploma), however, suddenly attributed their behaviour to circumstances: "I draw because I get a reward for doing it." In short, they forgot they could have fun doing it. They were now only interested in the reward.[10]

Lepper's research was ground-breaking and has been the catalyst for a slew of follow-up studies that have demonstrated how the same thing happens with adults. Whether it's drawing, studying or motivating employees or cyclists, all cases add up to the same thing. When people are rewarded for doing something they liked doing anyway, the chances are good that their motivation will decrease as soon as the rewards do. In a sense, rewards such as money and fame diminish the passion people or athletes have for their profession.

There are plenty of examples of riders losing their zest for cycling the moment the gain is gone. In some cases this happens when riders are so successful that a victory no longer provides them with the same thrill as it used to. Take Philippe Gilbert, who in 2011 won just about everything there was to win. In 2012, he was nowhere to be seen and did not appear very motivated. He had everything – what was left to motivate him now? At the beginning of his career Gilbert seemed to be a cyclist who was very passionate about his profession; following success, it took him several years to find his mojo again.

Most riders, however, become demotivated when the rewards dwindle as a consequence of results dropping off. It's a trap, because even the most successful riders – whether your name is Mark Cavendish or Jon Aberasturi – experience one certainty in cycling: you'll lose many more times than you'll win. Setbacks are guaranteed. And just as with children who don't want to draw anymore without reward, riders will lose their motivation to bike when recent success goes missing. It seems like a catch-22: the best way to cope with the lean years is by maintaining a true passion for cycling; but this passion will ultimately diminish when you are successful.

Luckily, there's a way out. As we saw earlier in this book, the manner in which riders interpret their own performance and behaviour is key.

When a rider is aware of the risks that come with his success, he can then learn to view rewards for good performances in a different light.[6] Instead of taking money and fame for what they are – extrinsic rewards – a rider can teach himself to view them as feedback on his race behaviour. For example, when he's very driven to improve himself every time he races, he could start to register the amount of interest other teams show in him (or even the media attention he gets) as *information* showing him how much closer he's getting to his intrinsic goal.

Research shows that people who can bend the meaning of rewards in this manner, become *more* intrinsically motivated, as opposed to less.[5] The trick is that you have to learn how.

First of all, you need to be aware of the risk that success poses to your motivation to bike. Next, you need to learn to interpret the extrinsic qualities of success. If one of these steps is skipped, the chances are that a rider will bike with reduced motivation. Getting help is therefore essential. Studies done amongst professional swimmers showed that a coach is a good support for an athlete in this regard.[11] Support staff often play an important role in a rider's mental development.

It does not *always* hold true that an intrinsically motivated rider races more quickly and more determinedly than one who is extrinsically motivated; Maurizio Fondriest's Milan San-Remo is a demonstration of this fact. The Italian was unbeatable on that day in March – not because he had such a good time biking, but because he wanted to dedicate a victory to his daughter no matter what the cost. He was biking for something other than himself. Fondriest is not unique here. The Spaniard Carlos Sastre, for example, exactly 10 years later at the 2003 Tour, arrived solo at the finishing line after a brutal stage across the Pyrenees, with a pacifier in his mouth. The stage was dedicated to those who had motivated him to push beyond his every limitation: his wife and newly-born baby.

It seems that the rare cases when a rider exceeds his ability are possible because of goals that have nothing to do with a passion for racing itself. A new father's motivation is something quite different to everyday extrinsic motivations such as wealth and glory. And this is precisely the point. Intrinsic and extrinsic motivations differ mostly in the *duration* they can keep someone motivated, and not so much in the *degree* of motivation. Someone who loves getting on a bicycle can last many more years doing that than someone who requires external incentives. Having said that, external rewards can influence the degree to which they motivate someone.

Research into the brain tells us that we come equipped with a so-called reward system.[12] When this system is activated we experience pleasant sensations. Drugs, for example, are enticing because they 'turn on' this reward system. The same goes for sex or a greasy snack. We know, in turn, that the reward system does not come with an on/off switch. It's more like there's a dimmer switch. Some rewards activate the reward system only a little, others a great deal.[12]

The reward system is itself linked to motivation. When a certain outcome is very rewarding – such as having sex – it will make some people very motivated to do whatever it takes to get to that desired outcome.[13] And the bigger the rewards, the more you want to work for them. One of the most extreme examples of this is a series of animal tests from the fifties.

The research that James Olds, one of the founders of modern brain research, did with his then-colleague Peter Milner was ground-breaking as they were the first to demonstrate the existence of the reward system. They called it the pleasure centre. To reach this discovery, they operated on rats and inserted electrodes deep into their brains, near the reward system. The rats were then placed in a cage with a lever. When a rat pressed the lever, the electrodes in its brain were activated, stimulating the reward system.[14] Pressing the lever felt good!

As it turned out, the rats continually pressed the lever. By directly stimulating the area of the brain they created the strongest possible rewards. The lever gave the rats such a feeling of ecstasy they wouldn't stop. To the rats, no other reward even came close to this rush and they were no longer interested in other things. They lost their interest in food and drink, even to the point of dehydration. They just kept pressing the lever.

The rats' motivation to activate their pleasure centres became even more apparent from their willingness to make sacrifices and endure pain. During one of the experiments, the researchers set up a test cage where the animals had to walk across an electrified floor (where they were shocked) in order to reach the lever. Normally, no animal would walk across the floor, but here the rats did. They were so motivated that the shocks just became a necessary evil.[14]

Humans are no different. There are things that are so rewarding that they can motivate people to the extreme. To accomplish a goal, a person can transcend themselves and face deprivation that would normally sink their plans in a heartbeat. Just as the rat was willing to experience electric shocks to accomplish his goal, the cyclist is prepared to experience pain to achieve his (a win). This sometimes goes so far that a rider, so completely worn out at the finish line, has to be put on a respirator at once.

What drives riders to reach that deep? There is a branch of psychology – for which we can thank Charles Darwin – that studies the way our behaviour is influenced by evolutionary principles. This field of study has provided us with insight into what motivates people to extreme degrees. One such thing (which was discussed earlier in this book in relation to the fear of descending) is accident prevention.[15] There are three others that also play a part in sports cycling.[15]

The first is the need for power and status; the yearning for glory and wealth is more or less an example of this. Some riders are extremely sensitive to this, and do much to reside in the limelight. But the degree to which the need for status and power can motivate an individual becomes even clearer when riders provoke and push each other to outperform one another. Subsequently, they soar to new heights and rise far above the competition together.

Take the famous struggle between the old Catholic Gino Bartali and the young and liberal Fausto Coppi in the 1940s. In their desire to prove their superiority over each other, they raised the bar to such levels that no one could follow them. Coppi was able to bike faster because of Bartali, and Bartali made Coppi bike faster. There's a reason why Coppi won the Tour of Italy five times and Bartali three times. Both of them also won the Tour de France twice.

Another comparable battle is the one between old-timer Roger de Vlaeminck and his younger team mate Johan de Muynck in the 1976 Giro. De Muynck wanted to show his rival what he was made of; De Vlaminck wanted to demonstrate why he was the captain of the Brooklyn team, the man who had already won the Tirreno-Adriatico five times, Paris-Roubaix three times, and had placed as third runner-up in the 1975 Giro. He was not about to be outshone by a rookie team mate. The Giro resulted in a struggle that made both riders better (motivated as they were by their desire for power and status). De Muynck ended the Tour of Italy in second place, only 19 seconds behind the winner, Felice Gimondi. De Vlaminck had to give up, but not after obtaining no fewer than four stage wins.

Aside from the need for power and status, there is another factor that is equally important from an evolutionary point of view: providing safety for your immediate family (sometimes even the entire family). Kin survival is its name in evolutionary theory.[15] Fondriest and Sastre demonstrated that riders can also be motivated to extremes by their family (and especially important events, such as a birth (or death)). Both performed far above expectation, driven by the birth of their children.

Another example in this case is the Italian Claudio Chiappucci, who was one of the best climbers in the peloton in the nineties. Everywhere he went, *la mamma* followed. His mother was his muse.[16] Or take Leontien van Moorsel during her participation in the Tour Féminin, the female equivalent of the Tour de France, which unfortunately – and shame on sports cycling – no longer exists. Looking back on a stage which had the finishing line on top of the Alpe d'Huez, during which she suffered unimaginably, she said, "I was keeping myself going, by […] continually repeating that I'm not just doing it for myself, but also for my mom and dad, and for my sisters."[17] Van Moorsel, in a single sentence, thus summarises the essence of the power of family as a source of motivation.

And then of course we have love. That love can force people to extremes has become a well-worn Hollywood cliché. It's true nonetheless for professional athletes as well. To illustrate I'll tell a story from the 1999 Vuelta a España, on a stage from Murcia to Madrid across many mountains. As happens so often in the Vuelta, a great number of riders were at the start with no other motivation than covering miles in preparation for the World Championships; riders you'll hardly notice except maybe for one or two stages where they test their legs to monitor their physical fitness. Finishing the thing is not part of the game. After two weeks they'll back out to save their strength, so they can start the World Championships well-rested.

One of the riders in 1999 was Frank Vandenbroucke, a Belgian cyclist who had already been quite successful that season. The Vuelta was perfect for him to get into fighting shape. Seeing how he'd won Liège-Bastogne-Liège earlier in the year, he was the favourite at the World Championships in Verona, which was going to be ridden across similar terrain. His plan was to bike along in Spain for two weeks, in preparation for his surge to victory during the World Championships. He did not have any ambition for the Vuelta itself. But things would turn out quite differently, as Vandenbroucke was caught and impassioned by love.[18]

Anyone who's ever visited a professional cycling race knows that everything around the race is a madhouse. Two hours before the riders start to arrive at the start there's a long and colourful procession of cars and motors spewing out a whole slew of promotional material. Flyers, pens, hats, key fobs, flags, coasters, giant rubber hands, plastic dolls, glasses, shirts, cans, bottles… you name it. The same thing happens at both the start and finishing lines: a whole moving village takes up temporary residence.

After the 6th stage – the first mountain stage – when Vandenbroucke surprisingly ended up in third place, the blonde rider shifted his gaze disinterestedly to these advertising nomads. His gaze stopped at the promotional booth of coffee machine manufacturer and cycling sponsor Saeco and – as is expected of an Italian sponsor – the coffee booth was run by beautiful women. One of them drew the Belgian's eye. He was instantly enamoured… and determined to meet her.

A few stages later, the Cofidis captain let his Italian teammate – Massimiliano Lelli – introduce him to the gorgeous coffee lady. They paid a visit to the Saeco stand for an espresso and Frank met Sarah. The beautiful Italian, to his utter disappointment, barely noticed Vandenbroucke. But it only made him more determined. If she's not impressed by me, I'll make sure she will be. There's only one goal for Vandenbroucke, his only desire: Sarah.

Chapter 10

Gold was struck on the 17th stage with the extremely motivated Vandenbroucke proving unbeatable on a course that ran through a windy, hilly Aragon. Then, he won with ease in Teruel, a city coincidentally known for its medieval mausoleum of the Lovers of Teruel, the Spanish version of Romeo and Juliet. The flowers went to Vandenbroucke, who immediately presented them to Sarah – this stage was for her.

After two further days of effort, the love-struck cyclist finally succeeded: Sarah agreed to a date! Vandenbroucke wanted to see her that same night but she was an hour's drive away. The fact that he needed to ride an important mountain stage the next day was irrelevant to him. Of course, his manager felt differently, but after the rider threatened to leave the race immediately if he was not permitted to visit Sarah, he was left with little choice. Vandenbroucke left straightaway, and only returned to the team hotel in the early hours of the following morning.

The next day, he once again gave the performance of his life. That he was so driven to race was due to a deal he had made with the coffee lady the night before: if he won the stage that finished in Avila, she would sleep with him. This motivated the Cofidis captain so much, that no one could equal his incredible pace going up the cobbled road to the fortified town. He passed the finishing line all alone and… ahem… conquered more than just the stage.

Okay, stories such as Frank and Sarah's love match are rare. And yet, the effect of being motivated by a (desired) lover is an eternal one and frequently occurs in the peloton. Indeed, research shows that just reading the name of the one you love is sufficient to stimulate you and improve performance. [19] It activates the reward system in the brain, and even makes people who are in love feel less pain.[20] Isn't that convenient during a race?!

Some things can motivate people so much that they become capable of much more than they normally could (or that others can); things like Fondriest becoming a father or Vandenbroucke's love. Early fatherhood and burgeoning love share something else which acts as a performance-enhancer, in addition to – or better said, as a consequence of – the psychological aspect. Young parents and lovers see several hormonal changes take place. For athletes the most important one is the rise in adrenalin levels in the body. It gives people a sense of excitement, which benefits the athlete in particular. There's a reason why several forms of doping – such as cocaine and ephedrine[21] – stimulate the adrenalin system. Adrenalin contributes to good performance.

This chapter started out with the claim that a rider driven by a passion for cycling performs better than one driven by outside goals. And yet, things *other* than a passion for racing turned out to be even more motivational. At first glance, this may seem contradictory, but it isn't.

Vandenbroucke, for example, climbed to great heights in order to conquer Sarah. He won two stages, several podium places and, on the last day in Madrid, obtained the points jersey for good measure. In the time between the end of the Vuelta and the start of the World Championships, he and Sarah left for Italy, where they locked themselves up in a cottage in the languid and romantic Tuscan property owned by Mapei cyclist Andrea Tafi. If Vandenbroucke was mostly intrinsically motivated to cycle he should have been able to find the motivation to prepare as best he could for the important race ahead, considering the landscape and the circumstances. But the expected winner of the World Championship did nothing of the like. He had obtained what he had set out to get. What reason did he have to even touch his bicycle? The answer came to him quite quickly – he didn't – and his Cofidis bicycle was relegated to the back lot of the estate during those weeks.

The Belgian managed to end up in the top ten in Verona, based solely on his extreme talent, and an obvious conclusion can be drawn. An extrinsically motivated rider will lose every reason to bike when he's accomplished his goal or when he thinks he'll never be able to reach it. Of course, it can be good for each cyclist to set challenging goals for themselves, and in some cases these can be outside cycling. Indeed, it can be an enormous help, as the following chapter will make even clearer. Still, intrinsic motivation is essential in the end. Extrinsic motivation helps a cyclist to one legendary victory, while intrinsic motivation helps him throughout his career.

11

Setting Goals: Jalabert's Fata Morgana

The 18th of May 2014. The Giro d'Italia.

The day's schedule was a tough bit of road, from Lugo to Sestola. Despite finishing uphill, the days ahead made it unlikely that the big names would show much of themselves. Indeed, the Italian manager Luca Scinto nicely summarised general expectations: "These are the days where you have to consider a lot and be cautious, certainly when we look ahead at what's coming. While it's clear the winner will be an excellent climber, it's unlikely to be someone high in the GC."[1]

In short, May 18th looked like a day for escapees but not the lightweights – it was a day for a rider like Pieter Weening and it was no surprise that the Dutchman broke away after 50 kilometres, with 13 others. Eventually, the stage victory boiled down to him and the excellent climber and time triallist Davide Malacarne. Weening ultimately prevailed and managed to best the Europcar cyclist in a duel.

For Weening, it was no less than his second stage win of the Tour of Italy, following a previous victory in 2011. In that year, the tour's management had included a stage that would take the peloton across the dusty *strade bianche* – the white gravel roads – just like the good old days seen in black-and-white television pictures. Racing across sunny Tuscany was sure to promise some excellent sights. The reality, however, was quite different – riders were soaked to the bone by rain and when they reached the white gravel roads they had to traverse rivers of mud. Not used to such weather and slick roads, most GC cyclists biked around with clenched buttocks, hoping they would make it to Piombino without too much time or skin loss.

To old cyclo-cross riders Weening and John Gadret, mud was familiar terrain. They got further and further away from the GC cyclists. Weening turned out to be the stronger of the two. Aside from the stage win, he also got the prized *maglia rosa*, which he was able to hold on to for several days.

Chapter 11

Currently, the Netherlands has a number of riders like Weening who are capable of winning big race stages, one example being the controversial (but heroic) Tour de France stage that Lars Boom won on Paris-Roubaix terrain in 2014. But still, Weening has long been the number one when it comes to transforming quality into results. This may be due, in part, to the plain old bad luck that some of the other riders have had to face; men like Wout Poels or Robert Gesink who have had terrible crashes. On the other hand, Weening's success almost certainly relates to a quality that makes all people perform better: he seems to be very good at setting goals – in his case, stage wins.

Weening analysed his 2011 success: "I knew it was a stage with my name written all over it. Nico Verhoeven, one of the Rabobank managers, had the same idea. We'd been working on it days in advance, even discussing this stage before the Giro started. Not to win it, but because you have to set goals for a big race, find stages that suit you."[2]

Three years later, joining in with a small escaping group was once again no sudden whim. It was a conscious – and very sensible – choice by Weening to focus completely on the stage win and not struggle through overthinking a good place in the rankings. What does it matter, overall, if you end up tenth or thirtieth in the rankings when you can chalk up a stage win on your list of victories?

The importance of focusing on a few main goals during the cycling season is not uncommon: there are quite a few cyclists, for example, who focus completely on the Tour de France, and barely ride for a win over the rest of the year. Setting goals is important because it helps provide that bit of extra power and energy at the exact moment you need it. A clear objective increases an individual's motivation to train, to focus, and give one's all in a single moment. In addition, after having completed the main goal, ever-increasing tension and stress can be dialled down; indeed, the realisation that the stress will end upon goal completion helps a rider push through for longer. Research even shows that after achieving a goal, motivation can completely dissipate and disappear.[3] Someone will have given everything – not just physically but mentally – and nothing's left. This is the reason why many riders perform well in the Tour of Flanders and could easily handle the Amstel Gold Race, but oftentimes don't even enter the latter – or only perform disappointingly if they do.

The most important function of setting a goal is that it provides someone with a point of reference, something to work towards. You know exactly when and where you have to be in fighting shape. You can chart your progress: is everything going according to plan or not? People who have a goal seemingly become more motivated to give that little bit extra when they're behind on their schedule. If they're ahead, they unknowingly take their foot off the pedal, to save up on energy.[4]

Take, for example, Greg van Avermaet – one of the stars in the spring of 2014. Only Fabian Cancellara was ahead of him on the Tour of Flanders and it was the first time the 28-year old Belgian came close to a legendary win, though not for the last time, as later races showed, like his 2016 Tirreno-Adriatico and Rio 2016 Olympic road race victories.

Van Avermaet's spring success turned out to be the result of the goals he set. "The Flemish classics were my big goals, and the Tour of Flanders *the* main goal. You start working towards the Flemish classics in November. Performing well there is constantly in the back of your head. It helps being more relaxed about other preparatory races."

By using the Tour of Flanders as a focal point, the man from Lokeren became more dedicated in his preparation. A focal point also helps a person to cope better with setbacks. "It's just like making a deadline at work. A fall or illness can slow down your preparation, but you just need to compensate for that with training or extra races. It doesn't change the deadline." When you have a clear goal in mind and you adjust your entire preparation to meet it, there's an additional advantage, so says Van Avermaet. Indeed, you become more self-confident. "Trust is very important, it gives you the feeling of having done everything right when you get to the starting line. Also, my goal was linked to something I'm good at. You get a route you excel at thrown in your lap! So you know you're competing among the best."

When you look at modern cycling, it seems impossible to win races without being goal-oriented, without choosing races where you need to perform. Other races – like Van Avermaet said – just become warmups, a bit like fancy training. If you don't finish them, or you finish with enormous arrears... well, that's just the way it is. You didn't come to win, so you didn't.

Chapter 11

And yet, this was once completely different. Men such as Eddy Merckx or Fausto Coppi biked well throughout the year and often won races across the whole season. In those days, people seemed much less involved in working towards specific races. You'd race all year long and if you had qualities like Merckx's, this yielded victories from early spring to late autumn. It's therefore unlikely there are, or will be, riders who can equal Merckx's victories: 525 in total.

The seventies saw the turnaround in sports cycling and The Netherlands led much of this change. Hennie Kuiper, who started his professional career in 1973, has been characterised as a pioneer by, amongst others, former cyclist Wim Albersen: "Hennie was far ahead of his time. He always had something to aim for. Always had a goal."[5]

The increasing importance of goal-oriented racing in the seventies coincided – not by chance – with another development in cycling: professionalism. The Raleigh team, founded in 1974, was the first truly professional team. It was Raleigh who had mechanics servicing and maintaining bikes during big races, rather than letting cyclists do that themselves (as did other teams).[6] The coaching of riders also improved in the seventies. Nowadays, all these things are the norm.

Professionalism enabled racers to focus on goals. Professionalism raised the level of riders and it thus became more difficult to distinguish oneself – on a general level – from competitors which ultimately led to greater and greater rider specialisation, for example in time trials or climbing. In turn, riders tried to peak at certain times of the season (with Hennie Kuiper as *primus inter pares*). This became *the* method of winning races, and it still is today. The path of professionalism in the seventies changed – most would say improved – cycling forever. Somewhat sadly, however, we did have to say our goodbyes to riders who could shine all year long.

At the same time as cycling became professional, psychology was undergoing developments of its own. In the late sixties, psychologists Edwin Locke and Gary Latham noticed that many companies tried to motivate their employees with exhortative remarks such as: "You have to try your hardest, you know!"[7] Locke and Latham felt that generic remarks such as this were unlikely to bring the best out of people, for 'what' should you try your hardest, and 'when' exactly? An employee was hardly able to try their hardest on everything all the time. As such,

Locke and Latham started a series of studies into the way people should set goals[7] and the conclusions garnered from their multi-year studies will sound familiar to many modern employees. In short, goals should be S.M.A.R.T.

- Specific
- Measurable
- Attainable
- Realistic
- Time-bound

Being measurable and time-bound are usually not an issue for a cyclist. The races in which they need to peak can be planned a year in advance and they don't need to make any effort to measure the results: race management will do that for them. A GPS chip, attached to the riders' bikes, exactly measures at what position each hill, each mountain, and each intermediate sprint was taken. In the last few years, they even measure what per cent of time a rider was leading a group. The tricky part of setting race goals therefore lies with *attainability*, in particular making it realistic and specific. How do you do that? Furthermore, is the importance of these kinds of focal points equal for all riders? The importance to a captain is self-evident, but seems less so for a domestique, whose role (by definition) is to support.

Making a goal attainable and realistic is easier said than done. The trick is setting a goal that is achievable and at the same time challenging. It can't be too simple. For example, if a rider focuses on a spot in the top 20 of the Clásica San Sebastián, and he's already been on the podium five times, that goal is attainable but hardly motivational. There's a reason why athletes regularly say they need challenges to get to a higher level.

To set a challenging goal for yourself, you need self-knowledge: what are you capable of? How much did you grow over the past year? And what could you achieve if you kept on following the same path? The risk here is that a rider sets goals that are *too* challenging. They are no longer realistic, which oftentimes proves very demotivational. Sometimes, young talents are strenuously put to work by their teams *for the whole year* but it can be too much to ask: they give their all, and yet they never fully meet expectations. Again and again they fall short. Such talents therefore rarely develop greatness.

There are plenty of examples of riders who demonstrate that they've set the bar too high, leading to diminished performances. Despite being one of the most successful French riders of his generation, Laurent Jalabert is a typical example of such a cyclist. Even though having a good insight into your own abilities is crucial in setting challenging goals, the full extent of his abilities seemed shrouded in mystery. The Frenchmen started his career as a sprinter and at the 1993 Vuelta a España he won no fewer than seven stages and the sprinter's jersey. A born speedster, but one of the few who also managed the hills well.

At the 1994 Tour de France, Jalabert and his direct competitor Wilfried Nelissen biked straight into a police officer taking photographs during a full-on sprint. For a moment it seemed Jalabert was to be ejected from sports cycling at the hands of this policeman.[8] His face was covered with blood and medical inspection showed teeth, cheekbones and his collarbone were broken. The Frenchman promised himself and his wife never to engage in this style of riding again.

But the driven, determined rider surged back to his old level – and exceeded himself. A year following the accident, the ONCE racer couldn't just cross hills, but mountains. Suddenly he was able to make it into the rankings. Absolutely no one knew what Jalabert was capable of achieving – including himself. It resulted in him setting the goal of winning the Tour de France.

It was challenging, to say the least. But fairly soon, long before he ultimately gave up hope, a Tour victory turned out to be unattainable. But there was one issue for Jalabert that was the elephant in the room… he experienced at least *one* bad day in every big race out there, losing a lot of time. He was indeed renowned for his *jour sans*. It always happened completely unexpectedly, and even though the ONCE captain would try to hide his feelings behind a poker face – as if he was not suffering – these events took their toll.

We discussed breaking points in an earlier chapter – moments when a rider feels his efforts no longer influence the outcome. Jalabert's off days created breaking points. If he charged on a bad day, like the 10th stage of the 1997 Tour, he immediately saw his goal – the final victory

– shatter into pieces. He should still have been physically able to limit the damage on days like these, but the Frenchman visibly broke down. His poker face crumbled little by little, kilometre after kilometre. Disillusioned and annoyed, he'd bike around with his hand gripping the handlebars only lightly, as if he couldn't be bothered. He lost a great many minutes doing this. In 1997 for example, he clocked in 19 minutes behind the 10th stage winner Jan Ullrich.

In 2001, Jalabert entered a new period in his career, one with new challenges and new goals, in a new team: CSC-Tiscali. The yellow jersey was no longer Jalabert's purpose: this time he would focus on the polka dot jersey. This was also not a goal to be taken lightly – the Frenchman was already in the latter part of his career and not the best climber in the peloton by far. On the other hand, he had no trouble getting over mountains, he was strong, and the polka dot jersey can be won despite bad days every now and then.

This challenging but at the same time realistic goal for the Tour de France signalled Jalabert's resurrection. His presence was not to be missed. Every stage upon which mountain points could be earned, the Frenchman would join in a long-lasting escape. In this way, he succeeded, and entered Paris wearing the red-dotted jersey. The tactic of joining long-lasting escapes was fruitful in any case; aside from the polka dot jersey, the CSC racer obtained two stage wins, including a difficult stage across the Elzas, which was ridden on the 14th of July, the French national holiday. He became a national hero.

A year later, Jalabert finished the Tour once again wearing the polka dot jersey. It was only after he adjusted his ambitions that he found success. This is the exact reason why it's so important to look at goals critically. It was only at the end of Jalabert's career that they were optimal; challenging, yet attainable and realistic. Pieter Weening handled matters similarly, by focusing on stage wins in big races, and less on final rankings. It made Weening one of the most successful Dutch cyclists of his generation.

Aside from realistic and attainable, a proper goal is also specific. This partially means that a rider, for example, focuses on specific races. But a goal such as 'riding well in the Tour' is not enough. It's better when you focus on obtaining the polka dot jersey, as Jalabert did. More specific, and thus better, would be to split up this reasonably large goal into smaller items. You can set goals at the stage level, for example, such as aiming to join in with the big escape on the 9th stage. The question, of course, is what works best for a rider in the end?

The former Dutch professional Gert Jakobs is very experienced when it comes to this. For years, Jakobs was a valuable domestique in the famed PDM team, but in the eighties and nineties he also biked for teams such as Festina and Superconfex-Yoko. While at PDM, Jakobs solicited sprints for his faster-than-lightning captain Jean-Paul van Poppel, who won multiple stages in big races. The mentality that Jakobs had whilst biking is something he succinctly explains: "I was happy riding point very fast and for a long time."

Jakobs was an eternal domestique but didn't have any issues with this. "No success without domestiques," he made clear. "Van Poppel would never have won those races if all those brave and experienced helpers didn't bike with everything they had. Everyone matters in a team." That a domestique would have experience in setting good goals for the season might, at first, seem surprising. Isn't that the job of a captain? After all, they have to show their mettle before everyone else.

Jakobs' answer is unambiguous. "A domestique focuses on the goals that have been set as much as anyone. Sure, you have to be able to do more diverse work than the captains. For example, during my days with PDM, I had to be good at biking classics like the Tour of Flanders and Paris-Roubaix; I'd bike for men such as Sean Kelly, Rudy Dhaenens or Dirk de Wolf. I would never see Breukink in these classics, he was biking a completely different programme. And yet, once in the Tour, I'd be his main domestique for the flat stages." So, domestique and captain are equals when it comes to the importance of goals.

The question here that's especially interesting is what kind of goals did Jakobs set for himself? How detailed did they need to be? It mainly seemed to come down to focusing on a few races in the season. "The Tour was very important to us, as were the major classics and the Tour of Spain. That's what you work towards."

But much more important, according to Jacobs, was setting goals *in* those races to optimise the chances of success. "Finishing a tour was never an option or a goal for us – just finishing means nothing. You had to be the best in the Tour, because Van Poppel *had* to win. In short, we had to ensure that there would be a sprint. This means that, during the Tour, you're only looking at stages where you have a chance of winning. The other stages are not important at all." That this way of setting goals worked well, needs little explanation… Jakobs accompanied Van Poppel in the 1988 Tour de France to no less than four sprint wins.

Jakobs did include a sidenote to his story. Goals are not to be made scripture. A goal can help you deal with adversity (as Greg van Avermaet also indicated) but sometimes it can be too late for that. "You're continually balancing on the wire. You can deliver the best planning you can, but illness or falls during the race, or races you weren't supposed to ride and you find yourself riding anyway – this is run-of-the-mill stuff. It necessitates the ability to continually adjust your planning."

It's that flexibility that can be difficult to some athletes. This becomes very clear in multi-day races with riders who have lost a good spot in the rankings. While some can very easily turn that switch in their heads and focus on stage wins, there's a large group of riders who fail to do so… as if the entire race is lost when you lose your spot in the rankings. Personality plays a role here.

The importance of personality proved evident in psychological research with soccer players. In 2009, a group of German researchers was interested in the toughest part (psychologically speaking) of a soccer match – penalties – and uncovered some very interesting findings.[9]

How a footballer could best deal with penalties turned out to depend on a specific personality trait, in that people *either* focus on the achievement of certain outcomes, *or* are preoccupied with avoiding negative outcomes.[10]

To draw an example: one person studies to get a good job, whilst someone else studies to prevent ending up in a bad job. This personality trait is equally present in sport: while a rider such as Alberto Contador is always trying to win and looking to attack, a compatriot such as Miguel Indurain was always busy keeping his head start, trying not to lose the race.

Interestingly enough, the German research showed that this character trait also correlates to roles. Defenders are naturally inclined to prevent the other team from winning and are therefore prevention-oriented; attackers try to win and are therefore deemed promotion-oriented. This phenomenon not only applies to soccer but to many other team sports.[9]

The person taking the penalty literally has the goal in sight. But what about the goal he's set in his mind? Back with our German researchers, soccer players were given an assignment of taking five penalties. A number of players were given the additional assignment of *scoring* at least three times, whilst a separate group were told they could only *miss* two at the most. The difference may seem small: both cases come down to the soccer player having to get the ball between the posts three times. And yet, there was a clear difference. Players with a prevention-oriented personality performed better when they focused on the goal of not missing more than twice. Players with the opposite personality scored better when they focused on the goal of scoring at least three times.[9]

In the end, there seems not to be one definitive truth when it comes to ideal goals for an athlete. Goals should be measurable, time-bound, specific and attainable but also challenging. The exact form, however, comes down to a customised, personal solution. When an athlete succeeds in setting such goals for himself, he will be optimally prepared – physically and mentally – to start a race and perform to the best of his abilities. To what degree an athlete actually performs to his best during a race, or in other words how *far* he can go, depends on yet another personality trait – but not one we've discussed before – *willpower*. Let's have a closer look at that!

12

Willpower: The Strength of the Lion of Flanders

It's 2002, and the Roubaix cycling track was very slippery. The weather was not good, and the riders were expected to cross the finish line one by one (although you would hardly be able to recognise them, their faces all masked in clay). Retired cycling superstar Hennie Kuiper was also present at the finishing line. Resplendent in his suit, he was the day's host for a number of corporate visitors.[1] They followed him wherever he went.

The unpleasant surroundings did not bother Kuiper and probably summoned up mostly positive memories of the 1983 edition, when the weather was similarly horrid. Kuiper won after a scintillating finale. Many older cycling enthusiasts can still instantaneously recall the image: Kuiper on point, solo, and destiny striking on a stretch of cobbles at Hem. Due to a bang on the cobbles, he couldn't use his bike anymore and there he was – completely covered in sludge – standing by the road, waiting until a new bike was delivered by his support car and he could continue. The moment seemed to last forever, but that eternity was brief enough to stay ahead of the peloton and win!

In 2002, the weather had cleared up a little at the end of day. While the asphalt was still stained with dark water marks, a pale sun broke through to welcome the winner, and Kuiper and his guests were anxiously looking forward to the first rider. They already knew who it would be. Just as in 1983, the rider would arrive solo… a man who had already broken away over 40 kilometres before the finishing line.[2] To the unknowing bystander, the mud on his clothes and face made it nearly impossible to identify him but the winner turned out to be Johan Museeuw, also known as the Lion of Flanders. The grim circumstances had left the competition floundering – just as they had done for Kuiper in 1983. The man in the muddy cycling jersey and the man in the crisp suit undoubtedly shared something: Museeuw and Kuiper were both riders with exceptional willpower.

Chapter 12

Cycling is a tough sport, both physically and mentally. And willpower is one of the most important mental qualities for a rider for a reason. Steven Rooks (himself part of the pantheon of Dutch cycling due to his legendary victory on the Alpe d'Huez) even calls it *the* most important quality for a professional cyclist. So, let's take a close look at what willpower precisely means.

Psychology describes willpower as the extent to which someone is able to resist short-term temptations to focus more successfully on long-term ambitions.[3] To a student, for example, willpower will mean being able to resist the temptation of procrastinating while there's studying to be done. In cycling, by contrast, willpower can equate to resisting the temptation to ease up on your legs, biking through pain to win a race, and biking long races without losing your pace.

A typical example of Kuiper's willpower in this context is that he wanted to bike the gigantic Bordeaux-Paris race during his career.[1] In 1985, that moment finally arrived, three years before the last edition was ridden. What had Kuiper been looking forward to so much? One race, one day, 585 kilometres on a bike. A race that the Belgian Herman van Springel won a record seven times, by the way.

Riders with a lot of willpower or perseverance get a lot further than others. Even with less talent, a rider with strong willpower will be able to win races. Indeed, research tells us that willpower has a positive influence on athletic performance with athletes better able to deal with pain, sacrifice more for their sport, and able to suffer more.[5] More broadly, sport is just one aspect of life, and people with a lot of willpower appear to enjoy better scholastic performance, a more stable and better social life, are less aggressive, and enter into dangerous situations less often. Some research has even concluded that there's a statistical relationship between willpower and the number of convicted crimes.[4] Greater willpower leads to fewer crimes.

Willpower is also influential outside actual races. Indeed, it can be a decisive factor when someone has to deal with an enormous setback. The last chapter, for example, showed us that a rider who becomes ill, or who falls, returns more easily to his old level if he has a clear goal to work towards. But what if someone falls so hard or becomes so ill that it's not clear whether they *can* return to the peloton? It demands the utmost of a rider. Aside from a clear goal, he's going to need a lot of willpower.

Johan Museeuw, for example, started the Hell of the North on the 12th of April 2002 as the absolute favourite. He'd never reach the finish, however, with his race ending that day on the famous and notorious Trouée d'Arenberg. "Biking into the Forest of Arenberg is a bit like descending into a mineshaft," the Lion of Flanders himself said. "It takes courage, as danger is constantly lurking from every corner. [...] That year as well [...] the further we penetrated the forest, the sludge on the cobbles became thicker and thicker. Falling down was only a matter of time."[2]

Museeuw fell and hit his knee on the sharp edge of a cobble. A subsequent infection with the Clostridium bacteria, noticed too late by doctors, meant the rider nearly lost his leg. Amputation was only narrowly avoided in the end, but his leg was worthless; Museeuw couldn't move it but giving up was not an option. Museeuw only wanted one thing: to race again at the highest level!

In a book by Ruben van Gucht, physical therapist Lieven Maesschalck tells the story of how he helped Museeuw recover. Many people thought he would never return to the saddle, yet, "The goal to get out there again was very ambitious, but [Johan] had so much willpower that I could go far as a therapist. The leg was completely stiff, and every day we would try going a little further. As I tried to bend his leg millimetre by millimetre, he was lying there, swearing and stuttering, stomaching the pain, shouting and crying."

Slowly but surely, the Lion of Flanders fought back. After a lot of exercise he was able to bend his leg again, after which he clambered back aboard his bicycle. A little later on, he found himself on a race bike, and a year afterwards he was competing for victory in 'his' Paris-Roubaix. An unlikely achievement considering the journey Museeuw had to take. "I immediately realised that he was far from a regular athlete," said Maesschalck. "That didn't show itself to me in performance, but in obduracy you only rarely see."[2]

Thus far, I may have given the impression that riders like Museeuw and Kuiper are exceptional when it comes to willpower because most riders lack it and give up at the slightest setback. This is certainly not the case! As we'll see, it's very likely that *all* professional cyclists possess a great deal of willpower. Otherwise, someone would never even make it into the professional ranks. But it's definitely true that it varies widely among riders. Whilst the previously-mentioned Museeuw and Kuiper were able to win a large number of races based on their mental strength, others succeeded based more on their physical talent.

Just as one person has (on the face of it) a greater talent for cycling than someone else due to congenital physical strengths, a person's level of willpower also seems to be congenital. Research has shown that small children and even four- and six-month old babies already differ.[4] The Austrian psychologist Walter Mischel conducted a number of experiments in America in the early seventies with children between the ages of four- and five-years old. In his work, a child was first placed in a small room with a table, a toy box and a tin cookie jar. The researchers first took the toy box and showed the child all the toys inside it, and told them they would be able to play later. But before play commenced, the child got to choose something from the cookie jar: a marshmallow or a pretzel.[5]

It was at that exact moment of the research that the Austrian introduced a clever and simple way of measuring willpower in children. Directly after the child had picked, for example, a colourful marshmallow, the researcher said: "You know what? I have to leave the room for a bit. If you wait until I get back, you can eat two marshmallows. But if you eat this one when I'm gone, then you won't get another one. So if you wait until I get back, you get two marshmallows."[5,6] And then the child was left alone, sitting by itself, on a little chair. A delicious pink marshmallow sat right in front of the child, who knew that another marshmallow was coming their way if the first one remained uneaten.

Walter Mischel and his colleagues observed how long a child could wait and the experimental protocol dictated that the researcher would only return to the child after 15 minutes. Many of the test subjects never made it through those 15 minutes. They would stare at the marshmallow without interruption, momentarily twisting their gaze away so they did not have to see their temptation. They'd press their fingers into the soft gooeyness, and then quickly pull them back. Some children would sit on their hands to diminish the urge to take the food. Some even licked the treat. After all, they were only told they couldn't eat the marshmallow. But then, suddenly, they couldn't take it anymore and would grab the marshmallow off the table with lightning speed, devouring the treat in one swift bite.[7]

It was remarkable to see the differences between the children. Some seemed perfectly happy to wait the full 15 minutes, whilst others couldn't last a minute. This inequality exactly demonstrated differences in willpower. What's simply known nowadays as "The Marshmallow Experiment" is willpower at its purest: resisting a short-term temptation (one treat) to get something even better (two treats) over the longer run.

Mischel's research isn't just a means of illustrating the willpower of children; it's mostly significant because marshmallow task performance predicts the amount of willpower someone has as young adult.[4,6] Someone who already has a lot of willpower as a child, will most likely profit from it later in life.

Hennie Kuiper is anecdotal proof of this. As a child, he would often pedal around on a small racing bike, racing around for fun with some of his friends. When he was 14, he got up early one morning to compete in his first actual race: the tour of Wierden. He was planning to go together with his bike buddies but the promise of bad weather led them to decide otherwise. To Kuiper, however, rain was not an insurmountable hurdle and he left for the starting line by bike. He was soaked through before he reached Wierden, with 40 kilometres already behind him. Arriving only just in time, he had to make extra efforts to even be allowed to start. He was too late to register and receive his race number (to affix to his cobbled-together cycling gear) but he managed to convince officials to let him race and officially started his cycling career that day in Wierden. His first race ended in a place worthy of Raymond Poulidor: second. Time to enjoy his good performance was not on the agenda though: he had to bike 40 kilometres home again. Finally, he reached his parents' farm in the dark, *with* a shiny trophy, which he proudly showed to his bike buddies the next day.[1]

The manner in which the young Kuiper set himself apart from his racing companions, in terms of perseverance, can be compared to the child with a tempting marshmallow waiting patiently for the researcher to return. The above-average willpower of the *boy* Kuiper indeed related to that of the *professional cyclist* Kuiper.

Chapter 12

In 1973, for example, Kuiper participated in the Tour of Flanders for the first time. Many of his HaRo teammates were making their first appearance, just like him. They all knew perfectly well what they were in for: 260 kilometres separating them from the finishing line. Most of the rookies would never make it to the finishing line at Meerbeke that day, and were not even planning on it. The first Tour of Flanders is for experience; you don't need to finish. The day before the start, Kuiper's teammates conveniently parked their cars at the first supply point. Having reached that point, there was little doubt they'd get off their bikes, climb into their cars, and head home.

Kuiper, however, was a cyclist with a completely different mentality. As opposed to his colleagues, he planned on finishing, and he succeeded – granted, miles behind winner Eric Leman, but he did manage it. He reached Meerbeke exhausted, then got in his car and drove back home, where he didn't arrive until late into the night. Despite this, he was back on his bike in a clean jersey at nine o'clock the next morning, ready to train.[1]

Kuiper's story illustrates how there can be innate differences in the reservoir of willpower that riders possess. That's not to say a racer can always draw from it. Research also shows that stress can cause the reservoir to become drained.[6] The more pressure that is placed on a rider, the less he is able to access his willpower.

A previous chapter showed us that one rider can better withstand the pressure of being captain than another. The difference lies in whether pressure – stress – is actually *experienced* as stress. If it is, a rider will not be able to properly utilise his willpower due to the forces of stress; even if the racer has a natural perseverance, it will not show itself on account of the circumstances.

This seems like bad news for riders who do not hold high levels of willpower in their youth. Luckily, however, such riders don't need to throw in the towel!

Over the past few years, we have seen an accumulation of evidence that willpower may be partially innate, but that it can also be learned. Or in other words: you can train it.[8] Roy Baumeister and his colleagues made this discovery when they identified a parallel between mental and physical strength.[9] If physical strength is powered by muscles, the

Americans reasoned, can't mental strength be something similar? Can willpower be viewed as something like mental muscle? Earlier research had already indicated similarities. Just as muscles become temporarily tired after lifting ten kilos of potatoes, willpower can become exhausted if it's used rigorously.

The researchers demonstrated that willpower does indeed work like a muscle and can be trained as such.[9] They did this by asking a large number of students to do daily exercises that required willpower for two weeks. The idea was that the mental muscle would strengthen from this mental fitness. After the training period, the students' willpower was compared to a pre-exercise measurement. Exactly as the researchers had predicted, the test subjects were shown to have increased their willpower strength over the period.[9]

As people use willpower across many different scenarios, there are many ways of training it. During the research mentioned above, for example, one group was given the assignment of consciously focusing on their posture for two weeks. Am I sitting correctly on this chair, do I have the right posture, back straight? Continually focusing on this takes a lot of mental effort. Another group was given a different message: they had to focus on their mood and emotions and try to be aware of how they were feeling. In other studies, subjects were given instructions on training their willpower by focusing on their language for weeks, or by only using their left hands for certain periods of time.[8]

The training methods varied from physical to emotional exertion and yet the results were always the same: willpower increases when you consciously train it. Compare it once more to the analogy of physical training. It doesn't matter if you train by using dumbbells, by bench-pressing, or by dragging around sacks of potatoes or rocks. The muscles you need are the same. In the same way, the mental strength being trained through different forms of training is the same. And just as training with dumbbells makes it easier to lift heavy grocery bags, exerting willpower over, say, your emotions will lead to greater willpower when peddling on your bicycle.

For recreational cyclists and other amateur athletes, willpower training undoubtedly makes a difference in improving performance. For professional racers there's a catch, however. Each professional has to work on their sport and their body each and every day, and will have to get on their bicycle, even if they don't want to. They'll have to eat treacly food from weird little packets, even though they'd much rather devour a hearty meal. By working in this way, a cyclist is training his willpower at the same time. All professionals, including those who were born with less willpower, are *already* exercising willpower as part of their profession. It's unlikely, therefore, that they'll be able to boost it with focused training.

There are still some opportunities for professional riders, though. Not so much in enhancing willpower, but by reloading it faster after expending effort, or using it less often thanks to simple techniques. These techniques benefit both amateur athletes and professionals.

Willpower is, to some degree, a finite resource that needs to be replenished when it gets used (think of it like water in a reservoir). Time is one good way to replenish willpower (i.e. a rest from using it) but another good example of reloading willpower after exertion is mindfulness. Mindfulness meditation is essentially focusing your complete attention on the 'here and now', and accepting everything fully without judgment. Recent experiments have shown that applying mindfulness meditation – like consciously sensing your chest moving on the rhythm of your breath – helps people to persevere in top gear more freqently.[10] It specifically helps individuals to recover faster after a high willpower episode.

A similar effect can be attained through yoga. Just as with mindfulness, yoga is about being aware, although yoga has a more physical component attached to it. The Belgian sprinter Eddy Planckaert, who garnered an impressive list of victories in the eighties, practiced yoga during his career. He said it helped him considerably to maintain calmness during the race, to 'be there' when necessary.[11]

Also, a rider with relatively limited perseverance can apply another tactic: avoiding the need to utilise willpower too much. The previously-mentioned marshmallow experiment illustrates this. It showed that some children simply could not wait for the researchers to return and see their patience rewarded with an extra piece of candy. Those with more willpower managed just fine. Later experiments with the same study design showed that children were able to wait more easily if they applied 'tricks' that diminished their need to deploy willpower.[7] Those same aids that helped children remain patient when the researcher was gone, turned out to be of equal help to adults – including cyclists. One example is to visualise the desired outcome: the finishing line, those final metres, the podium. Reinterpreting discomfort is another help. For example, you can take the cutting pain in your legs and see it as the pain you inflict on the others in your group of cyclists.

Finally, the refocusing of attention can be a tactic. When you've completely hit rock bottom, when your willpower is in danger of being fully drained, try focusing attention outward – from your body (and thus the pain) to your surroundings. As per chapter 1, focus on the trees that are slowly coming into leaf, a beautiful woman standing along the race course, the colourful billboards. The pain will decrease. The chapter on time trials mentioned that riders can benefit a great deal from this approach during such episodes: riding against the clock demands an enormous amount of willpower and perseverance. By lowering the sensation of pain, less willpower is needed to continue.

Not every professional cyclist is the new Kuiper or the next Museeuw. Each generation of cyclists produces a number of riders who stick out due to their extreme willpower and who, thanks to this innate trait, are able to win races. Luckily, this is not all there is to it; the competition does not need to meekly observe from the side-lines. In the end, willpower is as flexible as the person itself. It can still go in any direction.

This book has focused on the psychological phenomena that can help underpin great cycling performances. But there is one chapter left and it is on a topic that one might not immediately associate with psychology… *doping*.

13 Doping: Psychology in Practice

As we have seen in this book, cycling is a sport where a number of psychological processes play a major role. Many of the topics covered, so far, impact performance in unison with one another and can be applied to different aspects of cycling. When analysing cycling, in practice, it is important not to focus on a single psychological phenomenon, but to look more broadly. For example, an athlete who possesses a great deal of willpower might have the wrong motivation to take part in a particular sport, and will thus be less successful. Or he has the right amount of willpower and motivation, but sets the wrong goals, and therefore utilises his willpower at the wrong times.

One of the most interesting psychological areas to examine is doping. The use of performance-enhancing drugs might seem to be medical territory (and not psychology) but in this chapter we shall shine a psychological light on its use.

Before we take a look at doping, it's important to ask whether athletes perform better when using illicit substances. An odd question perhaps (surely they always perform better?) but one where the answer is not always affirmative. Scientific research has shown there to be a slight reduction in performance when using substances such as amphetamines, and no effect at all with several other substances including insulin and anabolic steroids.[1,2] The notorious drug EPO does lead to improved performance in some studies, but only marginally so; an athlete is likely to improve around 2% at the most.[2] The Dutch professor Harm Kuipers, an expert in doping, puts it nicely: "You can't use doping to turn a Ford Tempo into a Ferrari. A rider who performs well with doping can do so without doping."[2] These values are in stark contrast to doping perceptions in the peloton, where expected improvements range from 15 to 40 per cent.[1,3]

That the effects of doping are as large as some riders expect can easily be disproven. A performance improvement of, say, 20 per cent should be identifiable from a rider's average speed during a race. But this is not the case. In 2005, Lance Armstrong biked the fastest Tour de France ever, at 41.65 kilometres per hour. That's only 10.6 per cent faster than Tour winner Gastone Nencini in 1960. That's little improvement over the course of 45 years, certainly when you take into consideration that the 1960 Tour was no less than 565 kilometres (two full extra stages) longer.

On top of that, the biggest innovations in cycling over the last few decades have come in equipment and nutrition.[2] Bicycles have become much more aerodynamic, and riders have perfected their posture in the saddle. Both the bicycle alone and the bicycle with a rider get extensively tested in wind tunnels. And while the riders in 1960 enjoyed regular food, in 2016 they cycle around with specially-designed gel caps bursting with energy. The progression of the last few decades has much more to do with food, equipment, and shorter race distances than with illicit drugs.

Regardless of the actual physical effects of doping, it's interesting to note that expectations into their efficacy are high in the peloton. An earlier chapter, after all, showed us that an athlete's expectations will influence his performance. So, doping can affect performance based solely on the expectation that it works. In 1952, cycling legend Fausto Coppi was already aware of this: "[The mysterious bottle I carried around in the race] is an extra set of legs, made up of secret ingredients the most important of which are: dextroamphetamine and the rock-solid conviction the stuff works."[4]

To summarise, if riders believe they will bike 20 per cent faster by taking certain substances, this belief alone will make them bike faster. *Even if the substance itself has no real effect.* If they didn't have that belief, they would not bike faster. Nowadays, there's sufficient proof from research studies that the power of a person's expectations is indeed this influential,[5] and the term that is used to identify the effect of belief is world-famous: the placebo effect.

The placebo effect can be demonstrated, for example, in people who suffer from amnesia. In one study, young adults who had amnesia were given a pill and half of them told the pill had a soothing effect. The other half were told it could cause physical agitation. In reality, the pill was useless. And yet, it had an effect. People who were naturally restless, and who took the pill that (they thought) elicited unrest, fell asleep faster. This was because they ascribed their active mind to the pill and not to themselves; in doing so it was easier for the insomniacs to 'let go' of their restless thoughts and thus fall asleep.[6]

You might wonder how the placebo effect impacts upon professional athletes. After all, they operate at such a high level that placebo effects may no longer apply. In reality, this is not the case. The effect continues at all levels, and according to American psychologist Walter Cannon, the placebo effect can have such extreme consequences that people may die as a result of it. He based this conclusion on research he carried out amongst Native Americans and Aboriginals in the 1940s where people were known to die after being 'cursed'. These voodoo deaths only seemed to occur in populations where people believed in the power of black magic, it should be added![7] It appears that when a person was cursed, they were subjected to mortal fear and the stress caused a whole chain of physical responses which ultimately prevented them from looking after themselves by eating and drinking properly. If someone truly believed they had been cursed, they could even die within a relatively short period of time.[7]

If the placebo effect can have such extreme consequences, we might rightly assume they play a role in professional sports as well. Indeed, there are studies within sports psychology and kinesiology (the study of the mechanics of body movements) that demonstrate how athletes partially improve their performance after, for example, doping or after high-altitude training, because they *expect* it to enhance their performance.[8] This placebo enhancement boosts performance somewhere between 1 and 3 per cent.[8] That may not seem like much, but compare it to the effect of EPO, and you'll see it's similar.

So, it seems that doping effects are *partially* a consequence of psychology – an unwavering belief that the stuff works. In that sense, illicit substances are, psychologically speaking, nothing more than something like new tires, a new outfit, or even a relic like a rosary that makes someone 'believe' they'll perform better.

Aside from the effect that expectation can have on performance, there is another psychological element that can negatively impact performance. As seen, a rider can develop the belief that strong performances are the result of doping and this means he places the cause of his success *outside himself*. The consequence is that that same rider will perform worse if he stops using illicit substances; he won't hold the belief that he can be successful without these substances. He won't believe he has *control* over his success. We've shone a light on this phenomenon before, in the chapter about choking; it's a variant on the learned helplessness effect.

The phenomenon of learned helplessness with regard to doping can be seen, in practice, with riders who return to the peloton having served a suspension for several years due to positive tests. Some of them, such as Alejandro Valverde or Alberto Contador, soon return to their former prowess; others, such as David Millar or Thomas Dekker, never reach the old heights again. It's striking in these cases that it's oftentimes riders who were caught at an early age who never make it back to their previous level. These riders had been doping from the very start of their careers and do not have doping-free experiences to sustain them. They simply don't have the belief in their own abilities when they're forced to bike 'clean'. Older athletes, who had good performances before they started to use performance-enhancing drugs, will not experience this kind of learned helplessness. These are the riders who are most likely to make a successful return to competitive riding after a suspension.

If the efficacy of performance-enhancing drugs can be partially explained by psychology, it will come as no surprise that an athlete's decision to use these substances is also driven by psychology. Again, you'll see it is not a single psychological aspect that determines an athlete's choice, but more likely a combination of factors, ones we've seen earlier.

First of all, an athlete's personality plays a major part.[9] The role of personality traits has been identified multiple times in previous chapters, especially with regard to social dilemmas, or the dilemma of the rider having to choose between self-interest or group interest. That personality plays a considerable role when it comes to doping is no coincidence. The choice to use illegal drugs is linked with a dilemma between self-interest (better performance because of drugs), group interest (a doping-free sport) and a fundamental insecurity (not knowing whether other athletes are doping). This combination tempts a number of athletes and they cave in.[9] Generally speaking, this will be determined by the same personality traits that influence social dilemmas.

Research shows that there are a number of specific personality traits that relate to whether or not an individual uses illicit substances. An athlete's moral convictions are very influential. Someone who greatly values 'fair play', for example, is disinclined to dope.[9]

One character trait that increases the odds of someone doping is a propensity for risk-taking.[9] Some people are naturally inclined to avoid risks – they like to be as careful as possible – others, however, get a kick out of risk. They actively look for it. Someone who takes risks is much more inclined to enjoy extreme sports, for example, or invest his money in higher risk ventures, than someone who avoids risk.

And someone who doesn't like taking risks will not be quick to dope. After all, it comes with dangers. Take potential negative health consequences, for example, or the risk that a rider is caught and the possible sanctions that follow. Or the (likely) risk of the team letting the rider go, and the difficulty of finding a new employer. The risk-avoiding cyclist will be quickly deterred by worst-case scenarios.

Another personality trait that increases the likelihood of a rider giving in to the temptation of illicit substances is anxiety. We saw this term before when examining the pressure a captain feels. We saw that a captain with high anxiety will be quicker to fail when put under pressure. However, research shows something similar with other athletes who turn to doping when the pressure increases.[9] Such athletes become so anxious of not being able to perform that they cave under the pressure and want to use any means possible if it helps them succeed. Indeed, the ever-increasing pressure in sports cycling for athletes to bike longer, faster, and harder, is regularly cited as a reason for doping.[2]

One final personality trait specifically linked to doping, is an individual's sensitivity to peer pressure.[9] Some people are more sensitive to other people's opinions and their behaviour is more strongly influenced. This partially correlates to age. Teenagers are a notorious example of a group that is sensitive to peer pressure, with it decreasing as individuals age. But this sensitivity only partially depends on personality. It also depends on an athlete's surroundings. When his surroundings accept doping as a normal behaviour he'll become more inclined to use drugs. But if his surroundings give off the signal that doping is definitely not on the table, he'll be much less inclined to start.

That the choice to dope reaches far beyond personality is demonstrated by the fact that one generation of cyclists seems to find the use of doping much more acceptable than another. Compare the zeitgeist of the nineties with the situation some 20 years later. In 1998, the use of doping seemed generally accepted and commonplace within the peloton. In hindsight, the Tour de France had over thirty cyclists who admitted to using EPO and two entire teams – Festina and TVM – had to forfeit the Tour after doping was discovered.[10] Shortly after so-called Festinagate, all Spanish teams left the Tour – not on account of their colleagues' cheating, but because of the rigorous manner in which the French Justice department looked for doping. Around 20 years later, far fewer cyclists are caught doping and there are fewer scandals, but more strikingly there is a different attitude in the peloton. Riders cheer stricter controls to combat cheating and speak in highly disapproving tones about doping and what took place in the nineties.

The chances are slim that this difference came about because one generation of cyclists had different personalities to the next. Instead, cycling saw a shift in culture. That culture could affect a rider's behaviour is not that strange. All people are strongly influenced by the culture they live in. And as your local culture is so woven into daily life, you are unlikely to be aware of culture's stealthy impact on your opinions and behaviour.

The influence of culture and norms, and values in a group in particular, were examined in this book previously, in the context of team atmosphere. We saw that the more close-knit a team is, the more a rider feels obligated to abide by its unwritten rules. When we look at not just one team's culture, but that of cycling as a whole, a new question surfaces: how can it be that – at one point – doping was normal in cycling, while the outside world was appalled?

After all, riders are part of the same culture as the sport's observers. Take riders such as Stefan Schumacher, Jan Ullrich or Erik Zabel. All these Germans doped at a time when it seemed normal in the peloton. But at the same time, Germany was extremely strict in punishing doping scandals. The Tour de France was not even aired on German television for several years because it was seen as tainted by cycling's many doping scandals. If the German pill poppers were so strongly influenced by German culture, shouldn't they have viewed doping similarly? The answer is no.

Race cyclists will actually be less influenced by the opinions and customs of their country than those of their fellow cyclists because cycling is a subculture: a society of its own with its own customs, own ideas, its own norms and values. Cycling is not unique in this – there are a great many subcultures. Almost every company has one, as anyone who's ever switched jobs will know. It often takes a while to get used to how your new environment plays the game.

What is different from some other subcultures is that cycling seems very closed off.[11] Research has shown that closed cultures mostly occur in groups of people who work together under extreme circumstances, or who live in extreme isolation. With that in mind, it's not so odd that cycling is closed-off. After all, the sport is defined by racing all over the world, and riders are always together and not often home. In turn, everything takes place in a highly competitive climate. The consequence – and another characteristic of a closed culture – is the formation of a strong sense of togetherness: 'us cyclists'.[12] People feel strongly connected to one another, as well as the sport and its laws.

While this togetherness is essentially positive and – as discussed earlier – contributes to creating close-knit teams, it can have negative consequences if a number of unwanted norms and values take hold within the culture. In the case of professional cycling in the nineties, it seemed more the rule than the exception for people to accept doping. If this is the opinion within a close-knit subculture, it becomes the main behavioural instigator. That the outside world reacts very negatively is of less concern. The 'laws' of the subculture are much more influential and as long as a rider meets the 'we' laws of cycling he won't really experience the moral objections of wider culture (the outside world).

He won't feel it's wrong to use illicit drugs, and if something doesn't feel wrong, it's more difficult to say no. What's more, in what is sometimes referred to as a 'doping culture', it can feel as though someone's 'denying himself' something when he does not join the rest. As if a rider doesn't want to do everything it takes to win!

Chapter 13

When you compare the cycling culture of the nineties with today's culture, you'll see a major difference. Take Lance Armstrong's opinion. In a 2015 interview, he indicated that if he lived in 1995, he "would probably use doping again," as (in his mind) it was necessary because everyone else was doing it. But… "If I was racing in 2015, no, I wouldn't do it again."[13]

With Armstrong, we come to a final, more psychological, element that can seduce or stop an athlete from finding comfort in drugs, and that is *power*. An earlier chapter explained that the patrons of the peloton, like Armstrong, have the power to maintain and adjust the unwritten rules of the peloton. More so than other athletes, it's the leaders who can change the stance on doping, and who can influence novice athletes. In 2015, for example, you could see Marcel Kittel's efforts to utilise his rising stature to tighten the rules regarding doping by calling for lifelong bans.[14] Armstrong, on the other hand, tried to do the exact opposite. He didn't use his position of power to halt the tide of doping for the better; instead he instigated refined and professional doping. In hindsight, this is one of the things he seems to regret. "I didn't invent the culture, but I also didn't try to stop the culture."[15]

While doping may, at first glance, seem like a topic that his little to do with the brain, the opposite is true. A whole arsenal of psychological themes apply here as well. As with all sports situations, it's a combination of mental aspects which determine the course of events.

Take Hennie Kuiper's 1983 Paris-Roubaix win. It became the stuff of legend as Kuiper tore his wheel to shreds in the heat of the finale. His victory was a magnificent feat of willpower, but he also won because he was well-prepared, had set proper goals, was motivated and could handle pressure well.

A cyclist who wants to improve should not then directly start working on any single subject in this book. He should first take in all the themes and see where his strengths and weaknesses lie, and work on those. The hidden motor of the mind is no different to any other motor; all parts need to be continually adjusted for it to function as best it can. But once it is working at peak performance, an athlete can utilise no better or more powerful means to push forward and triumph.

References

Prologue

1 See for example: http://www.youtube.com/watch?v=8Nd13ARuvVE

2 Hahn, B. (Ed.) (2013). Opmerkelijke uitspraken uit de wielerinterviews van Hugo Camps in weekblad Elsevier [*Remarkable quotes from cycling interviews of Hugo Camps in Elsevier magazine*]. Elsevier, Onze Tour.

3 Images of this stage still exist: http://www.youtube.com/watch?v=n36Q-Fk1Byk&list=PL8601B5412ED5F072

1. Time Trials: How Strong is the Lonely Cyclist?

1 Triplett, N. (1898). The dynamogenic factors in pacemaking and competition. American Journal of Psychology, 9, 507-533.

2 Tony Martin in an interview with Cyclingnews after his third world championship time-trialling golden medal (www.cyclingnews.com).

3 Dansie, S. (2013). Fabian Cancellara: Ik ben gemaakt voor Vlaanderen en Roubaix [*I am made for Flanders and Roubaix*]. Procycling, jaaroverzicht, p.44-51.

4 Zajonc, R.B., Heingartner, A. and Herman, E.M. (1969) Social enhancement and impairment of performance in the cockroach, Journal of Personality and Social Psychology, 13, 83-92.

5 On pain perception under distraction, see for example Dillen, L. F. van (2008). Dealing with negative fealings: The role of working memory in emotion regulation. Proefschrift Vrije Universiteit Amsterdam.

6 Meumann, E. (1904). Haus- und Schularbeit: Experimente an Kindern der Volksschule. Die Deutsche Schule, 8, 278-303, 337-359, 416-431.

7 http://nos.nl/video/42102-cancellara-thank-you-holland.html

References

2. Lead Groups: Speedsters versus Slowpokes

1 Kravitz, D. A., & Martin, B. (1986). Ringelmann rediscovered: The original article. Journal of Personality and Social Psychology, 50, 936-941.

2 Forsyth, D. R. (1999). Group dynamics. Belmont: Brooks/Cole Wadsworth.

3 Zajonc, R. B. (1965). Social facilitation. Science, 149, 269-274.

4 Harkins, S. G. (1987). Social loafing and social facilitation. Journal of Experimental Social Psychology, 23, 1-18.

5 Karau, S. J., & Williams, K. D. (1993). Social loafing: A meta-analytic review and theoretical integration. Journal of Personality and Social Psychology, 65, 681-706.

6 Fotheringham, W. (2002). Zabel sprints to a Norman conquest. The Guardian, July 13. (http://www.theguardian.com/sport/2002/jul/13/cycling.tourdefrance2002)

7 Michaels, J. W., Blommel, J. M., Brocato, R. M., Linkous, R. A., & Rowe, J. S. (1982). Social facilitation and inhibition in a natural setting. Replications in Social Psychology, 2, 21-24.

8 Klehe, U., Anderson, N., & Hoefnagels, E. A. (2007). Social facilitation and inhibition during maximum versus typical performance situations. Human Performance, 20, 223-239.

3. Team Spirit: A Team is More than its Members

1 Randewijk, M. (2004). Op zoek naar de ware aard van de renner [*On a quest for the true nature of the cyclist*]. De Volkskrant, 10 juli.

2 The psychological movement originates in the early 20th century, but the quote itself is much older and goes back to Aristotle.

3 Forsyth, D. R. (1999). Group dynamics. Belmont: Brooks/Cole Wadsworth.

4 Zaccaro, S. J., Gualtieri, J., & Minionis, D. (1995). Task cohesion as a facilitator of team decision making under temporal urgency. Military Psychology, 7, 77-93.

5 Quotes relating to the special feeling of being part of a close team can be seen in diverse interviews with racers (both in cycling magazines, as in interviews I had with several pro-cyclists) or for example in the book The secret of Raleigh (J. Holthausen; 2008).

6 Aronson, E., & Mills, J. (1957). The effect of severity of initiation on liking for a group. Journal of Abnormal and Social Psychology, 59, 177-181.

7 Hamilton, T. (2013). Secret Race: Inside the Hidden World of the Tour de France: Doping, Cover-ups, and Winning at All Costs. Bantam.

4. Great Expectations: Coppi's and Giant-Alpecin's Trust

1 Rosenthal, R., & Jacobson, L. (1968). Pygmalion in the classroom. New York: Holt, Rinehart & Winston.

2 Feldman, R. S., & Prohaska, T. (1979). The student as Pygmalion: Effect of student expectation on the teacher. Journal of Educational Psychology, 71, 485-493.

3 Babad, E. Y., Inbar, J., & Rosenthal, R. (1982). Pygmalion, Galatea, and the Golem: Investigations of biased and unbiased teachers. Journal of Educational Psychology, 74, 459-474.

4 Website www.wielerflits.nl published a lengthy interview with Iwan Spekenbrink, of which some quotes are presented in this chapter; see:

http://www.wielerflits.nl/nieuws/24705/interview-spekenbrink-deel-iii-nu-bedanken-organisatoren-ons-in-plaats-van-wij-hen.html (16-04-2014)

5 http://www.wielerupdate.nl/wielernieuws/19894/cipollini-andy-schleck-is-een-twijfelaar/

References

6 Heider, F. (1944). Social perception and phenomenal causality. Psychological Review, 51, 358-374.

7 Rees, T., Ingledew, D. K., & Hardy, L. (2005). Attribution in sport psychology: Seeking congruence between theory, research, and practice. Psychology of Sport and Exercise, 6, 189-204.

8 Kelley, H. H. (1973). The process of causal attribution. American Psychologist, 28, 107-128.

9 Delaney, B. (2013). Chris Horner: Mijn prestatie is legendarisch [*My achievement is legendary*]. ProCycling, jaaroverzicht, p.172-179.

10 Haynes, T. L., Perry, R. P., Stupnisky, R. H., & Daniels, L. M. (2009). A review of attributional retraining treatments: Fostering engagement and persistence in vulnerable college students. In J. C. Smart (Ed.), Higher education: Handbook of Theory and Research. New York: Springer Science & Business.

11 Backelandt, F., de Jong, W., & Vanfleteren, S. (2012). Fausto Coppi. Veurne: Uitgeverij Kannibaal.

12 Buzatti, D. (1998). The Giro d'Italia: Coppi vs. Bartali at the 1949 Tour of Italy. VeloPress.

13 Rasle, O., LeFoll, D., & Higgins, N. C. (2008). Attributional retraining alterns novice golfers' free practice behavior. Journal of Applied Sport Psychology, 20, 157-164.

5. Mental Breaking Points: How to Lose the Tour de France

1 Veltkamp, M., Aarts, H., & Custers, R. (2009). Unravelling the motivational yarn: A framework for understanding the instigation of implicitly motivated behaviour resulting from deprivation and positive affect. European Review of Social Psychology, 20, 345-381.

2 Fiske, S. T. (2004). Social beings: Core motives in social psychology. New York: Wiley.

3 Eisenberger, N. I., Lieberman, M. D., & Williams, K. D. (2003). Does rejection hurt? An fMRI study of social exclusion. Science, 302, 290-292.

4 Skinner, E. A. (1996). A guide to constructs of control. Journal of Personality and Social Psychology, 71, 549-570.

5 Ajzen, I. (1985). From intentions to actions: A theory of planned behavior. In J. Kuhl & J. Beckmann (Eds.). Action control: From cognition to behavior. New York: Springer.

6 Biddle, S. J. H. (1999). Motivation and perceptions of control: Tracing its development and plotting its future in exercise and sport psychology. Journal of Sport & Exercise Psychology, 21, 1-25.

7 See for example Slater, L. (2004). Opening Skinner's box: Great psychological experiments of the twentieth century. London: Bloomsbury.

8 Seligman, M. E. P., & Maier, S. F. (1967). Failure to escape traumatic shock. Journal of Experimental Psychology, 74, 1-9.

6. Fear: The Fall of Wiggins

1 http://www.cyclingnews.com/news/savoldelli-wiggins-problem-on-descents-is-fear-not-material

2 Ekman, P. (1999). Basic emotions. In: T. Dalgleish & M. Power (Eds.). Handbook of Cognition and Emotion. Sussex, UK: Wiley & Sons.

3 Schmidt, N. B., Richey, J. A., & Maner, J. K. (2008). Exploring human freeze responses to a threat stressor. Journal of Behavior Therapy and Experimental Psychiatry, 39, 292-304.

4 Walk, R. & Gibson, E. (1961). A comparative and analytical study of visual depth perception. Psychological Monographs, 7, 15.

References

5 Verhofstadt-Deneve, L., van Geert, P., & Vyt, A. (1995). Handboek ontwikkelingspsychologie: Grondslagen en theorieen. [Handbook of developmental psychology] Houten: Bohn Stafleu van Loghum.

6 Watson, J.B. & Rayner, R. (1920). Conditioned emotional reactions. Journal of Experimental Psychology, 3, 1–14.

7 Nelissen, J. (1994). Leven voorbij de pijngrens [*Life beyond the pain treshhold*]. Maastricht: WIN Publiciteit.

8 http://www.cyclingnews.com/news/pinot-to-drive-racing-car-to-improve-descending (25-07-2014).

9 Dillen, L. F. van (2008). Dealing with negative fealings: The role of working memory in emotion regulation. Dissertation Vrije Universiteit Amsterdam.

10 Mulkens, S., Bogels, S. M., de Jong, P., & Louwers, J. (2001). Fear of blushing: Effects of task concentration training versus exposure in vivo on fear and physiology. Anxiety Disorders, 15, 413-432.

11 Cover Jones, M. (1924). A Laboratory Study of Fear: The Case of Peter. Pedagogical Seminary, 31, pp. 308–315

12 Raes, A. K., & de Raedt, R. (2012). The effect of counterconditioning on evaluative responses and harm expectancy in a fear conditioning paradigm. Behavioral Therapy, 43, 757-767.

13 Abt, S. (1990). Cycling: Rider taking classical approach. The New York Times, July 3rd

7. Social Dilemmas: The Decision in the Amstel Gold Race

1 www.tomjelteslagter.nl

2 romankreuziger.com/en/

3 Luce, R. D., & Raiffa, H. (1957). Games and decisions. New York: Wiley.

4 Forsyth, D. R. (1999). Group dynamics. Belmont: Brooks/Cole Wadsworth.

5 Lange, P. A. M. van, Joireman, J., Parks, C. D., & Dijk, E. van (2013). The psychology of social dilemmas: A review. Organizational Behavior and Human Decision Processes, 120, 125-141.

6 Axelrod, R. (1984). The evolution of cooperation. New York: Basic books.

7 Klapwijk, A., & Van Lange, P. A. M. (2009). Promoting cooperation and trust in "noisy" situations: The power of generosity. Journal of Personality and Social Psychology, 96, 83-103.

8 Lange, P. A. M. van, Otten, W., Bruin, E. M. N. de, & Joireman, J. (1997). Development of prosocial, individualistic, and competitive orientations: Theory and preliminary evidence. Journal of Personality and Social Psychology, 73, 733-746.

9 Madsen, M. C., & Lancy, D. F. (1981). Cooperative and competitive behavior: Experiments related to ethnic identity and urbanization in Papua New Guinea. Journal of Cross-Cultural Psychology, 12, 86-102.

8. The Balance of Power: from Raleigh to Sky, from Badger to Spartacus

1 Horst, H. van der (2010). Nederland: De vaderlandse geschiedenis van de prehistorie tot nu. [Dutch history from prehistoric times untill now] Amsterdam: Bert Bakker.

2 Procycling (2013). Interview with Bradley Wiggins. Giro edition Procycling.

3 Het Nieuwsblad (2010). Cancellara: "Solidariteit primeerde op egoisme." 5 juli. & Het Nieuwsblad (2010). Actie Cancellara zaait tweedracht in het peloton, 6 juli.

4 Vugt, M. van (2006). Evolutionary origins of leadership and followership. Personality and Social Psychology Review, 10, 354-371.

References

5 Spisak, B. R., Dekker, P. H., Kruger, M., & Vugt, M. van (2012). Warriors and peacekeepers: Testing a biosocial implicit leadership hypothesis of intergroup relations using masculine and feminine faces. PLoS One, 7:e30399.

6 Gladwell, M. (2013). David and Goliath: Underdogs, misfits and the art of battling giants. UK: Penguin.

7 Holthausen, J. (2008). Het geheim van Raleigh: De biografie van een bijzondere wielerploeg. [*The secret of Raleigh: Biography of a speical cycling team*] Amsterdam: Arbeiderspers.

8 Hogan, R., Curphy, G. J., & Hogan, J. (1994). What we know about leadership. American Psychologist, 49, 493-504.

9 Elijzen, M. (2013). Ongeschreven wielerwetten [*Unwritten cycling laws*]. hetiskoers.nl/2013/ ongeschreven-wielerwetten.

10 Driel, M. van (2003). Hoffelijkheid kan Ullrich de Tour kosten [*Courtesy can cost Ullrich the Tour*]. De Volkskrant, 22 juli 2003.

11 Kort,L. de (2013). Jan & Joop: "De Tour is een heiligdom" [*The Tour is sacred*]. ProCycling, 100 jaar Tour de France.

12 Withers, S. (2013). De heerschappij van Indurain [*Indurain's dominance*]. ProCycling, 100 jaar Tour de France.

13 Images can still be found on: http://www.ina.fr/video/CAB88034476

9. Leadership: Oh Captain, My Captain

1 Aarsbergen, A., & Nijssen, P. (2004). Kampioenen twijfelen niet: Geschiedenis van de wielersport in 100 portretten. [*Champions don't hesitate: History of cycling in 100 portraits*] Amsterdam: Arbeiderspers.

2 Green, R. D. (1999). Leadership as a function of power. Proposal Management, Fall, 54-56.

3 Goleman, D. (1998). What makes a leader? Harvard Business School.

4 Den Hartog, D. N., House, R. J., Hanges, P. J., Ruiz-Quintanilla, S. A., & Dorfman, P. W. (1999). Culture specific and cross-culturally generalizable implicit leadership theories: Are attributes of charismatic/transformational leadership universally endorsed? The Leadership Quarterly, 10(2), 219-256.

5 Kenney, R. A., Schwartz-Kenney, B. M., & Blascovich, J. (1996). Implicit leadership theories: Defining leaders described as worthy of influence. Personality and Social Psychology Bulletin, 22, 1128-1143.

6 Lindsey, J. (2004). Armstrong hunts down rider: Personal disputes mar Armstrong's perfect Tour. ProCycling.

See: http://www.bicycling.com/news/pro-cycling/armstrong-hunts-down-rider

7 Lehrer, J. (2010). The power trip. The Wall Street Journal, august 14. See: http://online.wsj.com/news/articles/SB10001424052748704407804575425561952689390

8 Haanstra, M. (2011). Top 5: Eeuwige talenten [*Eternal talents*]. HetisKoers, Zie: http://hetiskoers.nl/2011/top-5-eeuwige-talenten/

9 Baumeister, R. F., & Showers, C. J. (2006). A review of paradoxical performance effects: Choking under pressure in sports and mental tests. European Journal of Social Psychology, 16, 361-384.

10 Bijleveld, E. H., & Veling, H. (2014). Separating chokers from non-chokers: Predicting real-life tennis performance under pressure from behavioral tasks that tap into working memory functioning. Journal of Sport & Exercise Psychology, 36, 347-356.

11 Beilock, S. L., & Carr, T. H. (2001). On the fragility of skilled performance: What governs choking under pressure? Journal of Experimental Psychology: General, 130, 701-725.

12 Peifer, C., Schulz, A., Schachinger, H., Baumann, N., & Antoni, C. H. (2014). The relation of flow-experience and physiological arousal

under stress - Can u shape it? Journal of Experimental Social Psychology, 53, 62-69.

13 Ramirez, G., & Beilock, S. L. (2011). Writing about testing worries boosts exam performance in the classroom. Science, 331, 211-2013.

10. Motivation: Fondriest's Milan-San Remo

1 Hermans, W. F. (1991). De laatste roker [*The last smoker*]. Amsterdam: De Bezige Bij.

2 Nelissen, J. (1994). Leven voorbij de pijngrens [*Life beyond the pain treshhold*]. Maastricht: Win Publiciteit.

3 Vallerand, R. J. (2004). Intrinsic and extrinsic motivation in sport. Encyclopedia of Applied Psychology, 2, 427-435.

4 In a television interview Kroon tells about this (July 18th 2014)

5 From an interview of the author with Henk Lubberding.

6 Deci, E. L., Koestner, R., & Ryan, R. M. (1999). A meta-analytic review of experiments examining the effects of extrinsic rewards on intrinsic motivation. Psychological Bulletin, 6, 627-668.

7 Abt, S. (1999). Vantage point: As the scandals tarnish bike racing, a fan gets back to basics. The New York Times, june 1. See: http://www.nytimes.com/1999/06/01/sports/01iht-bike.2.t.html

8 Driel, M. van (2003). De ongekende wilskracht van Der Jan [*The extreme willpower of Der Jan*]. De Volkskrant, July 12th.

9 Lepper, M. R., Greene, D., & Nisbett, R. E. (1973). Undermining children's intrinsic interest with extrinsic reward: A test of the "overjustification" hypothesis. Journal of Personality and Social Psychology, 28, 129-137.

10 Bem, D. J. (1967). Self-perception: An alternative interpretation of cognitive dissonance phenomena. Psychological Review, 74, 183-200.

11 Mageau, G.A. & Vallerand, R. J. (2003). The coach-athlete relationship: A motivational model. Journal of Sports Sciences, 21, 883-904.

12 See for example Berridge, K. C. (2007). The debate over dopamines role in reward: The case for incentive salience. Psychopharmacology, 191, 391-431; or Shizgal, P. & Conover, K. (1998). On the neural computation of utility, Current Directions in Psychological Science, 5, pp. 37-43.

13 Aarts., H., Gollwitzer, P. M., & Hassin, R.R. (2004). Goal contagion: Perceiving is for pursuing. Journal of Personality and Social Psychology, 87, 23-37.

14 Olds, J. (1958). Self-stimulation of the brain. Science, 127. 315-324.

15 Griskevicius, V., & Kenrick, D. T. (2013). Fundamental motives: How evolutionary needs influence consumer behavior. Journal of Consumer Psychology, 23, 372-386.

16 Nelissen, J. (1994). Leven voorbij de pijngrens [*Life beyond the pain treshhold*]. Maastricht: Win Publiciteit.

17 Hahn, B. (Ed.) (2013). Opmerkelijke uitspraken uit de wielerinterviews van Hugo Camps in weekblad Elsevier [*Remarkable quotes from cycling interviews*]. Elsevier.

18 Antonissen, J., Graux, G., & Perre, S. v/d (2008). Frank Vandenbroucke: Gevallen voor Sarah [*Fallen for Sarah*]. Belgasport, Season 2, Episode 2. This impressive cycling documentary gives an overview of the Belgian's career. The love affair with Sarah is described in-depth.

19 Bianchi-Demicheli, F., Grafton, S. T., & Ortigue, S. (2006). The power of love on the human brain. Social Neuroscience, 1, 90-103.

20 Younger, J., Aron, A., Parke, S., Chatterjee, N., & Mackey, S. (2010). Viewing pictures of a romantic partner reduces experimental pain: Involvement of neural reward systems. PLoS ONE, 5, e13309.

References

21 Davis, E., Loiacono, R., & Summers, R.J. (2008). The rush to adrenaline: Drugs in sport acting on the β-adrenergic system. British Journal of Pharmacology, 154, 584-597.

11. Setting Goals: Jalabert's Fata Morgana

1 http://www.cyclingnews.com/giro-ditalia/stage-9 (16-4-2016)

2 Kort, L. de (2014). Laat me m'n gang gaan, dat werkt het best: Pieter Weening. ProCycling, Giro d'Italiagids, 34-41.

3 Forster, J., Liberman, N., & Higgins, E. T. (2005). Accessibility from active and fulfilled goals. Journal of Experimental Social Psychology, 41, 220-239.

4 Carver, C. S., & Scheier, M. F. (2001). On the self-regulation of behavior. UK: Cambridge University Press.

5 Elshout, D. (2003). Alleen vooruit: Hennie Kuiper, kampioen van het volk [*Move on alone: Hennie Kuiper, champion of the people*]. Amsterdam: L.J. Veen.

6 Holthausen, J. (2008). Het geheim van Raleigh: De biografie van een bijzondere wielerploeg [*The secret of Raleigh: Biography of a special cycling team*]. Amsterdam: Arbeiderspers.

7 Locke, E. A., & Latham, G. P. (2006). New directions in goal-setting theory. Current Directions in Psychological Science, 15, 265-268.

8 Aarsbergen, A., & Nijssen, P. (2004). Kampioenen twijfelen niet: Geschiedenis van de wielersport in 100 portretten [*Champions do not hesitate: History of cycling in 100 portraits*]. Amsterdam: Arbeiderspers.

9 Plessner, H., Unkelbach, C., Memmert, D., Baltes, A., & Kolb, A. (2009). Regulatory fit as a determinant of sport performance: How to succeed in a soccer penalty-shooting. Psychology of Sport and Exercise, 10, 108-115.

10 Higgins, E. T. (1997). Beyond pleasure and pain. American Psychologist, 52, 1280-1300.

12. Willpower: The Strength of the Lion of Flanders

1 Elshout, D. (2003). Alleen vooruit: Hennie Kuiper, kampioen van het volk [*Move on alone: Hennie Kuiper, champion of the people*]. Amsterdam: L.J. Veen.

2 Gucht, R. van (2014). Museeuw. Veurne: Kannibaal. Quotes from page 88 and 123.

3 Bauer, I. M., & Baumeister, R. F. (2011). Self-regulatory strength. In K. D. Vohs & R. F. Baumeister (Eds.), Handbook of self-regulation: Research, theory, and applications, p. 263-283.

4 Eisenberg, N., Smith, C. L., & Spinrad, T. L. (2011). Effortful Control: Relations with emotion regulation, adjustment, and socialization in childhood. In K. D. Vohs & R. F. Baumeister (Eds.), Handbook of self-regulation: Research, theory, and applications, p. 263-283.

5 Mischel, W., Ebbesen, E. B., & Zeiss, A. R. (1972). Cognitive and attentional mechanisms in delay of gratification. Journal of Personality and Social Psychology, 21, 204-218. Note that this specific test is not the same as the one conducted with four month old babies described in the paragraph above.

6 Metcalfe, J., & Mischel, W. (1999). A hot/cool-system analysis of delay of gratification: Dynamics of willpower. Psychological Review, 106, 3-19.

7 For those interested there are some interesting and well-explained videos to be found on YouTube, for example one by world-famous US psychologist Philip Zimbardo, also containing nice images of the children trying to resist https://www.youtube.com/watch?v=y7t-HxuI17Y (16-04-2016)

References

8 Muravan, M. (2010). Building self-control strength: Practising self-control leads to improved self-control performance. Journal of Experimental Social Psychology, 46, 465-468.

9 Muraven, M., Baumeister, R. F., & Tice, D. M. (1999). Longitudinal improvement of self-regulation through practice: Building self-control strength through repeated exercise. Journal of Social Psychology, 139, 446-458.

10 Friese, M., Messner, C., & Schaffner, Y. (2012). Mindfulness meditation counteracts self-control depletion. Consciousness and cognition, 21, 1016-1022.

11 Eddy Planckaert described how he did this in a television interview, July 24th 2014 (RTL television).

13. Doping: Psychology in Practice

1 Rozendaal, S. (2013). Waarom slikken en spuiten ze? Vier soorten doping: Van vertragend tot onzin. Heren wielrenners, het werkt niet! [*Why they dope? Four kinds of doping: From slowing down to nonsense. It does not work!*] Elsevier, Onze Tour.

2 MUMC TV (2012). Harm Kuipers tells on doping use and effectiveness in sports. (in Dutch: http://www.mumc.nl/actueel/mumc-tv/1847637896001-harm-kuipers-over-doping-de-sport).

3 Denaeghel, J. (2008). De Planckaerts: Kroniek van een wielerdynastie. [*Chronicle of a cycling dynasty*] Antwerpen: Standaard Uitgeverij. Quote p. 270.

4 Backelandt, F., de Jong, W., & Vanfleteren, S. (2012). Fausto Coppi, (p.78). Veurne: Uitgeverij Kannibaal.

5 Greenwald, A. G., Spangenberg, E. R., Pratkanis, A. R., & Eskenazi, J. (1991). Double-blind tests of subliminal self-help audiotapes. Psychological Science, 2, 119-122.

6 Storms, M. D., & Nisbett, R. E. (1970). Insomnia and the attribution process. Journal of Personality and Social Psychology, 16, 319-328.

7 Cannon, W. B. (1942). "Voodoo" death. American Anthropologist, 44, 169-181.

8 Halson, S. L., & Martin, D. T. (2013). Lying to win: Placebos and sport science. International Journal of Sports Physiology and Performance, 8, 597-599.

9 Petroczi, A., & Aidman, E. (2008). Psychological drivers in doping: The life-cycle model of performance enhancement. Substance Abuse Treatment, Prevention, and Policy, 3, 1-12.

10 http://www.cyclingnews.com/news/frensh-senate-releases-positive-epo-cases-from-1998-tour-de-france

11 Sturm, E. (2011). De cultuur is nog te gesloten [*Cycling culture is still too closed*]. Trouw, March 1st.

12 Keating, C. F., Pomerantz, J., Pommer, S. D., Ritt, S.J.H., Miller, L. M., & McCormick, J. (2005). Going to college and unpacking hazing: A functional approach to decrypting initiation practices among undergraduates. Group Dynamics: Theory, Research, and Practice, 9, 104-126.

13 http://nos.nl/artikel/2015563-armstrong-ik-zou-het-waarschijnlijk-weer-doen.html

14 http://www.nu.nl/sport/3537384/kittel-pleit-levenslange-schorsing-dopingzondaars.html

15 Randewijk, M. (2013). Armstrong heeft spijt, maar vooral van het feit dat hij ontmaskerd is [*Armstrong has regret, but especially of the fact that he was unmasked*]. De Volkskrant, 18 januari.

Index

Index

Other Books from Bennion Kearny

Tipping The Balance: The Mental Skills Handbook For Athletes

By Dr Martin Turner, Dr Jamie Barker

"The ability to produce a world-beating time is about how you use your mind to allow your body to function with freedom and fluency."

Many athletes grow up with the philosophy that their mental approach to performance is fixed. They do the same things over and over again and expect excellence. But we know that mental approaches are not fixed. They are extremely changeable and adaptable, and therefore the greatest athletes can develop their mental approaches to fulfil their potential. Athletes who can deal with pressure enjoy their sport more, achieve excellence and are resilient to the demands of competition and training.

Tipping The Balance offers contemporary evidence-based and highly practical mental strategies that help an athlete to develop the crucial mental skills that enable them to thrive under pressure, perform consistently when it matters most, and enjoy the challenge of the big event.

This book is about empowering you - the athlete - no matter what level you perform at. In this book you will discover the secrets of how the world's greatest athletes draw on cutting edge psychological skills to use what's between their ears to maximize performance.

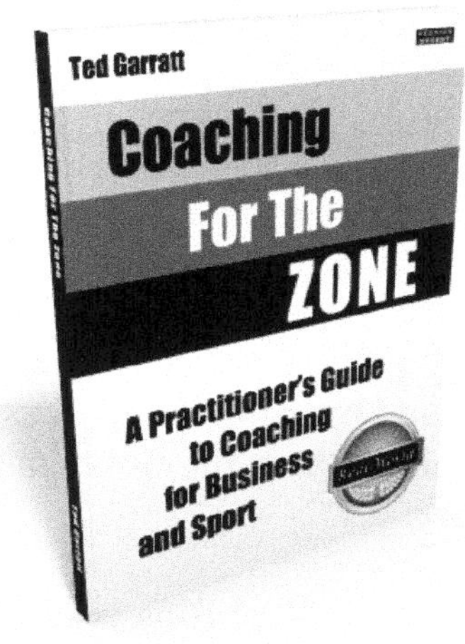

Coaching For The Zone: A Practitioner's Guide to Coaching for Business and Sport

By Ted Garratt

Attaining exceptional levels of achievement and performance • Total confidence in doing the right thing • Going beyond the self • Automatic and Effortless Actions

These are descriptions of being in The Zone and are phrases many people use when describing their greatest performances, often without explaining how they achieved it. In sport, coaches and managers will describe their players (or teams) as being in The Zone, again without explaining how it happened. The Zone can happen any day, in any context or situation, and can be planned for and coached.

Many people think The Zone is a matter of luck; it either happens or it doesn't. Because of this they don't plan for the Zone and when it happens don't know how to repeat it. In *Coaching For The Zone* leading coach practitioner and trainer Ted Garratt guides the reader through the process of training clients to enter The Zone. He demonstrates how to coach for The Zone to equip individuals with the skills and confidence to break through barriers and transform their abilities.

The book is split into two sections. The first section follows an 8-part coaching programme with a coachee in a business environment, but also includes examples and case histories from sport. The second section contains Key Skills and Exercises that the practitioner can use when coaching clients for The Zone.

Explore The Zone and its power to transform performance • Plan for The Zone • Learn Key Tools and Techniques required to help Achieve The Zone • Contains Examples of Real Life Experiences of People being Coached to get into The Zone • Filled with Practical Activities for coaches to Follow and Practice for Accessing The Zone

The 7 Master Moves of Success

By Jag Shoker

One of the most common clichés about success - that it is a journey, not a destination - has concealed one of its most defining qualities. Success really is a dynamic and ever-moving process. It is about making the right moves at the right time.

In this absorbing and uplifting book, Jag Shoker – a leading performance coach to business leaders, sports professionals and creative performers – brings the science and inspiration behind success to life. He reveals the 7 Master Moves that combine to create the high performance state that he calls Inspired Movement: the ability to perform an optimal series of moves to create the success you desire most.

Drawing widely on scientific research, his extensive consultancy experiences, and insights into the successes of top performers in business, sport, and entertainment, 7 Master Moves is a synthesis of the leading-edge thinking, and paradigms, that underpin personal performance and potential.

Building upon key research in fields such as neuroscience, psychology, expert performance and talent development - 7 Master Moves represents an evidence-based 'meta' theory of what really works. Compelling to read, and easy to follow, the book incorporates a strong practical element and shares a number of powerful and practical exercises that can help you apply each Master Move and achieve greater results in your life and work.

Regardless of your profession or passion in life, the 7 Master Moves will reward those who are prepared to work hard to achieve the success that matters most to them.

Other Books from Bennion Kearny

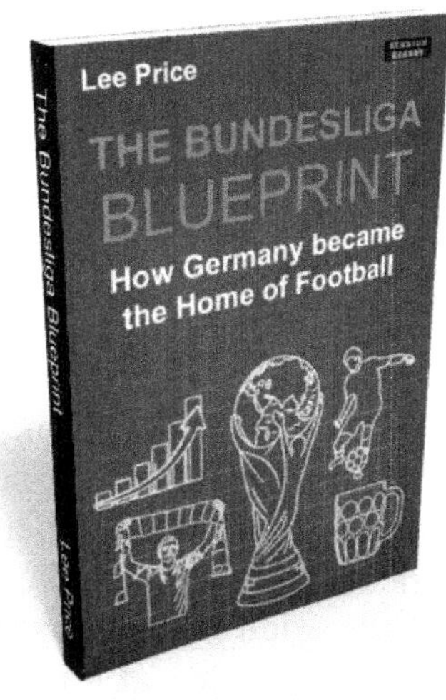

The Bundesliga Blueprint: How Germany became the Home of Football

By Lee Price

German Football is on a roll: winners of the 2014 World Cup, club sides leading the way in Europe, a production line of superb talent coming through the system. Yet, fifteen years ago – at Euro 2000 – it was all so different. Germany suffered one of their most humiliating tournament exits as dismal performances saw them finish bottom of their group with just one point… Immediately, the German FA set about fixing things. And rather than fudging matters, they introduced a raft of major changes designed to return German football to its sporting pinnacle in just 10 years.

In this entertaining, fascinating, and superbly-researched book, sportswriter Lee Price explores German football's 10-year plan. A plan that forced clubs to invest in youth, limit the number of foreign players in teams, build success without debt, and much more. The Bundesliga Blueprint details how German fans part-own and shape their clubs, how football is affordable, and the value of beer and a good sausage on match days.

The book includes interviews from Michael Ballack, Jens Nowotny and Christoph Kramer, and the movers-and-shakers behind Germany's leading clubs including Schalke, Dortmund, and Paderborn. There is no doubt that German football is the envy of many nations. There is no doubt that, thanks to them, lessons should be learned by everyone else.

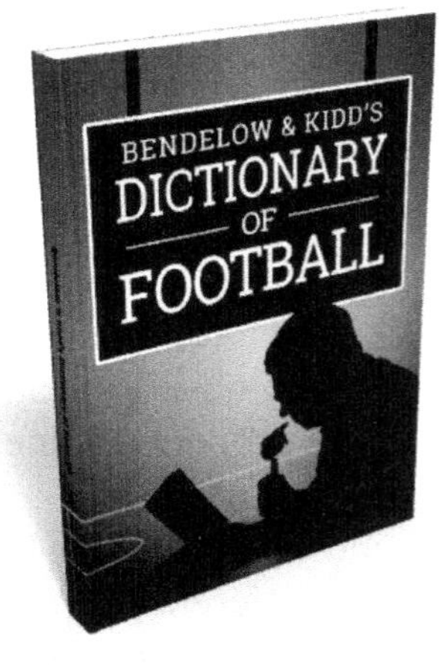

Bendelow and Kidd's Dictionary of Football

By Ian Bendelow, Jamie Kidd

Over time, the language of football has developed into something quite unrecognisable, a melting pot of hyperbole, idioms and exaggeration. Many of football's terms would be seen as bizarre in any other walk of life; a doctor would never diagnose a patient with having the dreaded metatarsal, and only commentators seem to feel the need to tell us who was at number one the last time a team won at a certain ground.

Join Bendelow and Kidd as they produce a barnstorming run through some of the best-loved (depending on how you look at it) phrases and sayings which come out of the mouths of players, managers, pundits, journalists and of course, you, the fans.

From trigger happy chairmen to the want-away striker, football offers us a unique language which can be amusing, and at other times simply infuriating. That's right, the lads really did give it 110% out there today, as they silenced the boo boys, in the relegation six-pointer.

A book which will make you laugh out loud, nod your head in agreement, and hopefully offer a few surprises, *Bendelow and Kidd's Dictionary of Football* should have its place on every true football fan's bookshelf.

Other Books from Bennion Kearny

Golf Tough: Practice, Prepare, Perform and Progress

By Dan Abrahams

"Too many golfers incorrectly believe that within lower handicaps lies better technique. And too many golfers believe that the only way to shoot lower scores is to improve their technique. Wrong and wrong!"

Golf Tough is an original and inspiring book– a book that will transform your game.

Dan Abrahams is Lead Psychologist for England Golf, as well as a former touring professional golfer, and PGA coach. In Golf Tough, Dan offers you a powerful blueprint for improvement and a detailed plan for consistent high performance no matter what your standard of play. If you want to significantly lower your handicap, compete with greater consistency, win tournaments or reach the next level on the course, Dan's simple yet powerful philosophies, tools and techniques will help you break through your current barriers and reach your golfing goals.

This book will show you how to practice to build skill, technique and confidence - your visits to the range will become more productive and purposeful than ever, and your practice more deliberate. Dan also reveals the secret processes golfing champions employ to prepare to compete under the most intense pressure, as well as how all golfers can learn to stand on the first tee brimming with self-belief.

Taking a unique viewpoint on performance and progression, you will learn from some of the top authorities in the game – the world's leading golf statistician, one of the premier coaches in Europe, a putting coach to the stars, and a former caddy who spends his days teaching players to plot their way around the course. This accumulated wisdom, combined with Dan's cutting edge approach in sport psychology - and with up-to-date scientific research, practical lessons, and eye opening anecdotes from golf and a variety of sports - makes Golf Tough the essential golfing read.

Other Books from Bennion Kearny

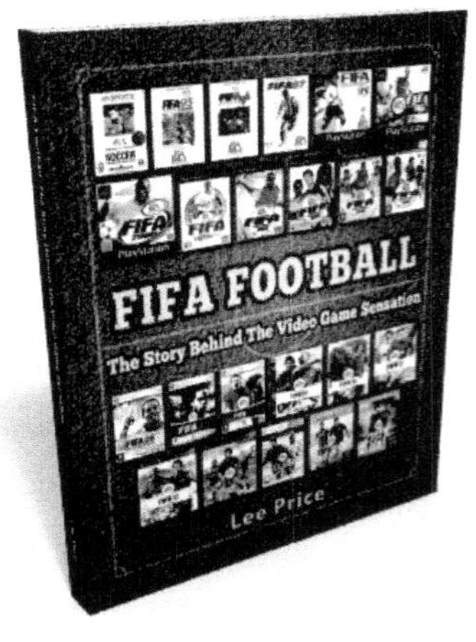

FIFA Football: The Story Behind The Video Game Sensation

By Lee Price

EA's most beautiful game – the FIFA series – has proved a global success. It has sold a record-breaking number of copies, garnered numerous plaudits and awards, and established itself as the leading sports title on the market.

But it almost never was.

Back in 1993, when the Premier League was still in its infancy, the Champions League a new-fangled term, and Lionel Messi had just started to kick a ball, EA Sports took a punt on the FIFA license for their first 'soccer' game. But, with the World Cup rights secured by a rival ahead of USA 94, bigwigs at the Canada-based firm started to fret that *FIFA International Soccer* would flop, and almost pulled the plug on what would become a seminal release.

Instead, the game confounded all expectations and – despite being released in December – became the best-selling game of the year. EA had unwittingly stumbled upon a diamond.

In *FIFA Football*, author Lee Price explores the history of the series including its gameplay and unique isometric camera angle, the battle with Pro Evolution Soccer for gaming supremacy, and the hi-tech software used to put together *FIFA 16* – a release which includes women's teams for the first time. It's a series which continues to innovate and exhilarate.

The book includes exclusive contributions from key figures in the FIFA story as well as behind-the-scenes insights from EA's HQ in Vancouver. It also details the futuristic head-scanning process that captures the players you love, the world of FUT, YouTubers, competitive gaming, soundtracks, FIFA's spinoffs, and so much more.

This is the definitive story of the FIFA video game.

Lightning Source UK Ltd.
Milton Keynes UK
UKOW05f1918240117
292801UK00018B/504/P

9 781911 121114

OUZO The GREE

A YEAR IN THE LIFE OF
A GREEK RESCUE DOG

WHO Chains YOU PUBLISHING

Lisa Edwards

Published by Who Chains You Publishing
P.O. Box 581
Amissville, VA 20106
www.WhoChainsYou.com

Cover and interior design by Tamira Thayne

ISBN-13: 978-1-946044-46-4

Printed in the United States of America

First Edition

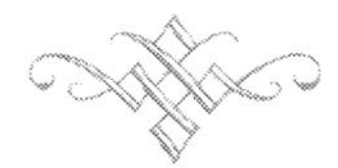

DEDICATION

Believe in angels, because they exist.

For my first love Ermioni Giannakou. My saviour, my heroine, and my very own guardian angel.

Table of
CONTENTS

INTRODUCTION
Who Am I?

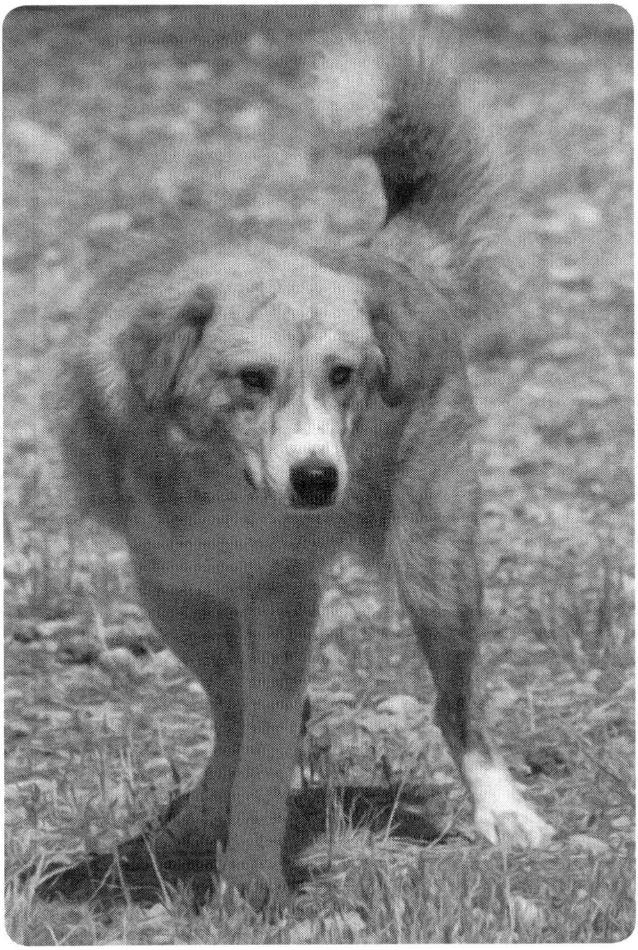

After being hit by a car and left for dead on the streets of Greece, I was rescued by my heroine and first love, Ermioni. With broken bones and open wounds so severe my flesh was beginning to rot, the only option was to amputate my leg.

Ermioni nursed me back to health and I lived for a time at the Diasozo Animal Rescue shelter. However, I was becoming depressed, as the healthier dogs were pushing me out of the way when there was food to be had.

My guardian angel continued to look out for me and share my story on social media all around the world, until one day I found my very own Mama and Papa, in little old England.

And this is where my story begins.

WEEK 1
My First Memories of England

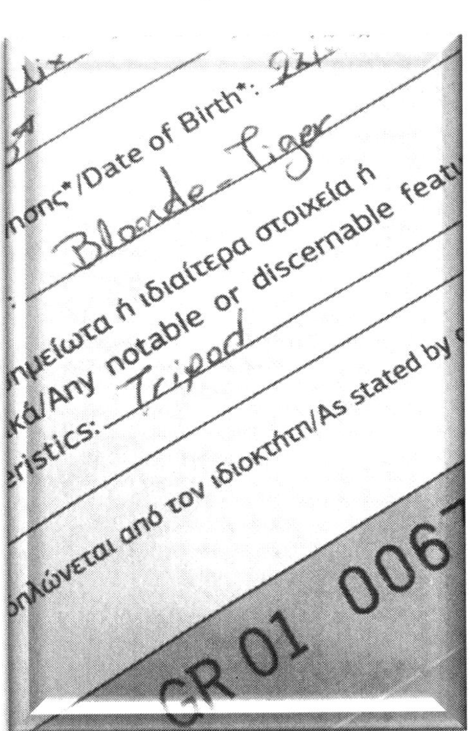

My first memory of England: cruising down the M40 in the back of a van on the way to my new life, as the one they call Mama opened my passport and scanned the details. I could sense the concern in her voice as she read out loud, "Description, blonde tiger, tripod." She exchanged glances with the man, aka Papa. What did those glances mean? Was there something wrong with me?

My first time in a house: my sensitive nose was accosted by lots of smells, mainly cats. Cats! For the love of God . . . I'd spent four days travelling across Europe, had a bit of a respite with a lovely lady named Juliet, and now I'd arrived in my forever home . . . with a crazy cat lady?

The crazy cat lady's house contained a few tricky obstacles, too—for example, a glass coffee table, which I gave a wide berth after cracking my head on it. See-through furniture? Just bizarre.

I quickly discovered one advantage to being in a house: sky raisins. They fly in through the open windows and can't get out again, which is perfect because I can catch them in seconds and swallow them whole. I no longer touch the bumble nuggets—they have a sting in their tail, much like a discarded Vindaloo (hot curry) I once tried on the streets in my homeland. Bad choice.

Men have not always been kind to me—yes, a few have, but many others have chased me, kicked me, and beaten me. I understandably became very wary of them. But I quickly learned that Papa is one of the good ones. He speaks softly and gives me my space. He also feeds me and slips me treats. Hence, I am growing fond of him, and follow him around in case he's carrying any of the afore-mentioned food. (You never know.) He takes me out too, and we sit happily together in the park and watch the world go by.

I was told if I got in the van we could drive to the beach, but I ain't going nowhere near another van . . . not for now, anyway.

Cats, did I mention this? Well, as it turns out, there is just the one, a big one. She's a fierce-looking brute who goes by the name of Daisy, aka Mrs. D, or Madam Le' D, due to the fact that she's French. She is also a rescue animal, spending a year in the care of the Cats Protection organization as no one wanted her—because she has no ears. That's what I'm told. But I think it's more likely it's because she's the evil ruler of the dark side. She likes to stare at me through the stairgate that stops me from reaching her; pfft, like I'm even going to try. Apparently one day this gate will be left open so we can share the sitting room, but I'm in no rush.

My new mama tells me she has just come out of hospital and has to rest. Is that true? I'm not sure, but I'm starting to suspect she's just a lazy old woman who enjoys bossing around her house boy (Papa), who waits on her hand and foot.

She gives a good back rub though, so she is growing on me, although she does have the annoying habit of constantly asking me who is a good boy? How the hell am I supposed to know. I get her back by stealing her book—while she's reading it. I creep up and gently take it out of her hand and she has to get up to steal it back from me. Hey, it's a fun game, and she needs the exercise.

Random things:

Presents. Mama has been given flowers from people she calls friends, who all wish her a speedy recovery. I don't have any friends; however, the strange thing is that I have been given exactly 18 presents—17 more than Mama—and 16 more than Mrs. D (the cat, remember?), who received a couple of feathery things that made her sniff and walk away with a look of disdain on her no-eared face. She's not very grateful.

I like my gifts; they're fun, but I don't know what you're supposed to do with a ball? I watch them throw it and listen to them telling me I am supposed to bring it back to them, but you know what? I only have three legs—get that damn ball yourself.

Barking. Our neighbours are great. There are a bunch of senior citizens that live in a block of flats overlooking our garden. My adorable sister-from-another-mister cares for some of them, so they all know who I am. Trouble is, with a name like mine, it's somewhat barking (mad, that is) when they lean out the windows shouting Ouzo—because anyone who doesn't know us thinks they're yelling for liquor.

Bed. What is this thing? Apparently I'm supposed to lie on it, sleep on it, or some such nonsense. Why? I'm perfectly happy sleeping on a bit of cold concrete—it's much more fun to simply chew up the dog bed and spread the stuffing around the floor. And no, Mama, I'm not really interested in how much it cost.

Final word: I'm not complaining, but you need to understand that my life so far has been difficult. If you see me out and about—in the park, the store, or wherever—I might wag my tail at you, but I am still very anxious. Please, for now, keep your distance. It's going to be a while before I am fully relaxed and understand that I am here with Mama and Papa and that darned cat for life.

Editor's comment: This don't impress me much.

WEEK 2
English Eccentricities

I have learnt a thing or two this week, including that there's an English tradition called 'Bank Holiday Monday', which appears to involve everyone staying home from work as it rains so much no one wants to leave the house. Also, on a Sunday we have a 'Sit-down Dinner'. The rules of the house specify that when the people eat, they sit at a table and ignore me. Rude. Apparently this is so I don't become a nuisance and scrounge for food and know my place, etc. . . . or maybe they just think I have an unhealthy interest in crockery and don't want me to have a smashing good time with it. I am Greek after all.

Anyway, back to the point. In the evening, if we're lucky, the leftovers are shared out between me and that darned cat. Delicious, I hear you say? Well, not when they shove a load of left-over carrots and broccoli on the top. I'm a street dog, not a character out of Watership Down. I made my point by leaving the offending items of, quite frankly, rank vegetation untouched.

I've been pondering the beauty of the English language—or not—as the case may be. The English language is a bit much for us Greek pups to learn. But I already know sit, down, wait, come, and be nice to the cat.

I have also heard a few new words which Mama has said I am not to repeat, or not until I am proficiently fluent in the English language and know how to use these particular words in the correct and most meaningful contexts. Ummm, like I understood any of that jibber jabber!

I think these words are of a similar ilk to those that I picked up from the Spanish dogs whom I shared my 'dogs on tour—drive of destiny' trip across

Europe on our way to a new life. Harsh times.

While I have you here, I'd like to mention a few more likes and dislikes. It may surprise you that, although I have never been in a house, I have no qualms whatsoever about things like vacuum cleaners, postmen, washing machines, or the suchlike. Everyone else seems calm about it, so I just follow suit.

I like most foods, toys, my new collar, and my concrete ramp to get in and out the door. But most of all Papa—I really like him.

And dislikes? Yeah, I have a fair few of these, which I don't mind listing for you. They consist of most men, strangers, oh, and Mrs. D, aka That Darned Cat. I totally admit that I growl at men I don't know. Hey, I can't help it—self-preservation and all that—plus I am used to being out and about and being able to run away from people I don't trust. I've found being in a house is kinda groovy, but I do feel a little trapped, which I'm not used to yet.

We have had a couple of gentleman callers, a gardener and a musician so I'm told. They were cool and gave me my space, but I still had a little growl at them. Mama says it's early days, and once I feel settled and fully trust her and Papa, I will be more relaxed around the males of the species. Whatever. Just between you and me, I'm not sure I will ever feel fully relaxed around that four-legged, no-eared fluffy she-devil. That's right, the cat.

Mama and Papa mostly get asked how I'm settling in. I can tell you that I'm adapting to the routine of daily life, this new life in a new country. I sit with Papa in the garden whilst he has his morning cuppa and a smoke. Then we often go to the park, where I met a couple of fellow Greekies this week; nice chaps, but as I am not allowed off the lead yet, I admit to feeling a bit nervous around them. I can't run away, so we just exchanged pleasantries via the courtesy rear end sniff and carried on about our business.

Papa makes me breakfast and Mama makes me dinner, and in between we chill, go out a couple more times for potty breaks, and play. I have only been here for two weeks, and I can't help but wonder where I might be taken to next. Mama and Papa tell me I am here forever and they will look after me, but I can't help but feel anxious at times.

I used to lick my feet when feeling a bit tense but Mama said I shouldn't so I licked my lipstick instead. Mama said I shouldn't do that either. Too many rules.

And finally, thank you to the following people who have given me more presents! Auntie Janine, thanks for the edible envelope—awesome, but I think the cash got lost in the post? Nana, Lou-Ann, Katz, (yes I have a friend called Katz), and ex-cop Karen, sorry for growling at you, old habits die hard, and all that jazz. Big love.

Editor's comment: You disgust me.

WEEK 3
That Darned Cat

The stairgate is down. Do you know what this means? The beast of darkness, aka That Darned Cat, has full access to my quarters. I do not have full access to her quarters. The damned creature has her own penthouse suite on the top floor of our building! Unnecessary.

We have had a few encounters, I don't mind telling you. I thought I would show her who's boss and do a bit of teeth snarling, lip curling, growling, etc. She just licked the claws on her paws, or b*tch slappers as she calls them, and flicked me a repugnant glance before casually strolling off through her very own door. Unreal.

The next meeting I tried a more friendly approach and greeted her in the favourable manner of rear end sniffing. Dear Lord. I have never heard a creature make such an enormous yowl of outrage, before, once again, casually leaving the building through her very own door. When I see her now I take the tried and tested fashion of playing dead. Seems to work.

Editor's comment: When meeting a bear in the wild it is advised you should lay down and play dead. This is good practice for when you will actually be dead in about one minute. The mutt is learning.

This brings us to other, more important topics: my foot fetish and Donald Trump. Yup, I have one—a foot fetish that is, not a Donald Trump. Ew. On three occasions over the last three weeks I have gone a bit bonkers and started to chew my own foot. Mama says if I was a person I would be diagnosed with post-traumatic stress disorder, but as I am a dog I will just be labeled a psycho. Rude!

Mama says this is ok, though, as being a bit weird makes life more interesting. Mama and Papa just use distractions to get me to stop. The first two times Papa took me out for a walk; the third time Mama tried a different tactic—actually about a billion different tactics—until she stumbled across the solution . . . an interactive Donald Trump meme on social media. I don't know who this fella is, but it had me so engrossed I forgot all about my manic foot eating.

Mama said this is the first useful thing he has ever done—Donny that is, not me. Then she got a bit carried away, thinking she is funny (like she does sometimes), and told me a joke about an Irish Wolfhound who laid in the corner chewing on a bone. When he got up he only had three legs. She laughed, but methinks it might be Mama who is the unhinged one.

Dog Treat Man. So my brother-from-another-mother came to visit again. I am still scared of this guy and won't go near him; to be sure he knows of my distrust, I growl from a safe distance. However, I have to admit that he has this aroma I find compulsively intriguing. Mama, or 'she-who-must-be-obeyed' as I am starting to think of her, instructed Treat Man to sit calmly without looking at me and then every now and again ping a bit of the good stuff in my direction. Oh yeah baby, that's the ticket!

So now I'm confused. I'm still scared of him, but a little interested in him too—just a tad. When he left he gave me a glance and I winked at him. Treat Man turned to Mama and said, 'That dog is a hustler.'

Mama is AMAZING! I have used capital letters to accentuate the way in which Mama keeps telling me this. I haven't heard anyone else say it, but according to Mama that is because they already know. I am beginning to think she may be deluded in addition to unhinged (see above); however, she has actually done something rather amazing. She has found my first love, Ermioni.

As a young pup of about six months I was found abandoned in a village in my homeland of Greece. A local lady contacted the Diasozo animal rescue team (Diasozo means to rescue—you teach me English, I teach you Greek) and informed them of a dog that was hiding in fear, aka me.

I was in pain and very scared, and it took them several hours to catch me. They think I had been hit by a car, and the injuries to my feet and legs had started to rot my flesh. For two months, under the instructions of the vet, Ermioni cared for me, cleaning my wounds and exercising my feet and legs, but sadly my front leg could not be saved.

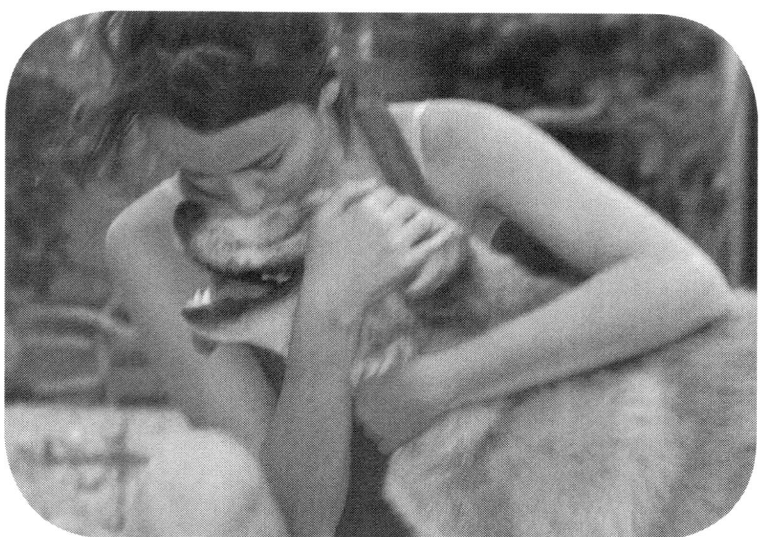

After my operation I lived for a time in the Diasozo animal rescue dog shelter in Karditsa with 50 other dogs, and every day I saw Ermioni. She holds a special place in my heart as one of the few people I had ever trusted, and I would always go to her for love and affection.

If it wasn't for Ermioni I wouldn't be where I am today—in my **forever home** that she helped me find. So thank you Ermioni, from the bottom of my heart, I will never forget you.

 Editor's comment: Man up.

WEEK 4
Life on the Street

I'm up to my old tricks. I am street dog, therefore I pilfer. (You know, like 'I think, therefore I am.') A life on the street teaches you to become somewhat of an expert in the art of getting what you want. The rules are 'if you don't ask, you don't get', and 'if you can't speak the local lingo, simply steal it'.

To be fair, Mama and Papa do provide the essentials, but old habits die hard. Sometimes I would like a bit more attention, so I have utilised my larceny skills for new and devious purposes. For example, my one friend (I have loads of them now), sent Mama a magazine with an article on three-legged dogs. Mama does not need to waste time reading such things when she has her very own three-legged dog balancing right in front of her. And did I mention he was in need of a hug? So I stole that magazine, and then I ate it. Sorry Juliet.

I've also supplemented my thievery with some new tricks. It turns out I am rather intelligent, or at least that's what they tell me. I can sit, lay down, and wait on command. I also come when I am called—relatively quickly if I am standing up, but it takes much longer if I am laying down, as I just do my impression of a commando crawl. I am not allowed off the lead (officially) until my final adoption papers have been signed, sealed, and delivered. Dull.

Of course I have a rather cunning plan to forget all about English words and their meanings the minute I am set free. As I am sure you are aware, dogs have an uncanny ability to read peoples' minds—we know exactly what you are thinking . . . at all times. For example, Mama and

Papa are thinking I might forget my English words when the time comes to let me loose. Turns out Mama and Papa are rather intelligent too.

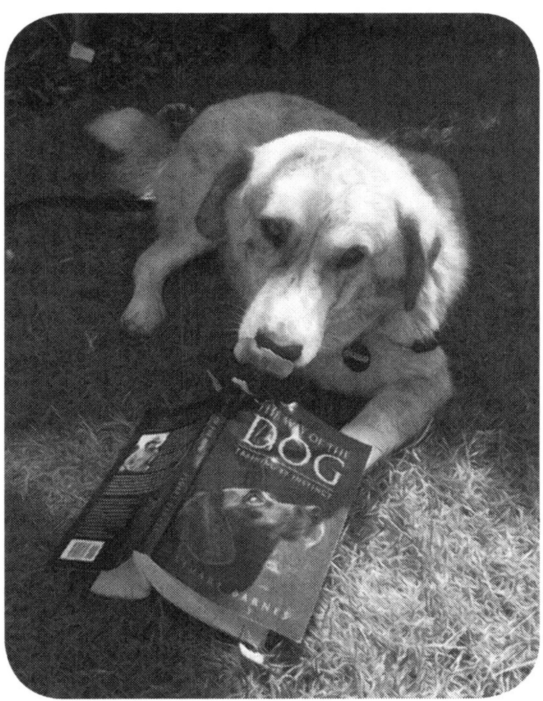

Both Mama and Papa started reading yet another book, *The Way of the Dog: Training by Instinct*, by Stuart Barnes. They said it was brilliant and full of really good advice, so I stole it, and then I ate it. Sorry Stuart Barnes.

In more news on That Darned Cat, I've been told the beast from the dark side has nine lives. 9. Do you know why? I believe it's because when these feline creatures reach the Pearly Gates they loiter at the entrance, thinking, 'Hmmmm, shall I go in? Shall I stay out? Shall I just sit in the threshold and lick my personal area?'

By which point Saint Peter lets his halo slip as he shoos the annoying creatures away, telling them to come back when they have their minds made up. And that is why they have nine lives. Grrrrr. So it looks like this heinous ball of fur is here to stay for some time.

To make matters worse, Papa went to Waitrose, yes Waitrose, the posh shop, and returned with extra special and expensive CAT food. Unbelievable. I made my protest by initiating a staring contest with the beast until Mama noticed and said, 'It's about time you four-legged creatures started to get on', followed by 'Sorry, Ouzo'.

How very rude. Jokes at the expense of my missing leg? Now I've heard it all.

That damned cat is my nemesis who haunts and taunts my every move.

What's with this Barkin' Mad Brexit stuff? I am a dog and quite frankly do not care for your ridiculous politics, but I do actually have a view on this whole Brexit deal. Four words: The great European Union. I am from Greece, a European Country, where it is hot, the beaches are golden, the ocean is warm, and the skies are blue.

Here in England, Mama and Papa took me to the beach—the English beach, mind you—where the wind is strong, the skies are grey, the sand is rocky, and the sea is FREEZING. Referendum, hah! In the words of Donny T, that's just Fake News (that fella is barkin' too, makes me LOL, a lot). The truth of the matter is you got chucked out for being cold, wet, and basically bland. Let's face it, you never see the Queen of England leaving the house without a hat on. I heard Papa ask Mama how come I can instantly recognise other Greek rescue dogs when we are out and about. Mama said, 'It's because he understands their language—we hear woof woof woof, he hears 'it's freaking cold here'.'

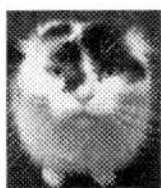

Editor's comment: You could always go back.

WEEK 5
Summer Lovin'

Summer lovin': In the words of Olivia Newton John, 'it happened so fast'. When I was given my passport and told I would be emigrating, I fantasized about a life in Paradise City, where the grass is green and the girls are pretty. In my defense, they did say I was going to a better life.

I continued to hold onto this little dream on my epic trek in the back of a van—for four long days and nights—until I rocked up in England where it would seem your summer lasts exactly five days. As a dog with three legs, my main concern is now Rickets.

She-who-must-be-obeyed, aka Mama, has announced she is now fully fit and has returned to work after her surgery. Papa commented that I may be feeling a little anxious in her absence, but trust me, my only trepidation is for her work colleagues—I myself am enjoying the peace. She is a little bonkers, but I am a tad fond of the old girl despite her strange habit of rolling her eyes every time she says the word 'Papa'.

When Mama returned from work on her first day back, I went to the door to meet her but That Darned Cat got there first, blocking my path and doing an impression of a three-legged amputee just to steal my limelight. Grrrr.

Karma is THE BEST THING EVER. So, it turns out I have an Aunt in Australia, Auntie Tina. She lives on this mahoosive farm with lots of animals, a couple of groovy cattle dogs (shout out to Rowf and Snitter), horses, chickens, cows, oh and a cat. (Those damn creatures are like a plague. Noah certainly messed things up there.)

I think I would like to live in Australia with Rowf and Snitter, although I would also like to live in the big posh house on the beach that Mama and Papa have to drag me away from every time we walk past it. Decisions, decisions.

Anyway, Auntie Tina bought me and the creature from the dark side a present. Turns out mine is still enroute, but the cat's arrived through the post this week. . . . when no one was home. (You see where I'm going with this.) It was just me and that cat, who was chilling upstairs in her penthouse suite. I grabbed the parcel the minute it hit the floor and ripped the begger open. Oh, joyous joy. Papa came home and caught me in the act, but whatever; I just wagged my tail and proper smirked.

Cat was furious. The no-eared beast was even more furious when she realised the present was actually a fluffy cat hat with ears. LOL.

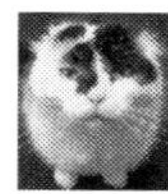 Editor's comment: I will end you.

A word about this foreign language you call English: I wish it was all Greek to me. I get the come, sit, wait, down, and all that jazz, but sometimes my belligerent streak comes out and my only response will be 'I no speakey the Engleesh' and then I ignore you.

I'm a street dog, not a sheep dog; 'come bye' (a phrase used to train sheep dogs, I learnt) still don't mean nout to me. Just sayin'.

Mama says it would be more useful if Papa trained me to follow him around the kitchen shutting cupboard doors and checking that the oven is turned off after he's used it.

If we're talking hashtags now, mine would have to be #mysquad, I've met so many dogs. The Snapster, a Jack Russell Terrier, and I had a bit of a romp, until I heard his Mama tell my Mama that The Snapster had the mind of a cat and did whatever he wanted. I made a quick exit.

I've also befriended three Greek rescue comrades, rough collies who aren't rough at all, plus a Russian Borzoi and a couple of Hungarian Vizslas that were all born in this country and can only speak English. Barking mad. Although I am pretty sure I got a whiff of vodka from the Borzoi—fair play to that fella.

I meet up regularly with Susie, another rescue dog who came all the way from South Africa. Her Papa and my Papa kinda' get the rehabilitation process for us canine nomads, so they make a big deal out of greeting each other.They shake hands or maybe give each other a pat on the back, reckoning this gives us dogs a feeling of ease. You know, welcome to our pack, that sort of thing; it's all about the body language.

If they start sniffing each other's rear ends, I'm using my passport to get the hell out of here. I must say, it does actually help though . . . I don't growl at Susie's Papa anymore, and I will take treats from his hand but I don't let him touch me—Stranger Danger and all that, and I'm certainly never getting in his van.

Speaking of which, in big news from this week, I have overcome my massive fear of Papa's van! I refused to walk past it at first, but now, thanks to the advice in Stuart Barnes' book (that I chewed up), I jump right in and wag my tail. Thanks, and sorry again, Stuart.

And now it's time for a little reality check, from me, the expert: don't get a dog unless you know the real deal. The first thing you'll need is buckets of patience and understanding. Mama and Papa think I'm great, which of course I am. But life has been harsh for me, and I am still scared. I LOVE a tummy tickle, but Papa made the mistake of trying to tickle my tummy with his foot one time and I ran a mile. It's early days still, as Mama keeps saying, and even though they both tell me I am here forever and they will never hurt me, I still ain't so sure—not yet anyway.

But if you can take these words to heart and still share the love, remember, saving one dog won't change the world, but for that one dog the world will change forever.

Shout out to the guys I left behind.

 Editor's comment: Harsh.

WEEK 6
Revenge of the Cat

Life is . . . a walk in the park. Except it's raining. And cold. And I'm homesick. I'm missing the sunshine, like seriously. How do you people live like this? We went on a recent trip to the park on a wet and windy wonderful English summer's day, and I managed to climb inside the cricket practice cage to make myself feel at home. It was just like the old days at the pound in Greece—except for the artic cold and rain, of course.

Papa had to climb in to get me out. I don't know why, he only had to call me and I would have come—if only it wasn't for that residual stubborn streak Papa says I have. To be fair, I may loiter a bit around the odd tree or shrub, but I have a lot of sniffing to do; I'm trying to learn the language, after all.

Back to the Treat Man. So, as a three-legged Greek street dog who was stuck in a van and spent many a long day and night travelling to this land of plenty, I ended up with a brother-from-another-mother who has just been on holiday to Greece of all places. Not only that, but he went with a lady friend who works at the English dog rescue centre that wouldn't let Mama and Papa have a dog because they already own a cat.

Hang on a minute, they do have a point there: I need to meet this woman, she will understand my dilemma. Anyway, my rock-and-roll bro brought back a bouzouki and a kalimba (Greek musical instruments, for the uninitiated), plus a bottle of Ouzo for Papa, which lost its lid in transport. This meant not-so-rock-and-roll bro had to walk through customs smelling like an alcoholic Bertie Bassett.

He came round to show Mama and Papa his photos, but as I have been there, done that I took the opportunity to take a nap in my boudoir. (The cat is teaching me French, plus it sounds posher than the converted cupboard under the stairs.)

The cat has finally had her revenge. If you remember, last week the creature from the dark side got a present from down under—a fluffy cat hat with ears from our lovely Auntie Tina. Mama got a photo of her wearing it, which made the evil beastie mad and me chuckle. This week my present arrived—a dog hoodie to keep me warm on your English summer nights.

It's kinda cool, and I suppose it's the thought that counts, but had Auntie Tina actually thought about it she may have considered what am I supposed to do with the one-too-many leg holes.

Admittedly, the cat and I are in the midst of a sibling rivalry. The cat is well jel (that means jealous, for those of you without the lingo). I know Mama loves me more than her—she must, she picks up my poop.

The feline fur bag has to dig her own hole in the garden to do her business, like she's on some sort of Bear Grylls-style camping trip. In the evenings, when Mama has settled down on the sofa, we like to play a little game called 'who can get the most attention'. We sit on either side of her and wait to see who gets stroked first.

Mama normally ends up on the floor so she can pet us both at the same time. Mama is too kind.

Speaking of siblings, my adoption papers arrived in the post. Turns out Mama and Papa are going to be my real Mama and Papa in just a few weeks after all. Bring it on.

Watch out pussy cat, this bad boy is here to stay.

 Editor's comment: Game on.

WEEK 7
Amber Retriever

Mama and Papa are starting to think I may have actually lost my leg due to some sort of undercover drug cartel bust. Pair of oddballs. The reason they suspect this is because Papa's Amber Leaf tobacco fell out of his pocket without him realising it during our walk in the park. My thieving instincts kicked in, and I picked up the packet of nicotine-flavoured drugs and returned it to Papa, who was very impressed with my skills. However, this later backfired when Papa decided to have a smoke and extinguished the disgusting roll up and flicked the end into the bushes. Big Brother got out of a car and approached Papa, informing him he was an undercover litter officer and issuing Papa an on the spot £50 fine. Personally I think I should have been given £50 for picking up litter in the first place. But hey, lesson learnt—Papa should know better. Mama may have said a lot worse.

In other news, my Nana sent me an article she cut out from the paper, 'The Daily Express', about a no-eared cat who had finally been adopted from some rescue centre across the pond in the USA. I am not sure why this is newsworthy, but since it is, I took it upon myself to contact 'The Daily Express' and explain my circumstances: I'm a two-eared three-legged dog adopted into a family with a four-legged no-eared cat from hell. I'm sure they'll be very interested, and I'm hoping to be offered my own column, 'Ask Ouzo', so I can be of assistance to other refugees who are rehoused to shared accommodation with a death beast.

Well, this was embarrassing, as it was indeed a bad hair day. I had a bath (against my will, mind you), and I smelt like a girl, but looked like a lion. It wasn't so bad; in fact, I was almost a little bit excited as the last time

I had a bath it was with the lovely Juliet before being handed over to Mama and Papa. I had a little hope that this time I was going to be moved on to the big posh house on the beach that I have my eye on. No such luck. I'm still in the semi overlooked by the charming old folk who still lean out their windows shouting Ouzo.

Having only three legs, Point 1: The trouble with having three legs means you can't trot, so instead you sort of bounce, which makes your tongue flap about a lot and smack you in the eye. Like every three seconds. Annoying.

Having only three legs, Point 2. Wherever we go everyone wants to know what happened to me, which is very kind of them. The trouble is Papa has to give Mama 'that look' to stop her from bigging it up and telling everyone 'it's a government secret, involves the SAS, bomb disposal, that sort of thing, can't be discussed any further, but you know, if you employ a colour blind dog he's gonna cut the wrong wire'. Barking (mad).

Life is good.

Editor's comment: Moron.

WEEK 8
Ouzothegit

So, whilst Papa was out and about grafting hard to pay for my adoption fee, Mama took me out for the first time all on her own. I had to get into her car. This was not good. Van . . . yup, no worries. Car . . . nope. Scared. It took her awhile to get me in—one large, scared dog with only three legs = tricky. But hey, I trusted her so I eventually, albeit warily, complied and squeezed myself into the little thing and off we headed to the beach. I was glad I did because I had fun, apart from one obnoxious dog who had the audacity to cock his leg on my head. How very rude. We were out for a long time, but I like being out and so I did what I always do; I loiter a little as we get nearer to the van, or in this case the car. I use the word loiter in its loosest term, because what I really do is just flop down and refuse to budge. And then this happened.

Mama: 'I am the strong, confident pack leader, he will follow me.'

Me: 'I can't be arsed.'

Mama: 'I will keep walking steadfastly and he will soon get up and follow me.'

Me: 'I can't be arsed.'

Mama: 'I will walk to the end of the path and no doubt I will soon hear the jingle jangle of his collar as he starts to follow.'

Me: 'I can't be arsed.'

Mama: 'I may be a fair distance now but I know he will soon get up and run towards me.'

Me: 'I can't be arsed. Hmmm . . . if I sneak through these bushes I could reach the dustbins on the other side.'

Mama: 'Ok, I am at the end of the path. I will use treats to tempt the way-ward creature to come when called. Hmmm . . . where has he gone?'

Me: 'I have discovered a maze of alleyways with dustbins and interesting smells; me likey.'

Mama: 'OMG, where has he gone?'

Me: 'Not really sure where I am, but I'll just follow my nose.'

Mama, running now, shouting: 'Ouzo, Ouzo.'

Random woman: 'Yes please.'

Mama: Death stare.

Me: 'Ah ha, now I know where I am, where the hell is Mama?'

Mama: Panicking, still running, still shouting, still giving evil eye to the not-so-hilarious random woman: 'OOOOOOOO-OUUUUUUUUUUZZZZZZZZOOOOOOOOOOOO.'

Me: 'I am bored waiting for the old girl, and it's tea time; best head home.'

Mama: Still panicking, still running, still shouting, still giving evil looks to the not-so-hilarious random woman who has now been joined by another random person also saying 'yes please' . . . . The phone rings, but it's a new number, and Mama considers not answering as she is anti-social but thinks better of it. 'Hello.'

Caller: 'Hi, it's Penny.'

Mama: Penny is her friend of almost 30 years; she considers saying, 'Good to hear from you, but now is not a good time.'

Penny: 'I've just found a three-legged dog'.

Mama: Instant relief: 'Where are you?'

Penny explains.

Mama is now running faster with still a long way to go. She's kinda' pleased she doesn't have to keep shouting Ouzo, whilst also regretting smoking so many fags. She finally makes it up to the road where she sees the amazing Penny and me.

Our reunion was short lived, one because Mama could barely breathe, and two, because Papa came past in his van, didn't spot us, and carried on to the beach in his quest to join us on our relaxing walk after a long day.

Mama thanked Penny profusely, and I was also very kind and let Penny stroke my head. Funny thing is, even though Penny and Mama hadn't seen each other for many years, Penny had been reading my blog so knew not to try and grab me as it would have scared me away.

The wonders of the modern day world wide web, eh?

Anyway, we had to get a move on as Papa had parked and was frogmarching along the beach trying to spot us. Mama did try to ring him, but he didn't have his phone, so there was no option but to run, yes, run, the whole way back, this time with Mama shouting 'Papa' at the top of her lungs. Parents, they're so embarrassing.

Another thing that happened this week is that I finally got to stay home alone! I don't know why Mama and Papa worried so much about leaving me on my own. It's awesome. I get to sleep without being disturbed—well, apart from the radio they insist on leaving on. We also have a chap called Postman who pops round and puts bits of paper through the door. I proper love him, it's kinda like someone popping a treat through the letter box and I get to chew on some junk mail, which, to be fair, is a nice distraction from The Archers.

But there's always a downside. When Mama comes home I hear her car and get excited. I can't wait to see her! Except That Darned Cat also hears Mama's car and finally slinks down the stairs from her penthouse suite, where she sits in the hallway blocking my access to Mama when she comes through the door. I think I've complained about this before, but I wanted you to know it's an ongoing problem. To make matters worse, the sly beast demands attention first, and she just wallows in her specialness whilst giving me smug 'she loves me most' looks.

However, this time I got the last laugh, because, after diligently chewing my way through double-glazing leaflets and Saga offers (a magazine with special offers for over 50s—Mama and Papa must be really old), I discovered a postcard from the vet saying Daisy was due her annual check-up.

This could be wishful thinking, but I was hoping for a needle in the neck, pill down the throat, and a thermometer in the rear end. Being the decent chap that I am, I waited patiently until the beast from the dark side had been given her stupid fuss and her stupid sweeties and then I gave Mama the very important letter from the vet. Mama said I was a very good boy!

Share the love man. Sweet.

Editor's comment: Utter nonsense.

WEEK 9
Feeling at Home

I'm starting to feel at home, although some of this indoor stuff is still a bit weird: light, for example. One minute you are just chilling on the rug at the end of a long day, and the next minute Papa gets up and flicks a switch on the wall and bam . . . total darkness. Another thing that is different for me is possessions; I've never had any before, but I've been seduced by your material world and I kinda' like it. I might be liking it a bit too much, as I got myself into trouble when I was given a toy I wasn't so keen on giving back. It turns out flashing your pearly whites at your new family is not the done thing. Mama declared a toy amnesty, and I had to hand everything over. Dull.

I'm just starting to get them back, and I gloriously ripped a stuffed chicken apart the other day; 'twas much silly fun. I also have a ball on a rope that we take out on walks. Mama got very excited the other day when she chucked it and I actually 'retrieved' it. I haven't done it since, and the only reason I did that time was because the silly mare threw it into the bushes by mistake, so I thought I would do the decent thing and bring it back for her. My bad. She whooped a lot then chucked it again and, yup, it ended up back in the bushes. I left her to it.

Apart from the occasional psycho moment, I am actually doing rather well in my new life. Yeah, I know I did a bit of a flit last week and lost Mama, but it all turned out ok in the end, didn't it? That's really all that matters. This week I was actually the best-behaved dog in the village. There I was, sniffing about and minding my own business, when two dogs with two different owners approached me from either side. Mama was way ahead (apparently having forgotten last week's incident), but keeping a beady eye on me. She doesn't like me going up to dogs on leads when I am loose as she says it's not fair, so she shouted at me to wait, and I did. Actually I was just glad for a bit of a lay down.

The trouble was that both dogs on leads started to drag their owners towards me, so Mama quickly threw out her magic word, and wham bam thank you mam I ran to her like a bat out of hell (although Mama described me as more of a blundering three-legged lummox). Rude.

What's this magic word business, you ask? The magic word is a new tool that Mama and Papa invented after my misdemeanour last week. I know many words now—and am pretty good at all of them—but there are times when it's easy to get a bit distracted. Hence the need for a magic word.

Years ago, when Mama and Papa rescued an imbecile chocolate Labrador, Cactus Jack, they needed a failsafe way of getting him to come back, so they chose a word that was not part of their daily conversation. They picked 'Buddy'. Every time Cactus Jack got fed they shouted the magic word. They made him work for it, even hiding down at the end of the garden, or at the back of the garage with his food bowl in hand shouting 'Buddy'. It turned out that Cactus Jack was a great foodie, so the very mention of the B word and he flew like the wind back to Mama or Papa as he knew this meant FOOD, his first love.

It worked beautifully until one day when it all got a bit weird. Mama was up on Highdown Hill when she heard a woman shouting 'Jack'. Cactus Jack decided this unknown woman was calling for him, so he ran up to her and jumped all over her. I did mention that he was an imbecile.

Anyway, Mama had to drag him away and apologised to the lady, explaining that his name was Jack. The lady understood and said that she was calling her dogs who had vanished chasing rabbits but she would call the other dog's name instead. As luck would have it, you guessed it, the other dog's name was 'Buddy'.

Mama had got some distance when she had to go all the way back to retrieve her Retriever, explaining to the rather perplexed woman that his other name was 'Buddy'. So. Awkward.

Back to the point. The crazy lady and the dodgy old man, aka Mama and Papa, had decided to train me with the same hocus pocusness. My magic word is 'Ela' which is Greek for 'come'. (Bizarrely whilst typing this page Mama put this word into google translate, and clicked on the little speaker icon. The google translate lady said 'Ela' and I came hopping in to the room, like magic!) So there you have it. If you ever happen to see a mad old lady holding one arm in the air shouting 'Ela' you will also see me coming pretty quickly too. Probably. No promises.

There's always more news: good news, bad news, and other news. The good news is Mama and Papa went to a book launch, and this book launch had a famous author but more importantly the book launch had a buffet. Mama brought home a doggie bag, and there were treats for me! Although, in order to get said treats, I had to run round the garden chasing Mama who was of course shouting 'Ela, Ela, Ela' holding one arm in the air waving my tasty morsels!

For the bad news, on a hot day I like to snooze in my little groove I have dug out for myself in the garden, because it reminds me of my past life. Except in Greece you don't get cats pooping in your very own personal area. The nerve! I am furious with the filthy beast.

In other evil cat news, That Darned Cat caught a mouse, Cecil the VIII, who moved into the cupboard under the sink and ate all the cat treats! Mama had to catch him herself in the end, and it turns out he was missing part of his tail, a fellow amputee. Mama considered keeping him, but instead she released him into the wilderness and told Cecil the VIII to stay out this time, for his own good.

Editor's comment: I am innocent.

WEEK 10
Summertime Feelin'

Mama has announced it's the summer holidays and she is done. . . but with what? She seems very happy about it. Once upon a time I was 'done', too, but I was not very happy about this. It would appear that Mama's 'done' means she gets to stay at home instead of going to work. This has thrown a wrench into my daily schedule. So this is how we now roll. . . .

Mrs. D (aka That Darned Cat): '6:30am, breakfast time. Mama is still asleep. I will wait patiently. 6:32am. Mama is still asleep, I will no longer wait patiently. Scratch at door until it opens, meow loudly, go under bed and climb into storage drawer. Roll around on plastic vacuum packed winter duvet, make very annoying scrunching sounds. Meow loudly. All efforts in vain. 6:37am. I am now in imminent danger of starving to death. Decisive action is required immediately if I am to survive this ordeal. 6:38am. Jump on bed, purr loudly as I approach my target. Reach target. Bite hard on the back of the neck. Target activated. With much moaning and groaning (what's she angry about?), fresh food is placed in my bowl. I sniff it and walk away. Summer holidays, not my problem.'

Me, the Good Dog, Ouzo: 'Day one of the summer holidays. Yay! Mama still smells strongly of Prosecco after her late night shenanigans, however, this means a lazy day of snuggling followed by a long and gentle stroll along the beach. Day two of the summer holidays. Uh oh. Mama is energised and quite frankly annoying. When Mama finally settles down to watch Escape to the Country and calls me over to sit with her, I take myself to my boudoir and lay in bed with my back to her. I am hoping these summer holidays don't last too long.'

Papa: 'Mama is home so I better look busy. Hmmm, let me think. Ah yes; 17 years ago Mama asked me to re-turf the lawn and finish the sunken seating area. I must get on with this straight away. Oh, and I have sourced the finest timber with a super duper price tag that I have to collect from Heathrow. Miles away. Perfect. Laterz Mama.'

Mama: 'SUMMER HOLIDAYS WHOOOP WHOOOOP! I get to stay home and chill, AND spend loads of quality time with Papa and the fur kids—they will all be so happy.'

As it turns out, Mama has plans. Apart from spending a lot of time talking to me in the voice of Foghorn Leghorn every time she stuffs her face with yet more chocolate, that is. 'I say, I say boy, these mini eggs are mine, I say mine, so you can take your greedy little eyes off them.' (See what I mean about annoying.) Unfortunately for me, she also has decided this so-called quality time is also training time. For the love of all things edible!

I know how to sit, wait, and how to respond instantly to my all-time favourite magic word, so you can now leave me alone, surely? No. On day two I was set the task of getting into the car, riding to Sainsburys, and then sitting in the car all alone—how very cruel!—for almost 7 minutes whilst she bought Papa's tea. Then, oh yes, the cruelty didn't end there, because we went to Pets at Home. I have never been in a shop before and I had no intention of entering this one.

But she-who-must-be-obeyed just stuck me on my leash and I had no choice but to walk in right next to her. Double cruel. At first I was afraid, petrified even, so I slunk to the floor and commando crawled next to Mama's side . . . until we reached the rabbit pen which was more like it. You have my interest now. Until Mama had to ruin it by saying I couldn't stop there and marched ever onward to the dog sweetie section.

I will admit, though, this wasn't a bad thing. I got to choose my own snacks, so I had a jolly good sniff and picked out a large bag of very expensive and beautifully wrapped goodies. Mama looked at the price tag and frogmarched me off yet again to the next aisle where she allowed me to choose from the reduced section. We got three bags of acceptably heavenly goodies and then headed for the checkout. Mama gave me a treat for being so good, but I spat it out in defiance and instead took one offered by the lovely checkout assistant. I hope that has taught her a lesson.

On Day 3 it became obvious that Mama needed to return to work as soon as possible. The plan for this day was seriously screwy, and I may need doggie therapy as a result. I may have mentioned that the creature from the dark side received news from the vet that she was due her annual check-up. Well Mama, in her infinite wisdom, decided to drive to the vets to make the appointment. Yup, you guessed it, she took me with her. To be fair, she did ring first to make sure no one else was there, so we rocked up with Mama once again attaching my lead and marching me into the building with no escape route in sight.

The place smelt funny yet familiar, and I started to wonder if maybe I would be getting my leg back—or better still my other parts which were removed without my consent. I had a good old sniff and then the nice lady came out and gave me treats. That part was acceptable. Mama asked her not to touch me, and she listened, but I still obliged her by taking the food. I'm no fool.

When she stopped feeding me I edged closer wearing my finest smile, which worked because she went and got me more treats. Apparently she owns a three-legged cat, and her friend has a no-eared, one-eyed cat. Bizarre. In the best news, Mama made an appointment for That Darned Cat to have her jabby stabby immunisations next week. Mama said I would be going back next week too, but only to have some more treats. I reckon I'm up for that.

On Day 4 we went to a tea party. Yup, we got an invite to a Greek Animal Rescue tea party reunion, which sounds great in theory, presuming there were treats to be had of course. But sad to say, it all went a little bit wrong. First off, I rolled in fox poop so I had to get another bath. (I don't know what Mama has against that brand of perfume, smells good to me.) Then Mama put my lead on and I refused to get up. Most unusual. When I did try to stand it hurt a lot. I had my chest on the floor and my butt in the air, I was panting heavily and retching, and I couldn't stop tinkling. What was happening to me?

Mama and Papa called the vet and explained the symptoms and they said 'bring him straight in'. On the way there Mama told Papa the vet had asked if I had a favourite toy I had been playing with, which Mama thought a bit strange. After we arrived at the vet's and I was examined, the question made a bit more sense: I was diagnosed with an erection. Awkward.

The vet explained that a dog's 'lipstick' has a bulbous end at the base so to speak, under the skin, which had 'enlarged' and therefore my 'lipstick' was unable to go back down. One good old-fashioned ice pack later, and Bob's your Uncle. . . . that means all back to normal, for the Americans in the audience.

Mama said she could never eat frozen peas again. And yes, I am castrated, thank you; apparently I'm just enthusiastic about life. If you must know, the condition is called Paraphimosis. And Mama needs to clear her google search history.

So, in other words, just another Saturday morning around here. We then upped and offed to the tea party. It was nice to meet more fellow rescued Greekies, but at the same time it was a little overwhelming. Mama thought she had done the wrong thing by bringing me, but considering how packed the little village hall was, I was rather well-behaved. I did say rather. I only vomited once from the car journey, but I ate it again and it was just like it never happened.

There were people and dogs everywhere . . . stepping over me, stroking me, and I only growled at three people. Since it's only been 10 weeks since I came to this freaking country, Mama says that's not too bad. I am getting there slowly, and grateful for the new chance at a 'normal' dog's life. Plus I believe lots of money was raised for those I left behind, so this makes me happy.

 Editor's comment: Weirdo.

WEEK 11
Grand Socialisation Scheme

Mama's still home, Papa's still busy in the garden, and I'm still being dragged around various areas of West Sussex in Mama's 'grand socialisation scheme'. For example, we went to Halfords, which is a car and bike accessory store. Why the hell did she take me there? Do I look like I need a bicycle or a pink fluffy steering wheel cover? I've also been to Pets at Home, where I didn't buy anything but I did have a sneaky freebie from the counter.

We also went to Pampered Pets, where they have the rabbit pen—amazing—but a rude look-don't-touch policy. Then there was a pub, where Mama said they also had a look-but-don't-touch policy in regards to a dropped packet of crisps, and finally to two cafes. Exhausting.

The first cafe was down by the river, and I got a bowl of water whilst the old folk got a full English breakfast. Harsh. However, by looking cute and appealing I managed to obtain a tidbit of my own, which is nothing you need to know about. The second cafe was a little more tricky. Mama, being Mama, dragged me into the village and sat on a bench so we could watch the world go by . . . the idea being to expose me to lots of people, lots of traffic, and lots of scary learning stuff.

The thing is, Mama does attract a certain kind of fellow oddball. Before long, one of those fellow oddballs called us over to join her at her table outside the cafe. Marvellous. She was proper nice, and proper nuts, too, my kinda' person. She also had a vast array of dog treats in her handbag, as you do when you are slightly eccentric. I was calm, cool, and collected and took up position in the doorway so everyone had to step over me. Why not? After all, I have been learning from that no-eared French cat creature. The kind lady gave me a treat, whilst Mama explained my fear of people. Now the nice lady was a tad mad, loud, and completely insane—much like my favourite person to stalk online, Donny Trump—yet she was more empathetic than psychopathic.

She told me all the best places to visit in the local vicinity, which was very nice of her except Mama had already dragged me around to all of them. She then tried to stroke my head, despite Mama's warning, and said what a good boy I was. Mama contradicted her by saying I was in fact a bad boy, as I was showing the nice lady my teeth. People! What can I say.

Oh, and a word of warning; when visiting Pets at Home, never purchase anything from the lower shelves, trust me on this one. I have a good sniffer, and I can tell you a lot of dogs have visited that shop—and a fair few have taken a whiz on the merchandise. Just sayin'.

We saw a load of ponies down the beach, a great gang of the hoofing huge monsters. Mama sat with me as we watched them go past, and it was all very cool and magical until she whispered in my ear 'Ouzo the Greek, see them there ponies; they are the pets I really want'. Charming. Well, I would rather have the Mama that lives in the posh house by the beach but hey, I got you and you got me. Deal.

Speaking of property, Mama and Papa have decided they want to live in a little house on the prairie, well, more sort of Gloucestershire. They have chosen the one they want, it only costs just under a million. It's kinda' uber groovy. The trouble is, Mama and Papa don't even have a million in Vietnamese Dong. Which is just as well, because it's not somewhere I particularly wish to relocate to, given the menu out there.

The place they want is a little two-bedroom folly set in two acres of idyllic woodland. Papa said they need to win the lottery, which will never happen, but Mama said they could afford it if only I learnt to do something useful like a one handed cartwheel. Then I'd be an overnight internet sensation and make loads of dollar, property in the bag, that sort of thing.

Mama has plans to buy Kunekune pigs and a flock of bad boy geese, whilst Papa would just keep busy loving the land as he does. Pigs and hard core geese don't do it for me . . . so no one-handed cartwheels will be learnt and any lottery tickets will be eaten. End of story.

Editor's comment: I would just like to point out that I once made it to the top 10 in Britain's Cleverest Cat competition.

Dear Lisa and Daisy

Thank you for entering our 'Felix presents...Britain's Cleverest Cat' competition!

You and Daisy successfully made it through to our top 10 cleverest cats in the UK!

It has been enormously difficult to choose the Britain's Cleverest Cat finalists from the many hundreds of amazingly talented cats and unfortunately, your cat Daisy didn't make it through to our final 3.

The good news is that you have won a pair of tickets to a live show of Britain's Got Talent!

I hate that cat. And what a naff prize—VIP tickets with backstage passes to Britain's Got Talent. Mama said she rocked up with her friend, and they ended up pilfering teabags from Union J's dressing room to take back to their cheap, and quite frankly, dodgy hotel room.

Anyway, if I won the lottery I would help my homeless comrades. There are so many of them. Sadly, one of the Greek rescue shelters, with over 150 dogs and cats in their care, is facing closure. These animals will be placed in municipal shelters, where life is grim, but they can't take them all so the rest will be dumped in the mountains to fend for themselves. Yes, this is factual.

All of us are only here for a very short time, once. At least as far as we know. So just be nice and look after all creatures great and small. (Apart from spiders.)

I know I'm one of the lucky ones. My life is now cushty.

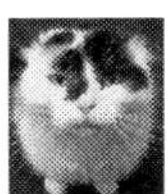

Editor's comment: Please just go now.

WEEK 12
A Bit of Baggage

It's been 12 weeks folks, but I am still nervous. I arrived with baggage, what can I say, and some of you still scare me silly to this day. Think about it . . . if everyone you met came up to you and started patting you on the head, you might just get a bit snarky about it too. Welcome to my world. Believe me, since starting my new life here in little old England I have met a lot of people, and the majority have been simply marvellous. But then there are the others.

1. The Annoying Person.

Yes there is always one annoying person. Let me introduce you to the 'know it all' of my local haunt.

Annoying Person: 'Darlings, what a wonderful dog.'

Mama and Papa: 'He is nervous of strangers please don't touch him.'

Annoying Person: 'Darlings, darlings, darlings, he will be fine with me, just you see.'

Mama and Papa: 'Please don't touch him.'

Annoying Person: 'Come on darling, you wouldn't growl at me.'

Me: Growl.

Annoying Person: Dog-whispering ego slightly dented . . . exits the scene.

2. The Mistake.

A truly lovely old gent. Out with his lady friends and a pack of mischievous little Chihuahuas. The old boy carried walking sticks, a fear of mine, but I sat calmly as he approached.

The Mistake: 'What a wonderful dog; here boy, come say hello.'

Mama: 'He is nervous of strangers, please don't touch him.'

The Mistake: 'Come along old fella, come and say hello.'

Me: Tense.

Mama: 'He really is nervous of strangers and best not touched.'

The Mistake: Bends forward, walking sticks akimbo, 'Come on old fella, come on'.

Me: 'Grrrrr'.

Mama: 'HE IS NERVOUS OF STRANGERS, PLEASE DO NOT TOUCH HIM.'

Lady friends: 'Sorry love, he is deaf.'

Mama: Feels bad, makes apologies, and takes me away.

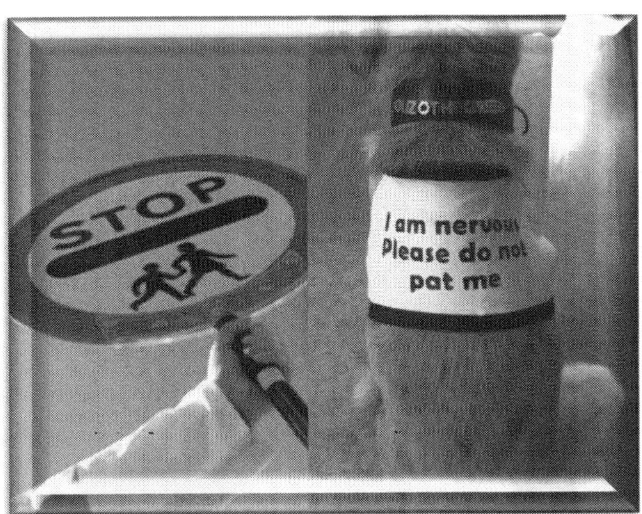

3. Cunning plan to stop it.

Now there is a ridiculous jacket that Mama makes me wear everywhere. Admittedly, I am starting to love Mama a little bit, so if she says I have to wear it, then so be it. Trouble is, I look like a lollipop lady.

As Mama is the wise one (allegedly), I now wear my fluorescent jacket when I am out and about. It kinda works, though, because when people read what it says, they usually back off. Usually.

4. The Pear Shaped.

Wore my snazzy little number down the beach. All was good in da hood. Until . . .

Pear Shaped: 'What a lovely dog; oh what does it say on his cute little jacket, hmmm, all dogs love me. Come on boy, come on.'

Me: Ignore him, he will go away.

Pear Shaped: 'So if I touch you, you'll growl at me? Well I have the answer to that.' Gets down on all fours and stares in my face. 'Come on boy, come on.'

Mama: Out loud says, 'Not a good idea.' Inwardly, she says something I'm not allowed to repeat.

Me: Run away, but only as far as Mama.

Mama was exasperated, but Mama and I went home and Mama drank a glass of wine; then she drank another one, and then she was ok.

Mama says some people need to learn manners, but that means I do too. I like a snuggle, a bit of scrummy love, fuss, and attention. Share the love man, it's what makes the world go round, right? But I'm a dog. I have no idea of your strange customs and conducts. For example, I like to lay at Mama's feet of an evening, airing my smalls (yes, my private parts). Mama tells me I have to behave in a more conservative English manner and cross my legs. Utter random nonsense.

We watched a bit of TV this week, a show called Animal Rescue Live. It made Mama happy to see animals being given a second chance, but it made Papa say 'no' a lot. In particular, he said 'no' to a fellow named Sausage the Parrot. This particular parrot was a nice-looking chap, but he had the language of a sewer rat. This made Mama laugh, but it made Papa say 'NO' even louder.

To be honest, Mama needs to stop flattering herself as the great animal rescuer. She is just an old bird after all. Speaking of birds . . . these seagulls? Annoying as hell. They shout non-stop at 3am every morning, fighting over who got the best Maccie D's out of a dustbin. They do my head in. Mama told me she once wrote to the local newspaper, tongue in cheek so to speak, asking if it was legal to shoot seagulls at 3am and how to go about gaining a gun licence. Big mistake! The local community went nuts, it even sparked a debate on the local radio too. Mama was the most-hated person in the village with everyone talking about how the seagulls were here first. Mama claims that actually the longest living sea bird was a Herring gull that could live for as long as 49 years. Mama is 51 so she says she disproved their point.

Dogs. I just like dogs. They are easier to understand despite their country of origin. Oh, and rabbits.

Editor's comment: Madness, my friend.

WEEK 13
A Second Chance

I am a quarter of the way through my 52-week diary, and my how things have changed.

I arrived with baggage. Yes, I am damaged goods. But I deserved a second chance—like every other dog, in my opinion at least. In my two years on this planet, I have been used, abused, run over, and left for dead. Harsh. My first love, Ermioni, rescued me and cared for me throughout my recovery after losing a leg. Not only that, but she then continued to share my story to help me find a forever home. Thank you Ermioni. I will never forget you.

We haven't really talked much about Juliet yet. The wonderful Juliet offered me a foster home with her, and so I was brought to England with a bunch of streetwise Spanish strays. Juliet and her team cared for me and the Spanish dogs, and cared for us well. Juliet introduced me to Mama and Papa. She was honest and explained my fear of men, which I reinforced by showing my teeth a few times; but hey, Mama and Papa took me anyway. And so our journey began. . . .

This might be a bit smarmy, but I admit that I am becoming fond of Mama and Papa, although I am still not fond of That Darned Cat. I am getting the hang of what is expected of me, and sometimes I partake in the art of following instructions. Sometimes I don't.

Because of this, Mama has decided to give me a middle name, that way I know when I'm in serious trouble. So if you ever hear someone shouting 'Ouzo the Enigma Greek', you can be pretty sure you'll come across a ranting old lady, Mama, clambering about in the flora and fauna and somewhere nearby there will be me, with my head stuck down a rabbit hole. Gotta love a bunny.

When I first arrived, I was terrified of so many things, yet also somewhat courageous, in my humble opinion, in trusting Mama and Papa. I have had my ups and downs. I have growled at visitors to our house, I have growled at that scary printing machine, a lot, yet I am happy for the parents to vacuum around me as I can't be bothered to move. I am a teenager in dog years after all. I point-blank refused to go anywhere near the van, shied away from traffic, and nearly had a coronary when we walked past the war memorial statue of a solider holding a gun above his head. I have had manic episodes of chewing my three remaining paws. I had no idea what to do with a dog bed (unless you count chewing it up, which I've learned is frowned upon).

Now, I get in the car and the van, sleep in my bed, no longer chew my paws, and will happily sit with strangers—I have even sniffed a few! Just don't touch me, still, because that is pushing it too far. I have been in shops, the vet's, and visited most of West Sussex. I will even allow the cat to sit with me when I'm relaxed, but I draw the line when she tries to get in my bed—it's the first one I've ever had and I'm not sharing. End of story.

I still have a few quirks, but who doesn't. For example, when we're out walking I sit down a lot. Mama and Papa used to think it was because I was tired, what with only having the three legs and all that. This is true to some extent, but I also sit down when I see people coming because I get nervous, so I wait until they've passed.

Papa is away at the moment, so Mama is getting up at the crack of dawn to take me out, which I think makes her a little grumpy. Papa usually walks me to the park each morning, but on one particular morning this week it was pouring rain, as it seems to do a lot in this country. Mama kindly drove me to the park, at 6:30am, so I could save my energy and have more of a romp when I got there. Mama is a funny fish.

I was grateful for the lift, but we arrived to find the parking lot locked; it was a tad early, so Mama parked up in a little car park reserved for village hall users only. We began our wander around the park in the delightful British weather, I did my business and all that jazz, and then took a seat. I carried on sitting whilst she threw a ball a couple of times, and then went and fetched it herself. Mama was quite wet by this point, and muttered something I didn't understand while declaring that we were going home.

About time too, my furry butt was getting damp. I walked back to the car, listening to Mama muttering something else that I did not understand as she discovered some idiot had put traffic cones all round her car. Yes, it was still virtually pre-dawn at this point, so whoever did that was a bit of a jerk. Turns out the cones were too heavy to move, so a muttering moist Mama just drove through them. Mama is cool.

Papa is pretty cool too, as it turns out he has managed to get us a week's free holiday in the beautiful Dorset, and we are leaving tomorrow. I can't wait!

 Editor's comment: Dorset you say; don't hurry home my friend.

WEEK 14
Our 'Free' Holiday

I went in the van with Papa to some place called Dorset while Mama drove behind, since she had no idea where we were going. Neither did I, and after awhile I started to grow concerned. 3 hours? Where was this place, the moon? Apparently Mama was also concerned. She fessed up to Papa later that as she followed us at a ridiculous speed (she was not impressed with his 'white van man' driving), she became so miffed that had there been an accident she would, in fact, have rescued me from the carnage first. Papa was not surprised.

When we finally arrived, we met the nice man and the lovely lady whose house we would be staying in. I was polite, of course. I later learned this was a free kinda holiday, as Papa was helping them fix up their new house. Then I met the electrician. I was not so polite.

He'll get over it. Everyone left then, so I relaxed and chilled out in what was truly a beautiful place. But then the fun stopped—a fierce-looking nine-lives devil (that's a cat, people) rocked up into the garden and stared at me through the window. I'd just escaped one . . . now there was another?

Papa was mainly working, which left Mama and me to our own devices. Mama has a thing for weirdness, so we popped off to see the Cerne Abbas Giant. Now the thing about driving in Dorset is that the roads are teeny weeny and very up-y, or very down-y, depending on your direction. There is a lot of stopping and starting involved. Unless you're Mama. As we weaved our way through little lanes we met a few oncoming fellow travelers. Most of which seemed to be mahoosive with the 'I'm bigger than you so I am not stopping' sort of attitude. Until they met Mama, whose answer was a little-known international hands-free signal, whilst shouting 'three-legged dog on board—we're coming through.'

Thankfully we made it to the big man in one piece, after a lot of cruising up and down the A35 with no map or sat nav and a lot of words I'm not allowed to use. We hopped out and took a look at the big fellow. Mama said she was half-impressed and half-disappointed, which was par for the course. I took one look and thought he needed urgent veterinary treatment. Been there, done that.

A coachload of younger people chugged up and they all piled out to take in the view. Now Mama was trying to get a photo or two, but the younger people all walked in front of her and held their phones up and grunted a bit. Mama complained that when she was their age she was lucky to have a day out at the neighbour's house, playing on their coveted Atari Tennis, with maybe a random butterscotch angel delight thrown into the mix. After a bit of tutting, Mama came up with a cunning plan and we trekked over to the other side of the little valley and made our way to the foot of the Cerne Man, where we loitered in peace.

As me and Mama sat at the foot of the big giant everyone on the other side of the valley continued to take their photos. Mama said there would now be loads of pictures circling social media of a giant chalk man with a big doodah, and when they zoomed in there would be a little old lady and a three-legged dog sitting at the chalk man's feet. Sorted.

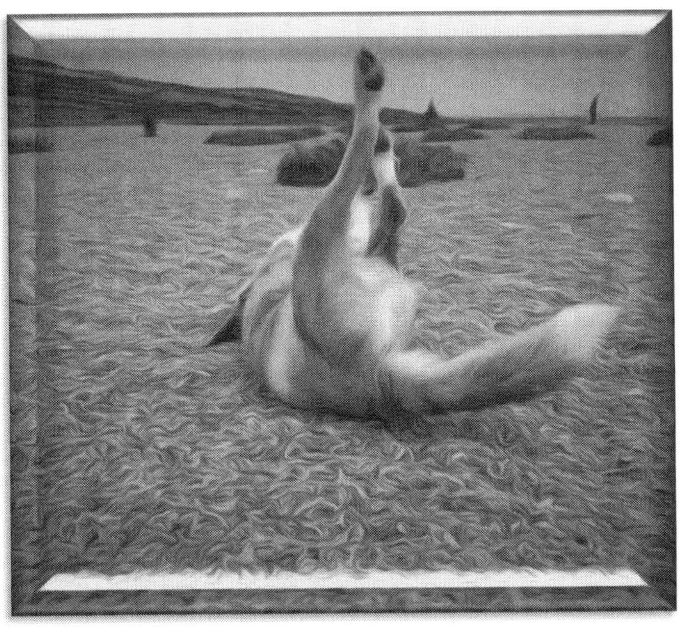

Dorset beaches were lush. In general, I am not a beach fan. At least not in my newfound home town: cold, seaweed, rocks, that sort of thing. But Dorset beaches were pretty as a picture, and the cliff top coastal paths were even better. Turns out I have a bit of a thing for living on the edge, and even though there were warning signs to stay away from the eroded cliff edges, I was still drawn to them. Mama had a tiny coronary every time I raised a leg to take a whiz. A two-legged dog balancing on the top of a cliff is a bit much for her heart, apparently. We saw a snake, Mama was soooo excited, and turns out it was an adder. She chatted to a local dude and discovered the place was full of them. And so our daily cliff top walking got a little more precarious. Awesome.

Chilling . . . it needed to be done; I was on holiday after all. Papa brought home some literature on the National Trust, such as where to visit, what to do, and all that jazz in the local area. That was too much information; I wanted to relax, so I ate it.

Mama and Papa celebrated their 17th wedding anniversary while we were there! We went out to the pub to celebrate. Papa booked a table for two adults and a three-legged dog. The manager laughed. And then we arrived, and he realized we weren't joking. The pub was called 'The Three Horseshoes', which was a little ironic, I think. The dinner was amazing. I sat at the table (on my best behaviour, of course) and after Mama and Papa had finished eating I got some leftovers, including rhubarb custard of all things. Mama scraped it out of her bowl and let me lick her fingers.

Mama had had two glasses of wine by then, so all manners were forgotten. She then had another glass and things really kicked off. She met a hilarious woman who claimed she was the owner of the most badly behaved dog in the world.

In fact, he was so bad he was not even allowed inside the pub. Of course Mama had to go and meet him then. I tagged along and was introduced to this bad boy. Digby. He was a proper fun chap, a Corgi, who was turned down by the Royal family for inappropriate behaviour—something to do with his lipstick. So we sat on the outside bench just shooting the breeze. Good times.

Even though we were on our 'free' vacation, we still had a routine. Every morning Mama dragged me up a hill, and halfway up there was a rest point. I found a marvellous place to chill, just inside the gateway. I even took to digging it a bit, just to making it more comfy and seem more like home. You can take the dog out of Greece, but you can't take Greece out of the dog. I loved it. After my five minutes of respite, I was back to being full of holiday beans and made Mama run down the hill—the very steep hill, really, really fast. Karma, Mama dearest. Hey, she survived.

We also visited the Melplash Show. It was huge! There were people everywhere, plus stalls, dogs, sheep, ponies, alpacas, pigs . . . I even rolled in pig poop, it was the best thing ever. I've never been somewhere so packed. People were brushing past me, touching me, in pushchairs, using electric wheelchairs—all my biggest fears. I'm proud to say I met them, dealt with them. Done. Except for that one freaky moment with a balloon, I was actually perfect.

Mama, on the other hand, wasn't. The local Wessex radio station were there, and Mama decided I had to have a mention. I am special, apparently. She spent a long time chatting to a very interesting chap, Mama liked him. However, she had to wait for his boss to request a mention on the Dorset airwaves. She got there in the end. The boss was not so nice, and just made a hmmph noise and went back to his important text messages.

Mama made a mental note to delete the Wessex numpty from the car radio as soon as she turned on the ignition on our return journey. When we finally left, as promised Mama revved up the little old car and boom, Wessex radio gone. Oh, hang on, they're playing an 80's classic, Bananarama, Venus. Mama said this was a tune, and sung all the way back to our holiday home. I am not sure what sort of tune it was but Mama certainly was not the best part of it. I concentrated on balancing on three legs during the up-y-down-y not stopping journey, and slightly envied the cat and her no-eared advantage.

I kinda liked the big house in the country, but do you know what I like more? Home. I came home. And it was my home.

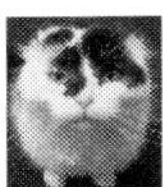

Editor's comment: I forgot the party. Welcome home, mutt boy.

WEEK 15
A New Job

The holidays are over, and Mama has a new job so has had to go back to work earlier than planned. The trouble, is Papa is still down in Dorset working on the big house. And it's not easy getting a dog sitter for a dog that is scared of everyone apart from Mama and Papa. A bit of a conundrum. Mama said after spending many a long hour during Year 6 maths working out how to divide 46 melons, two chocolate cakes, and a sack of potatoes between 13 people—one of whom was a vegan plus two with nut allergies—travelling at 56mph and needing to eat before they reached their final destination in the Outer Hebrides, that we didn't really have a problem at all. (The answer is easy by the way; the train cancelled so the 13 people took a bus, then a plane, and during the flight they chose their own food from the nut-free and vegan-friendly British Airways menu).

Now my new daily routine starts at the crack of sparrows so to speak; it's a bit too early even for me, and definitely way too early to deal with the car-parking jobsworth. Yep, him again, the one who insists on the no-parking rule in the vast empty spaces in the car park reserved for village hall users only, even though the second car park, the one for recreational park users, is not unlocked until 8am.

We got blocked in again. Mama persisted in her unlawful car parking throughout the week, but just parked at a more jaunty angle to make it a bit more fun when we vacated the randomly located traffic cones. On Friday, as we were approaching the car, we met the traffic-cone obsessed chap in person. And he said, I kid you not . . . 'Oh Ouzo, it's your car, well that's ok then'. I kid you not. He carried on talking to me and appeared to know all about me; turns out I'm some sort of urban legend at my local park? Who knew. He never said a word to Mama, didn't even look at her; but I did, and she was just standing there with her mouth open, yet no words came out. A first.

With Mama at work, I have enjoyed my 'me time'. I get to snooze or gnaw my chewie or even play with my peanut-butter-filled big rubber toy thingamajig. Mama feels guilty leaving me, but it's not for that long and there's no need to worry.

There was one strange thing that happened, though. Mama came home to what can only be described as a scene from 'Tales of the Unexpected'. A random explosion had occurred right in our sitting room! My little old bed had somehow flown out of my boudoir and . . . BANG! Exploded. Just like that. No idea how it happened. Scared me half to death, so it did. Mama asked me to explain EXACTLY what had taken place. So I did just that by replicating my surprised/shocked doggie face. I'm not sure she fell for it, but I'm sticking to my story.

Papa's in the doghouse. Without him there, it was a week of waking up before the dawn chorus, which is not actually a bunch of birds singing 'oh what a beautiful morning', but in fact a small minority of birds squawking and complaining. Well, that's what Mama told me, at least. Back to the point. All the early starts, with work, walks, and daily life add up to both Mama and me being a bit tired and missing Papa.

But hey, he was coming home on Friday! Yay. Much excitement all around. Papa was due home at 7pm, so Mama rushed home from work, dealt with the sitting-room catastrophe and cleaned the house, prepared a scrummy tea, and then took me out to my favourite bit of beach. All was well in the world. Until Papa called and said something about having dinner up at the big house with the family, so he would not be back until around 10pm.

We were a tad bit deflated, to say the least. So Mama poured some wine—after she hid Papa's craft beers—as there are always consequences to incorrect decisions in life.

During glass one, we googled shoes. It's the thing to do apparently. Mama said it was a good job I didn't require any, as finding a trio of shoes could prove tricky. Shoes for Mama were purchased, though, and oh, a rather snazzy cable-knit jumper found its way into the online shopping cart, too. How'd that get there?

During glass two, it was time to enter the spoof John Lewis Christmas advert competition. Mama said I couldn't jump on a trampoline because it would be a potential health and safety hazard, plus it was old news, so instead we went for a more topical theme; a transgender Donny T plus me and That Darned Cat.

Glass three turned out to be two too many. Mama started looking at online Dog Modeling agencies, and tried to persuade me that a three-legged dog hopping up to a vast banquet table and stealing a loaf of bread in the background of a Poldark episode would make it much more fun. I did my puppy-dog-eyed face and Mama thought better of it.

Cup of tea. Mama manned up and we sat together on the rug watching Celebrity Master Chef and holding hands. I love you Mama.

Papa is now home and forgiven. All is once again well with the world.

 Editor's comment: Reckless vandal.

WEEK 16
Down in Deepest Dorset

All is not good in the hood. Papa is STILL working down in deepest Dorset and I am still being left ALL ALONE for a few hours a day whilst Mama goes to work. This is not the forever home I had hoped for. My dear friend Nicholas suggested leaving me with a bit of smooth Maria Callas playing in the background; but no, Mama just abandons me to Radio 4, which is getting on my nerves. Quite frankly I do not care for your 'thought of the day', your 'shipping forecast', or your 'woman's hour'. I am a dog. A Greek street dog. Give me some music, man, and chuck an olive in my direction. Blah.

Unbelievable. That cat, that no-eared, four-legged evil eyesore—have I mentioned I dislike her? Mama came home from work, and all was lovey dovey; there was lots of fuss and attention, yum yum, happy days, and then it happened . . . IT swiped my nose with its super-sharp b*tch slappers. OUCH. I admit that I proper yelped man, scared me half to death. I did nothing and then WHAM. There was almost blood and everything.

I still do not like your English beach, and I don't mind mentioning it again. It's cold, it's smelly, it's covered in rocks. Where's the fun part? We had a little evening stroll out, along the greensward at the top of the beach, where the bunny rabbits live. Now that I like. The tide was way out, and Mama said it was beautiful, but I think Mama was not wearing her glasses. Mama decided we would walk back along the sand, even though it was not my cup of tea. I obliged. She made me run, a lot, it was getting late, she mentioned something about wine.

6:30am comes way too early. Ugh. I was up yet again in the middle of the night and off to the park. My foot hurt. I didn't make a fuss because I am a good boy, but thank God the parking cone man now lets us park in the car park. I hopped out, hopped a little bit more and then . . . OW. I just couldn't hop anymore. Mama was at a bit of a loss.

What do you do with a three-legged dog who has voluntarily collapsed in the middle of a park and is way too heavy to pick up? Mama is small. We kinda loitered for awhile listening to the birds screaming whilst Mama weighed the pros and cons of returning to the car and driving across a football field to rescue me. Mama had done a similar deed before and it didn't end well—plus parking cone man would be furious.

And then an angel appeared. A wonderful woman who was out for an innocent early morning stroll with her own little ginger dog. Mama accosted her, explaining that we were in dire need of help, and would she mind awfully picking up a dog that was somewhat likely to bite her and help carry the poor chap back to the car? The angel had no choice. Mama asked her to grab my rear end whilst she took the potential bitey bitey end and together they carried little old me back to the car. I was most grateful. I even let the lovely angel stroke me once we reached our destination. Thank you angel lady. xxoo.

Now I was down to two legs. So after travelling for many a day and night with my Spanish friends, in a van, over land and sea, I end up in a little three-bed semi with a sore nose and just the two useable legs. Hmmm. Time for the vet's office again. I have been already on a few visits. I can't say that I mind the place that much. They have nice nurses, a few treats on offer, plus they were nice to me on that other occasion which we don't talk about—a tad bit awkward.

Mama asked for a muzzle; how dare she, as if I would bite such kind people. But then I had to have my foot shaved, and the last time that happened I woke up with a missing limb. I admit I was scared. It turned out I had only scuffed a pad, so the world wouldn't end after all. I had an injection of painkillers, which was nice, and then they removed the muzzle and the nice vet gave me a stroke—not in the medical terminology kinda way, just the touchy-feely kinda way. I was so good and Mama felt so bad.

And then I got a shoe! And Mama got the bill!

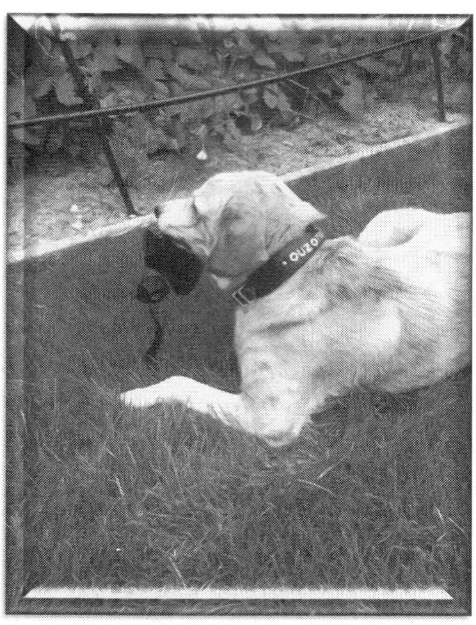

We travelled back home, a long 10-minute drive. I usually sit nicely in the foot well of the car, doing a bit of balancing whilst Mama drives in a careful fashion shouting at other drivers, but this time it was different. I climbed onto the seat, just my front end, and howled the whole way home, whilst wearing a shoe, a neopad Velcro shoe. Once we got home Mama packed up her recently-purchased new shoes, and the rather snazzy cable knit jumper, and sent them back to where they had come from. Apparently we could only afford the one shoe now. And then I was grounded.

Thank God for modern technology. I was housebound, virtually bed-bound, had just the two legs, and I was still recovering from a sore nose after the cat attack. So I had a bit of a catch up with my fellow four-legged friends on social media.

Mama felt guilty. It was Mama after all who insisted we gallop home along the beach which is where I did the damage, so Mama bought me a new bed. I ate the last one (or it exploded, one of the two). It is a big, fluffy, soft, enormous thing. She said it cost a fortune even though it was on sale. I have made my point by refusing to go anywhere near it. Guilt Mama, feel it deep.

After a few days of bed rest without actually getting on the new bed, I could suddenly walk on three legs again. What a relief. Mama said I could go out as long as I wore my Ouzo-Jimmy Choo shoe.

So I howled like a demon and refused to move. Mama removed the Ouzo-Jimmy Choo shoe and BAM, I was off like a greyhound in a stadium.

Life is good once more.

Editor's comment: Dream on tiger.

WEEK 17
Good Old British Postman

I do like a bit of good old-fashioned British post in the morning. Whilst sitting at home, all alone, having some me time, listening to Radio 4 and keeping up to date with current affairs, I also keep an ear out for he-who-I-call Postman. He's a decent chap, I expect; he chucks a load of stuff through the letter box every day, which I appreciate. I assume he realises my predicament, and likes to contribute some daily reading material. My sister-from-another-mister had some packages delivered this week—did you know that Mac make-up is very expensive? I could tell it was quality by how good it tasted. I left the lipstick untouched. . . well, you know, it just didn't seem right. 'Nuf said.

In other news, Papa knows this chap who runs some sort of musical production company, and it so happens they are putting on a performance of Oliver. The pianist was overjoyed as her little dog was going to play the part of Bulls-eye. Or so she thought. The man in charge announced there was in fact another dog up for the part—a three-legged Greek immigrant called Ouzo. It was up to the cast to take a vote to decide which dog should play the role, and guess who got a unanimous decision? That'd be me. One cast member had been thinking of resigning, but after hearing about my star qualities a mind was quickly changed under the conditions that backstage dog handler was in the cards.

I rather fancied a bit of Hollywood Ouzo the Greek walk of fame, but then again I'm not really an all-singing, all-dancing sort of three-legged dog, so I regretfully declined.

Mama claimed that was all part of me getting way too big for my boot.

The thing is, you teach your dog something new every day, even if you don't realise it. I had learnt, after my sore paw experience, that if I didn't want to walk I didn't have to. I was getting mighty bored of getting up at the crack of sparrows, driving to our now-reserved illegal parking space, and hopping around the park. So I chose to lay down instead. I also chose to have selective hearing.

Apparently these traits are quiet annoying for one's 'mistress' when standing in the freezing cold rain at 6:30am in the middle of a football pitch. Mama tried attaching my lead, but nope, I wasn't going anywhere and you can't exactly drag a three-legged dog across a field. I know my rights, I had read the RSPCA leaflet that my friend Postman had delivered to my door. I watched Mama stomp back to the car, way over in the distance, and when she got there I decided I would indeed get up and follow her because I did want breakfast after all.

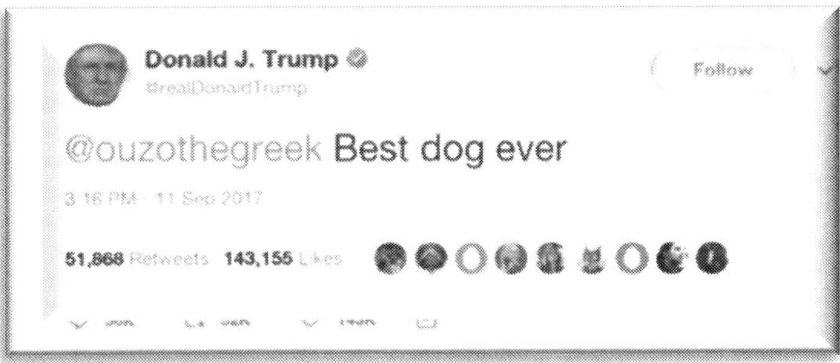

Mama decided I was obviously feeling at home in my new forever home and was starting to push my luck, so a new regimen would be enforced. Don't know why, my mate Donny T thinks I am the bee's knees and who could not agree with his perfectly sane and rational opinions? Fake news . . . never.

We now go out at 7am for a 15-minute stroll round the streets and the local alleyways, on the lead at all times, with no opportunity to lay down. Harsh? Not. I'm a street dog, lest she forget. I love the smell of roadkill in the morning, and last night's kebab litter is right up my alley thank you very much. I still have my evening fun off the lead chasing rabbits, plus a bit of chasing other dogs thrown into the mix. I seem to be remembering my manners as well as my name when Mama calls. Mama said that should

I chose to wear my boot again, which I will not, it would probably fit once more.

Good news! Papa is coming home next week, and I can't wait as I am not the only one getting a little carried away with myself.

Mama spent Saturday night drinking wine and chatting with my lovely foster mama Juliet about all the dogs that could be a new brother or sister for me. Juliet is amazing and is saving dogs from a life of misery from the killing stations in Spain. There are some truly heart-breaking stories, and Juliet is my new heroine.

Papa needs to get home quick before we have 101 Spanish mutts in residence, hogging all the attention. Oh, and all this drinking and planning was going on whilst a maniac was on the loose in my area! There were armed police, helicopters, etc., as some chap had gone bonkers and was roaming around Rustington with a machete. This guy ended up on the roof of an industrial building, but the trouble was he wasn't wearing a shirt, so when it got cold he had to come down to get a jacket. You can't make this stuff up. Barking mad. Come home, Papa.

 Editor's comment: 101 Spanish mutts? Over my dead body, sunshine.

WEEKS 18-19
Whatever, I'm a Dog

We had a bit of a blip, as you do, and all was no longer good in the hood. That kind of 'it can't get any worse' and then it does sorta thing. I had no idea what to do with a crying old lady before, but I do now. I just sit in front of her and let her hug me, and then I lean in on my missing leg side and very slowly collapse in a heap bringing the old girl down with me. Works a treat—Mama starts to feel sorry for me instead of herself.

Tonight we were the only odd couple on the beach; neither sight nor sound of man or beast, or even a seagull thankfully. Just us. And so we had some time to reflect. Did you know that a three-legged dog who has seen the harsher side of life yet keeps on rollin' does wonders for a miserable old woman? Mama says I am a belligerent, anti-social, unpredictable oddball, so in other words we are the perfect match. And yet I was still loveable. Go figure.

Mama cheered up after our talk, and then we came home. There was water dripping from the ceiling; can't say I was too bothered, I just wanted my tea, but Mama was not impressed. She did all the right things—turned the water off at the mains, drained the hot water tank, and other sort of plumbing type things. Mama did try to ring Papa, but there is no signal in deepest Dorset unless one is in the pub or Waitrose, neither of which we can afford. But hey, for now at least we are only on amber alert for potential ceiling collapse. Mama said she would be the one at work tomorrow who smelt a bit iffy, as well as being a tad thirsty. Hey ho.

As we are now dry Mama said she had no choice but to drink a glass of wine, even though it's only Monday. She's currently sipping something not so long ago she said she would never drink again, all whilst hanging out the back door puffing on a cigarette and telling the in-coming daddy long legs to 'think again'. (Apparently one of them chose to take its own life and dived bombed into the jug of water Mama had on standby.) Wise choice.

Papa returns home tomorrow. Praise the Lord.

Editor's comment: The jug of water is still sitting next to my food bowl, unacceptable.

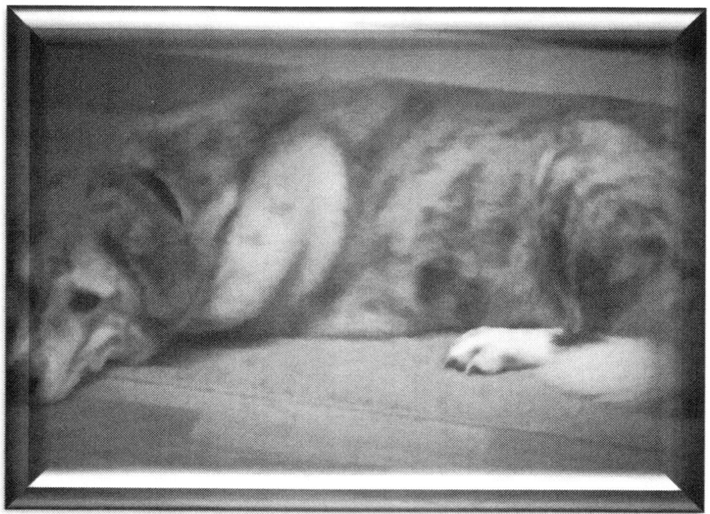

WEEK 20
Plumbing Disaster Averted

Papa came home and averted the plumbing disaster. Well, almost. The poor old boy had driven all the way back from the big house in deepest, darkest Dorset, picked up a new hot water tank enroute, and then fitted it, brass knobs, knockers and all. It was somewhat of a long day for the old chap and once all was declared up and running, it started running, again. Water, that is. Lots of it. Out the ceiling, down the wall, and then it began dripping out of the fuse box. Marvellous. We were back to draining the system once more—doors wide open, hosepipes, drainpipes, you name it. It was a tad late in the day by this point and also freakin' freezing, but Mama said not to worry as when the electricity blew up we would be toastie once more. Poor old Papa. But for one night at least we were all home together, even the beast from the dark side, sadly.

Papa has now returned to the big house and his chores in Dorset, which include more plumbing. Good luck with that.

Me and Mama are back to our early morning stints of walking the streets so I can splash my boots before being left all alone whilst the old girl goes out to work. I rather like it; I found a baguette down the alleyway one morning, as you do, but Mama told me to leave it. Believe it or not, being the good chap that I am, I left it.

It got grimmer after this. The next day I found a dead rabbit and the day after that a dead magpie. Mama thinks I should be an assistance dog to the Grim Reaper. She also still refers to me as The Enigma, as every time I find something I am not allowed to have I instantly obey commands to leave it. A bit odd for a street dog. However, when I am having one of my sit downs and Mama says to come I don't bother. I like to keep her guessing.

I got me a new bestie, Jazz, a young mutt who is tons of fun. Jazz makes both me and Mama happy, as I get a bit of a romp and I no longer keep Mama waiting while I have a bit of a sit.

There has also been a curious incident with the rabbits down the beach, as in they are no longer there. I used to enjoy my rabbit chasing around the beach huts, but the little blighters have gone AWOL. Haven't seen one in like forever. Mama said maybe they had all caught a mysterious virus that had previously been contained to Greece. Then Mama and I exchanged glances whilst sitting next to the aforementioned beach huts, and both silently vowed never to mention this again. Then, I got up and casually strolled away. Mama even whistled a bit as she also casually wandered off. Nothing more to see here.

Seeing as there are no longer any rabbits for me to chase, Mama thought she would cheer my up by taking me shopping at the local pet store where she let me chose my own treat. I went XXXL and selected the biggest thing in the shop, a buffalo horn. Mama had a bit of trouble getting the sticky label off and said in her 51 years on this planet she had never had to wash a buffalo horn before. She also said she never had to spend every evening vacuuming bits of such things out of the rug, but such is life since a three-legged Greek street dog moved in.

All in all it's not a bad life for a hound from the pound.

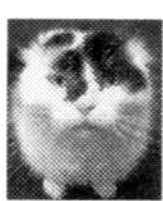

Editor's comment: I demand a unicorn horn.

WEEK 21
Heroes, Just for One Day

I am very quiet in the house; I don't bark at Postman, that sort of thing. Why would I? He brings me daily gifts. That is, until Friday night when I went a bit bat stuff crazy. Mama had to come downstairs and tell me in no uncertain terms to shut the hell up. Saturday I was still on edge, growling at the slightest sound, and went mental when someone knocked on the door. Mama told Papa of this new development when she spoke to him on the phone that evening, and they decided to add it to the list of oddness when the behaviourist comes for a visit.

Then came Saturday night. At 12:59am, Mama and I were awoken by a loud thud on the front door. She finally realized maybe I'm not bat stuff crazy, more like a German Shepherd Police attack dog. Proper fierce. Mama got dressed and came downstairs, and this time she didn't tell me to shut up. Mama saw a figure pass by the floor to ceiling window, followed by another. Then the outside lights turned off again, and I reverted to friendly house pet.

Now, many may say it was probably just a fox. However, unless this particular fox was 6-ft tall and was accompanied by a 5-ft-8 badger, I'm not so sure. Mama wanted to open the door and go outside like they do in the movies, but then thought better of it, since they usually die after that. We sat for a bit until Mama decided there wasn't much to be done about it so she went back to bed, fully dressed, with all the lights on. Then she got a bit hot and thought with me in the house she was in fact perfectly safe, so lights went off and the clothes came off and it was back to sleep—well, that is, until the cat came in and started shooting her mouth off.

Mama said the cat was the only witness as she had been outside, but since she was a cat, a French one at that, Mama couldn't understand a word she was meowing so could she kindly shut it.

The cat then bit Mama on the arm. When Mama came down in the morning I was still asleep by the front door where I had slept all night, just to be sure.

The next morning, as we hopped down the local alleyway with Mama picking up broken beer bottles so I didn't cut my feet (been there/done that), Mama told me I was her hero. She also said there was nothing in our house worth stealing, the last burglars should have spread the word on that. But last time they didn't have me in the house. Actually, I was the only thing worth stealing, but somehow Mama thinks no one would ever manage that unless they had a Taser and full body armour at least.

We were so busy talking about how I'd saved Mama's world, that we didn't notice the two sweet old ladies coming down the alleyway on their way to church. One tried to stroke me as she passed, and I growled at her. Mama said 'Sorry 'bout that', and the little old lady said she would pray for me.

As they wandered off Mama eyed them up and down muttering something about it's always the quiet ones but 6 ft and 5-ft-8 they weren't.

No one is going to steal my Mama.

Prior to this, we had enjoyed a relaxing evening, and I had even managed to get on Mama's lap before That Darned Cat stuck her nose into my business, like always.

In other news, Mama has been a bit of a numpty. She was bored, so she started surfing the net to find me a brother or sister—someone looking for a home who is confident with people and therefore will help me overcome my fears. Although Mama did make sure to remind me I was allowed to be vicious to anyone poking about the house in the middle of the night.

The numptiness occurred when Mama came across the cute little Lisa, looking for her forever home on the Broken Biscuits facebook page. The thing is, Mama had closed her facebook account so had to send them a message using the cat's facebook page, which in hindsight was probably not the best thing to do, and also probably why she has not heard back. A cat enquiring about adopting a dog is not really the norm.

However, as the old man and his dog said to me in the park this week, everyone needs a friend.

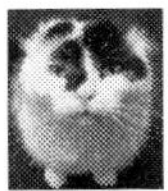
Editor's comment: Le Meow.

WEEK 22
My Family

Let's face it. They're an embarrassment. I don't know how to say it nicely. Last Saturday we had the burglar/badger incident, at 12:59am as someone was trying to gain access to our humble abode. This week Mama hears from a certain family member who rang up to say 'Sorry. It's a bit late to say sorry, but sorry anyway.' What? Turns out they had been in the local vicinity drinking alcoholic beverages until late into the night, last Saturday night to be precise. When they were walking home they got a bit caught short so to speak and had a beer induced 'Ah ha' moment when they passed the end of our street. They then thought it would be a good idea to use their key and quickly nip in to use the facilities, until they got one leg in the door and felt the wrath of a three-legged dog who was not expecting a late night visitor to our downstairs toilet. Hence their rapid exit. In their drunken haze they loitered for a while feeling guilty as they had woken up the entire neighbourhood, but decided they couldn't really try to come back in to explain for fear of losing a leg, so just wandered merrily off back to their own place a few miles down the road. Numpty. Mama said that it was just as well she had me because if she had been woken up whilst home alone and heard the toilet flushing she would have completely freaked. Worse still, what if she had slept through and then got up the next morning to find a random floater lurking under the lid? Shudder.

Mama is a fine one to talk, however, because she is also an embarrassment. As we pulled up at Highdown Hill one evening to go for a stroll, Mama spotted a three-legged dog in the car park. She leapt out the car, (rudely leaving me in said car), and ran over to the woman shrieking hysterically 'Oh my God, can I take a photo of your dog with my dog who also has three legs?' This poor stranger looked a tad scared of my Mama, who is in need of a bit of a haircut, and this wind doesn't help matters. Mama rushed back to get me out of the car for the photo shoot whilst the other three-legged dog was quickly whisked up and put safely back in their car before being driven away at speed. Mama was most disappointed. I was not. Cue doggie embarrassment.

As it happens, though, I must admit I am also a bit of a family embarrassment. Mama met a neighbour who said I had been barking whilst Mama was out, and that it really wasn't fair to leave me home alone—especially as I only have three legs. Mama agreed and said it was never the plan, regardless of how many legs I have, but things had gone a bit pear shaped with Papa's work at the big house. She then explained that he would be home this week, and should he need to return for a week or so he would be taking me with him.

Mama then went out, taking me with her obviously, and we bought some flowers as a peace offering for our other neighbours (the ones who are actually next door to us), and we went and said sorry. They said I wasn't that bad; in fact, I'm a very good guard dog as I only bark when someone comes down our drive. Trouble is, there are only four little houses on our road—and we all share the one drive—so there may well be a bit of coming and going. But they liked the flowers anyway, and we sat and listened to their dog yap whilst they went out shopping.

We did have another bit of an issue this week. I like my routine—walk, breakfast, chill out, bark at the neighbours whilst Mama is out, another walk, tea, and then an evening snuggle with Mama. One such evening we were having a lovely snuggle, coz I've decided I proper love Mama, when I got up for a bit of a stretch. Mama was on her laptop at the time, and as I went for a hop my leg got caught in the laptop wire and tripped me up. I was really scared, thought Mama had tried to hurt me, and wouldn't go anywhere near her.

It has only been five months of this indoor living luxury, so I am still settling in and I still get scared as life hasn't always been so easy. However, we soon made up and I am now back to snoozing on Mama of an evening, and Mama no longer has her laptop anywhere near me. Risk assessed and hazard free.

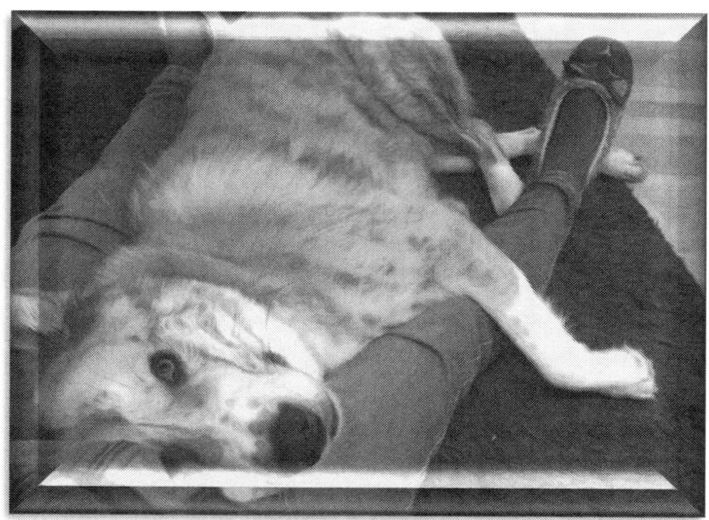

In other news, my-brother-from-another-mother had a birthday this week, and a birthday card arrived through the post for him at our house. I ate it. Oh, and the contents, of course . . . tasted minty!

Life has its ups and downs, but Mama says, and I agree, I'm basically headed in the right direction. We think.

Editor's comment: I think not. And Happy birthday, bro.

WEEK 23
Papa Comes Home

Papa came home and my life was complete once more. Until we both fell asleep and started snoring in perfect boy-bonding harmony and Mama had to wake us up as she was trying to watch The Undateables. Mama said we should in fact be on the show as a perfect example of a blissful match. Poor exhausted Papa went up to bed so he could sleep undisturbed, and Mama confessed to me that she actually finds it endearing listening to my gentle snores of contentment. The trouble is, when Papa snores Mama's mind wanders off to the possibilities of what one can achieve with a shovel. Hey, she loves us both big time and we love her too. Sleep easy Papa.

We made the most of Papa's week at home. We went out for breakfast, which I'd dearly missed, and we went to the forest, so many smells to be sniffed. We also met a nice family who were playing on a tree rope, and Mama and Papa reminisced about the time when their children were young and they did similar things, until the smallest child started to sing a little known Ian Jury song that has unfortunate lyrics about a wee lass called Ada. It was a tad awkward, so we wandered off rapidly. As rapidly as you can with three legs that is.

We also had afternoon tea down the beach. There we met a couple of Dalmatians, and their Mama was surprised by how interested they were in me. My Mama pointed out that there was a chip on the floor which both her dogs had spotted. Whilst they had been straining at the leash to reach the tempting morsel, I had in fact managed a commando crawl under the picnic bench and eaten it. Point for me.

We spent some time beachcombing, oh, and attracting nutters. Most people we meet are so lovely, they dearly want to stroke me, but they respect my insecurities. A real big and sincere thank you to those people, you are the ones who are actually helping me to relax and enjoy my new life.

On the other hand, Mama has developed a unique talent for spotting the body language of those who think they know better and she can tell people's intentions as they approach. We met a few of these this week, and yeah, you might be nice people, but you are not The Dog Whisperer you think you are. I might be happy to sit next to you whilst Mama repeats my life story, ran over/bomb disposal reject, depending on Mama's mood etc. But think about it this way: if my Mama or Papa sat next to *you* and had a little chat, yeah, things might be ok, but should Mama or Papa start touching you then you would feel a tad bit uncomfortable. That's how I feel. Look if you have to but no touchy.

Unfortunately, some folks still did try to touch me after being asked not to . . . twice. I growled at them. Mama warned them I would growl at them. Then they were surprised I growled at them. Really? Mama says she may have another jacket printed for me to wear, instead of my nifty little number that says 'Nervous, do not pat' this one might actually get the message across.

In other news, I now have a shrink. Maggie. Mama has been searching for the right one for some time; she didn't want just any old guru messing with my mind. Maggie comes highly recommended and works with The Dogs Trust and sounds amazing. Shout out to the beautiful Tasha for organising it. Maggie also has a degree in human psychology, so that should make things interesting. Mama and Maggie had a telephone conversation this week, and I earwigged when Mama told Papa all about it. Maggie told us we are doing the right things for now, and once Papa is home permanently from working on the big house she will come over for a home consultation. Mama did mention that it costs a fortune but hey, apparently I'm worth it. Mama then went on to say 'oh, and I have just spent £22.95 on the credit card'.

Papa said 'good for you, what have you bought?' To which Mama replied 'a flamingo dress with a monkey and a budgerigar sitting on a tea cup'. And I am the one seeing a shrink.

Mama has also apologised for leaving me home alone with the radio on. Whilst doing a bit of ironing, yep, the flamingo dress eyesore, Mama flipped the radio on and the delights of Elaine Paige wafted across the airwaves. Now Mama is the first to admit that she herself is annoying in many ways, but Elaine Paige—have you heard her laugh? Her show is on for two hours, two hours of that craziness. Mama said if she had to listen to that sound for two hours she would be barking too.

I'll leave you with one final thought for the week: fireworks. As a Greek stray with an enigma streak, I don't have problems with your outrageous explosions; I'm more than happy to snore my way through an evening. But my big sister, yes that cat from the dark side, is not so laid back. So on her behalf and as bizarre as it seems this rant is for her.

Seriously, don't you English folks have anything better to spend your money on? Watching 50 quid go whiz whiz, sparkly sparkly, BANG, in less than 3 seconds is ridiculous. Your Guy died in 1606. Get over it. Rant over. Go spend your money on an organised display, put some cash in the charity bucket, and give the pounds that you saved to something more worthwhile like people who are hungry and homeless. Or dogs. Or even cats.

I'm good.

Editor's comment: Erm . . . thank you, freak boy.

WEEK 24
My Soap Box. Deal.

As I assume you know by now, I am a three-legged Greek street dog who has been lucky enough to find his forever home. I travelled to the UK in a van full of Spanish rescue mutts all on our way to a better life. Others aren't so lucky.

I know we're having fun here, but we need to stop for a serious break. Did you know that thousands of dogs are killed every year in Spain? If they are abandoned, no longer useful as a working dog or a fun puppy, they end up in the municipal Perrera's, aka The Killing Stations. The dogs that live there are either chained, caged, or run loose and have a death penalty hanging over their heads. Some are killed by other dogs in the pound as chaos reigns. If no one claims them, then it's all over. It's simply a matter of time.

Recently, two operators working at one of these Killing Stations were prosecuted after a lengthy investigation which found they had euthanized the dogs in their so-called care by injecting the lethal dose into the dogs muscles instead of intravenously, and cutting back on the amount of the fatal drug used. Why? To save time and money. The dog's deaths were therefore prolonged and torturous, and the operators played loud music over megaphones to cover the sound of the dog's dying howls of agony. They killed a gruesome total of 2,183 healthy dogs and cats. No sedation, just held down, injected, then left to die whilst they moved on to the next one.

There are many Killing Stations in Spain and many dogs. Leonora is one of the dogs who ended up there.

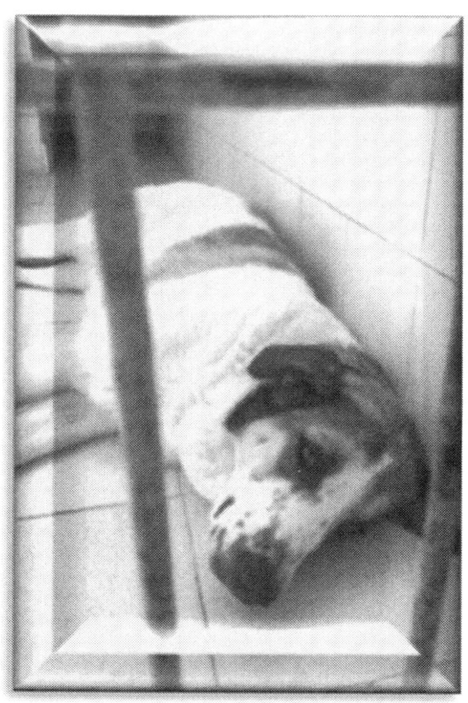

No longer wanted, Leonora was placed in the municipal Perrera and her life was allocated a number where she waited in atrocious conditions for her turn to die. The larger the dog, the more space he or she takes up; she would not be there for long.

There are many people, charities, and organisations who work tirelessly to help these poor tormented creatures. My previous foster Mama is just one of those special folks. Not long ago she saved some of these dogs and arranged for them to be released from the Killing Stations. These few fortunate creatures were then taken to a vet and treated for any infections or injuries and neutered or spayed before continuing on their journey to find a new life and their very own forever home.

But one person can't save them all. It takes an awful lot of dedication, time, and money for each and every dog that is rescued.

The group of dogs my previous foster Mama had agreed to help included a large Spanish Mastiff, who is also now safe and on the way to a better life. However, this large Spanish Mastiff looked very much like Leonora. So much so that when the dogs were released from the Perrera, the door to Leonora's cage was opened by mistake and Leonora slipped through the net. The dogs were loaded onto a vehicle and driven to their safe destination, with a cuckoo in the nest . . . Leonora.

Long story short, Leonora is now living in the UK with my previous foster Mama. Leonora is beautiful. I think I may even have a tiny bit of a doggie crush on her! But she can't stay in foster care forever, there are other dogs out there that need help, so big it up for Leonora and help share the love to find her forever home.

To Juliet, her wonderful team at Holly Farm Canine Centre, and all the other selfless people out there who don't just put themselves first. You are awesome.

In other news, yeah, I'm good. Tis squirrel season.

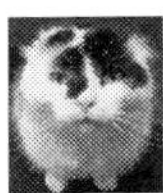

Editor's comment: I hate it when the dog is big-hearted.

WEEK 25
Grandchildren

We now have grandchildren. They are the sort of grandchildren Mama likes—furry with four legs. Today Mama accompanied my older brother to collect her three brand new granddaughters from The Rat Lady. Mama said it was the most amazing house she had ever been in, and Mama has been in a proper grand stately home, so it must have been amazing. One time Papa went for a job interview with an actual Lord, but he didn't get the job because when they were being shown round Mama shut the door to the library (which was an air-conditioned room and housed the prayer book of Henry VIII) and the 15th-century doorknob came off in her hand. Awkward. Mind you, this was after she had been caught gently stroking a stuffed badger perched on a sideboard. Double awkward.

Anyway, The Rat Lady was awesome apparently; she had a bunch of critters in her house: rats, mice, gerbils, parrots, dogs and something in a heated tank which Mama avoided in case it had more than four legs. My brother-from-another-mother was choosing from the litter of cuties as The Rat Lady explained there was in fact another sibling but the last visitors had dropped her and she was currently hiding under the washing machine.

Mama clutched the baby rat she was holding slightly tighter as she didn't want to make the same mistake, yet it was just then that she spotted another animal under the TV—a pig! There was a pig under the tele! Mama became overly excited as she is a huge pig fan, and so did the baby rat so it was a case of manically controlling a hyper rat whilst discussing the pig's heritage which turned out to be Lithuanian and The Rat Lady had picked him up locally for the grand sum of £65. I realise that this all sounds completely barking mad but I assure you it's all 100% true. Apparently, strange things occur behind the doors of stately homes and tiny terraced houses.

In other news, my Uncle Michael—who is not my actual Uncle but another adopted member of the family—challenged me to the latest facebook craze of posting black and white photo's for one week. Now this turned out to be a bit of a life saver. As we went for a hop round the park one evening Mama took some photos of me.

At the risk of sounding grumpy, I hate her God dammed mobile phone; she's always pointing it at me and snapping away. Get a life woman.

As I grew bored of Mama's inept photography, I took the chance to have a bit of a lie down as the old girl snapped away. And then we heard a dog approach, but we both just ignored it and carried on with the photo shoot. We could also hear a man shouting at this dog. Things did not seem quite right, so we stayed where we were. Mama shone her brand new poop-spotting torch but we couldn't see anything. We both decided to wait a bit longer.

And then it all went bad. A dog fight broke out, it was horrible! We could hear the screams from another dog and a woman shouting for help. We emerged from our hiding spot under the trees but we still couldn't see anything. The sounds continued for a bit and then all went silent. I stayed close to Mama. Mama stayed close to me. We were proper freaked.

Mama put my lead on and we set off to see if we could help. We soon found them; a man and a woman, who had been bitten, as had her dog, a large Doberman. Mama asked if they were ok and offered to assist in any way. They were all shaken but declined any help. Mama and I felt really bad, as we thought that would have been us if we hadn't been loitering in the bushes taking stupid photos for Facebook. Thank you Uncle Michael.

As it turned out Mama said the best black and white photo she had taken, that was supposed to describe your life, turned out to be the one of her sock covered in fur; sums us up nicely...

Papa is STILL working in Dorset, but he has been home for a few days rest which is proper good. I was only home alone a couple of times this week, which makes me a happy boy. On one of these days, Mama and Papa decided to take me to the vet for a bit of a check-up. Ridiculous. There's nothing wrong with me! The nice vet lady manipulated all my joints, checked out my heart, and declared me as fit as a fiddle.

Well, Mama and Papa, I could have told you that myself and saved you a tidy sum. The bad news is Mama and Papa now know that I don't actually have to sit down every five minutes to rest my three weary legs, so it has kinda backfired on me. This has forced me to pick up a brand new habit. Dark winter morning walks + dark winter evening walks = I have become a bit of a scent hound. 'Tis dark, my senses are a tad heightened, these things happen.

On one of these late evening strolls round yet another unlit dark park I caught the smell of something I really don't like—cat. The chase was on. Mama later told Papa I was like a greyhound on speed and as fast as her skinny little old legs could run, my fit and mighty fine three legs outran her. I was off. Mama used her poop-spotting torch and could not locate me, so she started to panic somewhat. As she crawled through the undergrowth where she had last spotted my good self she heard some passers-by, so she crawled back out and asked the local hooded youths if they had by chance happened to spot a crazy three-legged dog in the local vicinity.

They mumbled a grunted 'er, yeah, down there', and got away from Mama as fast as they could. Mama was most grateful anyway, and headed in the direction they had pointed, where she found me sniffing around someone else's front garden, hunting for cats! Mama was displeased but held her anger in, although I did kinda feel it was a bit of a 'my bad' moment.

The next day was better, as we headed out to the early morning park where I caught the whiff of a local squirrel, and off we went again. This time Mama had me on a long lead so she just ran like the wind with me. We never found that squirrel, but we did pass a number of early morning walkers with their 'more-normal-four-legged-pedigree-shop-bought-dogs'. Mama said she was grateful we were going so fast, as she had no intention of stopping to exchange pleasantries since she still had garlic breath from the night before and was wearing her jumper back to front.

'Tis nearly six months into my new life and I think it is all going to be just fine.

 Editor's comment: Chase me and lose an eye, buddy boy.

WEEK 26
Six Months

They say it takes a rescue dog six months to feel fully settled into his or her new home. It's official! Six months ago today I met a dodgy old couple and was put in a van and driven 167 miles from up North to down South to start my new life. Scared? . . . You betcha.

I was scared of men, including Papa, and I proved it by showing him my teeth on that first evening. He said they were a bit dingy, so now I have a serious Dentastix habit, but my teeth are beautiful.

I was scared of traffic, especially motorbikes and buses. Now I happily walk past Papa's motorbike without a care in the world. I still hate buses, but I no longer cower when I see one coming, athough I do occasionally have a random bark just to make my point.

I wouldn't go near Mama's car, and definitely nowhere near Papa's van without major coercion. But now I love the vehicles, as it means we're going out and about. Papa's driving is sometimes scary, according to Mama, but she can't talk as she really should concentrate more on the road rather than worrying about me balancing on three legs as she navigates a roundabout. After all, she's driving at a snail's pace.

I had a huge foot chewing obsession. I simply couldn't stop once I got started. I used to gnaw away like a maniac and Mama's ridiculous joke about an 'Irish Wolfhound who lay in a corner chewing a bone and when he got up he only had three legs' didn't put me off. Now? I stopped doing it, as I'm feeling mostly stress free—even though I still live with a cat from the dark side.

My coat has changed too, and even though I do say so myself, I am looking mighty fine.

I have adjusted to living indoors, I love having my own comfy bed (if you remember, I ignored the first one for a few weeks and then I ate it), I am used to the TV, washing machine, and all the other constant noises. I could care less about the vacuum, until I have to move which is annoying if I am comfy, and I love, love, love Postman.

I have been in shops, pubs, cafes, and the vets on five occasions, one of which shall still remain unmentionable, thank you very much. I have even been on holiday to deepest Dorset.

I have met so many friends—dogs and people—and had many a good romp in the park or the beach or the woods. I get about quite a bit you know. My people friends are mostly ok, but I still prefer not to be stroked by them; I will take a treat from their hand, sometimes, because hey, I like treats. We are still working on this, and I have my shrink appointment coming up soon so Mama and Papa will know best how to help me get even more confident.

All in all it's been a bit of a journey, but worth it, for all of us. Mama says she knows I'm happy, as I spend most of my time wagging my tail. So thank you again to Ermioni for rescuing me, and my foster Mama Juliet, and to Mama and Papa . . . I proper love you all.

 Editor's comment: I still don't like you.

WEEK 27
A Tale About Nothing

It finally happened—absolutely nothing. Best week ever. Plus tonight Papa is coming home from his job at the big house in deepest Dorset and he will be 'done done' so to speak. Whoop whoop! As I am now 6+ months into my new home and kinda groovy with life (settled/no unexpected behaviours lurking) I thought I would make Papa a surprise for his return, so I have dug a big hole in his relatively new lawn. Not bad for a three-legged dog.

I have also kept up my new 'scent hound' hobby. Mama thinks it may be the new pills I am taking, Yumove, prescribed by my mate Mrs. Vet. According to Mama, these scrummy little bad boys are fast-acting daily joint supplements for dogs which contain all the essential nutrients I need to maintain healthy joints, plus they encourage mobility and flexibility.

Now we do a fair bit of whizzing around after things that smell good; I get a whiff and whey hey, off we go. Squirrels are a favourite from our morning walks in the park. Met one today. Mama knew I was up to something as I was going a bit frantic sniffing round the trunk of a large tree.

Mama happened to be talking to a very nice lady at the time who had rescued a Romanian dog called Rosie. The nice lady was asking Mama how I had settled in and if I was well-behaved. Mama was proudly telling her that I was perfect—I came when called, and have no problems out and about whatsoever, apart from my fear of people so please don't touch me. In that moment I spotted the squirrel leaping from tree to tree, and that was me gone. Mama called me, and did I come back like the perfect dog Mama had just been describing? Hell no. I was busy.

There ensued some awkward glances between Mama and the nice lady, whose dog Rosie was indeed sitting perfectly next to her. Mama then shouted WAIT and I did, instantly; the other lady was most impressed, but Mama kinda knew I had only stopped in my tracks because the squirrel had listened to Mama and come to an abrupt halt.

All in all, daily walks have become much more fun with my newfound gusto. Given my level of success, Mama decided she would try a little self-medication herself, and has purchased some sort of women's trouble vitamin menopause jobbies; she's hoping she'll have more energy too.

Like I said, not much has occurred this week, which has been a pleasant change. My brother-from-another-mother did pop over yesterday, and he and Mama were talking for ages about my new nieces—the triplet rats—and I got bored. So I pawed Mama well hard with my extra-strength, nutrient-enhanced digging paw, and she finally gave in and sat next to me on the floor. I made my point by lying on top of her as she seemed to have forgotten I was there. Rude.

Beer's in the fridge for Papa as he will be home soon. Hoorah!

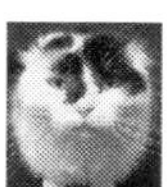 Editor's comment: Lummox.

WEEK 28
A Lost Dog

My wonderful Papa was due home Sunday evening. Did he come home? No. But we pretended we understood, as he'd been working really hard and finished late, and we wanted him to come home in one piece. So he stayed over another night and finally showed up back home on Monday at lunchtime. Home for good! Me and Mama were over the moon about it. Happy days were here again, and all that jazz.

Twenty-four hours was all it took for the honeymoon to wear off. Mama went off to work happy that I was happy. I was happy that Mama went off to work as I had Papa all to myself. Mama returned home later with much excitement and yelled 'Hi honey's I'm home' as she entered the too-quiet house. She was greeted by a small mew from the cat from the dark side, and a note from Papa that said 'out with the boy'.

Mama shrugged her shoulders, flicked the kettle on, and kicked off her shoes—and then Papa called. Mama flicked the kettle off and put her shoes back on. Papa had rung to say he had lost the dog. FFS.

Mama drove to Papa's last-known location relatively calmly, as she knew I would be ok. She spotted Papa's van down the little track and pulled up next to it. She also spotted something else. Me. Sitting patiently next to Papa's van. Mama got out in a rush and gave me a big hug and told me what a good boy I was and gave me a treat from her special treat box. Then she opened her car door and in I jumped.

Mama now had to find Papa.

Thank goodness for modern technology, am I right? Mama rang Papa, and when he answered I heard her tell him he was a numpty and to get back to the van pronto. Trouble was, Papa had followed me through the little hole in the fence around the park and as it was now getting dark he was somewhat lost in the vast gardens of the local RAF retirement home.

Mama was not impressed and muttered something about men and then decided to get back in the car and get the heater going as it was getting mighty cold. It was at this moment Mama realised that in her haste to leap out of the car to rescue me she had in fact lost her car keys. Parents. I despair.

Fortunately Mama discovered that the all-important keys were still in the ignition, so we soon toasted up nicely whilst waiting for Papa to find his way out of the nightmare he'd made for himself (having nothing to do with me). It didn't take long. Papa arrived and I was pleased to see him as I was worried about the old chap. Papa was pleased that I was pleased to see him, and opened up his van door so I could travel back with him to our humble abode.

I did a bit of sniffing and discovered the treat box that Mama had dropped during her key hunt, so I gave it back to her, then I hopped back into the toastie car. Mama and Papa exchanged glances and then Mama drove me home and gave me my tea. Papa came home and sheepishly made Mama her tea. Moron.

Papa is now getting back up to speed and fully retrained in the art of walking me. He realizes I'm good as gold—unless I see a squirrel or a rabbit, but I haven't seen one of those bad boys in a while. Papa has to stay one step ahead of the game and call me back before I become fixated. But Papa has also realised that even if you go out and about at 3pm, it's still dark in the countryside by 4pm, so he came up with a pretty smart solution. In the words of Rihanna I now 'shine bright like a diamond'.

Yup, Papa got me a flashing necklace. He was most proud of his purchase after scouring the many pet shops, and he doesn't even mind that I look like a tacky Christmas tree. On our next afternoon stroll Papa came home and told Mama all about it, 'Yeah it started to get dark but I could see him the whole time, knew exactly where he was and what he was doing.' He then proceeded to turn my lights on to show Mama and . . . battery dead. Mama just rolled her eyes.

Papa, being the determined type, scoured the entire world wide web for a sturdier replacement, and I am now the proud owner of what can only be described as a 1980's disco light which dangles from my collar. My street cred is now shot. If I had any in the first place.

Mama took me out to my favourite park nice and early in the afternoon, so no need for any glitter balls. It was heaving with dogs and people. I saw a man walking across the park and I ran over all tail wagging and smiley faced (Mama was most perplexed), until the nice man turned around to say hello and I realised it was not Papa. Surprise! So I did a little growl, my bad.

We met loads of other people and dogs too, and all was good until we met a particular woman. I don't like to be rude but Mama, well, she isn't as couth as me. She described her as Bet Lynch on steroids. The woman was tottering on high heels, wearing bright red lipstick and a leopard skin coat—in the park of all places—and then she came over to me to say hello. Mama did her usual spiel, 'he likes dogs but is wary of people so please don't touch him' etc. etc.

Well, Betty Steroid didn't take a blind bit of notice and teetered over and offered her hand right in my face. I did a little growl. Mama repeated her message and Betty Steroid replied 'I used to work for a world renowned dog rescue' and then shoved her hand in my face again. I did a second growl. Mama put me on my lead and we left before things got even uglier. Betty Steroid said 'well at least I got close to him.' Mama didn't dignify her rudeness with a reply. Well, she did, but only in her head.

In other unusual news, my-sister-from-another-mister, who I love, came round and was telling Papa and Mama about her work next door with the old folk. Apparently, some of these lovely people have dementia and can't remember her name when she calls in to care for them which is so sad, but they always ask 'how is Ouzo', which is kind of amazing. Big love to you all.

Editor's comment: Barking. Mad that is.

WEEK 29
Shrinks, Donkeys, Ducks, and Dogs

I met my shrink at long last. Mama threw a curve ball and changed her mind at the last minute about who we were going to see. She took advice from all the crazy rescuers who haunt the world wide web and picked Bone Canis to be my main man. Personally, I think she was a little worried that the one we were going to see had a qualification in human psychology too, and she had visions of being the one dragged off to a padded cell wearing a little jacket that made her hug herself. Wise choice.

Anyway, Bone Canis, aka Mark Bridger, was a top chap in my opinion because he had fishy treats. Mama and Papa held the same opinion, but for them it was because he gave good sound advice. Tomato, Tom-ah-to.

Diagnosis . . . I am not a psychopath like my mate Donny T over the pond. Phew.

His advice? When out and about 'be more fierce'—Mama and Papa that is, not me. If anyone comes up to me, Mama and Papa must say firmly 'he's in training, leave him alone'. And the best bit is, if they continue to approach me, then Mama has Mark's permission to be as rude as she likes. Lord help us all.

At the end of the day, no one should touch a dog without permission first. The more people I meet who heed this advice, the more confident I will become, and the less the odds are that an incident will occur. And should the worse ever happen and I end up biting someone, it won't be my fault, but it will be my life that will come to an end. A sobering thought.

Mark has also given Mama and Papa advice on how to react when we have guests in the house, how to keep my mind occupied as I am a bright sort of chap, as well as advice on walks, playtime, and lots of other stuff.

He also suggested that I may be part Anatolian Shepherd, which would explain my love of just lying down and watching my flock, or then again maybe I am just bone idle. Mark was also extremely honest when asked about a potential friend for me. A nervous or shy dog would definitely not help me. As for a more confident dog, it may well help but there is no guarantee. Taking on any sort of rescue dog is a challenge and each one is unique.

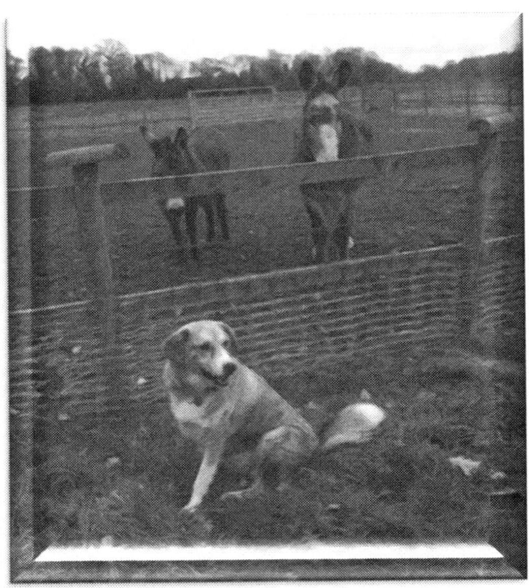

We also drove up to Surrey this week and met my Auntie Janine plus all my other extended family—a bizarre menagerie of donkeys, ducks, chickens, an elderly pony, and two little dogs. I was of course an angel. I loved playing with my little cousin canines Mosh and Raffa, and was most respectful of the donkeys and dear old pony. Ducks and chickens? Not a problem; I just laid down and did my newfound Anatolian Shepherd impersonation.

On our second stop we met someone else: dear little Orphan Annie. They invited me into their house but I didn't go in straight away. Mama and Papa went indoors and Mama asked if there was another dog in the garden, as she could see I was desperately trying to play with something—

I was all butt in the air, chest on the ground, jumpy jumpy, play with me, play with me. It turned out I was trying to charm a resin statue of a dog. Awkward.

So I went inside, deflated and embarrassed. Mama and Papa were seriously impressed with me, though, so that cheered me up a bit.

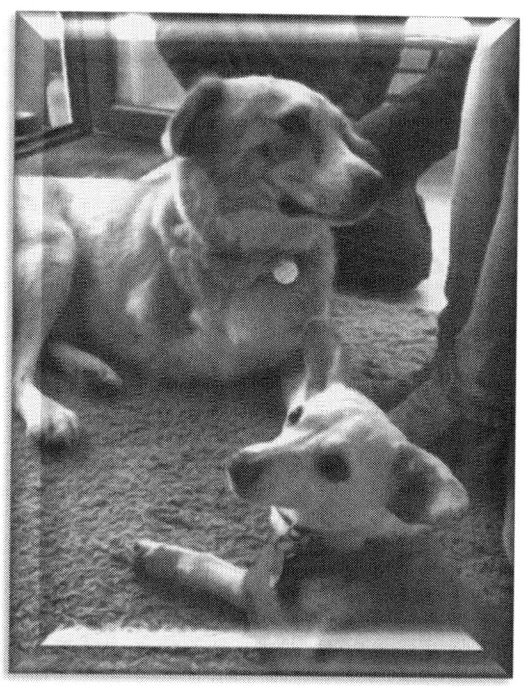

Not only was I relaxed, but I even sniffed this new lady's hand and let her stroke me. I then got a bit cocky and went to wander off into the lounge to have a bit of a look around, but Papa called me back so I did as I was told. I was then cordially introduced to Orphan Annie, who by all accounts is a real charmer. I liked her and I think she liked me too, because there was lots and lots of tail wagging. I took the plunge and asked her if she would like to meet up again, maybe come round to my place sometime? And guess what, she said yes . . .

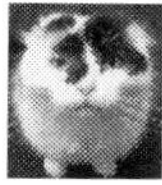 Editor's comment: No thanks. You can just stay there forever.

WEEK 30
First World Problems

Life is a funny old thing. This time last year I was living rough in Karditsa, and let me assure you, it was not fun. Who knew that a mere twelve months later, I'd be living in a foreign country in a cosy three-bed semi with a no-eared cat (from the dark side, of course) and a Mama and Papa who love me. My only troubles now are first world problems, like Papa couldn't fit me in the van as he had brought home some work, which meant the van was now full to the brim with a chandelier of all things. Papa said since he was unable to drive me to the park I could instead go wherever I wanted, so I led Papa down the drive, across the road, round the corner, down the alleyway, and into town. I hadn't been there for quite some time. Papa mused over where we were going until I finally sat down . . . outside the pet shop door. Papa refused to go inside, though, so I took him to the travel agent's and did a bit of window shopping, but the glossy ski brochures didn't do it for me so I took Papa to the butcher's instead. Those men didn't notice me begging for a treat, so I did one loud bark but nothing happened so I turned around and took Papa back home.

On Thursday Mama went out for her work's Christmas party. She came home late smelling of booze and yummy food and sat on the floor and told me what a good boy I was exactly nine times before abruptly announcing she was going to bed. And she thinks I'm peculiar.

Finally it was Saturday. The day my little friend Annie was coming over to play with me! Mama took the cat from the dark side to one side and explained that today was in fact apple cart day, and it was about to be upset. I took the opportunity to steal the post and was halfway through eating a small Amazon package before being caught by Mama who declared that was no way for a respectable Anatolian Shepherd dog to behave. So I stole her hat while she was busy putting up the Christmas cards in the front room in order to make it look like at least some people liked us before our guests arrived. Mama tsked as she retrieved her hat so I ate a Christmas card . . . just because.

And then she arrived. Orphan Annie. And my life was complete.

The other creature in the house, my nemesis the cat, was not impressed. The one who lurks upstairs in her penthouse suite has been thoroughly spoiled rotten, of course, as Mama says she is pet number one. On Saturday night she was allowed to sleep on Mama's bed (Papa slept downstairs with us tripaws to act as chaperone) so she made the most of Papa's pillow and used it as a nail file to sharpen her b*tch slappers. This was all done perilously close to Mama's face in an attempt to humiliate and assert her dominance—at least that's my opinion. Mama just told her to pack it in, so instead she pulled out and flaunted her loudest purr. Mama told the cat she was happy that she was happy and with that the cat jumped off the bed and returned to her own bedroom, just to be rude.

Annie is a delight . . . she loves everyone, and I hope that includes me, as I have quickly grown very fond of her. I have been on my best behaviour, and although I really want to play, I have been very respectful and let her do her own thing as she gets used to a new environment. I have even let her sleep on my bed, although she has a perfectly good one of her own.

Ouzo the Greek is being Ouzo the Gentleman. It is early days but I would really like it if she stayed forever.

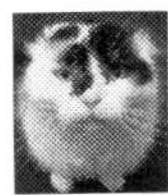

Editor's comment: I still vote no.

WEEK 31
Welcome to Annie

Mama's friend popped over for a cuppa. I'm not so keen on the old girl, as the first time I met her she rocked up with a broken foot and crutches . . . I just saw a stranger with two sticks and a loud mouth, and that was enough to set me off. She has been round many times since then, and I always keep my distance and growl a little bit. I don't like to change my mind.

Mama said she is a bird, aka a real good woman, although then she went on to say that she was actually more of a bird within a bird within a bird to which Mama's size 12 (plus a tad more) friend took offense. The big bird looked down at Annie and asked, 'What is that?'

Mama said, 'How rude, THAT is Annie.' The lovely, adorable, perfect little Annie who was curled up in her bed.

Then the bird asked, 'How many legs has she got?'

Mama replied 'Three.'

More annoying questions. 'Where did she come from, Uzbekistan?'

Mama replied, 'No and don't be so stupid, she is from Surrey, via Romania.'

The bird asked, 'Isn't there enough dogs in this country to adopt?'

(Note, that is a REALLY annoying question.)

So Mama said, 'Yup, but it's just a bit of sea in between us and the next country, and we're all on the same rock hurtling through space so what's the difference?'

Then Postman came, which enabled us all to cool down a little. Mama got up and brought the mail to the front room, and there was a Christmas card and a package. I like to think all packages are for me, so I got a bit excited. Mama did too, as she had no idea who it was from.

She opened the card first, and the bird asked, 'Who is it from?'

Mama replied, 'It's addressed to Ouzo and Annie, and it's from Auntie Janine, how lovely,' and the bird rolled her eyes.

Mama opened the package next, and we found out it was a book. The bird asked, 'Whose book is it?' and Mama replied 'Oliver's.'

The bird asked, 'Oliver who?' and Mama replied 'Oliver the Greek rescue dog, obviously', and the bird rolled her eyes until only the white bits showed and sighed deeply. I didn't mind it when she left.

The next day my sister-from-another-mister came round, and that's when Mama realised. Little Annie didn't jump up and run to greet her like she had before, and when Mama took her rose-tinted glasses off she remembered she didn't when her friend the bird came round either.

Now Annie is the most delightful, gorgeous, beautiful little being currently on this planet, and she just loves everyone. When Annie wags her tail her whole body wags with pleasure and excitement too. She is beyond words. But now Mama believed Annie was not happy in our home.

And this is the hardest bit . . . why? Unrequited love. Yup, that old thing.

To be fair, I am a self-confessed, socially awkward lummox, so I do understand. I love little Annie, I love little dogs. When out and about I love to play with a tiddy chap or chapess. I am gentle and respectful. I have been the same with Annie. The difference is, a small four-legged chap in the park can bugger off when it has had enough off me. Annie is a gentle three-legged fellow amputee, whose love for life was becoming a bit squished by my exuberance. I was respectful and left her alone when she retired to her boudoir, but when she showed her true personality, which was a real zest for life, I joined in and as gentle as I could be, my enthusiasm outweighed hers and that is not a good thing for a tiny little angel.

Should we have considered this before? Yes, of course, but we didn't realize, as previous experience had shown little dogs kinda like me too. No matter how many cups of tea Mama and Papa sat and drank whilst discussing every single possibility to ensure they were 'doing things right', the bottom line is actually 'doing the right thing'. For everyone, and that included Annie.

And so with much sadness all around, Annie has gone back home today.

Yes we are all heartbroken that this has happened. However, Mama and Papa have shown me that whatever happens you have to look for the positives because no matter how sad you are, if you look carefully you can find them.

Whilst Annie was with us her wonderful foster mama had a space so she took in two emergency rescue dogs with no place to go, and yesterday one of them went to their forever home.

Tomorrow is Christmas Day, and Annie will be where she is happy, and that is what matters the most. And the most bizarre thing of all . . . that cat from the dark side made her first ever friend, and actually sat on the sofa last night right next to little Annie.

The right thing to do is not always the easiest thing to do, but it is still the right thing to do. Annie deserves the best life, not the second best life. I'm sorry, Annie.

So all that is left to say is Merry Christmas to all those angels out there that give us four/three-legged beasties hope. May your day be merry and bright!

Big love from me. xxoo.

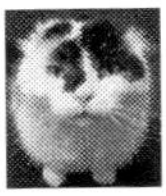

Editor's comment: Happy Christmas Annie, I actually liked you. Take care and blossom, sweet pea.

WEEK 32
The Good, The Bad, and The Beyond

Christmas Day is a new one on me, and a bit full on. We had visitors over, followed by a trip to the park where Mama and Papa spent time on the zip wire since all the local kids were indoors unwrapping presents from some guy in the sky. And you think I'm barking mad. This was followed by yet more family and a giant feast with much laughter and strange paper hats. I got presents too: a Meercat dressed as Santa from my truly beautiful Auntie Sarah (I chewed a limb off . . . just because). I also got a licky mat, one of those super expensive things you can buy on the world wide web but thanks to my mate Mark I got a whole pack of 6 for £4.99 from Amazon that were just branded with a different name. Up yours, marketing world!

And most importantly I got a package, albeit an empty one. It had Amazon written on it and I have a sneaky feeling it was the one that my economy licky mats came in but I wasn't bothered by that. Love, love, love a package! I chewed the beggar up with much gusto.

However, the best present of all? The advice from Bone Canis. Without this chap I couldn't have coped with all the madness of my freaky forever family. I even joined in the 'let's throw balls at Papa's basketball hat' Christmas party game, as you do.

I also got a bit of pocket money; well I didn't really, but my oddball family has a strange tradition of tree presents, and one of these contained a scratch card which had a £10 prize so Papa gave it to me. I finally went shopping at Pets Corner and got me some treat sticks which I carried all the way home. Hallelujah!

The ironic thing is my mate Mark gave some great advice on how I can tolerate visitors—distractions/praise/high value treats, etc. Yet now that we have a house full of smelly yet yummy distractions, not a lot of people have come a calling, which is not right in my opinion.

I'm not ashamed to admit I spent Christmas Eve crying because I missed my little friend Annie. It made Mama cry too, and Papa even had a bit of a wobble when doing something with a brussell sprout in the kitchen. It's not easy, this rehoming business, and Mama and Papa know they won't meet another dog as gentle and confident as little Annie. But a friend I need, so a friend I will find. One day.

Mama says she has two more possible suspects lined up: Ugly Olive and Normal Norman. I would kinda like a girlfriend, but Normal Norman sounds a tad more, ummm, easy on the eye.

It's the time of year to look back and ponder from whence we've come. In 2017 I immigrated to the UK, found a foster home up North, then a forever home down South. I also discovered I suffered from travel sickness, which isn't fun for any of us. I moved into my first house, I have been on holiday, I have been in shops, I have been to the vet's (including one unmentionable time), I have been to parks, woods, the beach (English beaches . . . ugh), cafes, and pubs. I have met so many people I can't remember them all, and a French no-eared cat that despises me.

I have also been left home alone—please don't leave again Papa! This year has been traumatic, epic, bonkers, and other English words I don't yet know and Mama says I don't need to know.

None of this would have happened if it were not for those amazing people out there: Ermioni my first love, Juliet, Sarah and the many, many others. And it is not just me. Little Orphan Annie, special little Orphan Annie, may have now found her very own forever home. We love you Annie, proper style.

And do you remember the cuckoo in the nest, Leonora? Well guess who had a special Christmas in her brand new home.

Dear amazing people, please keep doing what you are doing.

As for Mama and Papa, they just love me unconditionally, doggie smell and all. Mama and Papa, it's a ditto from me, your one and only great big aloof Anatolian Enigma.

Love, kindness and companionship, it is what life is about. Happy Christmas folks, from your three-legged friend.

Big love.

Editor's comment: I do like Christmas.

WEEK 33
Little House on the Contrary

As random as it seems for a three-legged Greek street dog to end up in a semi-detached house in English suburbia, it certainly is the right house for me. But it's still unreal, big time proper haphazardly mega time random. We are more little house on the contrary than little house on the prairie.

Let me tell you about my Auntie Janine who came to stay this weekend. She's a good sort, a dog walker in fact, plus she has her own small menagerie of dogs, donkeys, and ducks. This all equals her smelling kinda odd yet intriguing. Her car does too, a purchase made some time ago from a good Christian sort which still has that faithful fish stuck on the boot.

Now, as a dog I am not one bit religious. Why should I be, as the Catholic bible says I am not welcome in heaven? However, as a decent sort of dog, I endeavor to respect the beliefs of others, so pray for me if you wish but I have one small warning: I WILL eat your Watch Tower magazine if you put it through my letterbox. That is all.

Back to the point. Auntie Janine came to stay and we had a small adventure out. On our return to her car, I realised it wasn't just my immediate family who are bonkers, my extended family also attract random weirdness too. A lady, a very nice lady, was staring at Auntie Janine with a strange smile on her face which kept getting remarkably bigger.

Auntie Janine, being the good sort, smiled back and that was it. Mrs. Cheshire Cat Lady bounded over, flung her arms around Auntie Janine and declared 'Sister, I saw the car and then you! It's so good to see you, Sister, how are you and where do you worship now?'

There followed a short period of awkward silence until Auntie Janine blurted out a random made up name . . . 'St Augustus'. Something strange happened to Mama's eyebrows at this point but Mrs. Cheshire Cat Lady seemed delighted with this news. She then asked if the dog would like a drink of water followed instantly by, and I kid you not . . . 'Silly me, the Holy Spirit shines out of you and will let you know when the dog needs a drink.'

It was at this point we couldn't take it anymore and made our rapid farewells and drove off speedily with Mama making some comment about Jesus taking the wheel. Barking.

In other news my very own Papa was on the tele this week. We all settled down together one evening to watch a programme called DIY SOS and man it was truly heart-breaking. We are not ashamed to admit we all cried as we watched the story unfold of a truly courageous mother, Amanda, who had been involved in a horrific accident which left her paralysed from the waist down. Amanda and her beautiful family were amazing as they coped with life's newfound difficulties by simply loving and supporting one another.

Yet their modest home was just not suitable for wheelchair living, and Amanda had to struggle with everyday things that the rest of us take for granted. But struggle on they did until the DIY SOS team, along with 300 or so local volunteers, refurbished the family home from top to bottom in just ten days to meet all their needs. And Amanda got her wish . . . to be a mum again.

Amanda thanked everyone who helped and said her house had been made out of love. And do you know what, it had been. Faith in humanity restored.

Each and every person who contributed in whatever way is a legend because helping others is what life is all about. And Papa, well he summed it up nicely by saying our time is limited so it is the most precious thing we can give.

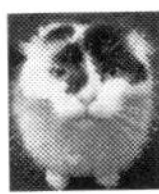 Editor's comment: He was my Papa first.

WEEK 34
Long John Silver

Suffering happens all over this planet regardless of species. The saddest part . . . you just get too used to it.

Once upon a time in a faraway land there was a dog. (No, not me for once, but I can see why you thought that.)A three-legged chap scavenging for scraps to keep himself alive. No one knows how he lost the bottom part of his leg. Rumour has it it was hacked off with a machete, but that is only a rumour, no one really knows for sure. Apart from Long John Silver, the dog, living on the outskirts of a train station in Amristsar, India.

No one paid attention to Long John Silver as he lay there amongst the bustling railway station with hundreds of people stepping over him each day going about their business. Just another doomed dog. Just another suffering soul. Until Cindy. Cindy was not well herself at the time and couldn't do much to help. But Long John Silver was constantly in her thoughts, and so she contacted a group called Guardians of the Voiceless. Now India is vast, like proper massive so I'm told, so what are the chances of finding a random three-legged dog who may just happen to hang around a train station which is a six-hour drive from the volunteers at Guardians of the Voiceless?

Using the power of social media, people went out to find him, but there was no news. Until Inder. Inder is a friend of Guardians of the Voiceless and having read about this particular dog went in search of him . . . and found him.

Inder was Long John's very own guardian angel. The rescue team was 300 miles away, so they got in a car and drove there. By the time they got there, things had changed somewhat, as they discovered Long John had his guardian angel but he also had a girlfriend, Clementine.

Then multiple groups came together to treat Long John and find him a better life—and Clementine too!

Mama first read this story almost a year ago, I had even shared his story on my own facebook page, and we often wondered what happened to Long John. Until now. The one and only Long John Silver is, and this is the bizarre bit, living just up the road from me in little old West Sussex, England, and he is looking for his forever home!

A perfect friend for me? I hear you ask. Well we have a lot in common—he wants a quiet home with no children, well ditto to that. He doesn't like cats . . . OMG he is my soul mate! Sadly Mama says our cat, Mrs. D from the dark side, comes first so it's a NO for us. Grrr. Long John is very friendly though and despite everything that happened to him, he likes people—I don't—and loves attention so here's hoping my little cat-hating soul mate finds a home.

As for Clementine, well she got lucky and found her very own home already, too.

So big it up for those that care, who see the suffering and react, because not only do they help those who need it most but they give the likes of Mama and Papa one of life's special things . . . a best friend.

Miracles can happen.

Editor's comment: I hate you too.

WEEK 35
Outed as a Lover of Women

I've been rumbled. It had to happen sooner or later. Mama and Papa believed that my grumpy behaviour towards two-legged creatures was due to my extremely harsh former life. To some extent this is true. Because of this I have met my very own doggie psychiatrist, who diagnosed me as an aloof Anatolian Shepherdy type dog, with a few, well, issues, to put it gently. Mama and Papa have labelled me as an enigma, which is also 100% spot on. But the deep down, real nitty gritty truth of the matter has now been exposed.

Earlier this week, Mama, being Mama, was checking my Facebook page, as apparently it's important to keep an eye on what us young'uns are up to, internet safety and all that jazz. Whilst scrolling through my timeline Mama spotted something peculiar. A friend of mine, a certain young lady, had updated her profile picture with . . . a photo of yours truly.

Now Mama has seen other photos of me during my previous existence with the wonderful Ermioni, who rescued me after my accident, and would always be my heroine. (Love you Ermioni).

Are you starting to see where this is going? The only visitor we have had to our house this week was Uncle Reg from Reading. Hmmm. Love you Uncle Reg from Reading, but with your bus pass and receding fringe (to put it politely) you just don't really do it for me. And yes I did growl, a tiny bit. Sorry, Uncle Reg from Reading.

I do love Mama and Papa, dearly, but as we are speaking the truth . . . Papa is a dead ringer for his brother, Uncle Reg from Reading, and Mama is on the cusp of a care home. All our visitors are dodgy and England is cold, wet and miserable, and oh yeah, muddy . . . slippy, slippy, slippy. This is not good for a three-legged dog who's just trying to take a whiz, let me tell you. But I digress. . .

The truth is out. I am, apparently, and from all evidence have always been, a good old-fashioned sunshine and ladies' man. Ain't nothin' wrong with that! In the words of David Bowie, 'Oh, you pretty things . . . driving your Mamas and Papas insane.'

I don't drive my Mama insane, as she already beat me there long ago. In her continued quest to find the perfect companion for me she has informed me that we are hoping to have a date with a potential new bestie, as early as next weekend. 'Joyous joy', I hear you cry. No. Mama has found me a boyfriend.

Let me remind you, I travelled for four long days and nights over land and sea with a bunch of Spanish chaps on our quest for a better life. Now little old England has a population of fifty-three million, six hundred and twenty-seven thousand, eight hundred and fifty-nine. And I got picked by number 53,627,858. Mama. There are also more than eight million, five hundred thousand dogs on this planet.

And Mama picks me a boyfriend? FFS. Don't get me wrong, there is absolutely nothing wrong with being gay. My predecessor, the odd Chocolate Labrador, Cactus Jack, was as gay as gay could be, and Mama and Papa were super proud of him. He even appeared on Radio One's Britain's gayest pets with Sarah Cox back in the day. If you love someone you love someone, and if they love you in return that is the most precious thing ever.

But having already pointed out that I am somewhat of a ladies man, I would really prefer a girlfriend. I see the way Papa looks at Mama, and even though she is as mad as a bucket of monkeys, he proper loves her. And that is what I want. My very own true love.

But it's not all about me coz that is just not right (at least not 24-7, I mean really.) There is a lot of love out there and this is for Claudiu.

Claudiu is a driver who transports rescued dogs from Romania to their new homes. Just before Christmas he was involved in a horrific accident. In the words of the rescue charities: 'Claudiu was always so amazing with the dogs, caring and dedicated beyond belief. Claudiu is highly respected and well-liked by all of the dog rescue organisations that have worked with him over the years.'

The accident left Claudiu in a coma, fighting for his life. His liver was damaged and his legs were crushed. Sadly his left leg could not be saved and has been amputated. His right leg has undergone several surgeries. Claudiu will never be able to return to the job he loved.

Claudiu has a lovely wife and young family to support but there is no benefit system in Romania to help and hospital treatment has to be paid for too.

Dog charities across the country are holding sponsored walks to support Claudiu and his loving family, to thank this wonderful man who helped so many rescue dogs. Now it is our time to help him. As a fellow amputee I have done my bit and hopped around Swanbourne Lake and made a donation.

At the end of the day it's all about caring. So share the love for Claudiu. And if I end up with a brother-from-another-mother instead of a girlfriend then so be it . . . if the boy needs some love then I am just the chap to share it.

Editor's comment: Just remember who was there when you woke up in the vet's without your personal bits, heroine indeed.

WEEK 36
Fashionably Late

It's been a bit of a week and a half. I was feeling poorly, like proper poorly. And to top it off, I was left home alone, for the first time in ages. Mama arrived home first and she did her usual—love, love, love—but That Darned Cat comes first, so I was given a quick treat whilst the creature from the dark side was given a three course meal upstairs in her penthouse suite.

Mama returned to my level and was surprised to find me still standing there in the hall, treat stick in mouth, not moving. Then Mama went into the sitting room and the reason for my bizarre behavior became apparent. Vomit. My vomit. Everywhere. Well, not actually everywhere—just on the rug that costs a fortune. The cheap sh*t rugs, wipe clean laminate flooring, and the dodgy old doormat were left untouched by the projectiles I'd produced in her absence.

Mama, being an angel, prepared buckets and cloths and began to deep clean the posh rug, and deep clean indeed as there were a lot of random carrot-looking particles hiding in that pile of lavish expensiveness. I remained in the hall, treat stick in mouth, horrified that I was expected to eat in such a disgusting environment.

Job finally done. Then Papa came home, and he looked a funny colour. What was going on here? He poured a beer, took one sip and declared he could drink no more. Mama considered dialling 999 at this revelation, but thought better of it. And so, ill we were, together, which was a little better than being ill alone, I guess.

Papa was, like proper poorly; but I just got bored and ate my snack in the hall. Mama cooked me rice and fish and prepared something soupy for Papa. And then we took to our beds. Thankfully, I was fully recovered in about 20 minutes, but Papa took much longer. We were both well worried about him.

The cat from the dark side was not well worried, though, and didn't appreciate the lack of attention; and so, in her cat-like fashion, she made the decision to hone her killer instincts by spending the next few days loitering on the stairs and leaping out only when Mama was passing by. In her very own cat-ninja-like discreet murderous way, of course. Thankfully her plot failed.

And then, Mama got a message from the wonderful Give a Dog a Home charity to say that two possible candidates for my forever friend had just rocked up into little old England. How exciting! Hello, and welcome.

I now had myself two dates in one day, just up the road in Brighton. As for poor sick Papa, well the medication was kicking in at last and so both Mama and Papa were my chaperones for the day. Hoorah.

Date number one: Dizzy.

Dizzy's foster mum was just lovely, and Mama and Papa went in first to meet him. Now Dizzy was not a dog they had really considered, yet as soon as they saw him knowing glances were exchanged. This was their sort of dog, just a wire-haired mass of gorgeousness. A silent decision was made in all but a few minutes. They liked him . . . a lot. Papa then went and got me and I brought me inside to meet my possible new bestie and I have to say he was fab. We both got on and yup, he was a top chap. Yet there was something not quite 'it' for me. Dizzy is a handsome young man, and he will make someone very, very happy. I admired the boy but he was not the one.

Mama got some great advice once, and this time she followed it: take loads of photos and then look back at them later. It gives you a better perspective of our dog body language. Try it, it is very revealing.

Take care my friend and find the best home for you.

Date number two. Rudy.

Did Mama follow this perfect advice and take loads of photos this time, no. Why not? Because I was a different dog here. I hopped into the house, happy as a happy thing on a happy day. I went out into the garden, said hello, then hopped right back in and settled down. There were Guinea Pigs, Tortoises, Rudy, Rudy's most amazing foster brother Andy (Mama was super impressed with Andy), Rudy's foster Mama, and foster Grand-mama. I rolled on my back and had a tummy tickle, if you can believe it. Yup, I felt right at home, no stress, no nothing, I even let the new strangers stroke me.

And Rudy? What can I say. Dizzy might be the most handsome chap in the world right now (lucky beggars that get to adopt him) yet Rudy was my cup of tea. He was a little friendly chap, who I am so hoping is going to be my very own new best friend. Yep, I got me a second date with the little guy.

There is the perfect home out there for all of us, remember that. It just takes some time to find, a bit like you weirdo human folk. Remember my first love—(well my second, since Ermioni, my saviour, is my first love)—little Orphan Annie, who I consider my proper girlfriend, is now living in her very own forever home. Much love Orphan Annie, we still love you loads.

Editor's comment: She was alright.

WEEK 37
Overwhelming Kindness

I have been a bit overwhelmed by kindness this week, and it's the most remarkable soul-soothing thingimajig ever. (I'm a dog, therefore I am articulate.)

Me and my old Mama have been dead worried about Papa; he might look all shiny and bright, but he has been feeling very poorly. Yet being the brave kind of chap he is, he has carried on regardless. Yesterday Mama and Papa were my chaperones once more on my second date with my new little bestie. As we were about to leave, Mama asked Papa if he needed the postcode to pop into his sat nav. Papa wearily replied, 'No, it's already saved in a folder named DOGS on my phone, so no need.' We love Papa.

Mama told Papa that she loved him and thank you. Papa told Mama that there was no need to say thank you, he was just grateful that no matter what happened, he knew his life would never be boring. I popped out for a quick whiz before the journey and did my usual back paw swipe once done. A few clods of turf flew over the neighbour's fence. Papa sighed and muttered something about the lawn costing £200 and a whole day's work, but hey ho, there will be two little blighters doing that soon.

So we rocked on up to Brighton, the home of the weird and wonderful. Mama had taken me out earlier that morning, and I had been my usual enigma self. I casually lolloped along without a care in the world, and then for no good reason whatsoever I barked at two buses and a van. Just because.

Brighton is busier that our little area, lots going on, and I like it. Not the traffic, of course, but there are more important things for a three-legged dog to delicately balance around whilst attempting to mark a stately tree-lined avenue.

Mama is useless in her current menopausal state, and completely forgot which house we were visiting, even though we had only been there a week before. She gaily marched right on past it, so I just sat outside and watched her jog on. Papa pointed out the error of her ways, and Mama returned to the correct abode whilst I just sat there, outside the entrance, casually waiting.

And then we went in. Again. Last time I was on my bestest behaviour, and this time . . . well, to Mama's surprise, ditto. My new bestie's foster Mama is awesome. Her own dog Andy is proof of this. Andy was poisoned and set on fire, but he was saved and is now thriving in his forever home, and is an absolute delight. I have added this remarkable lady to my list of heroines.

The Cypriot. Yep, my new potential bestest buddy is an immigrant from Cyprus, who was dumped as a puppy on Christmas day in 2016. The little chap and his littermates were cared for by the awesome Paws Dog Shelter in Paphos.

Each of the others got a brand new home, which is marvellous, but my little bestie didn't. He spent the last year living there without his brother and sisters, and was well-cared for of course, but the boy needs a family to call his own. With a bit of love, patience, and kindness—and I reckon it's my turn to give back—and he'll be just fine.

It turns out my little bestie was just as excited about meeting me again, and he even wore his best bowtie to make a good impression.

This time last year I was just a three-legged dog living rough. As I sat with my new chum, I listened to Mama tell Rudy's foster Mama why she had chosen me.

Mama and Papa had had dogs before—Cactus Jack and Scruffy Bucket—two old rescued souls who experienced a long and good life. When Mama and Papa discussed getting another dog, they were only interested in a rescue dog. Papa had visions of a hound that could accompany him on odd jobs in his van, as well as long runs across the English countryside. Mama shattered his dreams when she declared they were adopting a three-legged Greek beast who hated travelling in any sort of vehicle and was not up to jogging even on flat surfaces.

The reason being that Mama had seen my story on the world wide web, and it said I was becoming depressed because the other dogs would push me out of the way at the feeding stations. Plus, I was an anti-social man-hater with a penchant for attractive ladies. An oddball and an enigma . . . the perfect match.

And I'd be the first to say I'm a happy dog now. Mama and Papa love me dearly, and I love them too. Do they want another dog? No, not really.

But I want a friend. A dog friend. And Mama and Papa realise this; and so, being the loving doggie parents they are, they have continued their quest to find me a bestie.

When we got back home from our visit, I was super surprised to find a package waiting for me. I LOVE (to eat) packages, and this one had my name on it!

My super gorgeous Facebook friend Auntie Beverley had sent me a parcel, whoop whoop, and boy did I love it. Tore the beggar open and it was filled with toys! I LOVE YOU Auntie Beverley with all of my little heart, like proper love, you awesomely wonderous woman.

In other news I have heard from my first love, Orphan Annie, who is having the best time in her new home. This makes all of us a bit joyous—even the evil cat from the dark side—as we just loved her immensely. Go Annie, big love from us all.

Week 37. Who would have thought. I'm super happy! Thank you to all of you, but especially these guys who have simply been kind to me, which includes Give a Dog a Home and Auntie Beverley.

Oh, and it's date number three with my new bestie next week!

 Editor's comment: I will end you. Have I said that before?

WEEK 38
Enter Mr. Moussaka

I have a bestie. My very own best forever friend, and the best bit about having a bestie is that I am his bestie too! Excited doesn't even cover it. I am a hyper-happy-hoppy, three-legged, manically-super-over-the-moon Ouzo the Greek Complete. I am also exhausted, since my bestie, Mr. Moussaka, aka Rudy Moose, has one more leg than me and is super-fast and sprightly. He also has one more toe than the norm, and his back leg appears to be double jointed and bends in its own quirky direction, so that makes him the perfect match for our bizarre family.

Random fact of the day. We are now a three pet household, with a total of 3 tails, 4 ears, 11 legs, and 45 toes between us.

We're making adjustments. Mama and Papa have been thoughtful and considered how to make Mr. Moussaka feel welcome and safe. When I first arrived, I discovered see-through furniture when I bashed my head on a glass table. Ridiculous.

When my beautiful little Orphan Annie came to stay, Mama and Papa finally removed this apparently expensive piece of unsightly furniture so we would have more room to play. They also got rid of the expensive glass computer table and chair and replaced them with a good old-fashioned small and sturdy wooden coffee table, purchased from the exclusive online shopping experience known as Gumtree. This also served a very useful secondary purpose; Mama and Papa placed Orphan Annie's bed under this table so she had a safe and secure place to go should she feel the need.

However, my little Rudy Moose is a tad bigger than little Orphan Annie, so Mama instructed Papa to 'do something with that, love'. And so Papa did, and little Rudy Moose spent his first night on his very own super-duper comfy fluffy bed tucked under his very own pine archway.

As you can imagine, Mama and Papa have, as ever, put a lot of time and thought into pleasing Pet Number One too, aka The Creature from the Dark Side. After all, the poor old puss was in a shelter herself for over a year as no one wanted her either. I think this is because she has no ears and is a vicious, belligerent brute, plus she is also some sort of mixed breed as she is proper hefty at the front end and proper skinny at the rear end. Her back legs are also a lot longer than her front legs. In my humble opinion, she is a bizarre creature indeed.

Anyway, back to the point. Mr. Moussaka rocked up from Brighton to my humble abode and we were all prepared with stair gates, closed doors, and a natural remedy pet plug-in with calming diffusers all in place.

Until . . . yup, the very first tea time, as I was happily chomping in the living room and Mr. Moussaka was happily munching in the kitchen. Mrs. D chose that exact moment to enter the kitchen via the cat flap in the back door. Uh oh. Will this end badly?

But my brave and fearless companion casually trotted over to the Death Star and introduced himself. 'How do you do, and who does Mr. R. Moussaka have the great pleasure in meeting?'

Mama intercepted in a calm and casual manner and stood in between them, explaining to little Rudy Moose that this fluffy black-and-white ball of fur was in fact a bit of a ninja with nails, sharp ones, and it might just be best to give the old girl some room to pass.

Rudy Moose sat down. Mrs. D, being from the Dark Side, well, she just pushed him out of the way and started to eat out of his bowl. Harsh. And after much careful—yet not so meticulous—planning that is how they met.

The doors are now open yet the stair gate remains closed, as my mate

Rudy Moose has a lot to learn about the perils of the French feline femme fatale. Now, when the cat isn't sleeping on her very own single bed in her very own penthouse suite, she has taken to laying on the other side of the stair gate staring at her new target and plotting something very dark. In fact I do believe she is actually taking mental measurements so she knows just how big a hole to dig. Take care, Mr. Moussaka. I will endeavor to protect you, my friend.

Mama has mastered her very own technique for climbing over the stair gate, and Papa commented that it was actually good exercise and Mama should in fact consider taking part in some sort of competitive hurdling contest. While she may not be graceful, or fast, she gets the job done.

Or then again, she could just open the gate and walk through, closing it behind her. Whatever. Mama said not to be so stupid, what if she opened the gate and forgot to shut it? Then what would happen? Later that very same day, Mama forgot to shut the gate. Rudy Moose went straight up the stairs and ate all the cat food. That boy is my absolute hero. What a legend!

My dear little friend, Mr. R. Moussaka, has only been here for just over 24 hours, but I am pretty sure this rather beautiful relationship is going to blossom. Thank you to all at Give a Dog a Home, and most of all to Auntie Hannah, who gave Rudy Moose the chance of another life.

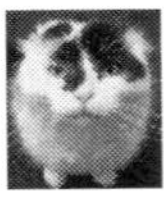 Editor's comment: Dog #2? What could possibly go wrong.

WEEK 39
Chinese New Year of the Dog

According to the experts, 'as the eleventh animal in Chinese zodiac, **Dog** is the symbol of loyalty and honesty. People born in the **Year of the Dog** possess the best traits of human nature. They are honest, friendly, faithful, loyal, smart, straightforward, venerable, and have a strong sense of responsibility.'

Yup, be more Dog. Stick that in your pipe and smoke it, Cats!!!!

I have this thing called a twitter account. I have no idea how it works because I am a dog. However, I had a little scroll through the other day and it was all 'Whoop Whoop, Chinese New Year of the Dog'. A wonderful thing to behold . . . maybe.

However, me being me, I'm a tad mistrusting of the human kind; I worry that we in the West may have misinterpreted this whole deal, as dogs are still on the menu in some parts of China. To my suspicious mind, the Chinese Year of the Dog could just be a tad bit more sinister, as in the Chinese version of a cheap and tasty dinner. I hope not.

Anyway, enough of my rambling and back to other matters.

I have banged on about this in the past, but Mama spends far too much time on her laptop. Personally I hate the damn thing, plus that godawful phone! Don't get me started. Marvellous, yet another photo of me on the world wide web.

Privacy Mama Edwards, privacy. But I have to say the world wide web did help Mama find me a friend, so she did good. She kept on telling me she was trying to find someone for me to play with, and yeah, I wanted one. My mate Rudy Moose, Mr. Moussaka to those not in the immediate family circle, is just my cup of tea. My cup of tea? What a very English turn of phrase . . . I seem to be turning into a right old English gentleman. Next I'll find myself saying cor blimey Guvnah and hanging around back yards full of homing pigeons and whippets. Who'd have thought it!

So this aloof Anatolian Greek street Shepherd, three-legged lummox who is developing an English accent, is now a big brother. And I like it. REALLY LIKE IT. Thank you Mama and Papa. I proper love you.

My little chap has been here for a whole week and he's doing great. He's no longer scared of curtains, plus he has learned to go through the glass patio door only when it's open. The vacuum cleaner is still a scary entity, but he'll learn; I just lay there and let the parents vacuum around me. Being the continental type he is also fond of a drop of wine.

Thankfully Mama is a lightweight in the alcohol department, and the glass of wine she left on the floor was actually only 5% proof and two thirds water; plus it was quickly retrieved once lapping sounds were heard. Most surprisingly, after only seven days the stair gates are now left open. The boy knows upstairs is a no-go cat-only territory, a sort of canine/feline Gaza Strip, and he only had to be told twice. Hmmm, just twice? He is a bit of a smart cookie.

Oh, and a cat whisperer extraordinaire too. We are quite a sight first thing in the morning when we all traipse out the front door, Mama, Papa, me, Rudy Moose, and That Darned Cat.

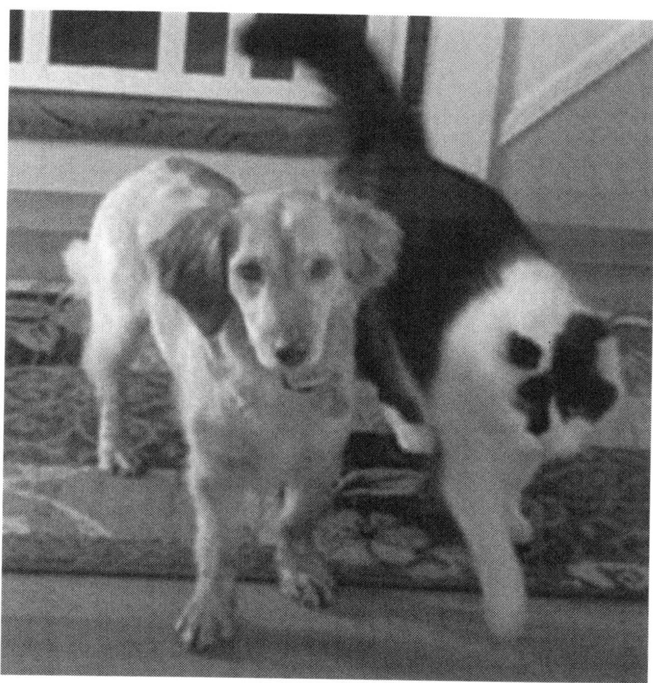

We went visiting the other day to Papa's mate, who lives in a proper posh countryside manor, just the kind of mansion I pictured myself in, before I realised my forever home was actually a bit of a humdrum, semi-detached suburban working class (slightly bigger than a rabbit hutch) abode. I still have my eye on that big jobby house on the seafront but Papa's mates house . . . OMG.

Rudy Moose was kept on a lead, since it's only been a few days and I am, apparently, expected to show him a good example. Mama, with her godawful phone took a snap of me looking out of the enormous Gothic window.

A whimsical look of hope? A look at all that awaits me in my new life … a gaze into the future? Nope. It's a beautiful photo, but I was just licking the window trying to grab a sky raisin, aka a poxy fly. The rich have them too.

My wee friend Rudy Moose took a little unwell on the journey and had a bit of an accident enroute. But hey, what's a bit of misplaced tinkle in the back of a van?

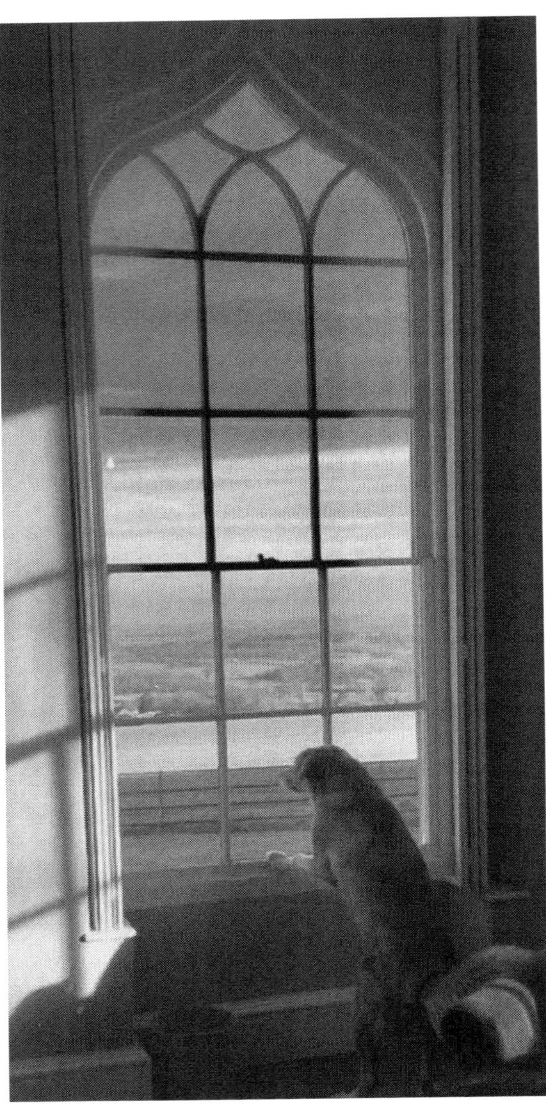

I manned up and attempted to make my boy feel at home on the return journey, but then had an accident of my own and did a bit of car sick projectile vomiting, all over everything, and I mean proper everywhere. Sorry Rudy Moose.

Me and my bestie are one week into our new relationship, but it feels like much longer. I wanted what Mama and Papa have, a special relationship, and so far so good. We are a little bit in love, but we are still getting to know each other. Toys, treats, and dinner are still a slow approach, just because . . . I still growl in my sleep. But now, with my new bestie I just snore.

Mama's boys are happy boys which makes a happy Mama.

Happy Chinese New Year of the Dog!

 Editor's comment: Ok, he can stay if he has to.

WEEK 40
Not Bothered

It's kinda groovy to look back, cuz boy have I changed. Sure, I'm still a lumbering three-legged aloof Anatolian lummox, but my new little mate Mr. Moussaka has made me realise just how far I've come. For example, my dear friend is scared of curtains, the vacuum cleaner, the van, Mama's singing (who wouldn't be), whereas me? Not bothered. In fact, today when my buddy was lurking in the kitchen whilst Mama vacuumed our plethora of combined hair—which according to Mama was enough to weave blankets for the local cats' home—I simply refused to move and allowed Mama to vacuum around me. Yep, I'm still scared of people, but Rudy Moose is all over anyone that comes to visit, so maybe one day I will relax with company just like my buddy will with Mama's singing.

OMG, I almost forgot, there is seriously bad news on the home front too. We no longer have a letter box! WTF. My deep love of Postman's daily visit has been thwarted. Papa has made the front door look like new, with no letter box, and fixed some sort of other feature for deliveries on the outside wall. I'm heartbroken, of course. There's nothing like a bit of post to chew in the morning. Gutted doesn't even cover it. Bad Papa. Apparently Papa doesn't want Mr. Moussaka picking up this sort behaviour, or as he put it, 'two of us morons eating the important information' that is diligently delivered to our home each day. I can only assume Papa is fond of those Saga circulars. Grrrrrrr. Or Grrrrrrr no more as the case may be.

Plus, we now have a new fence around the front garden. Another one of Papa's little jobs. As it turns out, my mate can fit through the cat flap; he hasn't tried yet, and maybe never will, but just in case Papa has built a

Mr. Moussaka potential escape picket fence—as you do. The neighbours commented on how nice it looked and enquired as to why Papa had, after all these years, decided to build such a lovely fence. Papa explained that a young dog named Mr. Moussaka, a homeless mutt all the way from Cyprus, had recently flown into Gatwick in his quest to find a forever home. Then because of this invention called the world wide web, Mama had found out about this and offered the wee chap a place to live; yet being a wee chap, he could fit through the cat flap, hence the new fence. The neighbours didn't ask any more questions.

My boy has been here for two weeks, and we have settled into a nice routine when we're not sleeping. We have a street walk in the morning—what with me being a street dog there is nothing better than a sniff around on a Sunday morning. Rudy Moose is a bit of a Speedy Gonzales, though, with all that 'arriba arriba, andale andale' Mexican muchness.

For Mr. Moussaka everything is dead exciting, and it's a bit of a mission to keep up with the wee chap. But keep up I do. Until we head home when it's a bit more mission impossible, so he has to wait for me whilst I have a bit of a lie down. Afternoons are more up his avenue. All that running about on grass nonsense—parks, greenswards, fields, galloping about and doing his rather remarkable gazelle impression. But, it seems to make the boy giddy. I am happy too, as long as when it all gets a bit much I can have my little lie down and watch Papa hide in bushes while Rudy Moose runs around like a looney trying to find him.

Some interesting facts about my new oddball friend. I may have already mentioned the double-jointed wonky back legs and the extra toe, but in fact he has two extra toes, one on each leg. Plus, I suspect he was last in the queue for ears and most certainly first in the queue when it comes to the lipstick department, if you know what I mean. A random mishmash of body parts make up our Mr. Moussaka, and I love him just the way he is.

But all is not a bed of roses, due to the creature from the dark side. The beast with the sheathed weapons is not to be trusted. Yeah, just look at the lovely Mrs. D, all sweetness and light. . . be my friend and all that jazz. Be warned, she has a cunning feline plan my friends, a cunning feline plan . . . beware of the dark side. Three hours after this beautiful little 'all is good in da hood' photo was taken, the she-devil revealed her true traits and had a hissy fit, taking a razor sharp swipe at my bestie. She missed, of course.

Papa told the she-devil that she was indeed an evil beast, and that she should apologise immediately. The cat said 'le meow' what with her being French and all that which roughly translates into something I could not possibly repeat. How very rude.

Later that evening, as us boys settled down for the night with our bed-time snacks in our separate beds, the feline fiend dared to stick her head round the door. I used my native tongue and let out a mighty Greek roar, go google translate that, you little French pussy cat.

And by the way, Mr. Moussaka has impeccable good manners, comes instantly when called, sits on command, and waits like an angel until told otherwise at feeding times. The boy is an angel . . . so far, at least!

Editor's comment: I said I liked him better than you . . . not that I actually liked him. Duh.

WEEK 41
The Arrival of Snow

In 2008, someone asked Mama 'Where do you see yourself in ten years' time?' Turns out the correct answer was loitering around the back of the butchers shop at 7am in sub-zero temperatures watching a three-legged Greek ex-street dog sniff a bin.

Mama got all excited at the arrival of snow and took us outside to get some pretty pictures of her boys frolicking in the winter wonderland. I sat down, as that's what I do, and Mr. Moussaka, well he did a poop, and then we went back in.

The snow wasn't exciting for the beast from the dark side either. Mama awoke one night to the sound of peculiar scratching sounds, followed by a loud thump. She got up to investigate and caught the no eared feline sneaking out of the bathroom. Mama's curiosity meant the cat came dangerously close to losing a life, as Mama discovered exactly what had taken place . . . the world's largest cat poop was still steaming in the bath tub.

Yes she has a cat flap. Yes she has a litter tray. Yes she is disgusting.

We're a hardy bunch though, so we still traipsed out each morning and afternoon, just a little quicker than the norm and not for so long. Boy was it cold. Three legs and snow does not mix well. I'm not keen on slippery mud, so icy snow was a precarious business, especially when one was doing one's business. Balancing on two legs to take a whiz on a daffodil who ended up at the wrong place at the wrong time, the only thing I could find protruding from the white landscape, was a delicate affair let me tell you.

Rudy Moose skipped about showing off on his four paws, enjoying every second of new sights and smells and brimming with excitement. Like me, he's keen on checking out the back of the food shops too on our morning expeditions, and then we both hurry home for warmth and breakfast. My buddie is a smart cookie, and has learned the one and only rule during our return journey: no cocking of legs on shop doorways, apart from the estate agents, as apparently no one likes them.

Mama was being a tad smug yesterday as she proudly boasted to Papa how good her boys were as she stood and watched us in the garden. She said compared to the neighbour's dogs we were simply amazing: so calm, well-behaved, and just no trouble at all. Well, apart from my anti-social tendency to growl at people, of course. Mama opened the door and called us in. Rudy Moose bounded in with his usual energetic abundant eagerness and I sat down. Mama called me again and I lay down. Mama went for the more authoritarian tone and instructed me in no uncertain terms to get up. Being the faithful companion that I am I did just that. Mama reminded me what a good boy I was and to come, so I set off the wrong way down the garden. Mama used a word that began with a 'b' but I didn't hear the rest as I was no longer listening.

Mr. Moussaka, according to Mama, is a completely different kettle of fish. Mama, according to me, talks nonsense, and this is the reason I don't always bother to listen. Papa is with me on this one. However, Mama is now very excited as she has enrolled my little Rudy Moose into training sessions with the wonderful Bone Canis. This means that starting at the end of the month Mr. Moussaka and Mama will be out of the house one evening a week doing all sorts of exciting physical activities whilst I will be left at home with Papa with nothing to do but lay down and snuggle. Marvellous.

We do like an evening snuggle with the parents. Just the other evening we were all cosied up, lovely and warm enjoying a snooze. Rudy Moose woke up and temporarily forgot he now lived in a house and had a little stretch then casually took a whiz on the rug. Mama said accidents happen and cleared it up saying at least it would take away the smell of treat sticks for a bit.

My buddy and I happily eat our goodies sitting next to each other now, while Mama hangs around like a boxing referee just in case any trouble breaks out, but no, we're great. Papa went on the world wide web to place another bulk order, which I'm never opposed to. Apparently our need for snacks has doubled with the advent of Mr. Moussaka.

Mama isn't a fan of the hairdresser's, but she went this week for a trim—a quick in, wash, cut, and out no nonsense affair, since sitting in front of a mirror talking drivel is not Mama's thing. There was some sort of mix up at the till, so Mama had to hang around for a bit which meant by the time she got home her hair had dried, au natural, and she walked in the door with a wild curly monstrosity on the top of her head.

Us boys took fright as we had no idea who she was. Papa asked if there had been some sort of psychotic episode in the salon and Mama replied, 'No; well, there nearly was when the hairdresser asked me how old my grandchildren were.'

After much use of various electrical appliances, Mama straightened herself out and we then went for a stroll. It was nice now that the snow had gone, just the usual rain instead. We all got a bit wet, but had a good rub down when we got home.

Mama laughed at my buddy and took a photo of his ears to share on the world wide web as they looked like they had been crimped. Papa said he should have taken a photo of Mama earlier and shared that on the world wide web too. We all chuckled and Mama told Papa something unmentionable, but it was all in fun.

Family life. It's good.

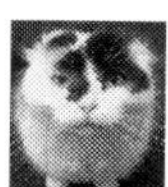

Editor's comment: Forget my birthday = I poop in your bathtub.

WEEK 42
Mama's Story

It's Mama's Day. So it's over to you Mama.

Mama's story:

I have three children—two boys and a girl. They are my world. I love them, and their quirky individuality makes me proud each and every day.

I have three pets—two boys and a girl. They are my world. I love them, and their quirky individuality makes me laugh, swear, and vacuum each and every day.

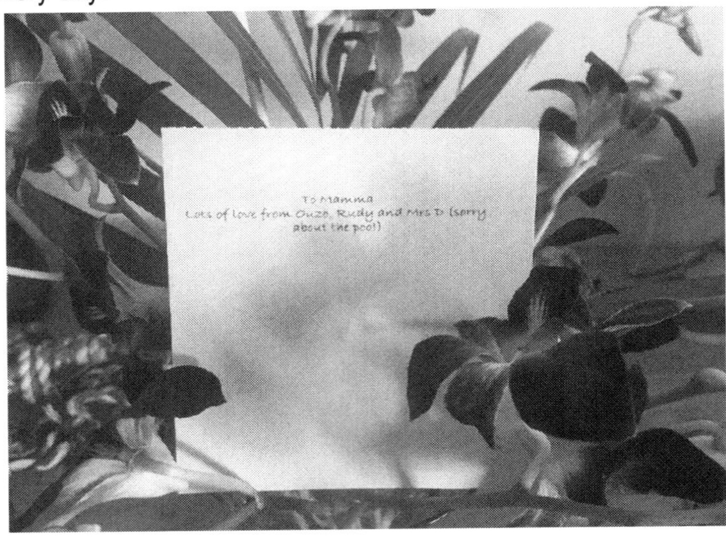

Ouzo the Greek came into our lives 42 weeks ago today. Two days after I had four hours of intensive surgery, Papa drove me almost the entire length of the country to go and meet him (against his will and with me pretending I was just fine when I wasn't).

The first thing Ouzo did was show me his teeth. It was hardly love at first sight. But his story had touched me; he'd endured so much in his short time on this barking planet, that I just knew he was 'the one'. There's no explaining it. The three-legged Greek street dog was in need of a forever home with a bit of old-fashioned unconditional love. And so we rescued a dog.

Regrets? Never. Mistakes? Yes. We could have done a few things a bit better, for him and for us, but we learnt and we grew. Would we be without him? God no. Ouzo has changed from an extremely tense, scared young man into a ridiculously loving, adorable doofus that we treasure immensely. He has given us his trust, he has given us his heart, and that's something you hold close and never let go.

Ouzo is stupidly handsome, stubbornly aloof, yet unbelievably responsive when needs must. He's a lummox, a reprobate, an enigma. He is the bee's knees, the cat's whiskers, and the dog's missing parts.

Oh, and don't forget the part about the potential candidate for an ASBO (anti-social behaviour order issued by police to unruly people) as he doesn't really like strangers.

The most important thing we learnt . . . it turns out we didn't really rescue a dog with a sorry story, we just inadvertently stumbled across our best friend.

We love you, Ouzo, and we've loved sharing your story with the world.

Yet our boy needed a friend—a dog friend. And so I became obsessed with finding my boy the best forever friend *for his needs*. This was not an easy task, and yes I got it wrong at first (we love you Annie, bucket loads) and there were some possible matches that were just too far away for my boy to meet, or too scared of strangers; or too big, too small, too boisterous, or worse, had an unhealthy interest in cats.

Until Mr. Moussaka came along. He is a little tiny tad of an angel sent not from heaven, but from Cyprus. The boy is a legend, and they sure love each other. I hope I got it right this time.

Four weeks later and things could not be better. Our boys are heart-meltingly adorable; they snuggle up, play, and yes, annoy each other . . . true brotherly love. Mr. Moussaka has given us exactly what we wanted, but I still have a fear that it's too good to be true.

And then along came the accidents.

After four weeks our boys had been trusted to stay home alone, all by themselves, with the cat, for two whole hours. I returned first and something peculiar had occurred. The strange thing I noticed on the rug turned out to be Mr. Moussaka's collar, ripped into several separate pieces. When questioned, the boys looked as bemused as me. Just a bizarre incident/accident with no explanation? It happens. Apparently.

Oh, well, no matter, as the young Rudy Moose still had his harness. I popped it on and took the boys to the prettiest park, where the oddest people hang out, for a bit of a jaunt. We were having fun but then I threw a stick—a stupid thing to do, but I did it. The boys both charged for it like Olympic athletes, para and standard, but it went horribly awry. Somehow, Ouzo's leg slipped through Rudy Moose's harness and Rudy twisted so both boys ended up on the ground with Rudy's ribcage being squished and Ouzo panicking with his leg trapped, one of his biggest fears.

The noise was horrible. There are four clips on the harness, and I couldn't find a single one to undo in the tangled mess. Ouzo could no longer contain his fear and screamed as he bit me in wild panic. He calmed again as I fumbled with the f***ing clips, whilst Rudy Moose looked terrified as I stumbled on trying to reassure them. Ouzo panicked again as the God dammed thing got tighter around his leg and he bit me a few more times until I finally found a clip, and then another one, and set them free.

Young Rudy Moose, the poor boy, was as cool as a cucumber and sat by my side as we comforted Ouzo, who was distraught (legs are important to him) and lay panting for some time with a sad look in his eyes. I couldn't read his mind, but I knew he felt bad for biting me; he was in a panic, I understood and no blood was spilt.

I reassured him and told him I loved him, because I do, and Rudy Moose too, and then we made our way home.

The boys were good; they even had another run around the park on the way back to the car. Happy days had returned. Once we got home the boys were fed and I went upstairs to change. My hand hurt a bit but things could have been worse.

Pet number one came to join me in the bedroom. She's my first love when it comes to my adoptive family, and she could sense my upset and gently mewed as I got changed. I was touched by her concern, so I patted the bed to encourage her and up she jumped.

That's when accident number three occurred. As a fluffy beast, sometimes there can be a slight problem with, you know, fur and stuff. Mrs. D ensconced herself in the duvet and then began to wipe her rear end across the bed leaving a nasty skid mark. For the love of God! Even though I was in pain, I washed and changed the bedding, deskanked the cats bottom area, and decided I deserved a glass of wine.

By this time my hand was too swollen to pick up the bottle or hold a glass . . . so instead I sat and had a good cry.

My fur kids. I wouldn't swap them for the world.

Ouzo's defense:

As an aloof Anatolian three-legged Greek enigma, I may not be bright enough to put into words how I feel about you . . . so instead I stole someone else's.

'In all the world, there is no heart for me like yours.In all the world, there is no love for you like mine.' —Maya Angelou

I'm sorry, Mama.

Happy Mama's Day. We love you.

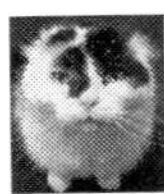

Editor's comment: Hey, sh*t happens.

WEEK 43
An English Winter

English winter—we're done with it, man. Mama said British summer starts soon, so bring it on; my bro and I are beach body ready, baby.

Not to speak for the rest of the family, but I think we're all in need of a bit of sunshine to defrost the bones. Especially the old folk, Mama and Papa, who seem to be going a bit winter stir crazy. On what felt like day 4,927, of your long and dark British winter nights, the old folk finally lost the plot and started to witter on about their wildest dreams . . . winning the lottery and escaping to a house in the country. Mama wants to change her name to Lady (something I can't possibly divulge) and Papa rather fancies being called Nigel Ponsenberry-Smallpiece. Whatever floats your boat I suppose? They plan on living in a tiny cottage, called Pallet Wood, hidden amongst a mahoosive private woodland, miles from anywhere.

They are anti-social, like me, it's why we get along so well, bizarrely. Since they are changing their names, they plan on reinventing their pasts, too. Then, during a rare and intimate moment, while they are sipping craft beer with the locals of their new community at the only tavern for miles, they will reveal their secret histories.

Mama will whisper that she is in fact an ex-Russian farm hand who had an unfortunate accident whilst learning a new skill: fake tanning with a man from America who turned permanently orange. Therefore, Mama had to go into hiding in deepest Wiltshire, or wherever. And Papa, her soul mate and saviour, is an ex-tobogganist who may or may not have been involved in espionage (no one suspects the tobogganist), who is also passionate about cheesecake.

And they think I'm barking. Then again, they might just carry on with reality, as cold and dark as it is. Mama did actually find Papa a job, check this out: Parking Cone man, from back in the day, has retired and his job is up for grabs. Park keeper of the local current community. Mama said he should go for it, since it's literally right up his street.

She told us boys we could rock up every morning and mess with his mind, parking at jaunty angles in the village hall users-only bays before the allocated time but Papa just raised his eyebrows—well kind of, that is. Let's just say he made his best effort after his recent misdemeanour with hair clippers and inappropriate settings.

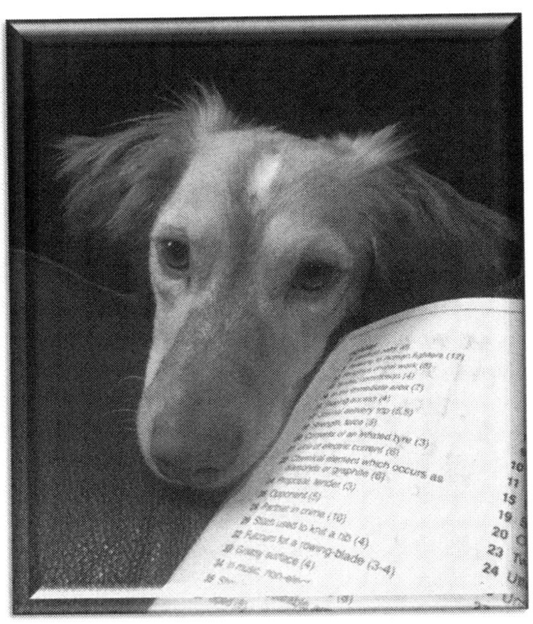

Mr. Moussaka did his best to dissuade these crazy musings, and used an adoring face to plead with them to just crack on with their crossword, sup up their Ovaltine, and break out the treat sticks. Top man.

I hope now you can see my problem—we miss you summer! The parents need to get out more, and should we ever win the lottery the first thing on the list is Oscar Pistorious' leg, for me.

As for me and my bestie? LOVED UP BABY. Winter weather is becoming a tad boring, sure, but we still get out twice a day, morning and noon, and have somewhat of a fab time regardless of the Arctic conditions. My Mr. Moussaka bounds about with bundles of energy, wearing me out just watching him, but it is such a pleasure to see him soooooo happy.

We met a couple of cyclists in the park the other day, and Papa told Rudy Moose to sit and wait whilst they passed; he did just that. When he sprints off super speedy in the wrong direction, he comes straight back when called. He loves other people (weirdo) and dogs, but he always comes back to me.

He even worries and runs round like a lunatic if he can't find me. And whilst the old folk play their own odd games, The Moose and I play ours . . . who can sit in the most annoying position. Tis much fun.

Plus, we found a new game called 'hunt the rock'. We found our first one yesterday, a pretty painted stone hidden in the village, and Mama turned it over to see a message on the back: '#cancerwiserocks pass it on'. Turns out it's a local volunteer group who supports families with cancer, a brilliant charity, so we joined the group and re hid the stone. Much excitement.

Talking of much excitement, Mama promised us an adventure, so on an English-Artic Spring afternoon we drove to the pet shop and I got to choose my beloved his own gift, one of the finest treats in the store. The only slight problem was that I took the bag in my mouth and made for the door before paying; Mama pointed out the police car outside, so I reluctantly waited whilst Papa paid and then we took our goodies home. Happy days.

Oh, and this morning I found another rock hidden in the village and this afternoon another one in the park.

Love this game!

Editor's comment: A big woohoo for #cancerwiserocks from me too, as I am a cancer survivor.

WEEK 44
Cancer, Charity, and Chile

I've been here for almost a year, and in all of those 44 weeks only one of them has been normal. #bestweekever.

My life has completely changed, because of charity and love. In my humble opinion, these are the best things in the world; so share the love, always.

Now I might harp on a bit about my past and all that, but it's what makes us who we are today. And today I am a three-legged ex-Greek street dog who's loving life. Mama says I'm barking (with just a tad of bonkers).

Here is the harping on about me and my past.

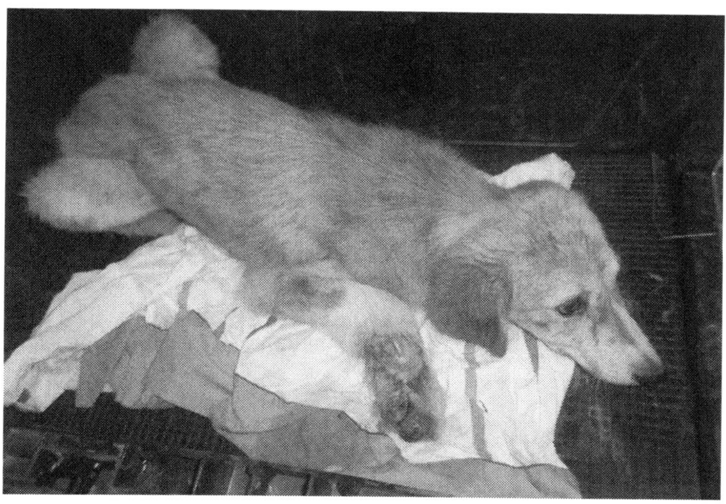

A reminder of where I have come from.

A reminder of my first love, my saviour, the remarkable charity worker to whom I owe my life.

My time to leave, my turn to shine.

People did amazing things: those who raised funds for my transport, my foster Mama, the wonderful Juliet, and of course Greek Animal Rescue. I will be forever grateful to a whole bucket load of people that gave me a chance, and did stuff I never thought any person would ever even consider. The good people. The ones you never hear about. If I had a hat, I would take it off to you. Big love from me to you all.

Now I live in a house with a bed—my own bed—it's warm, I get to snuggle all night long (even though it took me a couple of months to actually get onto it). I go out and about every day, and have even taken up rock hunting. I have breakfast and tea time plus treat sticks and dried stuff that stinks to high heaven and make Mama grimace and wash her hands a lot. I feel safe. I have a Mama and a Papa who love me ridiculously. AND I have a best friend . . . my very own Mr. Moussaka.

Oh, and I have a cat, that resident feline from the dark side. But such is life.

I am still a lumbering three-legged lummox with a penchant for growling at people who try to touch me. I still have bad memories. It has taken Mama all this time to realise why I do this, the daft mare, because it's actually obvious: the old flight or fight jobby. With three legs I can't do a runner, so there you go.

Other than that one slight quirky personality trait (well, there may be a few others) I am actually a rather happy chappie. And appreciative.

On to bettering our planet. Mama's Papa had cancer, and died at the age of 49. Mama's sister has overcome cancer, Papa's sister-in-law is fighting cancer, and our friend has terminal cancer. The cat from the dark side, the one with no ears . . . that's also due to cancer.

Recently I discovered a local charity that works with and supports people suffering with cancer. After several days of tripping over a brightly-coloured painted rock under my favourite tree for a morning whiz, we finally picked it up and read the message on the back.

Life is all about helping each other, no matter who you may be. I'm a prime example. Have fun, work hard, and listen to others. Be compassionate, be kind. Throw in the occasion growl just because.

I have made a financial contribution to this charity, and it was small maybe, but every penny helps. Now it was time to make my own rocks for other people to find. Picture the scene, a three-legged dog wearing a beret and sitting at an easel. This could all go horribly awry.

But I pulled it off and painted my famalam. My little rocks are now hidden around my favourite jaunts, so if you live nearby find, re-hide, and if you want donate a few pennies to this charity—or any other charity that floats your boat.

I was somewhat impressed with myself, until I compared my painting of Mr. Moussaka with the one done by his foster Mama, Auntie Hannah.

I had a bit of fun with it too, as you do. My rock is hidden right outside the pet shop door, because it's the best place in the world, let me tell you. The Moose's is hidden outside the local canine beauty parlour (because he's such a selfie boy) and the cat's? outside the dreaded vets! Ha! Sometimes I crack myself up.

As for Chile, the wee boy in the middle of my rock family, well he is still looking for his forever home, so I'm sending his rock to him so he can hide it in his own neck of the woods, and maybe it will not only raise awareness of the cancer charity but also my little Chile Dog too.

Because? Well Mama has told you this. She read my story and fell in love with me, and so it came to be. If Mama had read Chile's story (he was beaten so badly by his owner that he was left with a broken pelvis) and not mine, he might be living here now with my buddy instead of me.

And that is simply fate.

We love you Chile. Stay strong.

Charity . . . it may start at home, but it's going on across this whole rock we live on.

Editor's comment: You left my stone at the vets? How very dare you.

WEEK 45
Mama's Birthday

It was Mama's birthday this week; she turned 52, which in dog years is 364. One would think she might be a little wiser by now. However, I am almost 3, which in dog years is 21, and so I do believe I'm starting to mature. A corner just may have been turned. My present to my Mama? I have decided to be a well-behaved waggy-tailed chap who welcomes all visitors to our house.

The aloof Anatolian three-legged Greek street dog who hates everyone with a passion is, dare I say, becoming a little more interested in folk. I believe this is due to several factors:

1. Since I arrived in little old England no one has ever hurt me. (Well, apart from the time Mama tripped me up with her laptop wire and then again when Mr. Moussaka snared my leg in his harness. Oh, and that time Mama made me walk over stones on the beach and I hurt one of my three remaining paws.)
2. I may need to rethink point 1.
3. Having rethought point 1 . . . that freaking cat . . . ouch.
4. Mama and Papa have looked out for me. (Well, apart from the time Mama lost me down at the beach and I had to make my own way home before Auntie Penny found me, and that other time Papa lost me in the vast expanse of the RAF retirement home grounds and I had to find my own way back to his van.)
5. I need to rethink point 4.
6. People have been respectful of my phobia. (Well, apart from that time the 'know it all bird' at the beach who thought she was a dog

whisperer and insisted on touching me and then loudly pronouncing I was indeed vicious when I growled at her, and that old fella who got down on his hands and knees and stared me in the face, despite warnings and my very own flashy jacket which actually spelt out NERVOUS DO NOT PAT.)

7. I need to rethink point 6.
8. Treat sticks and various and sundry other delicious edibles.
9. I think about point 8 A LOT.
10. Bone Canis. Now here is a chap who did his job: making dogs feel better. And Mamas and Papas too. Sir Canis, you will always be known as 'The Fish Man' in our household. And yeah, our house stinks. THANK YOU.
11. Time; healing; love. (aka Mama and Papa).
12. Mr. Moussaka.

Speaking of stranger danger, a young Eastern European chap delivered a parcel to our humble abode this week. Now I love a package, when shoved through the letter box, but seeing as Papa has rudely sealed this up, the young man had to knock on the door. I growled, just a tad, and Mama told me to stop being such a drama queen (again, rude) before opening the door.

Now this young man had visited us before, and on that occasion he had a bit of a fright. Mama had opened the door, and as she was signing for the package the cat from the dark side made an ominous appearance.

The young man took a step backwards and in his delightful accent (with his eyebrows joining his fringe) declared, 'What dis dat, a kittydog?'

On this occasion I made my way towards him, and my tail was wagging (check me out), and this time he loitered (forever, despite the burning smell wafting from the kitchen) and Mama signed the little electronic thing with dumpling mix on her fingers as the young man sighed and said, 'I ave a dog, it haz moooor legz.'

That guy should be a comedian.

In news of my bestie, Mr. Moussaka, did I mention he can leap like a gazelle? He apparently got a little overconfident, and ended up in a little problem with one of those English seaside breakwaters. He somewhat misjudged his landing and ended up in a rock pool. Mama used to be a trampoline judge and said he only lost 0.5 of a mark. He is no longer scared of the vacuum cleaner or the curtains, but there was a bit of a curious incident with a hog in the night time.

Yup, the boy met his first hedgehog, which frightened him half to death and he refused to go into the garden again. The next day Papa was outside fixing the gate, and there was a bit of banging. Rudy Moose had a bit of a panic attack, until Mama picked him up and took him outside to prove it was in fact Papa and not some enormous hedgehog doing a spot of carpentry.

The Moose is also in dog school now. He and Mama were gone for ages, and I spent the entire evening laying by the front door waiting for them to return. When they got back, Papa asked Mr. Moussaka if he had been a good boy, and Mama replied 'sort of'.

Mr. Moussaka told me that he'd met a very nice Spanish lady (a rescue dog from Spain), and he was hoping to meet up with her again next week. As for the 'school' bit, well, it involved a lot of sitting down and eating snacks. I like the sound of this. Papa said he would take me to watch on the last night, if we're allowed. And then Rudy Moose crashed hard, coz dog school is very taxing, apparently.

Editor's comment: Dog training, Ha!

WEEK 46
The Enigma

Mama read a blog this week based on a recent study on dog behaviour and temperaments which, after much in-depth analysis, summed up that people choose dogs with similar personalities to their own. Mama looked at me curiously. Mama told Papa who looked at Mr. Moussaka . . . smugly.

They may call me an enigma, but I like to think of it as more of a 'unique personality'. And there is always a reason for everything.

For example, when we went to the forest, I ran like the wind up a very steep hill in my pursuit of pheasants. Mr. Moussaka came back instantly when called, however, I didn't because:

a) I couldn't hear?

b) I have three legs and couldn't possibly run down a steep hill.

or c) I was chasing pheasants which is slightly more important than being obedient.

Mama, I believe non-compliance is one of your strong points, too!

When we went to Highdown Hill, I refused point blank to walk at all. The reason:

a) I was enjoying a bit of a sit down and taking in the view; there's a bench there and it's there for that very reason.

b) I was entranced by watching Mr. Moussaka gorging on pony poop whilst Mama was frog marching through the mud to the wastebin, again.

or c) Just because.

She was a bit grumpy about the whole experience. (Yes grumpy. So maybe we are a tiny tad similar after all.)

We got more packages the next day. A giant box arrived and I thought it might actually be a ginormous ostrich leg, but sadly it was just a toilet.

Papa is fitting a new bathroom, which they seem to be excited about, but us? Not so much. There is a lot of banging and crashing going on, and my Rudy Moose has been a tad scared. I look after him and reassure him as he hides behind me coz I love him. Mama used to do this for me when I got scared, and it helped.

Mr. Moussaka has been back to school; he dragged Mama into the village hall and she assumed he was pleased to be there. He told me later that he was just keen to see the pretty Spanish girl again (maybe he is more like Papa then). The Moose is a little star at school, and follows every command. When asked to walk to heel and ignore the small pile of treats on the floor he told me he did just that, but only because he's smart and veered off to the left where the actual massive bag containing all the snacks was hidden behind the curtain.

Speaking of The Moose, he met his double this week, a wee young chap who was super excited. Mr. Moose was super excited too, and whilst he leapt about showing off on his four legs with his new buddy, I made friends with his owner. Yes, me, making friends with a strange man. I took several treats from him but when Mama explained I was usually scared he then tried to touch me and I did do a little growl. But it is still progress.

I also followed a very nice lady who was feeding her dog cocktail crisps and gave me a couple too. Mama was polite, yet disapproved of her choice of treat. I pointed out that last Friday night Mama consumed almost an entire bottle of wine, but she seems to think that's different.

We finally got around to visiting the post office to send my mate Chile Dog his stone. Mama was asked 'What does this package contain' to which she replied 'a rock and a treat stick'. The kindly assistant made an effort to ignore the stench whilst giving Mama a strange look, but Mama doesn't give a damn about what other people think of her (another similarity we have, me thinks).

Editor's comment: Mama chose me too.

WEEK 47
The Moose

Mr. Moussaka is the sort of chap that got made in the final five minutes of a Friday afternoon shift. His ears are too big, his feet are too big and as for his 'lipstick' well, there's a Great Dane out there somewhere wondering what happened. He has long hair, short hair, straight hair, wavy hair, and the skinniest tail with an abundance of hair. His nose is pink and his eyes are ginger. Whichever angle you look at him, things look just kinda 'wrong'. I have previously mentioned the extra toes and the double jointed legs that bend the wrong way, and which he likes to drape over me when he sits on top of me.

Mr. Moussaka's character is of a similar ilk, which I'd categorize as oddly variable. He's an outgoing adventurer who loves everyone and bounds around wherever we may be, delighted to meet and greet whoever we come across. But if there's a shopping trolley, a man with a metal detector, or scaffold poles—or Papa upstairs banging with plumbing—he turns into a quivering wreck and his face morphs from fun inquisitive puppy into an old man with the weight of the world on his shoulders.

It's sad to see him like that, but Mama reminded me that it wasn't that long ago that I was the one who was scared of many things, like motorbikes, war memorials, and men. Mama also pointed out that my three remaining feet are no longer pink as I no longer manically chew them when stressed.

Mama has a point, however, I will probably always be scared of most men. Mama says, still, I should be proud that the little boy looks to me for guidance and confidence as I have come a long way. And do you know what? I am a little bit proud, and I do reassure my mate The Moose that there is indeed no need to be concerned—unless of course I'm busy selecting which daffodil to take a whiz on, then I just ignore him.

Time my friend, time. I once had a panic attack when Papa picked up a broom, now I just lay aloofly whilst he sweeps round me. No one is going to hurt you with me around . . . well, beware of That Darned Cat.

My little bro looks out for me too. He may dash about like a gazelle on steroids when playing with other chaps down at the beach, but he always comes back to me and sits by my side when I am having one of my lie downs.

In the nine weeks he has been here, Mama has taken the slow approach to introducing toys and the suchlike, as I used to be a bit of an 'it's mine, get your own' kind of a chap. When you come from the streets, if you get your paws on something worthwhile, then you ain't giving it up for no man nor beast. A cat? Maybe.

I've found out that we are going on a summer holiday! Strangely enough, Mama and Papa like a bit of a quirky holiday experience in an isolated and rural location, as they are about as anti-social as me. The trouble with their suggested plan is how do you get a three-legged dog up a ladder to stay in a treehouse? This limits our options a bit.

Plus, long car journeys on a potentially blazing hot July day? Not really our cup of tea, so the holiday was looking like it was coming down to local options only. Oh, and price? Dear Lord! Mama and Papa didn't really fancy taking out a mortgage for a one-week escape to the country.

But Mama's stubborn streak is as broad as mine, and so in the end she did indeed find the perfect location, with the perfect price, and the perfect three-legged dog disability access. Betty the Bedford has been booked. Yup, we are glamping it up in a horsebox.

Mama finally found the time to take me to meet the lovely Emma this week, the organiser of #CancerWiseRocks. I'm super impressed with what she's doing, raising much needed funds for a charity that was on the brink of closing, a charity which helped her after her diagnosis.

She has generated much press and publicity, and funds are now coming in from local businesses, too. Seeing all the photos of the kids' smiling faces as they join in on the rock hunting is such fun. I did my little bit too, and donated some rock painting starter kits for kids who want to get involved but whose parents can't afford a holiday in a horsebox, never mind splashing out on paint. Massive respect to Emma from me.

Editor's comment: I refuse to holiday in a horsebox.

WEEK 48
Mr. Blue Sky

Well, hello sunshine . . .

No time to be writing when the sun is out, so here's week 48 in a nutshell:

1. Mr. Moussaka has taken to using my one remaining front leg as a useful third paw when holding his bone in place to have a gnaw.

2. Mr. Moussaka has discovered if you gallop through a rock pool it tends to get deeper.

3. Mr. Moussaka is scared of lawn mowers, not just ours, but any random lawn mower far away in the distant leafy suburbs.

4. Mr. Moussaka is not scared of thunderstorms.

5. Mr. Moussaka is doing brilliantly at dog school.

6. Mr. Moussaka was used as an example at dog school.

7. Mr. Moussaka was asked to sit, wait, and come by Mr. Dog Teacher.

8. Mr. Moussaka sat, waited, and carried on waiting.

9. Maybe Mr. Moussaka is not doing so brilliantly at dog school.

10. Mr. Moussaka fell asleep at dog school.

11. Mama is still barking.

12. Papa is still fitting a new bathroom.

13. Thirteen can only mean one thing . . . The Cat from the Dark Side is still going strong.

14. Me? I'm just marvellous, thank you. Even though it appears that the new kid's getting all the attention these days.

Not such a bad life for a couple of second hand dogs.

Oh, and farewell mud, for the time being at least. I won't miss you.

Editor's comment: One wishes the staff would get a move on with finishing the new bathroom.

Papa's comment: I have spent the week working elsewhere to keep you all in the manor you are accustomed to . . . so keep you hair on, Princess.

Note: Hair was not kept on, and fixing the vacuum has been added to Papa's never-ending list.

And that was the week that was.

WEEK 49
Stuff Happened

Week 49, and my little old book has nearly come to an end. Only three weeks left of my one-year diary, which means it's only three weeks until my very first 'gotcha day' and my third birthday. I will be 21.

Each week I kinda think hmmm, so what happened over the past seven days . . . and then I remember, living in England is barking!

So, yeah stuff happened. But if I can just go back a bit, to when my Mr. Moussaka arrived, I was super-excited and made every effort to keep up with the young fool. To be honest it was a bit exhausting, and after a few days I did have a kinda meltdown on the pavement during a morning walk, and refused point blank to move as it was all too much. Mama and Papa considered the options: wait for several hours for me to recover my strength? Return home to fetch a much-needed vehicle for me to be gently lifted aboard? But then thankfully a bus came along.

I was instantly energised and leapt up like a spring lamb, barking furiously at the GD thing, not because I'm scared, I'm so over that, but because it is such fun. So this week . . .

We went to the park one afternoon, a park I don't really like. Mama likes to take us to different places each afternoon, so our world isn't too boring. We have the beach, the woods, the park with the big pond, the park with the small pond, the prettiest park in the world with the oddest, most annoying people in the world, and the dull park (Parking Cone man park).

This particular afternoon's ramble was the dull park. It's blah. Been there, done that, as has every other dog in the local vicinity; I have smelt their pee-mail many times over. So I lay down—a lot. Sue me, I get tired.

There was a tractor cutting the grass on the football pitch, not bothered. Mr. Moose and I were cool, until I kinda perked up a bit and decided, yup, reckon I could bag me a tractor. So I got up and ran like the wind. Now, when Mama or Papa say 'wait', if I'm included I obey instantly and stop in my tracks. But not today. I thought . . . nah, I'm going for it.

Mama had a small coronary, as she thought I was going to get run over again, and sent Papa to retrieve me. Mama quickly popped Rudy Moose on a lead, but in her panic she kinda forgot the long lead was wrapped around her neck and didn't really explain to The Moose that is was walk nicely time. (You see where I'm going with this.) So she clipped it on in haste, then my boy ran like the wind hot on my heels.

Mama was temporarily garrotted. Me, well I was on a quest. I might only have three legs, but I did an entire lap of the football pitch hot on the heels of that tractor baby, with Papa in warm pursuit, and Mama, well she was still choking on a long lead getting tighter around her neck as my boy attempted to join in the fun.

And boy was it fun! The tractor driver stopped twice. So did I. And then he took off again. And so did I. I hunted my prey down until Mr. Tractor driver parked and gave up.

Mama and Papa then profusely apologised for my behaviour. Mr. Tractor Man was cool and reported to Mama and Papa that for a three-legged dog it was somewhat impressive as I had reached up to 12 miles per hour!

Mama was finally able to breathe again as she unleashed Mr. Moose and leashed me. Papa was a bit puffed out and me, well I growled at Mr. Tractor Man as he saluted my efforts and attempted to stroke me despite warnings from the old folks.

Been back to the dull park since. I did a bit of a lay down after a few paces and Mama just looked at me knowingly and yup, forced to get up. I may have blown my cover with that tractor stunt after all.

Mr. Moussaka went to school again this week and killed it again. Naturally. They had to do this thing where they had to wait at one end of the hall and then be called to the other end, but with a bit of a trick in-between. A row of delicious treats were laid out right across the floor. In the first attempt, Mr. Moose had a little snuffle and ate one tidbit and then came to Mama. On the second attempt, he listened perfectly and went straight to Mama. He was the only dog who did! Oh, yeah! Proud of you bro.

Another time, a treat was dropped in front of them with the command to 'leave' it. Now there is another dog who is also super cool, he stared at the treat whilst his Mama left the room and then returned and he was very, very good and did not touch the treat. Rudy Moose . . . well he was also very good. The treat was dropped, he listened to Mama and did not touch it, Mama left the room . . . and Rudy Moose followed. Mrs. Dog Trainer was impressed and said that meant Rudy Moose places Mama higher than a tasty snack left unattended on the floor. God bless that little love.

In other news, I have learnt how to share; yup, that small bro ends up with everything: toys, bones, the lot, and I don't mind. Those are big steps for me. Oh, and I licked him the other day, for the first time ever. I love Mama and Papa and will happily snuggle them, but I never, ever lick them.

Lastly, Papa took me and my little bro in to Mama's work, and I met Mama's boss. I growled at him. Mama said that was fine as sometimes she growls at him too. Afterwards we went to the beach and I kid you not we met two Greek dogs, three Romanians, a Spaniard, and a Polish mutt. Mama said it was like the canine United Nations and it made her happy. It made us happy too.

Mad dogs and Englishmen, you rock my world.

Editor's comment: Can one advise how a cat can obtain a tractor licence? Asking for a friend.

WEEK 50
Compassion

It's a funny old world, and a bit of a barking old rock that we all live on.

Two years ago I was at the end of my very short life, slowly rotting away, a sad and miserable death awaiting me.

I was scared.

I was rescued.

I was rehomed.

In 1935 a baby was born, several weeks premature. In fact, she was born on the 'guzunder', that old-fashioned potty thing that lived under the bed pre-indoor plumbing days. She was wrapped in cotton wool and placed in a bed with her Mama; the prognosis was that she would not make it through the night. But she did. And she grew.

In 1938 this same little girl, Elizabeth, suffered a ruptured appendix, was taken to a hospital and operated on with no parents allowed to stay at her bedside, and survived.

In 1939 WWII broke out. Elizabeth's father kept a gun by the front door, just in case of invasion, and many nights were spent in the bomb shelter, but thankfully Elizabeth and her family survived.

In 1948 Elizabeth was a beautiful, kind, and caring 18 year old, with the world at her feet. She was a professional dancer performing in the West End. And then she contracted tuberculosis. The prognosis was bad. Her hopes and dreams shattered, she spent 18 months in a hospital for TB sufferers. One lung was removed. Against all odds she survived.

Elizabeth is now 83 years old, and worked right up until a few years ago. Recently she took ill. A doctor was not available to come and visit her, so she was advised to dial 111. A kindly paramedic came to visit and diagnosed a chest infection and prescribed antibiotics. Elizabeth got worse. The doctor was still unavailable. Elizabeth was advised to dial 111 again, and so the kindly paramedic visited once more and told Elizabeth she could in fact go to the hospital, however, she would have to wait on a trolley for several hours before being seen and there was no guarantee she'd receive a chest x-ray.

Elizabeth declined his offer. Elizabeth was weak, and the antibiotics were upsetting her stomach. The doctor was called again, but he was still unavailable. The kindly paramedic arrived and told Elizabeth to stop taking the medication.

Elizabeth felt worse. The doctor was still unavailable but did take the time to do a 'telephone consultation'. The diagnosis? 'You sound fine, there's no need for me to come out and see you, and no need for you to be on medication.'

The next day Elizabeth finally dialled 999 and was rushed to hospital where she was diagnosed with pneumonia and a secondary lung infection. Elizabeth only has one lung. Elizabeth survived.

Today Elizabeth has been allowed to go home. She's weak and frail, but she's still a fighter.

Oh, and I forgot to mention, in 1966 Elizabeth gave birth to another fighter . . . my Mama.

Thank you, Elizabeth. Stay strong.

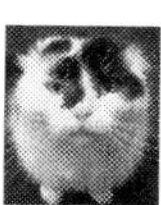

Editor's comment: Humble.

WEEK 51
Birthday List

Next week is my birthday AND my very first 'gotcha day' anniversary. Mama said I could have a very special present, as long as it doesn't cost too much. I have thought long and hard about this because I am the sort of dog that enjoys a good ponder whilst basking in the sunshine, so have come up with a list:

1. World peace. However, this would mean I would no longer be able to growl at strange people. So I changed my mind.

2. A leg . . . obviously. However, this would mean I might actually one day catch a random tractor that I was chasing and I am not sure what I would do with it if I did. So I changed my mind.

3. A girlfriend. However, this would make my Mr. Moussaka well jel. So I changed my mind.

4. That Darned Cat exterminated. However, Mama said that was vicious and unkind. So I did not change my mind.

5. Hang on, I know exactly what I want. I have asked Mama and she said YES! I am now super-excited! I'll keep you in suspense . . .

In other news, well there has been a lot.

My lovely Nannie has been proper poorly but is now slowly recovering and we wish her lots of love coz life is harsh. Get well soon Nannie.

Mr. Moussaka graduated from dog school. Now in my humble opinion that's a massive achievement. His class was full of canine beasts from all over, and all were marvellous. Yet Mr. Moussaka was the only hound who had spent his entire life in the pound, and, only been part of our little family for six weeks when he first started school. For a little second-hand chap that no other bugger wanted, he is an absolute legend. He has learnt loads: he walks to heal on a lead, walks to heal off a lead, sits, lays down, leaves, waits, comes when called, shakes hands, and bows. The stairgate is no longer required, and he never ventures upstairs to steal the cat's food, or wanders off if the door is left open. Next up is sniffer dog school, because that boy loves to follow his nose.

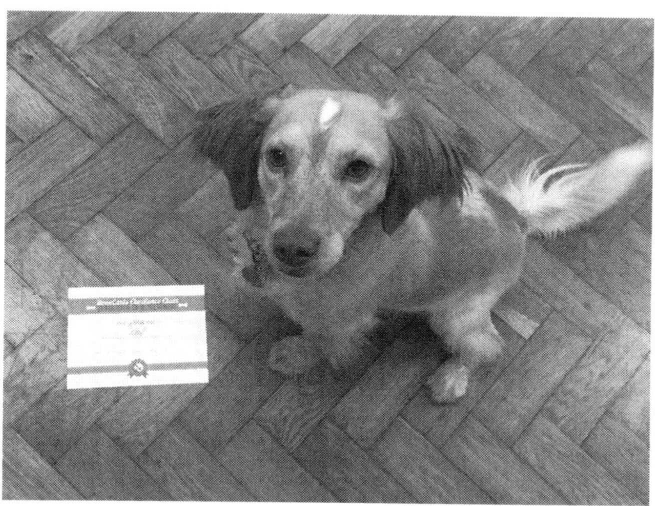

Oh, and he also learnt another trick. We were left home alone for an hour, and on the old folks' return something peculiar had occurred. Our water bowl is on a towel, because I'm a bit of a drooly drinker. (Hey, no one's perfect.) Somehow, as if by magic, when Mama and Papa returned the towel was on the posh thick rug, smack in the middle, with the water bowl still on the top! Tada.

Mama looked at Papa, Papa looked at Mama. Neither of them had put it there. No water had been spilt. Bizarre. The only little clue was just the tad end of the towel appeared to have a few little Cypriot dog tooth marks on it. The boy had apparently dragged the entire thing several feet, up and onto the big deep pile rug, and not spilt a drop. He is a freaking waiter in the making. Someone buy that boy a bowtie.

On another sunny afternoon—yes we're being spoiled here in sunny old England—we had a casual stroll around the park. Normal kind of a jaunt. On this particular occasion Mama gave up with me and my laying down and went off to play with the other fella, The Moose. All was good in the hood until a stranger approached. Mama called over and said, 'Don't touch the three-legged dog having a lie down,' and the stranger replied 'Mama Edwards, is that you?'

Turned out it was a colleague of Mama's, out with their own dog and so they had a little chat. Mama explained that I was a teeny-tad anti-social, and with only the three legs spent a lot of time just laying down. Mama's colleague replied, 'Well, actually I was in this very park last week and I watched your three-legged dog do an entire lap of the field at great speed in pursuit of a tractor.' My, good news travels fast! Doesn't Mama look like a bit of a idiot now.

In my defense, it's not only me who is occasionally bad. Mama is too. On yet another stroll around a different park Mama was very bad(ish). On this outing we met a very nice lady who was actually rather annoying. With her super-expensive handbag dog straining manically on its extendable lead she decided we were now her best friends. We weren't. She joined in on our walk with her poor designer dog behaving in a very unruly fashion.

Obviously me and The Moose were super-respectful of the poor wee beastie, whilst Mama explained the usual of how I had lost my leg and had been rescued from the streets of Greece before emigrating to the UK. However, Mama forgot to mention to the well-heeled lady in the park that when I had rocked up in little old England I had arrived with a lot of baggage.

And when the lady wasn't tripping over her own high heels she went to stroke me and . . . well, to be honest I can't be arsed to carry all that baggage anymore but she was incredibly annoying and as she reached over my remaining 'inner clutch bag' surfaced and grrrrrrrr. She left us to walk on without her. Papa said Mama should have warned her and Mama said she needed to learn dogs are actually dogs.

Also, I finally got to meet my Auntie Tina, who has flown over from the land down under, Australia. Yeah I was a tad scared, but Auntie Australian Tina, I think I kinda like you and your mailed treats a lot. Mr. Auntie Australian Tina ... not so keen, but I didn't bite you, just grrrrrrrr'd a lot. So there's that.

As for Mrs. Auntie Australian Tina, well, she said sit, I sat, she said down, I lay down, she said wait, I waited, she said come and yeah I came and took one of those treats right out of her hand.

Auntie English Janine also came a visiting, I like Auntie English Janine too but the fact that we had had a houseful for most of the week, I was a grumpy beggar, and growled at her every move. It's just the way I am.

Ouzo, the 'Enigma' Greek.

My penultimate diary entry. I never thought when I started this I would have made so many friends. My very own blog has reached every single continent across the planet with the exception of Antarctica and who wants a polar bear as a stalker anyway!

Editor's comment: Some people need to get a life.

WEEK 52
Gotcha Week

I started by saying 'I'm not really sure what life has in store for me, but seeing as I have one I might as well make the best of it.'

Pulling up stakes and starting a whole new life in a place where you don't understand anything is terrifying, but you know what? I *have* made the best of it.

Today is my third birthday. I am 21. But more importantly today is my very first 'gotcha day'. A year ago today. Mama and Papa drove umpteen miles, about 340 to be precise(ish), on a round trip to Birmingham to come and find me and take me home. The first thing I did was show them my teeth; they said I had very nice teeth and they took me anyway. I have so many people to thank, and trust me, I will.

This week has been a little bit epic. My boy, my favourite little love, Mr. Moussaka, has really started to relax into his new home and show his real personality. It is a little surprising, as he has many talents; for example, when left unattended he can take a CD off the shelf, take it out of the case, and destroy it. Let's just say he has a unique taste in music.

He hasn't done it again, so we assume the remaining collection is more his cup of tea. He has also started to make the cutest little noises, or the most bizarre noises, and Mama has declared that he does in fact have Tourette's. He leaps like a gazelle and goes 'grryap' and Mama says it is just a tick and it is rude to stare. We proper love him so much.

Number one: finding a forever home. Number two: finding my true love. Boy, can a guy get any luckier?

As you may well know, I am still a bit of an enigma. Mama read a blog this week about people taking their dogs all over the place, and that in fact the dog may well rather stay at home. Not me. Yup, I am an anti-social three-legged aloof Anatolian Shepherd dog, however, I am also an enigma. I'm not so keen on the car journey, but other than that, take me anywhere.

Just don't touch me. I'm more than comfortable around some people now; in fact, I even got into a spot this week when, on one of my jaunts around a local park, I approached a lady I know well and stuck my head in her handbag. Mama said that was ridiculously rude of me, but hey, the lady was busy stroking The Moose, so I just thought I would take a sneaky peak. Turns out this is bad manners. I am a dog, how should I know.

Mama and Papa had planned a whole weekend of birthday/gotcha day celebrations. For my birthday eve, Mama declared we were going on an adventure. Now Mama quite often declares in a rather annoying high-pitched voice that we are off on an adventure. This usually means going pheasant chasing in the forest or visiting the pet shop. Both of which I love, a lot.

But no, this was an epic adventure. We drove into the countryside and stopped for a full English breakfast. Well the parents did, but me and The Moose got to share some tasty pudding! Then we headed off again to . . . THE BIGGEST PET SHOP IN THE WORLD. Paws in the Park at the South of England show ground. OMG. I'm not sure where to start. So much to see, so little birthday time.

Papa and I watched Mama and The Moose take part in the search and rescue display. We also watched a bunch of dogs jumping through rings of fire! They were all rescue dogs, and seriously awesome with how they trusted their parents. Some of them did this little trick where they jumped through hoops; now Mama is surfing the world wide web to buy a hoop for Mr. Moussaka to jump through. Oh dear Lord. There are times I am grateful for only having three legs.

Mama and Papa went in search of actual human ice cream which turned out to be a bit of a mission as everything there was for us dogs! Enroute Mama spotted a little sombrero; Mama said making a dog wear a hat was ridiculous. Ten minutes later Mama went back and bought the sombrero. I have to say, Mr. Moussaka looked rather fetching in it and he was more than happy to spend the rest of the day trotting about wearing his new found millinery item, much to the delight of everyone in the show-ground. A three-legged dog and his small friend in a hat gained much attention.

A lovely lady from a trade stand rushed over to Mama and said, 'I love sombrero dog and his friend hoppy, please could we take some promotional photos of them both on our trade stand?'

Willingly we both obliged. Mama and Papa sat at each end of the advertising banner with us boys in the middle, me with my disability and my bro with his hat. Then the rather wonderful people, Autarky Dog Food, yup, I promised to ditto their publicity, snapped away. As a reward they gave us a bag of goodies and my, they are mighty fine. Thank you guys. Much appreciated.

Mama took a peak at their social media post later that day, they had cropped out Mama, and Papa, and me too, so it was just The Moose who was the star of the show.

We went off to watch dog agility, as Mama thinks Mr. Moussaka might like to take part in something like this. Seriously, those dogs are awesome, but there was me, basking under the shade of an old oak, thinking to myself . . . um, why? Just growl at people and then no one will ever ask you to take up show jumping with hazards.

Mr. Moussaka, well he was way too busy posing in his new sombrero for his new fan base to take photos to pay any attention to dogs doing amazing things.

Thank you Mama and Papa, for the best day out ever. Papa said 'it was the best day out ever . . . so far.' Sign me up for more of those!

There was also a royal wedding going on that day, which meant no traffic jams as everyone else was home watching the tele. Mama said a wedding is a wonderful thing, not because you are royal, but whoever you are, yet she would rather enjoy the love and devotion she has in her own family as that is a teeny tad more important. Well, for us bunch of oddballs anyway.

And now it is my birthday/gotcha day. I thought long and hard about what I would like as a present, and the most important thing to me is to give something back. Mama and Papa don't have a lot of money, but Mama did win £25 on the premium bonds last week, plus she has £75 in nectar points, so the weekly shopping was done with this and a handsome sum of one hundred pounds was given to me. Yup, me, a three-legged ex street dog just hit the lottery. My decision was hard, as there are so many people out there that do such a thankless yet fantastic job, but I followed my heart.

Ermioni, my first love, my saviour. There are sadly far too many dogs that your charity rescues, I could not simply pick one, so instead I have donated to your request for help in building shelters for all those that you give a second chance to. You helped me and now it is my turn to give a little bit of help back. Thank you Ermioni, you will always be carried in my heart.

Oh, and I also got breakfast with three sausages, as I am a dog and don't appreciate candles.

And there we have it, one year on, little old me, a three-legged Greek street dog; from destitute and dying, to rescued, rehabilitated, and rehomed. And loved.

But I would like to finish with it not being all about me, because this is a big old rock we are all on, and sometimes stuff gets blurred. When you take on a rescue dog, it works both ways. You may think you are saving a soul, but do you know what, us guys kinda save you too . . .

The second hand, the misfits, the unwanted and unloved, the soul soothers—this is for you.

Editor's comment: And the moral of this story? **The glass is not half full, or half empty. It is refillable.**

The end.

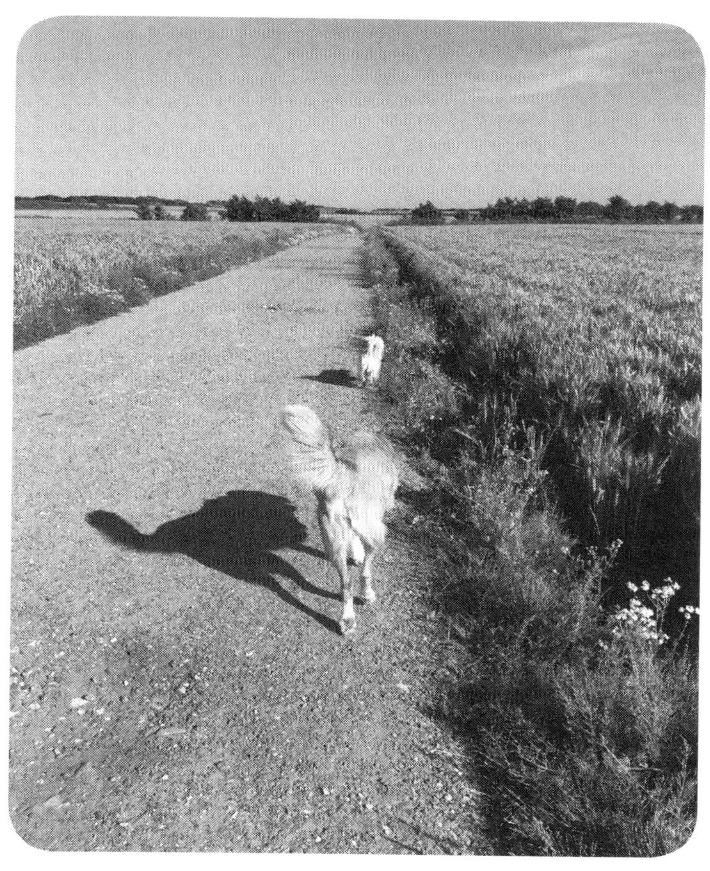

Our adventures continue . . .

THANK YOU & *Acknowledgements*

Thank you so much to the following people and charities that make this planet ROCK. Ermioni and everyone at the Diasozo Animal Rescue team; Diane and Greek Animal Rescue; Juliet at Holly Farm Canine Centre (big love to you); Lynne, Sarah and Hannah at Give a Dog a Home, can't thank you enough; Paws Dog Shelter Cyprus; Mark Bridger, a truly top chap plus the Bone Canis team; Dogs in Brazil; Madison; Monica; Angela; Lizzie; Lynne; Michael; Evi; Caroline; Louise; Beverley; Emma at Cancer-wiserocks, and all the rest of my barking friends.

Want more time with Ouzo? Visit these links to watch video of him today and see photos of his rescue in Greece:

https://www.youtube.com/watch?v=zVehBkpcTI8
https://www.youtube.com/watch?v=qCcsSFzVqHM
https://www.youtube.com/watch?v=VPQySkWs-bQ
https://www.youtube.com/watch?v=CvzT6Hq4zKs
https://www.youtube.com/watch?v=kI1dFYi9L0I

Link to blog:
https://ouzothegreek.blog/

Links to social media:
Facebook https://www.facebook.com/ouzothegreek
Twitter https://twitter.com/ouzothegreek

ABOUT
The Author

Lisa Edwards lives in a quiet village in West Sussex, England. With their children grown, Lisa and her husband Michael decided the time had come to search for a new family dog. Having rescued pets in the past, there was no hesitation in deciding to 'adopt' rather than 'shop'. Enter Ouzo the Greek, who joined Mrs. D, aka That Darned Cat, and more recently Mr. Moussaka. These three misfit second-hand pets completely changed Lisa's life.

Lisa spent over a decade working as an Executive Assistant in secondary education, but gave it all up to start a new career, where she is now employed at an animal rescue organisation. She hopes to make a difference to those still looking for their forever home, as well as write about animals and animal causes on a freelance basis.

As for Ouzo, well Lisa and Michael didn't just rescue a dog, they inadvertently stumbled across their best friend.

Thank you for taking the time
to read *Ouzo The Greek.*

COULD YOU TAKE A MOMENT TO GIVE THE BOOK A SHORT REVIEW ON AMAZON.COM? YOUR REVIEWS MEAN THE WORLD TO OUR AUTHORS, AND HELP STORIES SUCH AS THIS ONE REACH A WIDER AUDIENCE. THANK YOU SO MUCH!

Find links to
Ouzo The Greek
AND ALL OUR GREAT BOOKS
ON AMAZON OR AT WWW.WHOCHAINSYOU.COM.

Also from Who Chains You Books

THE DOG THIEF AND OTHER STORIES
JILL KEARNEY

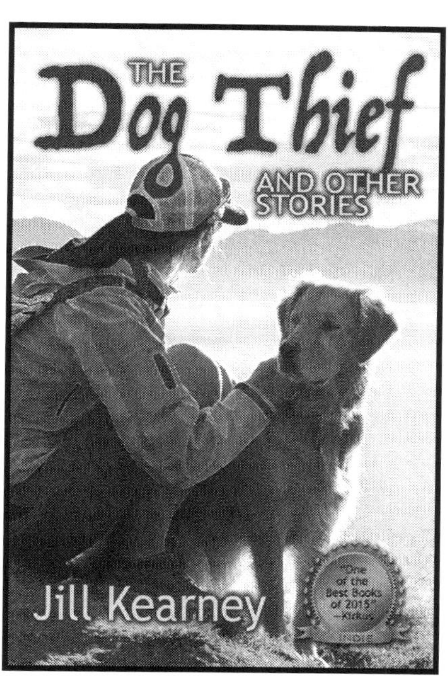

"Decrepit humans rescue desperate canines, cats and the occasional rat in this collection of shaggy but piercing short stories."

Listed by Kirkus Review as one of the best books of 2015, this collection of short stories and a novella explores the complexity of relationships between people and animals in an impoverished rural community where the connections people have with animals are sometimes their only connection to life.

According to Kirkus Review: "Kearney treats her characters, and their relationships with their pets, with a cleareyed, unsentimental sensitivity and psychological depth. Through their struggles, she shows readers a search for meaning through the humblest acts of caretaking and companionship. A superb collection of stories about the most elemental of bonds."...*Read more and order from whochainsyou.com, Amazon, and other outlets.*

Also from Who Chains You Books

Foster Doggie Insanity: Tips and Tales to Keep Your Kool as a Doggie Foster Parent

by Tamira Thayne

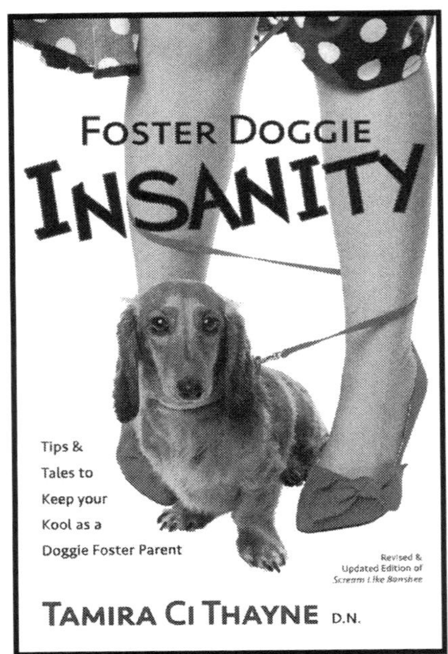

"I regularly buy books with a rescue theme but always felt a bit disappointed because there hasn't been a book that portrayed my rescue experiences. So I wasn't really prepared for Tamira Ci Thayne's book. It is the most honest account of the perils and pitfalls as well as the joy and fulfillment that rescue volunteers face daily. The book was beautifully written and brutally honest...Thayne's book feels like an embrace from a friend that understands what we all go through. It is a beacon of hope to let other rescuers know that they are not alone. It is a must read for anyone involved in rescue."—*Amy Snyder, Volunteer for Dachshund Rescue of North America*

Do you struggle as a doggie foster parent, and feel like you're the only one who finds it hard? Do you want to foster a dog, but don't know where to start, how to prepare, and what to expect? If so, this is the book for you...*Read more and order from whochainsyou.com, Amazon, and other outlets.*

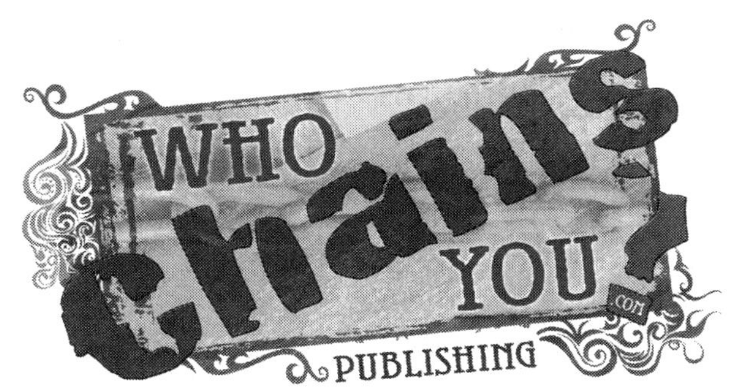

About Who Chains You Books

WELCOME TO WHO CHAINS YOU: BOOKS FOR THOSE WHO BELIEVE PEOPLE—AND ANIMALS—DESERVE TO BE FREE.

At Who Chains You Books our mission is a simple one—to amplify the voices of the animals through the empowerment of animal lovers, activists, and rescuers to write and publish books elevating the status of animals in today's society.

We hope you'll visit our website and join us on this adventure we call animal advocacy publishing. We welcome you.

Read more about us at whochainsyou.com.

Printed in Great Britain
by Amazon